PROS AND CONS

A NEWSPAPER READER'S AND DEBATER'S
GUIDE TO THE LEADING
CONTROVERSIES OF THE DAY

(POLITICAL, SOCIAL, RELIGIOUS, Etc.)

EDITED BY

JOHN BERTRAM ASKEW

FOURTH EDITION, REVISED AND ENLARGED

LONDON
SWAN SONNENSCHEIN & CO., Ltd.
PATERNOSTER SQUARE
1899

First Edition . . . . *April*, 1896.
Second Edition (Unaltered) . . *June*, 1896.
Third Edition (Revised and Enlarged) . *June*, 1897.

In the interest of creating a more extensive selection of rare historical book reprints, we have chosen to reproduce this title even though it may possibly have occasional imperfections such as missing and blurred pages, missing text, poor pictures, markings, dark backgrounds and other reproduction issues beyond our control. Because this work is culturally important, we have made it available as a part of our commitment to protecting, preserving and promoting the world's literature. Thank you for your understanding.

PREFACE.

The object of this little book is to place in the hands of the every-day reader and debater, in as fair and impartial a manner as may be possible, a concise, yet more or less comprehensive, statement of the opposing arguments advanced by the partisans of the several rival schools or theories which are at the present day striving to catch the ear of the public, whether in social, political, or religious spheres.

When we consider the enormous increase in the controversial literature of the last few years, and the number of the battles that are being fought out to-day in the pages of books, reviews, and newspapers, it seems likely that a work which digests and epito-mises all this floating and scattered material should, if properly executed, be of real service as an *aide-mémoire* to the casual inquirer, to the newspaper reader, and perhaps, incidentally, to the serious student of sociology, though the book is not sufficiently full or elaborate to be of service to the specialist in his own department. I cannot hope that the present volume is very perfect; but I believe it to be trustworthy, as far as it goes, great care having been given to adequately represent the chief points in each subject, and the attitude taken up with respect to them by each side. The arguments have been arranged in numbered paragraphs, under their respective headings of *pro* and *con*, in such manner that each *con* answers its corresponding *pro*, or at any rate that paragraphs bearing the same number deal with the same argument from the points of view of the respective dis-putants. It has been urged as an objection to this arrangement that it leaves the *pros* at the mercy of the *cons*, and, further, that there is a tendency to disregard *cons* to which no *pros* apply. These dangers I have sought to avoid, and have on occasions inserted *cons* without a corresponding *pro*, just as, similarly, *pros* sometimes appear with no *cons* to answer them.

My choice of subjects has been, I have no doubt, somewhat arbitrary. I can only say that arbitrariness is involved in the very conception of the book. It is, I am convinced, impossible to draw a hard and fast line as to what subjects should be admitted, and the rule adopted has been to admit such subjects only as seemed likely to interest any considerable section of the public. The subjects are not necessarily treated of in a degree of length that is at all relative to their respective importance. Here the rule adopted has been to treat them in such detail as seemed consistent with a due presentation of both aspects of the case.

I must express my obligation to Mr. Sydney Buxton, whose excellent *Handbook to Political Questions* has been of great service to me for those subjects with which he deals. These, however, are comparatively few; and I am mainly indebted, for much help and advice, to a number of ladies and gentlemen who are recognized authorities in their own several fields of controversy. I have sought, and nearly always obtained, help from all sides, and must here content myself with merely expressing my gratitude generally; individual recognition would be too lengthy, and, indeed, would in some cases—those, moreover, in which I am most deeply indebted—be against the expressed wishes of the contributors. While my own researches have been very laborious, and have extended over a considerable time, I am, I confess, not wholly satisfied with some of the articles which I have myself contributed; these, however, I hope, with greater leisure at my disposal, to improve in a second edition, should such be called for. Meantime, any criticisms, any indications of errors, whether as to omission or commission, will be thankfully received by me.*

J. B. A.

London, 1896.

PREFACE TO THE THIRD EDITION.

IN issuing this new edition, the third within little more than a year of first publication, I think it right to point out that several alterations have been made, both by way of condensation and of expansion. A number of articles have been made more concise, without, I hope, in any way sacrificing lucidity, whilst several have been added in order to bring the book quite up to date. For one or two of these I have to acknowledge assistance freely rendered to me by others who do not desire their names mentioned.

J. B. A.

June, 1897.

* Under cover to my publishers, Messrs. Swan Sonnenschein & Co., Paternoster Square, London.

CONTENTS.

	PAGE
Absenteeism	1
Abstinence, Total	1
Adulteration Acts	2
Advertizing, Public Control of	3
Advowsons, Sale of	3
Africa, Central	4
Agnosticism	5
Agricultural Banks	5
Agricultural Depression	6
Agricultural Light Railways	7
Agricultural Rates Act	7
Allotments and Small Holdings	8
Alsace-Lorraine	9
America and England	10
Anarchism	12
Anglican Church	12
Anglican Orders	13
Anti-Semitism	13
Arbitration, Commercial	15
Arbitration, Compulsory Industrial	15
Arbitration, International	16
Aristocratic v. Democratic Government	17
Armenian Question	18
Army Short Service	19
Asylums, Private	19
Authority in Religious Belief	20
Authors and Publishers	20
Bachelors, Taxation of	21
Bacteria	22
Bakehouses, Municipalization of	23
Ballot, The	23
Bank Holidays	23
Betterment	24
Bicycle Tax	26
Bimetallism	26
Bishops: Exclusion from House of Lords	28
Blasphemy Laws	29
Boycotting	29
British Museum	30
Broad-Church Party	30

	PAGE
Cabinet, Government by	30
Canada	31
Canada: Copyright Claim	32
Canals, Nationalization of	33
Canvassing at Elections	33
Capital Punishment	34
Cathedrals, Nationalization of	35
Catholic University for Ireland	35
Celibacy of Priests	35
Channel Tunnel	36
Charitable Relief	36
Charity Organization Society	37
Child Labour: "Half Timers"	38
Chinese, Exclusion of	39
Christendom, Reunion of	39
Christian Socialism	40
Christianity: its Divine Origin	40
Christianity: Is Dogma a Necessity?	41
Church Attendance	41
Churches and Social Problems	41
Civil Service (England)	42
Civil Service (India)	42
Civilization in Savage Lands	43
Codification of the Law	43
Collectivism (or Socialism)	44
Common Lands, Enclosure of	45
Compensation to Publicans	46
Conscription for England	47
Constitution, A Written	48
Contagious Diseases Act (Women)	48
Contracting-Out Clause	49
Co-operation and Capitalism	49
Co-operation and State Socialism	49
Corporal Punishment in Schools	50
Cremation	50
Criminal Appeal	51
Death Duties, English, Graduated	51
Deceased Wife's Sister	52
Decimal Notation	53
Degeneration	54
Disarmament, International	54
Disendowment of the Church	55

CONTENTS

	PAGE		PAGE
Disestablishment of the Church	56	Hospitals, Nationalization of	93
Disestablishment and Disendowment: Scotland	59	Husband and Wife as Witnesses	94
Disestablishment and Disendowment: Wales	50	Immigration of Destitute Aliens	94
Distress for Rent	61	Immorality and Public Life	95
Divorce	61	Immortality of the Individual	95, 96
Divorce for Women	62	Imperial Federation, British	96
Docks, Municipalization of	62	*In Camerâ* Proceedings	97
Drama and Social Questions	63	Income Tax, A Progressive	98
Drink, Free Trade in	63	Increased Armaments	99
Duelling	63	Independent Labour Party	100
		India, Child-Marriages in	101
		India: Home-Rule	101
Education, Mixed	64	Indian Defence	102
Education, Moral	64	Individualism	103
Education, Religious	65	Infallibility, Papal	104
Education, State	66	Insurance of Children	105
Education, State, Compulsory	66	Inter-Imperial Communication	106
Education, State, Free	66	Internationalism	107
Education, Voluntary Schools	67	International Money	107
Egypt, Evacuation of	70	Intestacy, Abolition of the Law of	107
Eight Hours' Day, An	71	Ireland: Lord Lieutenancy	108
Elections, Simultaneous	74	Ireland: Home Rule	108
Elgin Marbles	74	Ireland: Is she Overtaxed?	110
Employers' Liability	74	Irish Land Acts	111
Endowment of Research	161	Irish Members of Parliament	111
England: Why is She Unpopular	75	Irish Ministry of Agriculture	111
Entail, Abolition of the Law of	76		
Equality, Religious	76		
Equality, Social	77	Journalism: Are Signed Articles Desirable?	112
Ethical Movement, The	77	Jury System, The	113
Ethics as an Experimental Science	78		
Examinations, Competitive	79		
Experimental in Politics, The	79	Kindergarten System, The	113
Fagging at Schools	80	Land Nationalization	114
Fair Trade v. Free Trade	80	Leasehold Enfranchisement	117
Fair Wages Clause	82	Legal Education, Reform of	119
Farm Colonies	82	Liberty of Opinion, Speech, etc	120
Fashion in Dress	82	Life: Is it Worth Living?	121
Federal Government in G. Britain	83	Livery Companies of London	120
Free Libraries	86	Local Option	122
Free Luxuries for the Poor	86	Local Veto	122
Free Meals at Board Schools	87	London Self-Government	123
Free Shelters and Refuges	87	London, Unification of	124
Free Soup Kitchens, etc.	88	Lords, House of, Abolition of	125
Gambling in Commerce	89	Magistrates, Stipendiary	126
Gambling, Morality of	89	Manhood Suffrage	126
Gambling, Suppression of, by Law	89	Markets, Municipalization of	127
Game Laws, Abolition of	90	Marriage Laws, Reform of	128
Gas Supply, Municipalization of	90	Middleman, Elimination of	129
Gibraltar	90	Military Council The New	129
Gothenburg System	91	Minorities, Rights of	129
Greek, Compulsory	91	Monarchy v. Republicanism	130
Ground Values, Taxation of	92	Monogamy, Legal	131

CONTENTS

	PAGE
Municipal Dwellings for the Poor	132
National Party in Politics, A	133
Naval Adviser, A	133
Naval Reserve	133
Official Expenses of Candidates	135
Official Expenses, Parliamentary	135
Old-Age Pensions	135
One Man One Vote	137
Opium Trade; Suppression of	138
Outdoor Relief	141
Parliament, Members of, Payment of	142
Parliament: Delegates or Representatives?	143
Parliaments, Shorter	144
Parochial Boards	145
Party Government	146
Pauper Children, Boarding out of	146
Peasant Proprietorship	148
Police, Metropolitan	149
Population	149
Post Office, The	150
Premature Burial	151
Prison Reform	152
Professionalism in Sports	153
Profit Sharing	154
Psychical Research v. Science	154
Railway Nationalization	155
Rates	157
Referendum, The	158
Registration of Title to Land	159
Reversionists, Rating of	160
Rights of Animals	160
Scientific Research, Endowment of	161
Sea Serpent, The	162
Second Ballots	162
Sex in Fiction	163
Socialism	44
Socialism and Natural Selection	164
Special Assessment of Land	164
Spelling Reform, English	164
Sport	165
Street Music, Legislation against	166
Sugar Bounties	166
Suicide: Is it Immoral?	167
Sunday Closing of Public Houses	168
Sunday Opening of Museums	168
Taxation, Indirect, Abolition of	169
Taxation, Voluntary	170
Thames Steamboat Service	170
Theism	170
Thorough (or Deep) Cultivation	171
Tied Houses, Abolition of	172
Trades Unionism	173
Tramways Municipalization	174
Unemployed, The	175
Universal Language	176
University, Teaching, for London	177
University Extension Movement	178
Vacant Land: its Rating	178
Vaccination, Compulsory	179
Vegetarianism	181
Vivisection	182
Voluntary Schools and Rate Aid	184
Voters, Illiterate	184
Voting, Compulsory	185
Water Supply, Municipalization	185
Women and University Degrees	186
Women, Higher Education of	187
Women, Married, as Workers	188
Women, Medical Education for	189
Women Suffrage	190
Workmen's Accident Insurance	191

PROS AND CONS.

ABSENTEEISM: can it be justified?
Pro: (1) Property in land is on the same footing as any other kind of property, and personal supervision of it cannot reasonably be claimed. (2) Absenteeism tends to make the tenant farmer independent, and not to rely too much on the charitable assistance of his landlord. (3) Landlords more and more buy from Stores, where they obtain goods cheaper and better than locally: thus their absence has little effect on local trade.
Con: (1) Property in land cannot be put on the same footing as other property. (*See* LAND NATIONALIZATION.) (2) Absenteeism entirely destroys the relics of the kindly feelings which formerly existed between the landlord and his tenant. (3) Residence of a landlord on his property has an important effect on local trade; and his presence exercises a refining and civilizing influence on his tenantry. (4) His presence leads to a more far-sighted policy in the cultivation of the estate than is secured by the employment of an agent.

ABSTINENCE, TOTAL.
Pro: (1) The slight gratification afforded by indulgence in alcohol cannot weigh against the dangerous example it sets; for it is admitted that little that is noble and very much that is base has been done under its influence. Alcohol is the source of most of our pauperism and crime, thus leading to immense and unnecessary public expenditure and corresponding taxation. (2) The liquor industry employs relatively few hands, and is *pro tanto* an enemy of the working classes. The country gains little, general commerce is scarcely benefited at all, and the working classes are "kept under" by the drink trade. Millions of bushels of grain are annually destroyed, which otherwise would be available for healthy food. (3) Alcohol is not a food, since it passes through the body in great measure without chemical change. The habit of taking it is always unnecessary and frequently deleterious to health. Animals drink nothing but water, and no child requires alcohol during the critical period of its life up to fifteen years: indications that man in a healthy state should not need it. Many hard-working men have eschewed it, and yet remained strong. (4) The alcoholic *habitué* is greatly handicapped in illness; for while alcohol fails to act on him as a drug, many medicines cease wholly or in part to have their proper effect. (5) The mortality rate of Total Abstainers is lower than that of Moderate Abstainers by some $26\frac{1}{2}$ %. Some Life Insurance Offices actually offer a considerable rebate to Total Abstainers. (6) The alcohol habit is hereditary, and anything that increases the risks of a parent transmitting it to his offspring is a moral crime. (7) The alcohol habit, once contracted, cannot easily be overcome. The national Drink Bill remains much the same in bad as in good times. (8) It is often the immediate cause of insanity. (9) Where liberty leads to licence, and licence involves such enormous evil, the State is called upon to interfere by way of Prohibition. (10) Prohibition has proved successful in Maine, U.S.A., and elsewhere.
Con: (1) The innocent gratification afforded by alcohol, especially to hard-working men and to manual labourers, is a distinct factor in the

pleasures of their lives, and one that they should not be forced to forego. That its abuse is harmful no one can deny; but the true principle is to set an example of its right use, not to shirk responsibility by disuse. Moreover, the argument for self-sacrifice applies with equal validity to all pleasures: excess in everything is bad. Example, however, is rarely the cause of a drunken habit, which is due rather to the hardships and pressure of modern life: drunkenness is the effect rather than the cause of the problem it involves.   (2) The liquor industry employs a large number of hands. The national revenue derived from the beer trade is a very large annual sum, which our Exchequer could with difficulty spare; and, if spared, it would only be at the expense of general taxation. It is reasonable that alcohol consumers should pay their own taxation directly. If the millions of bushels were not wanted for the liquor trade, they would not be grown, or, if grown, the price for the grain crops would be still further reduced than at present.   (3) Alcohol is useful as a food: in moderation it has none of the ill effects commonly attributed to it. It interferes with no bodily function, nor does it lower the temperature (as is often asserted). There is every reason to believe that its action is on the whole beneficial, and its stimulating and recuperative influence on an over-tired man is beyond dispute. It has been resorted to by all the most progressive and intellectually and physically active races of the world.   (4) The moderate drinker is sufficiently influenced by all ordinary drugs.   (5) The statistics are valueless, as they include drunkards. Such Insurance Companies as offer reduced premiums to Total Abstainers, do so mainly in competition and for the sake of advertisement.   (6) There is no reason to suppose that moderate drinking is hereditary; and, even if it were, no harm would be done.   (7) All unnecessary habits which are beyond one's control are evils; but there is no reason why the drink habit should not be properly regulated by each man for himself.   (8) Alcoholism is a symptom of a disordered brain, rather than a cause of madness.   (9) Prohibition would be a gross infringement of the liberty of the subject: it is better for a nation to be drunkards than slaves.   (10) Prohibition has not succeeded in Maine, U.S.A., in suppressing illicit drinking, which is much worse than that done in public places under the eye of the public authorities.

ADULTERATION ACTS.

Pro: (1) The public, especially the poorer classes, are not in a position to inquire into the nature of the goods they buy, so that the Government is bound to see that at least they get what they ask for.   (2) It may be true that it is not easy to define what is popularly meant by any particular article, but the Government can at least make rough definitions, *viz.*, beer must not contain any noxious or deleterious matter, milk not more than a certain percentage of water, etc.   (3) Freedom of purchase acts only very remotely in the case of the poorest classes, who have to buy in their own vicinity at the cheapest rate, and whose taste has been deteriorated by cheap goods.   (4) Public opinion will not tolerate one class of men to enrich themselves by means of the ignorance of their neighbours. The only way public opinion can effectively prevent this is through the State: the worst cases are amenable to public opinion, but others escape. (Some) Public opinion is far too arbitrary to be trusted; and definitive legislation is imperative.   (5) It is true that an action for breach of contract might in every case be brought, but this would entail great hardships on the poor.

Con: (1) The Acts contradict the legal maxim *caveat emptor*, which leaves the buyer to find out whether the goods he buys are those he wants, and ought to receive for his money.   (2) It is not a duty of the State to fix the connotation of words; for, except in obvious cases of fraud (and even here many think the buyer must look out for himself), and of goods which are clearly definable, it is not possible to say what is generally understood, say, by beer, milk, cloth, etc. (3) The presumption is that, if the public buys, say, adulterated beer, the public likes adulterated beer. Under Freedom of Purchase evils of this sort are sure to right themselves, as it would pay others to sell good articles if they were in demand. (4) Public opinion is strong enough without an Act of Parliament to check the worst cases of adulteration. (5) Deception *ought* to be treated as a criminal offence, which would obviate the need of an army of inspectors open to possible corruption.

ADVERTIZING, PUBLIC CONTROL OF.

Pro: (1) Law ought to prevent the disfigurement of our towns and beautiful country districts by advertisements of enterprizing manufacturers. Sense of beauty is a most important trait in national character, and ought to be fostered, even at considerable cost, as a counter influence to the materialistic tendencies of a commercial age. (2) Legal regulation of advertizing would afford protection to manufacturers who object to the means of advertisement at present in vogue, and who do not wish to see our towns made hideous and our scenery spoilt, yet who are forced by keen competition to imitate the methods of their rivals. (3) This control would be feasible by giving the Board of Trade, or some other public body, power to license advertisements, and (as in some foreign countries) to enforce a small tax, which would not be seriously felt, but would bring in a considerable revenue for the relief of taxation generally. Though it might be hard to draw the line as to what and where advertisements should be admitted, public opinion would prevent any great abuse of the powers of the department. (4) Advertizing is a great tax on business; each trader is obliged to resort to it under penalty of seeing business go to his rivals. In this way the cost of goods is kept up, and the public gains little or nothing from the fall in wholesale prices. Were advertizing abolished, firms selling good articles could soon find other means of introducing them to the public; as it is, advertizing is chiefly adopted as a means of palming off worthless goods on the public. (5) Landholders and others hold their property only subject to the public welfare, and there can be no injustice in requiring advertizers to conform to such conditions as Society chooses to impose.

Con: (1) The State has no concern in the æsthetic culture of her citizens. (2) No manufacturer does, or would be likely to, object to extend his business by any honest means. (3) It would put too much power into the hands of a public body, since who is to decide what is a "beautiful spot," or where an advertisement should be allowed? Further, no Government would refuse a chance of making money: hence no real control would exist. Public opinion is no safeguard against abuse of power on the part of the Government; and such powers against a special class would make that class disaffected against the Government. Why subject this one class to a special tax? (4) By advertizing alone can a young manufacturer introduce his wares to the public; it thus affords a means of livelihood to many thousands who might otherwise be chargeable to the rates. (5) It would be very hard, especially in bad times, to cut off those having advertisement spaces to let from so fruitful a source of income. To pay compensation would be expensive; not to pay it would be dishonest.

ADVOWSONS, SALE OF.

Pro: (1) The sale of Advowsons has long been recognized as a legitimate form of barter; and there is no valid reason why it should be abolished, (Some) provided a patron be not allowed to appoint himself to the living within his gift. (2) If private patronage were abolished, it would be difficult to find an equally efficacious method of selection: bishops rarely make satisfactory appointments, and popular election has proved itself unsuccessful. (3) If the sale of Advowsons were made illegal, compensation would have to be paid; and whether paid by the Church or by the State, it would be a great and unnecessary expense.

Con: (1) The fact that an abuse has long existed is no argument in favour of its continuance. The whole idea of barter in connection with ecclesiastical appointments is anomalous: indecorous incidents and painful scandals frequently accompany such sales at the Auction Mart, rendering them a grief and a humiliation to all friends of the Church. Moreover, the patron need not even be a Christian. Under no circumstances should a patron be allowed to appoint himself. (2) The bishop is the natural and right person to appoint the clergy in his own diocese; he is at any rate not likely to be less competent than the average patron. (Some) The parishioners should elect, or at any rate have a voice in the election of, their own pastor. (3) Even if compensation were called for, which some deny, it would be money well spent, in view of increasing the efficiency of the Church.

AFRICA, CENTRAL: its value to Great Britain.

Pro: (1) Central Africa is of great value to England, because it helps her maintain her position among the Great Powers, and extend to savages the blessings of British rule and civilization. England has undertaken the duty of guardianship to less civilized races, fitting them for self-government; and, to be consistent, she ought not to withhold her benefactions from Africa. So far she has done her best to civilize the country, having already restrained the traffic in gin introduced by irresponsible traders, and partially suppressed the Slave Trade (recognizing, as regards the latter, that it is never wise to interfere too summarily with the customs of native races). (2) Where Englishmen have gone, the protection of their Government must follow them. England must show the world that she intends to defend the interests of her subjects at all costs, especially of those brave pioneers who have done so much to extend British dominion at the peril of their lives. (3) The mere fact of undertaking such reponsibilities has a valuable moral influence on a nation, since it is an admission that commercial objects are not the be-all and end-all of national policy. The argument that the Central African Colonies would be useful for exchange purposes with other States is, for a similar reason, morally bad. (4) We are absolutely shut out by high protective tariffs from German, French, and other colonies: hence new markets are indispensable to us. (5) Our Central African Colonies, apart from their value to us for defence purposes, have already opened up an enormous trade for us: they are some of the chief fields now open to Manchester goods, and, being merely in their infancy, are likely to become more and more important to us. (6) Precisely similar objections to those usually urged against our colonization of Africa might have been advanced against our occupation of India; yet few Englishmen lament our presence there, or doubt its mutual benefit to both countries. Africa, like India, shows traces of earlier civilization, and being at least as fertile, should prove equally profitable.

Con: (1) Central Africa is not a part of the world in which Europeans can permanently settle, owing to its unhealthy climate. The chief results of British (and other European) rule in Africa seem to be the utter demoralization of the natives, through the introduction of gin and other curses of civilization (see CIVILIZATION IN SAVAGE LANDS) and the continued toleration of the Slave Trade. (2) It is obvious that the Government must put a limit to the extent within which she is prepared to defend the "rights" of her subjects. Where a subject, for his own personal ends, enters the territory of a foreign power, which on account of religion or other causes is known to be hostile to the presence of unbelievers or foreigners, he does so at his own peril; and it is unreasonable to expect that his Government should endorse his action, at any rate until it can be proved that national interests would be thereby furthered. (3) The undertaking of such great responsibilities is bad for a nation, encouraging an attitude of mere Jingoism, which is most provocative of war. The Central African Colonies might be exchanged with some foreign power, and as Englishmen have not yet settled there to any great extent, few would suffer by such a transfer. (**4**) Though it is obvious that new markets are very desirable for England, Central Africa is not likely ever to become an important one. We do a far larger trade with certain foreign States and their Colonies than we do with all our African Colonies put together; and any policy that would be likely to jeopardize this is impolitic. (**5**) This trade is a decreasing one; nor is the decline likely to be merely temporary. (**6**) No analogy can be drawn between Africa and India, which was in possession of enormous resources and an ancient civilization before we took possession of it.

AGNOSTICISM.

Pro: It is fruitless to argue on subjects such as the existence of God, the Soul, the External World, or other problems with reference to which we can never verify our conclusions. We cannot know things (*noumena*), only appearances (*phenomena*), and must therefore hold our judgment in suspense.

Some of the greatest philosophers since Locke in England and Kant in Germany have recognized this, and endeavoured to turn philosophy from questions of Being (ontology) to those of Knowing (epistemology).

In the words of Professor Huxley, the author of the term "Agnostic":

"Agnosticism is not a creed but a method, the essence of which lies in the rigorous application of a single principle. Positively the principle may be expressed: In matters of the intellect follow your reason as far as it will take you without regard to any other consideration. And negatively: In matters of the intellect do not pretend that conclusions are certain which are not demonstrated nor demonstrable."—*Essays on Some Controverted Questions* [1892], p. 362.

Con: It is impossible for man to be satisfied with a mere negation or negative position. The regions of the known are widened by every fresh discovery, so that it is manifestly arbitrary to place any limit to the possibility of the knowable.

To say we only know *phenomena*, not things as they are, is to erect an unreal abstraction into the most important place in our philosophy. Things as they are, apart from possible human knowledge, cannot be said to exist; and the mere positing of an unknowable *noumenon* is an absurdity. To say that a thing exists is to say that it is knowable.

Epistemology is thus equivalent to Ontology.

AGRICULTURAL BANKS.

Pro: (**1**) One of the chief causes contributing to the depression in British agriculture is the difficulty our farmers experience in obtaining credit in comparison with our competitors abroad. Owing to this, they have been unable to enter favourably into competition with foreign farmers (Danish, German, French, etc.) for the supply of vegetables, eggs, poultry, etc., to the London and other markets; for these demand a larger capital proportionately than ordinary farming—a capital which the farmers of several other nations can obtain through their Agricultural Banks, but which ours cannot. (**2**) The present Banking System, while it secures credit to the average trader, is insufficient to meet the wants of Agriculture for the following reasons: (*a*) The loan is needed for an unusually long time, *e.g.*, if hops are grown, for perhaps several years, thus the risks are enormously increased. (*b*) The farmer has practically no sufficient security such as a Banker can recognize, excepting character and (in the case of the allotment-holder) his wages, since even in the case of the larger capitalist-farmer his capital is almost all sunk in his farm. (**3**) While the landlord may in some few cases act as a loan agent, this is impossible in the case of most landlords, and highly undesirable, since, in the case of the landlord refusing, it would be very difficult for the tenant to obtain credit elsewhere. (4) The difficulty of obtaining credit has already brought a large number of the farmers into the hands of the money-lenders and dealers, who charge most exorbitant sums for slight assistance, and are indeed often mere swindlers, who make no advances at all, but simply angle for "preliminary" and "enquiry" fees. (5) Worked on the Raifeisen System, Agricultural Banks have proved most successful on the Continent: whole districts have, through their instrumentality, been relieved from entanglements arising from Jewish usury. Banks do not often lose their loans; even in the most illiterate parts of Silesia one of these Banks has, in 15 years, lost only £150 out of a total of £6,400,000 lent. (6) Agricultural Banks, being on a co-operative basis and strictly limited to members, all of whom must be intimately acquainted with each other, are able to do a very much safer business, whilst at the same time they can lend when other Banks would not dare to do so. Where the liability of members to outsiders is unlimited, it makes each of the members very much more careful. (7) They are in no sense competitors to ordinary Banks, but, on the contrary, bring them a larger business by breaking new ground which the old Banks cannot reach.

Con: (1) The real cause of the decline of British agriculture lies in the fact that, owing to a combination of the possession of favourable soil, good climate, and low freights, our foreign competitors are able to sell huge quantities of corn at prices which our farmers cannot afford to take. And as regards poultry, eggs, butter, etc., all the previous experience in this line shows that it is the invincible ignorance and prejudice of the farming class, and not want of capital, that is at the root of this evil. Capital without a knowledge how to use it advantageously would simply lead to ruinous speculation all round. (2) No Bank could stand the risk of lending for several years in a risky business such as agriculture; and, whilst a run of luck may carry them on for many years, small co-operative Banks could not work on these principles. (3) The landlord, as knowing the tenant's resources, is the person most competent to lend money on fair terms, since he has a direct interest in keeping his tenant solvent and in improving his own land; and moreover, good tenants are hard to get, and probably still harder to keep. (4) It is impossible to expect that in agriculture the means for obtaining credit shall be as good as in trades where less uncertainty prevails; and in proportion as this is the case, so much the higher must be the terms demanded by those who take the risks. Of course the borrower must protect himself against fraud. No law can so adequately prevent a man from falling a victim to such a palpable form of deception as the "preliminary fee" fraud as can the man himself. (5) The experience of foreign countries can give us no idea as to how a system would work here. English farming under Free Trade, with hostile railway tariffs, is very different from the protected system of the Continent with State railways aiding them with low rates. (6) Banking worked on a co-operative basis could hardly ever prove as useful as Banks worked by a single man of business or a firm. For example: it is found in business that Banks worked by partners are much more accommodating to good clients in the matter of calling loans than are Joint Stock Banks worked by directors. (7) The Banks extend everywhere in England and to almost all classes, so that there is practically no new ground to break up, without interfering with the existing Banks.

AGRICULTURAL DEPRESSION: should remedies be sought?

Pro: (1) Agriculture is unquestionably our most important industry. (2) When agriculture is prosperous, its prosperity reacts on other industries, increases the demand for goods of various kinds, and thus helps to benefit the towns. (3) Agriculture supplies the men who form the backbone of Britain. Town populations can be kept up only by drafts on country districts, town families always having a tendency to die out. (**4**) Government cannot stand by and watch the conversion of agriculture into a huge monopoly, consisting of vast farms worked by a comparatively few hands with the aid of machinery. (**5**) Agriculture is in many ways unfavourably situated in regard to obtaining credit, etc., owing to the uncertain nature of crops and the many accidents to which they are liable. In view of the great importance of the problem, Government might reasonably give such facilities as would enable farmers to tide over their difficulties. (*See* AGRICULTURAL BANKS.) In former days high prices recouped a farmer in a bad year; now they do so no longer, as in bad seasons food is imported from abroad.

Con: (**1**) Agriculture is no more important to the nation than other great industries. (**2**) When any industry is prosperous, it reacts on all other industries, especially on agriculture. (**3**) There is no evidence that townsmen are necessarily more unhealthy than their country neighbours, or that town families necessarily die out. With the tendency to go further and further into the suburbs, encouraged by increased railway facilities, there is no reason why men should live in such confined places as they now do, or should not enjoy all the advantages of a country life. Moreover, with the introduction of electricity, it is prophesied that factories will more and more tend to go further into the country, and thus render the continued draft on village population unnecessary. (**4**) Government interference would do more harm than good by checking the necessary transformation of the industry from small to great. Large farms are worked at a greater profit and on better methods than small farms can be. (**5**) State assistance of agriculture would involve the same relief being granted to other industries, a policy which must soon land us in national disaster. Private enterprize is doing all that is possible.

AGRICULTURAL LIGHT RAILWAYS.

Pro: (**1**) As a partial remedy for agricultural distress the State should undertake the construction of Light Tramways in country districts along the roads, for such railways would enable the farmer to get his produce quickly and cheaply into the market, and would put him on a better footing as regards foreign competition. (**2**) The great cost of building railways on the present system has always told against their extension to country districts, whereas the proposed Light Railways could be made at a comparatively low cost. (**3**) Light cars would not travel fast enough to be dangerous to traffic, but quite fast enough to be a considerable saving of time. Horses would soon get accustomed to them. (**4**) They would not render superfluous the use of horses on the farm or for pleasure purposes; but, even if they were to, it would be no argument against their introduction.

Con: (**1**) Such railways have been tried and have failed in Ireland, nor does it seem likely that they would be much more successful elsewhere, or in any case go far towards remedying agricultural depression. (**2**) The expense of construction, except in very flat countries, would be great; but, whatever the cost, it would have to come out of the county rates, and thus accentuate the farmer's evil plight. (**3**) They would either be dangerous to wayfarers (especially children), stray cattle, etc., or too slow for practical purposes. Horses would no more get accustomed to them than they have to traction engines. (**4**) They would tend to destroy the value of horses. (**5**) They would cut up and render necessary the widening of country roads, and impair the beauty of our countryside. (**6**) They would involve the handling of goods at least once, sometimes twice, more than at present—a great expense and drawback.

AGRICULTURAL RATES ACT.

Pro: (**1**) In view of the distressed state of agriculture, the Government should at least do what they can to relieve the farmer of the burden of taxation on a basis fixed when the farmer was protected. The country having benefited by Free Trade at the expense of the farmers can afford to be just to the latter. (2) The Land Tax was originally a tax on all forms of property, and in view of this, when the succession duty was first imposed, land was exempted. The fact that it has been found impossible to impose rates on personalty is a good reason for relieving the local rates through the Imperial treasury, as it enables an injustice to be rectified. Even where it has been compounded, the Land Tax equally forms a tax on property, as a higher price is paid for such properties. Agricultural land forms only a small proportion of the national wealth, and should not be taxed to relieve the wealthy classes who live on invested capital. (3) Though the value of land has fallen enormously, the rates have risen in consequence of the smaller assessment. The rates in towns may have risen more, but so has the wealth of the towns. (4) The whole agricultural community who gave evidence before the Commission and the greatest Treasury experts agreed that land pays a more than proportionate share of public taxation, and the report was signed by those members of the Commission who had had practical as opposed to purely theoretical knowledge of agricultural questions. (5) The fact that the landlord may ultimately derive some benefit is no reason for perpetuating an injustice. Rents, it may be safely said, will not rise, as, though many farms are held on yearly tenancies, the rent never changes as long as the farmer remains, and no wise landlord will offend a good tenant.

Con: (1) The farmer has benefited almost equally with the manufacturer in the increased cheapness of machinery and manufactured goods, and even of food. (2) It would be impossible to reimpose a local tax on personalty. The Land Tax is not an ordinary tax at all, but more in the nature of a charge on the land. Land is undoubtedly the most fruitful source of income. What is wanted is, not to relieve it of all taxation, but to arrange taxation so that it shall fall more heavily on those lands which from proximity to towns have acquired an unearned increment, and which were very lightly taxed, and are by the recent Act almost exempt. (3) The rates on agricultural land have fallen enormously in total amount, and even on the rateable value, in the last few years, while those in towns have greatly risen. (4) The evidence of the farmers was chiefly directed to showing what protection would do for them. Sir Alfred Milner's figures as to the incidence of taxation were shown to be fallacious by Sir Robert Giffen. But the relief given is least in those parishes where the distress being greatest the assessment is low, and greatest in the case of those parishes where market gardens being most common the assessment is highest because the depression is hardly felt. (5) Rates are paid in reality by the owner, and, farms being held on a yearly tenancy, in most cases this will raise the rent—at least, the owners will not be so lax with arrears.

ALLOTMENTS & SMALL HOLDINGS EXTENSION.

Pro: (1) By the enclosure of common lands, etc., the labourer has been gradually deprived of all interest in the land. The provision of allotments would go a long way towards remedying this evil; and, while not interfering with his power to earn wages, would yet make him less dependent, give him an interest in life, and help towards keeping him on the land from which the present joyless condition of his life is too surely driving him. (2) It would lead to the better cultivation of the land. (3) The landlords are in law the tenants of the State; hence the State has a perfect right to interfere with a view to prevent abuses. (4) Since compulsory powers are necessary to secure the land at a fair price, extended powers should be given to the local authorities, County Councils, etc., to compulsorily buy land at a fair price for the purpose of letting it in allotments, etc., where they are satisfied that these are required by the people and the landlord refuses to supply them.

(5) Public opinion would always be able to guarantee the rights of any particular landlord against unfair treatment. (6) The tenant could easily sell his right. (7) Where allotments have been refused, it has generally been because the terms were so grossly unfair and the rents so high as to render the offer a farce, which it was often meant to be. (8) Allotment holders have cheerfully paid four times the farmer's rent; hence there ought to be no difficulty in making the purchase pay on the part of the community.

Con: (1) Allotments have not been popular; labourers have rarely troubled to take them. If numerous they would lower wages, partly because the men could not give as much of their time to their work as before, partly because they would be tied to the soil. (2) Where the farmer does not succeed, the labourer would have very little chance, especially when worried by a public authority and hedged about with all sorts of futile restrictions. (3) Though landlords hold their land directly from the Queen *in capite*, it is absurd that she should force them to part with it, simply to hand it over to another. In any case it would be unwise on the part of the State to do anything which would shake the popular belief in the sanctity of the rights of property. Sufficient powers are already vested in the authorities, so that any extra powers would benefit only a small minority at the expense of the landlord and the community generally. (4) The proposed legislation would allow local authorities to take the most valuable part of a landlord's property at a price which would not compensate him, and might lower the value of the rest of his property. (5) Public opinion is no sufficient safeguard against abuse of power on the part of local authorities. (6) Allotments would prevent the movement of labour, keeping it fixed in places where it might not be wanted. (7) It is better to leave such problems to the laws of supply and demand, bearing in mind that it is unreasonable to expect a landlord to let three acres at the same rate as thirty. (8) The principal claim of the labourer is that he should obtain land at "farmers' rents," so that the community could not get the rents at present paid for allotments. (9) Purchase of land for allotments by the County Council would raise rates.

ALSACE-LORRAINE: shall Germany cede it?

Pro: (1) Whatever may be the strategic reasons in favour of holding Alsace-Lorraine, they are more than balanced by involving on Germany the perpetual hostility of France, a hostility which not only weakens Germany by forcing on her a huge military expenditure, but complicates her diplomacy, as it has done in the unsuccessful attempt to prevent Russia from allying herself with France. (2) Were the Alsace-Lorraine question out of the way, the chief menace to the peace of Europe would be removed. (3) France will never agree to the present situation. The younger generation of Frenchmen are as keen as the old, if not keener, in their conviction that no friendship between France and Germany is possible while Germany holds these provinces. (4) France had had Alsace-Lorraine for over 200 years, and consequently her right was indisputable. (5) The idea that Germany holds these provinces so that by insulting France she may keep up the loyalty of the Southern States to the German *Bund* may be true, but in this case she pays a price out of all proportion to any possible gain she can acquire from German unity. (6) There is no reason why Germany and France should not agree to neutralize the provinces, dismantling the fortresses. Were this done, France, having got all she wanted, would not wish to attack Germany. (7) Germany has never secured the loyalty of the population, which in the 200 years of French rule had become French. The German officials with their brutality have never even attempted to conciliate the people.

Con: (1) Strategic reasons must alone determine Germany to retain Alsace-Lorraine, as the advantage which their possession in the case of war would

confer on Germany is enormous. Further, it is certain that the French would always have found cause for wrath in having to recognize Germany as a power at all, a country which she had always considered as a vassal, and in whose weakness she had always considered her strength to lie. Austria was in a totally different position, as, owing to her peculiar position, she needed protection against Russia—which could be accorded only by Germany.
(2) Such questions as Egypt, the Turkish Question and Constantinople, the Advance of Russia on India, and many other questions, would still remain, and exercize a much stronger hold than the memories of 1870-71, even among Frenchmen. (3) The Colonial movement, the revival of which was due to M. Jules Ferry and Prince Bismarck, has undoubtedly succeeded in drawing the attention of France and in diverting her energies from Germany. Whatever they may say, it is beyond doubt that no responsible French statesman or Frenchman would dream of attacking Germany alone, or could imagine that the Russian Alliance could be used for that purpose. It is much more likely that the latter is aimed at England—the occupation of Egypt being the burning question in France; and the alliance of Germany, passive or active, would probably be welcomed for the purpose of settling this question in the interests of France, while Russia took India. (4) Alsace-Lorraine had been most arbitrarily taken by France from Germany, and the restoration was undoubtedly popular in Germany as completing the idea of German unity. (5) Germany has a good motive in retaining these provinces, as, by keeping France hostile, it restrains all wish on the part of the disaffected States to leave the German *Bund*. The unity of Germany being a desirable object, this policy is perfectly natural, and enables the effect of years of separation to gradually disappear. (6) Germany has no object in consenting to a policy which, while no gain to her, would deprive her of all the trouble she has taken to make these fortresses, Metz, Strassburg, etc., impregnable, and would create endless friction. (7) The population of Alsace-Lorraine is much more loyal now than it was.

AMERICA AND ENGLAND: Union of the English-speaking Race.

Pro: (1) The great need of the day is that those races of the world which, so to speak, form the vanguard of progress should, as far as possible, combine their strength in the effort to overcome the forces of savagery and reaction. As speaking a common language, inheriting common traditions, and being very nearly allied in all forms of thought and government, it is eminently desirable that the English-speaking race should unite, as a preliminary to a possible wider confederation of the Teutonic and Latin races.
(2) The advantages of such a union will be seen as a factor making for peace, when we remember, for instance, that a trifling boundary question in South America between England and Venezuela, which now becomes for Americans (who naturally do not wish to see European powers encroaching on the American Continent) a grave question out of all proportion to its intrinsic importance, would raise no dispute were the foreign interests of both peoples the same. (3) Thus, to take Armenia as an example, instead of the whole English-speaking world being shocked by horrors which it was powerless to prevent, the question could have been at once settled by the English-speaking race, if united. (4) Whether under such a union Canada joined the United States or not would be a question between the two countries; but it is quite conceivable that the Canadians might remain independent if they wished it: though, as the advantages of a union to Canada would be enormous, it is probable that interest would overcome prejudice. (5) Both England and America are equally democratic, though the former may not be so in form, and few Englishmen, however much they may respect the throne and its present occupant, would allow that to stand in the way of a closer union with America. (6) The actions of nations are in the long run

governed by their interests, and not by their prejudices, or must be if they are to continue to hold any sway in the world. This consideration alone has made it possible to create the modern German Empire out of the mutually antipathetic countries, such as Prussia and Saxony, Prussia and Bavaria, etc. Prussia was and is still universally detested, though not so strongly by these other States of the Confederation; yet that does not prevent a union against common foes. In the same way when America, as Australia has already done, finds her trade in China and the Far East threatened by Russia and Japan (it may be a long time off), and sees that isolation is impossible, she will reconsider her position. (7) The difficulties of Imperial Federation have on the whole been exaggerated, but Imperial Federation, excluding as it does the United States, is likely to be looked at rather askance, especially by those of our Colonies which, valuing the goodwill of the States, would not like to take any step which could in any way be construed as hostile to them. Consequently a union which embraced the whole English-speaking race has probably a better chance of success than one which embraces only a part. (8) As India is and must remain a dependency for many generations, the government of India would be just as easy under a common government as under that of England alone. (9) The question of the predominance of one State or another, as involved in such questions as the Capital and seat of Government, etc., could be met by referring it to a referendum of the whole English-speaking world; as the probabilities are that it would resolve itself into a question of Washington or London, the common-sense and mutual accommodation of the two peoples would probably be easily able to settle this question. It is undoubtedly unnecessary that any power should have a predominating influence, nor could it under a really democratic constitution, *e.g.*, were a referendum to the whole English-speaking people made the final appeal. (10) There seems no reason why the question of tariffs should not be decided by each member of the union for itself. (Some) A customs union might be formed on the basis of reciprocal Free Trade with mutual advantage to all.

Con: (1) Nations need some much stronger ties than are afforded by mere identity of language. Were language the great bond of union, we might expect to see the various German-speaking peoples in Switzerland and Austria entering the German *Bund;* but, as a matter of fact, it is probable that only the pressure of external dangers keeps the *Bund* itself together. As the recent crisis conclusively showed, where national interests clash identity of language rather aggravates a crisis, by enabling each country to see the extreme view of fanatical jingoes on the other side. (2) It is not difficult to imagine occasions on which differences of opinion would arise within the Federation itself; and, indeed, the commercial and national jealousy of the two great States, of which the Venezuelan crisis was only a symptom, would go a long way to render union impossible. (3) No American Government would be justified in exposing the interests of its citizens to a war on behalf of the Armenians; but if they did, a treaty of alliance between England and America would be effective enough for the purpose. (4) Canadians, whatever desire a small minority may have for independence, repudiate any connection with the United States; and if the question of the union of the English-speaking race arose, it is difficult to see how it could get over the difficulty engendered by the jealousy of these two members of it. (5) The fact that England is in form and sympathy monarchical and aristocratic, and the United States as firmly attached to democracy, is sufficient to prevent any political union. (6) The disadvantages that would arise from a surrender of independent action would more than outweigh any advantages that an increase of strength could bring about. The chance of a common danger affecting the whole race is sufficiently remote to render discussion of the point futile. (7) If the difficulties of Imperial Federation are seen to be great, those of the union of the English-speaking races are infinitely greater. In fact, the chief advantage that the former has is, that it is supposed to be practical; but if this is not so, then the English-speaking Federation becomes a veritable myth. In a small way the same difficulties have been witnessed in the case of Australian Federation. Now it may freely be concluded that, if the Australian Colonies cannot agree over such a simple question as this, the prospects of Imperial Federation itself are exceedingly hazy. (8) The government of India would present almost insuperable difficulties to any such scheme, since it is more than probable that an attempt would be made to force on her a democratic constitution for which she is not ripe. (9) The question of the Capital, as deciding which State should have the predominating voice, would excite the keenest jealousy—notably between Washington and London; and it is not likely that the self-respect and pride of either would allow it to yield to the claims of the other; yet it is obvious that the Government must have a settled seat.

ANARCHISM.

Pro: (1) Universal suffrage and democratic rule constitute as great a danger to liberty in this age as the aristocracies and monarchies of the past did in their times. The Anarchists contend, as against the Socialists, that what is wanted to secure to every man his rights is not an increase in the sphere of government, but its total abolition. (2) The amount of work already done voluntarily shows what can be done in the absence of all contract, and without any idea of Government control. Neither fines nor compulsion are so effective as free agreements. Man can always refuse to work with or for those who have failed to act honourably. (3) A Swiss citizen belongs to at least a dozen Societies, which supply him with things considered elsewhere within the province of government, such as roads, fountains, etc. (4) Anarchy does not mean disorder—simply the absence of legal compulsion.

Con: (1) Some form of government cannot possibly be dispensed with so long as human nature remains what it is. Though Democracy, Aristocracy, and Monarchy may all have proved gross tyrannies, yet No-government would be a greater tyranny still. Instead of, at the worst, being the victim of the indignation of a whole people, an unpopular person would be at the mercy of any small body of men, or even of any single man, who chose to attack him. It is only through settled government that commerce, science, education, religion, etc., can exist at all. (2) It is precisely government which renders those voluntary agreements possible which are now used as an object lesson against it, while, in practice, the only way to ensure that a man shall carry out his undertakings is to attach some penalty to their non-observance. (3) The existence, or at any rate prosperous management, of voluntary associations, such as the Swiss Societies, implies a settled government behind them. (4) True liberty is only possible under Law.

ANGLICAN CHURCH (Modern): is it a branch of the Catholic Church?

Pro: (1) The Anglican Church preserves an unbroken continuity with her past, and her Orders have never lost their validity. (*See* ANGLICAN ORDERS.) (2) She has rejected no doctrine which was held essential by the Primitive Church, or which could be found in the Bible She has merely cleared away abuses which had grown up. (3) All the National Churches had power to vary customs and ceremonies; but none of them to add to the faith, as has been done by the Church of Rome. The fact that ignorance as to rights existed does not destroy those rights.

Con: (1) The Anglican Orders are not valid (*See* ANGLICAN ORDERS), and the present English Church is merely a political creature set up by Henry VIII. and carried out by his successors, to supply the place of the old Church of England. (2) The Church of England has erred deeply in doctrine.

(3) The so-called Branch Theory of National Churches is merely an argument started by the Ritualists in the English Church to justify their position. The great majority of Anglicans have always held that she is Protestant, and not Catholic.

ANGLICAN ORDERS.

Roman Catholic Attitude: (1) Rome has pronounced against Anglican Orders. (2) No record of the consecration of Bp. Barlow [1559], who consecrated Archbishop Parker, exists; and it is doubtful if he was ever consecrated at all. Cranmer, who kept his notes for his Register with great care, has no entry of it. (3) The Ordinal used at Parker's consecration—that of Edward VI.—shows a manifest intention of not making a Catholic bishop, as then and now understood, but of appointing an overseer, who, deriving his power from the Sovereign, should administer discipline, teach, and preach. Similarly the Anglican Ordinal for making priests, at any rate down to Charles II., bore on its face the intention not to make sacrificing priests, but a "Gospel ministry." (4) Even if the Anglican Orders were valid, they would not belong to the true Church. Catholics "know" that their Orders are valid because they are members of the True Church, and Anglicans "believe" that they belong to the True Church because their Orders are valid.

Anglican Attitude: (1) The Council of Trent was asked by Pius IV. to declare the consecration of the Elizabethan bishops to be invalid, but refused to do so. (2) Though the record of Barlow's consecration has been lost, sufficient evidence remains to show that he had been consecrated Bp. of St. David's, inasmuch as his nomination, election, and confirmation can be proved, as well as his installation, recovery of temporalities, summons to the House of Lords, voting there and in Convocation. Bp. Gardiner, writing to Protector Somerset, speaks of Barlow as a bishop; and Queen Mary's *congé d'élire*, naming Gilbert Bourne to the See of Bath and Wells, specifies the resignation of William Barlow, last bishop thereof, as the cause of the vacancy. The fact that Cranmer omitted to note the fact of consecration in his Register is accounted for by the carelessness with which that Register was kept, the names of no fewer than 8 other prelates having been omitted, though there is contemporary evidence to prove their consecration. Other public documents exist at Lambeth and in H.M. Public Record Office, which prove Barlow's consecration; but even if he had not been consecrated, it is undisputed that the other two bishops assisting in the consecration had been consecrated; and the Nicene canons ordering three bishops to take part in every consecration were adopted to meet a case of this sort, in order that B and C might supply any defects of A. Hence Barlow could not affect the validity of Parker's consecration. (3) All that is necessary for the validity of consecration is that a bishop, himself consecrated, should transmit the office through the laying-on of hands. England has never ceased to be Christian, and the line of consecrated bishops has remained unbroken. It is hard to draw any distinction between a "bishop" and an "overseer" [$\dot{\epsilon}\pi\iota\sigma\kappa o\pi o s$]. (4) How are we to know what constitutes the True Church, apart from its Apostolic Succession?

ANTI-SEMITISM IN RUSSIA.

Pro: (1) The anti-Semitic movement in Russia is in no way the result of religious intolerance, but is purely a social and economic movement on the part of the people of Russia to free themselves from the tyrannous exactions of the Jewish money-lender. (2) That Russia is most tolerant in religious matters has been testified to by competent observers of all nations and peoples; and, though full liberty is not given to dissenters from the orthodox faith, dissenting sects and so on, and proselytism is strictly confined to the State Church, this is only because the State Church is the outward and visible sign of racial unity, and the Czar, who is head of the orthodox Russian Church as well as of the State, cannot allow his rights to be entrenched upon. (Some) Many of the so-called persecutions of dissenters in Russia have been on account of doctrines subversive of morals having been promulgated thereby. (3) The Jews in Russia have always been notorious for the fact that they never live by manual labour, but are simply parasites living on the labour of others. The usury of the Jews among the ignorant Russian peasants has wrought untold mischief; it is notorious that when a Jew arrives in a village he never leaves it till he has ruined it. Again, though middlemen (which the Jews are always) may be necessary in small numbers, when they become so numerous as the Jews in Russia they are almost compelled to become parasites. (4) The Jews monopolize the whole trade of many parts of Russia, where their keen business habits and unscrupulous methods of killing competition by playing into each other's hands, has driven their rivals from the field. (5) Jews are to be found in every disreputable trade. They keep the gin shops, disorderly houses, etc. They are smugglers, and, with the aid of unscrupulous officials, manage to rob the State of large sums of money yearly. Russian women who are employed by Jews almost invariably lose their religion and morality, and sink into prostitution. (6) The Jews help to spread the seditious and subversive doctrines of Nihilism among the people. (7) The outrages on the Jews reported in the foreign newspapers have been very much exaggerated; in fact, the English Consular reports, 1881 (*Accounts and Papers*, 1882, vol. lxxxi., "Correspondence concerning the Jews in Russia"), show that, as an example, where the Jews had assessed damages at 300,000 roubles, 20,000 was the greatest value placed on it by independent valuers; and whole accounts of outrages, houses demolished, etc., were utterly unfounded, or grossly exaggerated; also that the Government, who were said to have aided and abetted, were absolutely blameless in this matter, which originated purely spontaneously, that it was, in fact, only owing to the prompt action of the Government that more damage was not done. Russia has no wish to become, like Austria-Hungary, a Jewish Empire; but it was obvious that if the Jews were allowed freedom to go where they liked this would soon be the case, since their alarming fertility and cleverness would soon enable them to overrun the whole of Russia. Among those who were charged with shirking military service, out of a total of 23%, the Jews were 20%. The Jews cannot complain of hardship when the Government merely puts in force a law which they (the Jews) were consciously breaking, with the connivance of the Russian official. For example, it was perfectly well known that St. Petersburg and Moscow were closed to Jews, yet at one time they swarmed in both — naturally by corrupting the officials.

Con: (2) Russia is not tolerant in matters of religion; though professedly allowing freedom to other religions, every device is taken to entice away adherents, who, when they are once classified as orthodox (even sometimes by mistake or against the will of the individual, as when whole villages have been converted *en masse*), are prescribed by the law against proselytism from returning to their previous worship: further, a father may not even, under penalty, dissuade his children from adopting the creed of the Czar. (3) Considering that, in the opinion of competent observers, eight-tenths of the Jews live from hand to mouth and possess no means whatever, they cannot be in a position to lend largely. Of the rest, half are artizans. They cannot take part in professions which are closed to them (as most are); and money-lending is, in fact, one of the few which are open to them, though even in this the rate of interest paid to the Jews is less than that paid to the native money-lender. Even were the rate of interest exorbitant, the best way to meet the evil would be in supplanting the Jew by institutions such as Land Banks (*See* AGRICULTURAL BANKS), rather than by harrying the Jews and rendering their property insecure, thus aggravating the evil. (4) The charges against the Jews of using unfair methods of competition are absolutely unfounded. A commission appointed by the Russian Government to investigate the matter, under the presidency of Count Pahlin, a former Minister of Justice, came to the conclusion that the Jews were a distinct benefit rather than an evil. The Jews in South Russia are entrusted by the foreign commercial establishments in the country to do the most private business. (5) The spirit trade was forced on the Jews by the Polish nobles; and so far from inducing the people to drink, the habit is far worse in those parts of the country where there are no Jews, than where there are. The Government returns showed that the spirit consumption in the latter was double that in the former. (6) The accusation against the Jews of being concerned with Secret Societies is absolutely false, though, considering the provocation they suffer through the imposition of unjust laws, it would be no wonder if the accusation were justified. (7) The outrages on the Jewish population were very serious, and though in some cases perhaps exaggerated, yet this in no way militates against the fact that they have been brutally ill-treated. Moreover, as Leroy Beaulieu clearly shows, there is every reason to believe that some of the outrages were directly connived at by the Government, and were in no sense a spontaneous rising. (*The Empire of the Czars*, vol. iii., p. 551.) By concentrating the Jews on a given area the Russian Government has done its best to aggravate the evil of which it complains; but nevertheless, even Poland, the most Jew-ridden province of Russia, is at the same time the wealthiest. The Jews, according to the military returns, provide a larger contingent of recruits to the Russian army than any other class in the community; moreover, where among Christians schoolmasters are exempt, among the Jews they have to serve, and, among other things, the Jews find it very much harder to escape military service than any other class in the community. The Jews have good reason to complain when laws which have lain dormant for years have been suddenly and without warning put in force (as in Moscow in the height of winter on a cold night, when the Jewish residents were suddenly turned out of house and home).

ARBITRATION, COMMERCIAL.

Pro: (1) Arbitration is a great saving of both time and money to the parties to the dispute. (2) It economizes the time of the Courts of Justice, and relieves them of technical work with which they are not wholly qualified to deal, leaving the decision in the hands of a trade expert.

Con: (1) It is no saving of money to the party to whom the verdict should belong if he loses his case or part of it, though saving most of his legal expenses. (2) The court is a better tribunal before which to bring disputes than a trade arbitrator, who cannot well be wholly free from trade prejudices, and who, at best, can be nothing but an untrained judge. His strong tendency always is to "split the difference" between the parties in dispute. It is also a good thing to occasionally have a judge's opinion on "trade customs."

ARBITRATION, COMPULSORY INDUSTRIAL.

Pro: (1) The damage arising from strikes is so immense that the State ought, in the interests of the public, to interfere and afford means for arbitration, which must be compulsory in order to render the award binding on both parties. (2) As the arbitrator would be appointed by both parties, there is no reason why either should object to abide by his decision.

Con: (1) There is already provision for legalized arbitration [5 Geo. IV. c. 96, Lord St. Leonard's Act of 1867 (30 & 31 Vict. c. 105), and Mundella's Act of 1872 (35 & 36 Vict. c. 46)], though this legislation has so far been inoperative. Granting that arbitration may at times be useful, why should it be compulsory? (2) There would be an almost insurmountable difficulty in obtaining a competent arbitrator, and in supplying him with the requisite facts. Moreover, an agreement as to the principles on which he should work could never be determined by the two parties to the dispute.

ARBITRATION, INTERNATIONAL: is it a Substitute for War?

Pro: (1) Arbitration brings reason and justice, in place of force, as the final arbiter in International disputes. (2) War settles nothing, but merely leaves behind a desire for revenge. Arbitration, on the other hand, settles disputes in an amicable and just manner. (3) The cost of war and the preparations against attack involve Europe in an immense and increasing taxation, which threatens universal bankruptcy or universal war, or both—to say nothing of the numbers of men withdrawn from industry. (Some) Over-production and over-population could be met, the former by a better organization of industry, and the latter by the exercise of prudence and restraint on the part of the various members of Society. (4) Nations do respect these decisions, as has been proved by experience, for the very same reason that they have kept other treaties. Arbitration is optional, and a nation will be hardly likely to ignore the decision of a Court to which they have appealed. (Some) Some form of European Federation ought to be aimed at which, leaving each nation free as regards internal affairs, might arrange the relations of those States to each other on a basis of mutual accommodation. (Some) A permanent tribunal of Arbitration might be formed to which nations should be bound to submit their disputes, and which should, if possible, be supplied by the various powers, with force to compel its decisions. (5) War has been got rid of between individuals; why then should it be impossible to abolish it between States? As civilization advances, competition gives way more and more to co-operation. War may have been necessary to teach man the value of the Social State, but, when this is learnt, the circumstances are altered. Co-operation between nations is a much more efficient means to the same end than competition. (7) International morality has made enormous strides within the last few years. Even wars are conducted with much less brutality: witness the conduct of the soldiers in the Franco-German War as compared with that of the men in the Napoleonic Wars. And it continually makes fresh strides, largely owing to the awakening of the popular conscience in various lands to a sense of the people's responsibility for the doings of their Government. (8) The fact that periods of struggle produced great master-pieces of literature and art in the past would not prove that it would do so now, or justify us in furthering war on that account. As a set-off also must be allowed the loss of human life, and the amount of energy diverted from useful elements to purposes of mere destruction.

Con: (1) Arbitration, save in isolated cases, can never supersede war. International law is far too vague to give any guidance, and there is no guarantee that the award will be adhered to. Arbitration is, usually, only possible where one nation agrees to abandon a portion of its claims. (2) Arbitration, like a lawsuit, leads to bickering and fraud. Nations put forward forged documents. Each country sees only its own side, and passions are just as much stirred as in war. Awards rarely satisfy. (3) War is the best cure for surplus wealth and population. In peace the productive powers of mankind have passed their powers of consumption; the markets are glutted and men thrown out of employment, in addition to a vast surplus over-population having accrued. War corrects these evils. Arbitration is possible only between nations of equal strength. Strong nations will certainly never go to arbitration on important matters with weak nations. (4) The attempt to organize Europe federally has been made by Emperors and Popes, but was rejected, as it meant a tyranny which no self-respecting nation would submit to. Arbitration is always unsatisfactory, and its awards have not always been carried out, *e.g.*, America refused the Behring Sea award. (5) War between individuals organized under a common State is very different from that between States. Were a Universal State possible, war might come to an end; but till all men speak the same language and reach the same level of culture the Universal State is impossible, excepting under a Cæsar, who is not likely to arise. At present the Individual State represents the ripest fruit of human organizing power. (6) Competition is a most essential element in human progress, and eliminates the unfit in nations as among individuals. By war alone has man become a social animal organized into a State. Men will always compete or stagnate; civilization has altered the direction, but not lessened the importance, of competition. (7) International morality is very weak. Neither public bodies nor nations have any conscience beyond utility. (8) Periods of struggle have invariably produced great deeds in action and thought, great masterpieces of literature and of art.

ARISTOCRATIC v. DEMOCRATIC GOVERNMENT.

Pro Aristocratic: (1) An Aristocratic Government is, by education and temperament, better fitted to govern society on broad principles, and with a view to the interests of the whole rather than to those of any particular class. Democracy, on the other hand, expects that each class will look to its own class-interests, and where, as generally happens, the lowest and least-instructed class happens to preponderate, that class will gain at the expense of the others. (2) We do not throw open the privileges attaching to the practice of medicine to anyone who proclaims himself to be a doctor, but enforce a certain training; nor do we even elect doctors by popular vote, but leave their qualification to experts: so, in government, it would be better to entrust ourselves to the hands of those who know how to govern or have had time to study the subject; for government as a profession is far more intricate than medicine, and makes even greater demand on time and energies. (3) Government by aristocracy concentrates all power into the hands of a few, who, being the cynosure of all eyes, are less inclined to abuse their powers than a democracy, which is under no such check. (4) Aristocracies are made up of men who have a very large stake in the country they are called upon to rule, and whose knowledge of history has taught them to avoid the errors of the past. (5) Aristocracies are always most particular to keep up the external splendour of the State, and thus to raise the nation in the eyes of mankind. (6) Aristocracies are much more stable than democracies, which are proverbially fickle, and hence offer a strong temptation to holders of office to secure all they can get during their brief tenure by corruption. In an aristocracy the tenure is neither brief, nor, as is often the case in democracies, does the Minister depend on it; hence he is much more likely to be disinterested. (7) Political as well as other qualities descend from father to son. (8) Democracy means government by catch-words.

Pro Democratic: (1) Aristocracies have invariably governed rather with a view to selfish class privileges and interests than to the interests of the nation as a whole. Democracy gives to each class a chance of having its views heard and its interests safeguarded. No one class can speak for the whole community, but each class can contribute something to the common wisdom. (2) No particular qualification or training fits a man to govern; but if such qualification exist it is certainly not possessed by the aristocratic classes, whose chief fault has been that they have never looked seriously enough on their duties, but always taken them in a dilettante spirit; in any case, the best guarantee lies, not in the formation of a political class, but in arousing all sections of the people to a due conception of their duties as members of the State. (3) Aristocracy has always led to nepotism and favouritism. (4) The interests of men with large properties do not always coincide with those of the community at large, but are often diametrically opposed to them. Nor are the members of this class remarkable for the knowledge they display of history. (5) Aristocracy tries to conceal its weakness, and impose on others by display and luxury. Democracy encourages simplicity, and seeks to appeal to the reality rather than the show of things, to a sense of right and an appreciation of good government. (6) Aristocracies suffer from the fact that the government gets into the hands of a few families, who may or may not produce good men: if they do, government works well, but if not (as is often the case), it is hard to get rid of a bad man with a powerful family influence at his back. (7) The doctrine of descent lends no support to the theory of an hereditary legislative class; in fact, the greatest men have generally either had no families or utterly incompetent sons. (8) Aristocracies are ruled as much by catch-words as other classes.

ARMENIAN QUESTION, THE, AND ENGLISH INTERVENTION.

Pro: (1) England, having been largely responsible for the maintenance of Turkey, and having, under the Cyprus Convention, undertaken special responsibilities towards securing the good government of the Asiatic provinces of Turkey, ought not and cannot allow the Armenians to be butchered by the Turkish soldiery. (2) The alleged Armenian plot is a pure myth, invented by the Turks as an excuse for their own brutalities. It is beyond all dispute that the oppression of the Turkish Government, and its utter inability to protect the Armenians against the Kurds, though they may have provoked reprisals, were responsible for the mischief. (3) It is necessary that England should make clear to Russia, as the only power who can help the Armenians, that England is not seeking her own aggrandizement, and that she has absolutely turned her back on the policy of opposition to Russia which she has followed since the Crimean War. It is not to be wondered at that Russia is hardly willing to take up the cause of the oppressed Armenians, when, having rescued the Bulgarians at the cost of much money and blood, she was robbed of the fruits of her victory by England, or that she should be unready to trust England again in view of the manner in which England turned Russia's discomfiture to her own advantage. Russia has repeatedly declared that she does not want Constantinople. (4) The Concert of Europe is, and has always been, a farce. Were England to have really shown her determination to act singly rather than not at all, it is certain that the Porte would have given way. The risk of combination against England on the part of the other powers was ludicrously small,—they would have had no common ground of agreement, as would have become evident had they attempted to take action. In any case, the assertion that England was going to take only diplomatic action was to render even that a farce, and was tantamount to an invitation to the Sultan to do what he liked.

Con: (1) England was powerless to interfere. Had she bombarded Constantinople—no easy task, as this forms one of the strongest positions in the world, and a hostile fleet would only with the greatest difficulty pass the Dardanelles—she would merely have incited the Turks to wholesale massacres which she would have been powerless to prevent, as they would have taken place many miles away, and inland. (2) The aspirations of the Armenians for independence (a wholly unrealizable dream for a scattered race living amongst alien and hostile populations), fanned by sympathizers in London and in Paris, caused them to rebel, which rebellion was put down, no doubt with considerable cruelty, by the Turkish soldiers. The Sultan's Government can, however, hardly be accounted responsible for the indignation of his fanatical subjects fighting, as they believed, for their creed (and here no doubt the language used by English politicians gave them good grounds for apprehension) against a race which is universally loathed and despised in the East by Christians and Mahommedans alike, much as the Jews are in the West, and for the same reasons. The so-called Constantinople massacre was the natural consequence of the cold-blooded attack made by the Armenians on the Ottoman Bank, when, having taken the Bank, they fired on the soldiers in an unprovoked manner. (3) The advice that England should invite Russia into Constantinople would be giving away what did not belong to us, would be very foolish (since it would put Russia in the very strongest position in the world), and would make the Black Sea a vast Russian lake, upon which her fleet could always fall back without much danger from attack: and would thus force us to enormously increase our fleet, proportionally to the Russian. It would not benefit the Armenians, who probably enjoy greater toleration under Turkish rule than their co-religionists in Russia, and who do not want to be subject to Russia. Russia's aims are undoubtedly to keep the question open, and to do this she has not hesitated to support the Porte against England, while at the same time inciting the Armenians to rebel. (4) The Concert of Europe is the only way reforms could be effected, short of a general European war, which would have followed had the English Government listened to fanatics.

ARMY SHORT SERVICE.

Pro: (1) Under the old system soldiers were kept abroad all their lives, or a very long time, and came to look on enlistment as only a last resource; hence our troops suffered in quantity and in quality. In India, for instance, a regiment sometimes stayed so long, that before it returned home all the original members had died out, having been replaced by drafts from home; which was certainly no economy. Short Service has given us a reserve, and, at any rate for India, a thoroughly efficient army, nor have the troops generally deteriorated. (2) Europeans never get acclimatized to India— rather the reverse: hence a Short Service keeps them more efficient, and is more humane. (3) Our Short Service is longer than the usual service on the Continent.

Con: (1) Under the old system, by long service, soldiers at least learnt their work. The army, though smaller than now, was more efficient, veterans being superior to the raw boys who go to India, and better able to take precautions against illness, etc. The Short Service system has, in fact, broken down in our Indian wars. (2) Troops learn to diet themselves in India, and the longer they stay the more competent they become. (3) Continental army regulations are no guide to the needs of the British Empire. (4) Short Service has abolished the old feeling of regimental *esprit de corps*, which had such an excellent effect on discipline, etc.

ASYLUMS, PRIVATE: ought they to be permitted?

Pro: (1) Doctors who own Private Asylums have every interest in effecting as many cures as possible for the sake of their reputation. They have no inducement to discharge a patient before he is quite cured, as often happens in Public Asylums. (2) Private establishments are now so closely under Government inspection that great abuses are impossible. (3) In Private Asylums it is possible to give much greater personal attention to individual cases, and to allow extra comforts, which is of much importance to certain patients, who ought to be allowed to have them if they can pay for them. (4) Private Asylums have every opportunity of becoming differentiated and noted for special classes of cases, instead of having all classes mixed up as in a public institution, which is classified by locality and not by disease. (5) Competition always affords a stimulus to introduction of improvements. (6) Gross injustice would be done to a hard-working class if they were not allowed to pursue a calling hitherto sanctioned by law; and compensation would be a great and unnecessary expense.

Con: (1) Asylums are institutions that ought not to be left to the working of individual interest. A cured patient retained in the establishment is just as remunerative to the doctor as a lunatic. (2) If no scandals occur in Private Asylums, why do we so often hear of them? Many great scandals have arisen owing to conspiracies between interested relations and doctors certifying sane people to be insane. Public institutions abolish this kind of danger. (3) It would be quite possible in a public institution to afford a patient such extra care as he may desire, or as may be thought desirable for him, provided he can pay for it. (4) In a public institution cases can be much more easily differentiated than in a Private Asylum. (5) Competition does not bring out good qualities so much as severe public inspection, which, in the case of Private Asylums, occurs only at intervals, and is not nearly so good as the disinterested service of professional men who are always on the spot. As a matter of fact, improvements have been brought about through Public Asylums rather than through Private Asylums. (6) The only interest to be considered in a case of this sort is the good of the public. Compensation would be comparatively inexpensive. (7) Since the superintendent necessarily has arbitrary power, it is advisable that he should be a public official.

AUTHORITY AS THE BASIS OF RELIGIOUS BELIEF.

Pro: (1) Authority enables a man to learn more than his unaided intellect could ever teach him, much in the same way as a microscope enables us to perceive more than we can see with the naked eye. (2) The majority of men have neither the time nor the ability to form opinions for themselves. In Science we are all bound to take the greater portion of our beliefs on the authority of others; why not in Theology? (3) Rationalism is a form of intellectual conceit.

Con: (1) Authority relieves man from the responsibility, which the possession of an intellect imposes, to find out the truth for himself. There is no analogy between the microscope and the authority of Church or Bible. The former admits of scientific verification, the latter cannot. (2) We are, it is true, obliged to take much on the authority of others, and are often deceived in so doing. Where our action, however, depends upon belief, we take all the means in our power to verify our hypothesis. (3) It is no more intellectual conceit to say that my reason is the highest authority I have, than to say that my eyes are the only organs I possess for vision. Reason is as much implied in the acceptance as in the rejection of any particular authority.

AUTHORS AND PUBLISHERS: are the former inequitably treated?

Pro: (1) The lion's share of the profits accruing from the sale of a successful book has hitherto gone to the Publisher, in spite of the fact that he never undertakes any venture (not excluding books by new writers) which involves him in financial risk. (2) Publishers thus grow rich, or at any rate well-to-do, whilst Authors, who supply the raw material, as a class remain poor. Successful Authors especially, who scarcely need a Publisher at all, are wholly inadequately paid. (3) In the case of "half-profit" ("partnership") books, Publishers make "secret profits" by charging against the joint account a larger sum for expenses than has really been incurred, and thus even in these cases fare better than Authors. Further, they sometimes make charges for warehousing, packing, and similar expenses, which should really be treated as establishment expenses. (4) In the case of "royalty" books, the royalties paid are far too low, and should be about doubled. (5) In the case of "commission" books, Publishers do nothing to promote their sales. Even if the present rate of commission were increased, Publishers would not treat commission books as though they had a permanent stake in them. (6) (Some) It would be advantageous for Authors to become their own Publishers, and thus save the payment to the middleman for mere distribution. (Others) An Authors' Publishing Association should be formed on co-operative principles.*

Con: (1) A successful book by a new and untried Author is often very profitable to the Publisher (such books, however, are few and far between); whilst unsuccessful "first books" frequently fail to bring back their cost of production and sale. Thus successes have to pay for failures—an invariable rule in speculative businesses. On the other hand, books by well-known Authors command adequate prices for their copyrights, frequently even more than the entire profits they earn. Occasionally *coups* are made by Publishers out of books even by famous writers; but these occur so infrequently that they may almost be left out of consideration. (2) Publishers, as a class, are by no means rich. Popular Authors, especially novelists, earn large incomes, frequently larger than prominent Publishers, although they have no capital at risk. The Publishers' contribution of money, experience, and trade machinery cannot be ignored. (3) "Secret profits" are wholly illegal, and therefore outside the scope of the present argument. Charges for warehousing, etc., are a matter of contract, and it is for the Author to see that they are properly provided for, and subsequently dealt with according to agreement. (4) Royalties have steadily risen for the past few years, and are still rising, owing to competition and the awakening of Authors to the financial value of a successful book. Really successful writers can and do now command almost their own terms; and it is questionable whether maximum royalties have not already been reached. (5) At the present rate of commission, books thus published scarcely pay the Publishers more than the incidental expenses of their sale, bad debts, and so on; they thus have no margin for vigorous "pushing," and, moreover, do not work their businesses for the sole benefit of Authors. (Some) Commission books receive all the advantages, apart from public advertisements (unless paid for by the Author), which their own ventures receive. (6) Experiments in the direction of amateur publishing have rarely proved successful (with one notable exception, that of Mr. Ruskin); and a Publisher's services, in the way of trade distribution, etc., are of real importance. A Publisher who provides all the capital for launching a literary venture is scarcely a middleman. If an Authors' Publishing Association were formed, it would be found that, unless run by a small clique of successful writers only, it would have to be conducted on lines identical with those of present Publishers.

BACHELORS, TAXATION OF (FRANCE).†

Pro: (1) Taxation should be based upon the resources and responsibilities of the citizen. (2) A family which contributes able-bodied children to the State is *ipso facto* contributing to the welfare of the country. (3) There is no class so well able to bear taxation as the bachelor. (4) Taxation of bachelors would encourage the idea that it is wrong to remain unmarried, and would reduce the risks of marriage, since the State would grant a bounty in proportion to the size of the family, with a view to counteract any decrease in the population of France. (5) The unmarried state is in itself an evil, since all men are the better for the responsibilities and influences of married life.

Con: (1) Taxation of bachelors would burden one section of society for the benefit of the rest, and is therefore opposed to the first principles of taxation. (2) It is not so much a numerical increase as an improvement in the quality of the population that makes a nation prosperous. (3) It

* An experiment of this kind has been initiated in France, an Authors' Society, under the style of *La Société Libre d'Edition des Gens de Lettres*, having started business on co-operative principles in August, 1895, under the Secretaryship of M. Henri Rainaldy, 11, Rue d'Ulm, Paris.
† On and after the 1st January, 1898, bachelors from the ages of 20 to 80 (!) are to be taxed in the Argentine Republic. The assessment is to be monthly, and to cease on the day of marriage.

would increase the difficulties of a poor industrious bachelor who is trying to save money with a view to marriage, which it would tend to postpone. (4) It would further encourage improvident marriages amongst the poor. It is better that a man should remain unmarried than that he should marry, only to throw his responsibilities on the State. In the case of childless marriages, presumably no benefit would accrue to those married. (5) It is beyond the scope of the State to enforce upon her citizens the alleged advantages arising from the married state.

BACTERIA.

Pro: (1) Bacteria (microscopic fungi) are very widely diffused, and on account of their great and constant activity play a most important rôle in the economy of nature, exerting a direct and beneficial influence upon the very existence of mankind. By their agency, dead organic material, which otherwise would quickly cover the face of the earth, is so broken up as to suit it for a useful purpose. (2) By their help substances which are very resistant to the ordinary means of disintegration become oxidized, and are thus rendered available for the nourishment of green plants. (3) They set up various kinds of fermentation, among the more important of which may be mentioned the conversion of starch into sugar, the rendering of cellulose soluble, the peptonization of albumen, the formation of vinegar from alcohol, the conversion of urea into carbonate of ammonium, and the transformation of ammonia into nitrous acid. (4) By the processes of putrefactive fermentation, the first stage of which is brought about by the bacteria which need abundant oxygen (aërobic forms), and the second by certain species which grow luxuriantly only in the absence of free oxygen (anaërobic forms), complex organic substances are split up into simple salts and gases, which serve as food for plants. (5) Some bacteria grow upon the roots of certain plants, and enable them to feed directly upon the free nitrogen which is always present in abundance in the soil, and by this means materially aid them in their growth and development. (6) They play a most important and salutary part in the purification of impure water. (7) Some of our savoury and nutritious foods can be produced only by their aid. (8) They are of the greatest importance to the animal body, owing to the help they give to the processes of digestion.

Con: (1) Owing to the extreme lightness of their spores and to their wide diffusion, food substances can be protected from them only by means of special and minute precautions, and hence, if it be not made use of whilst fresh, is soon rendered by them unfit for animal consumption. (2) The fermentative processes set up by them often render food unfit for use; for instance, milk is turned sour by the lactic acid fermentation which is produced by their agency. (3) As the result of putrefactive fermentation, substances called ptomaines are formed; these act as veritable poisons to man if they are eaten with the putrefying food containing them. (4) Some species which are parasitic upon plants set up diseases in them, which either cause their death or render them unhealthy and unfruitful. (5) They set up various diseases in man and other animals, either by mechanically blocking up the blood-vessels, or by setting free poisonous substances which circulate in the organism, and give rise to dangerous or fatal results. The chief diseases which are known to be due to bacteria are consumption, diphtheria, cholera, malignant pustule, erysipelas, pneumonia, typhoid fever, tetanus, relapsing fever, glanders, and leprosy. (6) Owing to many of the most dangerous species being able to live and multiply in milk and water, they render these fluids, if exposed to contamination, highly dangerous. Hence water, which otherwise is perfectly pure, may be rendered quite unfit for human consumption by their presence. This is especially the case with water infected with the bacteria of typhoid fever or of cholera, these diseases being largely water-borne. (7) It is essential that open wounds should be kept free from bacteria, since suppuration, gangrene, and various other dangers arising from surgical operations are due to the infection of the wound by these micro-organisms. (8) If, in the processes of digestion, the antiseptic action of the gastric juice and the bile is in any way interfered with, the presence and activity of bacteria result in the formation of various gases, which not only cause great discomfort and pain, but seriously interfere with the normal processes of digestion.

BAKEHOUSES, MUNICIPALIZATION OF.

Pro: (1) The baking of bread, being perfectly simple, might well be undertaken by the Municipality. (2) It is important that bread, our most necessary article of diet, should be baked under absolutely sanitary conditions, and its ingredients be perfectly wholesome. This end would be more economically and efficaciously secured if the Municipality took bread-making into its own hands instead of merely appointing Inspectors. (3) The state of our Metropolitan bakehouses is a scandal. The work is very often done in cellars, amid excessively insanitary conditions. (4) The working of bakehouses by the Municipality would enable it to shorten the long hours of unhealthy labour now obtaining.

Con: (1) The Municipal authorities have already more work to do than they can properly manage. (2) If the Municipality were to undertake the duty of bread-baking, it would soon find that there are other industries with equal claims upon it. Municipalization of industries, unless for the sake of public health, is an evil; and there is no evidence that much disease or death is traceable to insanitary bread. Moreover, few departments of State are worked at a profit, and the result could only be either that bread would rise in price, or that taxation would *pro tanto* increase. (3) The Metropolitan bakehouses can be effectively controlled by a body of Inspectors. (4) Municipal bakehouses would not "sweat" their employés any less than private establishments; no private firm sweats its workpeople as the Post Office does.

BALLOT, THE.

Pro: (1) The ballot reduces the fear of intimidation, and enables the voter (of special importance if he be a poor man in any way dependent on the candidate) to vote in accordance with his conscience. (2) It reduces the temptation to corruption, since it affords no security that an elector votes according to his promise. (3) Secrecy reduces the causes of rowdyism at elections, no man knowing how his neighbour has voted.

Con: (1) A man ought to exercise his responsibility publicly. No man who dares not give utterance to his convictions is fit to be entrusted with a vote. Moreover, by means of the ballot the employer, usually a cultured man, loses control over his illiterate workmen. (2) The ballot gives a man the opportunity of doing what he would not care to do openly, viz., to vote for himself. (3) The ballot has hardly reduced rowdyism at elections.

BANK HOLIDAYS BY ACT OF PARLIAMENT.

Pro: (1) It is right that Parliament should interfere to secure to hardworked employés, and even business men, a certain number of holidays to relieve the monotony of their lives. (2) By making it compulsory on the Banks to close their doors, Parliament has taken the most efficacious means to this end, since a consensus amongst employers as to fixed dates for holidays could with difficulty be attained, and if attained could not be enforced. (3) The Act has worked very well. A common holiday enables railway companies to organize cheap excursions to places which under ordinary circumstances the populace could never visit. (4) It involves no hardship nor any appreciable loss of trade.

Con: (1) It is not right that Parliament should interfere in such matters. As a matter of fact, most clerks, etc., have always contracted for fixed holidays, and Bank Holidays are nothing but an additional burden on the employer. (2) Extra holidays, if desirable, could easily be obtained by voluntary agreement, and would be no harder to enforce than any other contract. The Early Closing Movement has so far worked very successfully. (3) Holidays should be left to voluntary arrangement, one man taking another man's work in the same office or shop, and certain kinds of shops agreeing to close on certain days. At best, the Bank Holiday is nearly spoilt by the fact that it is universal, and can therefore be enjoyed only in a crowd. (4) Bank Holidays involve a great disturbance of industry; not only are the Bank Holidays *dies non*, but employés become disorganized, and in some trades do not return to work for several succeeding days. Railway goods traffic is practically suspended. (Some) Twice the number of holidays added to the summer vacation, and thus suitably distributed amongst the employés, would be preferable to the Bank Holiday system.

"BETTERMENT."

Pro: (1) Since the properties of landlords are appreciated by permanent improvements, towards which the owners contribute no more than the ordinary ratepayers, it is only just that they should be subjected to a special tax in proportion to the benefit received. (2) "Betterment" would be a just means of dealing with "unearned increment." It is unjust that landlords should benefit by improvements made at the cost of the community. (3) The principle of "Betterment" is already accepted, since a district especially benefited by an improvement contributes a larger proportion of the cost than the rest of the metropolis; hence the present proposal is only an extension of this principle, and the cost of such improvements would be still further localized, viz., by making it an individual burden. (4) By applying the principle of "Betterment" to individual properties, a more equitable system of taxation would ensue, since only those properties would be taxed which derive actual appreciation from the improvements. (5) No hardship would result from "Betterment," since the interests of each individual landowner would be taken into consideration, and the burden would be proportionate to the benefits received. (6) By this scheme landlords would pay only a fair share of the cost of such improvements, the balance being borne by the ratepayers. (7) At present a twofold advantage accrues to the landlord (*a*) by the remunerative sale of a portion of his property, (*b*) by the value of the remaining property being thereby enhanced. (8) The principle of "Worsement," *i.e.*, compensation to landlords, already exists. It is, therefore, only just that "Betterment" should also obtain. (9) "Betterment" would equalize the incidence of rates, which at present fall entirely on the tenant, and would extract from the real owner a fair contribution towards the permanent improvement of his property. (10) "Betterment" would allow of urgent public improvements being undertaken at once, a procedure which is at present impossible owing to the already heavy rates. (11) The difficulty of justly assessing the amount to be contributed by individual landlords has been unduly exaggerated, and would gradually disappear, and, as now in the case of compulsory sale of land, cases of difficulty would be settled by arbitration. (12) By the system of "Betterment" the London County Council would not be obliged to buy up properties for public improvements, and would thereby be relieved of the necessity of large and speculative financial transactions, and be free from the suspicion of corruption. (13) The system of "Betterment" has been adopted in the United States, and its principle in some of our Colonies.

Con: (1) Properties are appreciated not by improvements, but by the expenditure of capital on adjacent properties after such impovements have been effected. It would, therefore, be doubly hard on the landlords if they were compelled first to contribute largely to public improvements, and then to have to expend further sums in order that their properties might derive any advantage. (2) Public alterations are undertaken only if it is believed that corresponding benefits will accrue to the community. It would, therefore, be unjust to tax landlords higher than ordinary ratepayers, seeing that such improvements necessitate a corresponding expenditure on the adjacent properties. A landlord's income would be depreciated by the amount of this new tax if he did not speculate in improvements, and in many cases this would be financially impossible. (3) The principle of "Betterment" is already accepted, but it deals with the district as a whole, and not with the individual members of it. This is much fairer, since it is impossible to estimate the exact money-value of such improvements. (4) Any great public work, such as the opening up of a wide thoroughfare through a densely populated district, improves the whole neighbourhood, not only the adjacent properties. It would be the height of injustice to inflict the greater part of the cost of, say, a new bridge upon the riparian owners of the land. (5) Great hardships would be inflicted on landlords by the adoption of the system of "Betterment," since it would take time to alter the adjacent properties in accordance with the new surroundings, especially as it is possible that such alterations might result in financial loss instead of the anticipated gain. To tax prospectively such problematical increments would be manifestly unjust to the owner, and yet not to tax them, should they accrue, would be equally unjust to the community. "Betterment" to be equitable must be retrospective, and such legislation is abhorrent to Englishmen. Further, while a district was being "bettered," transactions in land would be suspended, and a consequent loss of income to the landlord would ensue. (6) At present the inhabitants of a district pay only a share of the cost of a local improvement, the balance falling on the rest of the community. To force landlords to be the unwilling chief contributors to a public improvement would be unjust. (7) An immediate disadvantage would accrue to the landlord when a district had been "bettered," since such improvement would involve him in the outlay of capital. (8) Compensation for "Worsement," though nominally, does not actually exist to any appreciable extent, and if the principle of "Betterment" were to be accepted, that of "Worsement" would logically have to follow. (9) Under the quinquennial valuation, rates are continually being readjusted; hence any "unearned increment" attaching to the property is of only short duration, and the application of the principle of "Betterment" thus unnecessary. To minimize the duration of any period to which "unearned increment" might attach, an *annual* valuation might be instituted. (10) "Betterment" would only increase local opposition to public improvements, and would tend to still further raise rents, since landlords would have to increase their rent-rolls in order to be able to meet the new demand. (11) The reassessment of properties after a district has been "bettered" would cause endless litigation and discontent, and no true estimate of prospective values could be arrived at. Arbitration would in this, as in most other cases, prove unsatisfactory to both parties. (12) Instead of freeing the London County Council from the necessity of buying up large areas of land, the acquirement of such properties, where urgent public improvements are demanded, is rather to be advocated, since, after the improvements have been effected, such areas could be resold at an enhanced rate for the benefit of the community. It would be unjust to tax landlords in order to avoid the suspicion of corruption attaching to a public body. (13) It has still to be shown that experiments in "Betterment," as made in the United States and elsewhere, work successfully. (14) The rent-charge under the scheme of "Betterment" would tend to convert a freehold into a leasehold property; eventually, also, this new imposition would inevitably fall upon the tenant. (15) The drawbacks to "Betterment" would be minimized if the landlord had the option of compelling the London County Council to purchase his property at its market value, in case he preferred this to retaining it under the new system. This would, indeed, be the only equitable basis on which the scheme could be adopted.

BICYCLE TAX.

Pro: (1) Those who can afford to buy a bicycle can afford to pay, either directly or indirectly, a small tax upon it. (2) A Bicycle Tax would add enormously to the revenue, and, if levied directly, be no harder to collect, say, than that on dogs. (3) Exceptions might be made in the case of those using bicycles for business purposes, or labourers going to their work; yet it would be no great hardship if even they had to pay a nominal annual tax, since that on dogs, which, as a rule, are pure luxuries, is not found to be prohibitive. (4) The proposed tax, though belated, is not thereby invalidated. Taxation generally tends to increase, in order to meet the growing national expenditure.

Con: (1) A Bicycle Tax, if levied on the manufacturer, would raise the price of bicycles; if levied on the owner, it would reduce the number of riders, in both cases tending to depress the industry. (2) If levied directly, it would lead to constant friction; if otherwise, it would merely increase the number of indirectly-taxed articles; and indirect taxation is a most undesirable way of raising revenue. (*See* TAXATION: DIRECT OR INDIRECT.) (3) Bicycles are a great boon, often almost a necessity, to working men, and, in addition, make it possible for them and other poor people to live in a healthy neighbourhood at some distance from their work. They also afford a cheap and healthy amusement to thousands of poor people. (4) If imposed, the tax should have been levied many years ago. It would now be extremely unpopular, and no Government would care to introduce it.

BIMETALLISM.

Pro: (1) All the professors of political economy in Great Britain are agreed not only on the possibility of an international ratio being stable, but also on the desirability of arriving at one. (2) The currency of the world has for many centuries consisted of gold and silver, circulating concurrently. Gold Monometallism was first established by England in 1816; but it was not until 1873, the date of the closing of the French mint, that Bimetallism came to an end in Europe and North America. (3) From 1803 to 1873 the Latin Union maintained the ratio of 15½ to 1 in spite of the gold discoveries and other disturbing causes; and it was not until Germany, fired with ambition by the example of England, decided to establish a gold standard and flooded the market with silver, that France closed her mint to silver. (4) British manufactures, trade, and agriculture grew and reached their highest prosperity under the Bimetallic system. Since 1873, for want of a Bimetallic system, they have had to struggle under difficulties which have increased year by year and month by month. (5) Gold is an unstable standard of money when not rated or linked by ratio to silver (with free acceptance of both metals as legal tender money). The injury to Great Britain from the gold standard has been greatly increased by the fact that since the Franco-German War (1870-71) Germany, the United States, Austria, and Italy have adopted it, and so created a still greater scarcity of gold. This scarcity of gold (*i.e.*, contraction of money) of course immensely increased the purchasing powers (*i.e.*, appreciation) of gold, and lowered the prices of produce. (6) The increasing appreciation of gold, and absence of the free coinage of gold and silver at a fixed ratio, constitute a fearful addition to debts, mortgages, and fixed charges of every kind. But even this is hardly the worst feature. Nothing is so discouraging to the trader as to bring forward goods for a falling market. Declining prices (*a*) reduce profits, check enterprize, and retard the productive investment of capital; (*b*) involve an increasing pressure of debts (private, public, municipal, national, international), under which every trade and nation staggers: *e.g.*,

India, being herself a silver country, is being rapidly reduced to bankruptcy by the burden of interest on her enormous gold debt; (c) discourage investments, enterprizes, and reduce wages and employment; (d) bring uncertainty of exchanges and loss of trade with the great silver-using populations, with whom alone we can trade unchecked by protective tariffs. (7) The premium on gold acts as a bonus to the produce of countries using silver or depreciated paper, and so develops their industries at the cost of ours. (8) The United States, Europe, and our Colonies, since 1873, have been forced to put up protective tariffs against us, in the hope of assisting their producers against falling prices. Since these tariffs, each fresh fall of prices has meant a fresh increase of hostile tariffs, because, the hostile tariffs being chiefly specific, each fresh fall leaves our manufacturers, after paying the hostile tariffs, a smaller profit. (9) Countries using depreciated paper are less and less able and willing to resume metallic currency. (10) No Bimetallist wants any nation by itself to establish the bimetallic ratio, but only by agreement with the other powers. The United States, France, Germany, Holland, Italy, Switzerland, Belgium, Greece, and Austria are now ready to do so, and England alone blocks the way. (11) Bimetallism would re-establish a means of steady exchange between those who use silver money (700 millions) and those who use gold (300 millions), because as long as there are mints open to receive both metals, as in France from 1803 to 1873, at the rate of 100 francs (£4) for one ounce of gold, and 100 francs (£4) for fifteen and a half ounces of silver, no one will give more or take less than those mints will give; and therefore, at the ratio of 14½ to 1, everyone everywhere will exchange silver and gold, and products priced in silver or in gold, at a steady exchange. (12) England acquired her commercial superiority long before she had a gold standard. Sixteen years before she adopted it the monopoly of almost all the trade of the world was in her hands. That monopoly is hers no longer. Her commercial superiority is due to the energy and determination of the Anglo-Saxon race, to her insular position, good harbours, the fact that she is the "carrier" of the world, and her two centuries of internal peace and accumulating capital. The gold standard has been from first to last a source of inconvenience and danger; but up to 1873 she was saved from the difficulties which have since beset her, by the double standard of France. (13) Bimetallism does not attempt to fix the value of gold and silver; it does not even attempt to fix their relative values; all it does is to create a demand for them at the legal ratio. Bimetallism is not, therefore, opposed to the laws of supply and demand, nor does it interfere with them, but is based upon them. The greater the number of mints open to the free coinage of gold and silver, the greater will be the demand for these metals at the legal ratio, the greater therefore the minuteness with which this ratio will be maintained. But should, by any chance, the market prices of the two metals deviate from the fixed legal ratio, an increased demand will at once arise for the cheaper metal, which will continue until the legal and the market ratio are again identical. Through this "compensatory action" Bimetallism secures in an automatic manner the constant equilibrium between the two metals at the legal rates. (14) England's greatest interests rest on the solvency and prosperity of her customers, both of which are now endangered by the insidious progress of the appreciation of gold.

Con: (1) The agreement among the leading advocates of Bimetallism is merely nominal, and does not extend to the enunciation of any specific practical proposals, which would at once reveal the "rift within the lute" of Bimetallism. (2) Gold has recommended itself, and is likely to increasingly recommend itself, to the richer nations of the earth by reason of its obvious convenience, lightness, and value; and we find that as nations become more prosperous, they discard a silver for a gold basis. (3) When Bimetallic practice existed there were periods when the ratio between silver and gold varied between 14 to 1 and 16 to 1, yet there have been other periods when great changes took place, *e.g.*, at the beginning of the 17th century, showing that Bimetallism in practice never prevents changes in the ratio, small as a rule in ordinary times, but great when occasion arises. (4) English prosperity has been due to Free Trade, which inaugurated a period of prosperity previously unknown. The depression since 1874 is fully accounted for by the vast armaments, hostile tariffs, etc., which have since prevailed in Europe. (Some) The fall in prices since 1873 is not explained by the demonetization of silver, for had scarcity of money affected prices it surely would have affected prices more or less evenly, yet this is far from being the case, and we find some extraordinary fluctuations in the various articles quite consistent with a general decline in prices, but still inconsistent with the even decline required. This, however, is better explained by the fact that since 1873 the number of competing nations has grown, and, whilst we had a virtual manufacturing monopoly then, we have entirely lost it now, and the productive powers of mankind have outgrown their consumptive power. Hence result stagnation and a fall in prices, which, as is natural, takes a more spasmodic and uneven form than would one from scarcity of money. (5) The experience of well-nigh a century has proved that our system of currency is suited to the wants of a great commercial country, and that to depart from it would probably be disastrous to our trade and credit. (6) The new supply of gold in recent years has been enormous, far beyond any currency demand, whilst the output in 1894 was the largest on record. The use of credit instruments (cheques, notes, etc.) has largely superseded the need of gold money. (*a*) The fall in prices is due to over-production of goods. (*b*) Bimetallism, to meet the pressure of debts on the individual, would practically compel his creditors to make him a present of a considerable percentage of his indebtedness. (*c*) By depreciating the currency we should be inflicting a heavy blow to thrift in all its forms; whereas the continued appreciation of gold, if such was the case, would encourage saving, and enhance the price of "gilt-edged" securities. (*d*) If each man had the option of paying his neighbour either in gold or in silver, the difficulties of exchange would probably be imported into the daily operations of our national life. (7) Germany, our most serious competitor, has a gold standard. (9) If it raised prices, say of wheat or cotton, Bimetallism would be a direct attack upon every artizan and labourer in the country, since their well-being depends, above all things, on the cheapness of the necessaries of life. It has yet to be proved that a mere increase of the stock of money would raise prices; unless it raised the demand for commodities, it would certainly not do so. (10) No such international agreement as that contemplated by Bimetallists is possible; even if it were, it is not such as England, being the chief creditor of the world, can assent to, for it would simply amount to an invitation to her debtors to pay her in a depreciated metal. (12) The monometallic gold standard of England has existed in practice not only from 1816, but from the beginning of the 18th century. (13) Open mints did not create a demand in any real sense, for when the silver was coined, people did not want it.

BISHOPS: their exclusion from the House of Lords.

Pro: (1) As the clergy cannot become members of the House of Commons, it is hard to see why Bishops should be allowed to remain in the House of Lords, since they cannot and do not represent the interests of the beneficed clergy. (2) Their work mainly lies in guarding their own temporalities. (3) Their presence in the Lords keeps them from their dioceses too long in the year, and their dioceses suffer accordingly. This is specially the case with the junior Bishop, who is *ex officio* Chaplain of the House. (4) Their presence in the Lords is a source of religious jealousy by the dissenters, who would, indeed, rather see the clergy sit in the Commons. (5) Bishops are rarely fitted by circumstances or temperament to be good legislators. They are the most anti-progressive of all the Lords, and their exclusion would strengthen the House. (6) The constitution of a State is justified only in so far as it fulfils a useful function; hence, though the position of the Bishops may be constitutional, that is no valid reason for their retention after their presence has been shown to be no longer beneficial.

Con : (1) By the exclusion of the Bishops, the Church would be deprived of all Parliamentary representation; since her clergy cannot sit in the Commons, although this privilege is allowed to dissenting ministers. (2) The Bishops do very useful work as guardians of the interests of the Church, and in educational questions their advice is of great importance. They take a statesmanlike view of questions of public policy. (3) Their presence in the Lords involves no interference with their diocesan duties, since, as they form the governing body of the Church, they are obliged to spend a certain part of the year in the metropolis. (4) There is no reason why their presence in the Lords should be regarded as a grievance by the dissenters, nor would their withdrawal weaken the cry for Disestablishment. It would be anomalous that the Church alone among public bodies should be unrepresented in Parliament. (5) They are among the few members of the Lords who sit by virtue of merit and not of birth, and their absence would decidedly weaken the House. (6) Their legislative functions are an integral part of the Constitution.

BLASPHEMY LAWS: their abolition.

Pro : (1) By the law as it stands any Unitarian or other non-Trinitarian denying the divinity of Christ, not necessarily offensively, may be indicted for blasphemy, which it is, in fact, impossible to distinguish from mere schism. (2) An orthodox lecturer beaten in debate can turn the criminal law on to his opponent. Freedom of opinion ought not to be thus needlessly restricted. (3) If Christianity is true, blasphemy laws are needless; if false, such artificial means will not avail to save it.

Con : (1) There are certain rules of morality which are so universal, and so deeply underlie the conscience of everyone, that speeches and writings which treat them with public contempt, and sap our simple faith in all that is noble and worthy, are rightly deemed a species of constructive breach of the peace. The more rigorous of the blasphemy laws are no longer appealed to now; many laws remain on the statute book which are never put into force; and it would be impossible to repeal all useless laws. (2) Blasphemy laws are useful for maintaining the decencies of life, and defending the religious convictions of by far the greater majority of the people from needless offence. Any undue straining of the Acts would certainly do more harm to the party who instigated it than it could possibly do to freedom of opinion; *e.g.*, such action, against say a prominent Agnostic or Unitarian, would have probably led to the repeal of the Acts. (3) Christianity is part of the law of the land; hence anything that denies the former comes into conflict with the latter, and cannot therefore be permitted.

BOYCOTTING.

Pro : (1) Boycotting is only a form of exclusive dealing. Its prohibition would be a further and improper attempt to extend the scope of State interference. (2) It is only right that a section of society, constituting practically a *vox populi*, should have the power to ostracize a man guilty of certain offences of which the law takes no notice.

Con : (1) Boycotting in Ireland was in itself the direct cause of social disturbances. The State has a right to impose what terms she thinks fit on those who trade under her protection, and to take any steps for the better preservation of the rights of all her members. If a man offers goods for public sale (as a tradesman does) he is thereby under a legal obligation to supply them to anyone tendering a cash payment for them. (2) The

State cannot tolerate an *imperium in imperio*, such as was constituted by the illegal claims of those who, in effect if not in name, governed Ireland.

BRITISH MUSEUM AND FOUR UNIVERSITY LIBRARIES: compulsory donation of books to.

Pro: (1) The compulsory donation by the publisher to the British Museum, the Bodleian Library, Oxford, the University Library, Cambridge, the Advocates' Library, Edinburgh, and Trinity College, Dublin, of one copy each of every book he may publish, is a great, almost indispensable, boon to literature. If much rubbish is received with the rest, it at least avoids the necessity of appointing a committee of selection, whose judgment would be always open to dispute, and who might be partial to some particular school or schools, while neglecting others of equal merit. (2) It has created libraries whose completeness for reference purposes, in English books, is unrivalled. (3) A man who enters the publishing trade knows that he will have to incur this obligation, and so it is no real hardship.

Con: (1) It imposes a great strain on the resources of the libraries, which are compelled to house and catalogue all that the publishers send them, the great majority of which but rarely, if ever, leave the shelves. The authorities are allowed no discretion in this matter, and much utterly worthless literature is thus stored up and perpetuated, at great and unremunerative expenditure of public funds. (2) A special tax on a particular trade, for the benefit of society at large, is unfair; nor would so serious a tax be required for the formation of large libraries, if they were eclectic. (3) The fact that a tax is a known quantity does not make it, if unfair, a good one.

BROAD-CHURCH PARTY: should it leave the Church?

Pro: (1) No man is morally entitled to become or act as a minister of the Church unless he believe in *all* her doctrines. (2) The doctrines of the Church are set forth with sufficient clearness to enable a man to see what is *not* to be taught; and in any case the formularies of the Church are incompatible with much of the teaching of the Broad-Church party. (3) Definite doctrinal teaching is absolutely necessary for the continuance of the Church: to ignore dogmas is practically to deny them. (4) The members of the Broad-Church party ought either to get the doctrines of the Church relaxed, or else to leave the Church.

Con: (1) The Church of England, by her acts and confessions, has always claimed the right to revise her doctrines and ceremonies. The terms of subscription have been expressly widened to admit of the wider interpretation. (2) It is absolutely impossible for anyone to be strictly orthodox, because the Prayer Book is the outcome of two contending schools, and contains contradictory principles; hence there have always been at least a High-Church and a Low-Church party. Why should there not be an intermediate or Broad-Church party? (3) It is much better that the Church should yield where she is wrong, and retain her hold on the best minds of the time, than dwindle into a mere sect. (4) It is always better, where possible, to remain and reform existing institutions from within, than to go out and add one more to the number of hostile sects.

CABINET, GOVERNMENT BY.

Pro: (1) Under Cabinet Government each Minister is supreme in his own department, whilst benefiting by the collective advice and support of his colleagues on questions of general policy. (2) By allotting to each department a chief of wide administrative experience, the prejudices of the permanent officials, from whom he obtains all his detailed information, are best counteracted. (3) Cabinet Government brings the executive into direct connection with the legislative branch of government, and protects the departments from unnecessary interference on the part of the Commons.

(4) It has succeeded very well on the whole, has been the admiration of foreign Governments and political philosophers, and has found numerous imitators.

Con: (1) Cabinet Government relieves a Minister of responsibility for his departmental administration, and compels his colleagues to support his conduct of affairs, whether they approve it or not. (2) Ministers are rarely experts in any special department; they have to depend upon the permanent officials, who, not being themselves responsible or trained in habits of responsibility, are not always trustworthy. (3) Cabinet Government makes the policy of the executive altogether dependent upon a chance vote of an ill-informed House of Commons, voting on party lines, or, worse still, subordinates well-informed and capable officials to the ignorance of a chief whose sole qualification may be devotion to his party or the length of his purse. The State would be better served if the latter had supreme control in their own departments, and were directly responsible to Parliament.

CANADA: should she join the United States?

Pro: (1) The geographical position of the two countries is such that fusion is their natural and inevitable policy. Considerations of contiguity, when considered in the light of political and commercial expediency, are apt to weigh very heavily in the scale against those based on history, and the effect of increasing intercommunication extends, whilst that of history becomes yearly more remote. (2) The chief trade of Canada is already with the United States, and, were all barriers removed, this trade would still further develop. She is a poor country, and her trade is her very life. (3) Her union with England would be a source of great danger to her in the event of a war between England and the States (*e.g.*, the Canadian frontier would be very hard to defend); while, for England, the independence of Canada would remove the principal chance of war. (4) Canada and the United States have far more in common than can be possible between countries so unlike in every way as England and Canada. (The Canadian Parliament, in order to capture the Irish vote, passed a vote in favour of Irish Home Rule.) (5) The English Government has made many mistakes in the government of Canada, and done much harm by ill-advised interference. Amongst other things, it has allowed the Roman Catholics to get such a hold over the government of Quebec as they no longer possess in any other country of the world, save perhaps Spain: from this gross injustice to the Protestants of that province the United States would have protected them. (6) The votes of the loyal Canadians would neutralize the votes of England's enemies in the American Senate and Congress. (7) There is no reason why political separation, unaccompanied by any bitter memories, should tend to develop a difference. In spite of all assertions to the contrary, and attempts to develop national differences, the United States and Great Britain have strong features in common, but it is hopeless to expect that any two societies will develop in exactly the same manner, any more than the England of to-day should agree with the England of yesterday. (8) Canada has lost enormously by not joining the United States, notably by the McKinley Tariff. The States are the natural market for Canadian goods, and no loss of this kind can be made good by the inconsiderable trade with Great Britain.

Con: (1) The fact that two countries form parts of the same continent is no reason for their political fusion. Social and political traditions are infinitely stronger than mere geographical contiguity, and nations are guided by other than merely commercial considerations. As time goes on, new causes of bitterness will arise between the two peoples, such as the incursion of Fenians backed by the United States; and, though the Canadians are brought into closer social relations with the States than with England, that is scarcely calculated to make them wish to join the Union, seeing—as they cannot fail to see—the weak points of the American system. (2) Canada does a large and increasing trade with Great Britain. There is every reason to believe that she is really a far richer country than America. While the latter lacks timber, and her wheat fields are being exhausted, Canada has a rich supply of both, besides large coal fields and plentiful supplies of fish, etc. It will be much more to Canada's interest to deal with Great Britain than with the States. (3) Canada occupies a unique geographical position; and her frontier, though hard to defend, would be equally hard to attack. Her military and naval position is such that, if she passed from England, the Empire would be much weakened, and her position as an independent State would be almost impossible. Canada has made wonderful sacrifices in the last 20 years to bind her people together and strengthen her position; and there are no sufficient political grounds for her fusion with the States. Canadians are not likely to join the States on the grounds of the danger to Canada arising from a hypothetical war between England and the States; her action during the last crisis showed them to be infinitely superior to paltry considerations such as these. (4) Even the greatest advocates of separation do not pretend that union with the States is popular in Canada, but admit that it is bitterly opposed; they allow that America has many problems from which Canada is free—among others the negro question, the diversity of marriage laws, corrupt politics; that America is, moreover, becoming less and less English and increasingly German, etc. The Canadian constitution, based as it is on the British model, is much more democratic than that of the States, and offers no possibility, such as the latter affords, of a Ministry remaining in power after they have been condemned by the popular vote, but makes them responsible to, not independent of, the Representative Chamber. (5) Greater consideration on the part of Britain would prevent any avoidable friction arising in future. (6) Loyal Canadians neutralize the votes of England's enemies much more effectually by remaining outside the Union than they would by becoming a minority within it. (7) Countries, when once they have separated, tend to develop their differences rather than their similarities to one another. (8) What Canada has lost by the McKinley Act she has gained in energy and self-reliance, as well as in the stimulus this Act has given to her trade with Great Britain.

CANADIAN COPYRIGHT CLAIM.

Pro: (1) Canada, whose population is over 5,000,000, is at present dependent for her intellectual sustenance on the almost prohibitory editions of English books on the one hand, and on the often worthless piratical issues of the United States on the other. (2) Canadians should be allowed to undertake, at their own individual discretion, the republication of such books by British authors as they think desirable, subject only to their having to pay royalties to the authors or their representatives, the royalty being fixed at ten per cent., to be collected by the author or his representative. (3) Canada is on the American continent, and cannot be treated as merely an outlying possession of Great Britain without reference to her connection with the United States. (4) The manufacture of such reprints would give employment to many hands in the various Canadian industries. (5) The Canadian market for British books is very small at present. If it were encouraged by native reprints, it would become large, and thus Canadian royalties would practically be a net additional gain to British authors or publishers. (6) Grace would be given to the British publisher, by which he could himself undertake a Canadian reprint, and thus retain his copyright. (7) It would cement and strengthen the ties which bind Canada to the Mother Country, if the House of Commons in London would respect the unanimous claim of the House of Commons of Canada for self-government in a matter of such importance as this. (Some) Canadians have a right to self-government, and even to self-misgovernment if they so choose. (8) A large portion of the cotton interests and iron interests in England would be glad to see a reversal of the present tariff policy; and if British authors and publishers persist in taking a narrow view, it must be remembered that there are larger interests at stake than theirs.

Con : (1) Canada is a British colony, and there is no reason why Canadians should be privileged to undersell their fellow-subjects, or Englishmen deprived of control over their books in Canada. (2) Royalties due from Canadian reprinters could with difficulty be collected by the British owner of the copyright, more especially as he would first have to discover if reprints had been made, and, if so, by whom. As a matter of practice, Canadian editions would probably be mainly undertaken by just those publishers who never intend to pay royalties at all. (3) Geographical situation has no direct bearing on the relations between a Mother Country and her Colonies, though in wisdom a Mother Country should do all she can to further the just claims of her Colonies, so long as they are not inconsistent with the rights of her other subjects. (4) The whole of the present agitation emanates from a few leading Canadian *printers*, who would no doubt benefit largely, as printers, by the proposed legislation. (5) The Canadian market for British books, though not large, is an increasing one; and as it grows, British publishers will no doubt find it worth their while to themselves undertake cheap editions of popular books for that market, as is occasionally done in the case of other Colonies, notably Australia. If Canada herself produced large numbers of good authors, she would not think it fair that she should be ousted from British protection. (6) The British publisher, as a British subject, cannot equitably be called upon to set up the type and incur the costs of printing his book twice over, in order to enable him to protect his rights in Canada. (7) The right of self-government has nothing to do with the question, which is purely one of equity to the British author and publisher. Several leading publishing firms already issue cheap "Colonial Libraries," which Canadian booksellers can import if they desire.

CANALS, NATIONALIZATION OF.

Pro : (1) Most Canals are in the hands of the railway companies, who have closed them to prevent competition. (2) Owners of property in means of communication have no right to abuse their powers. (3) Canals are a suitable industry for the State to work, as their management is very simple. (4) Compensation would not be heavy in the case of disused Canals. (5) Canals are a most useful means of transport for heavy merchandize, where cheap freight is more important than speedy delivery. (6) Nationalization would encourage competition, and thereby compel the railways to reduce their rates.

Con : (1) Canals are not all in the hands of the railways; some are worked by private companies. (2) Property conveys the right to its owner to use it as he pleases. (3) If Canals were nationalized, mismanagement would ensue. (4) The costs of compensation alone would be very great, but those of reopening disused Canals far greater. (5) Canals have not paid for a long time, and are not wanted. If reopened, they would benefit only a small class. (6) The intercompetition between the railways is already free, and their rates as a whole are fair and legal.

CANVASSING AT PARLIAMENTARY ELECTIONS.

Pro : (1) Canvassing enables a candidate to explain himself more fully to his constituents than is possible at a public meeting. It brings him into close contact with his electors, and thus, in the event of his election, he can better represent them. (2) All undue influence is now prevented by stringent Acts. (3) It would be impossible to stop all canvassing, especially that by the candidate's friends and admirers. (4) Prohibition would be an unjustifiable interference with personal liberty. (5) It would give an undue advantage to local candidates, and local influence is already over-represented in Parliament. (6) It would be impossible to draw any hard-and-fast line between "conversation" and "canvassing," and thus lead to an increased number of election petitions.

Con : (1) A candidate has sufficient opportunity to express his views in his address and at public meetings, where electors have the power to question him on points he may not have dealt with. (2) Canvassing should be forbidden absolutely, because it leads to undue influence, and makes the election depend more on side-issues and personal qualifications than on national policy. It frequently leads to deception by electors as to the disposal of their votes, and by candidates and their friends in their promises. At best, personal canvassing is undignified. (3) It would, perhaps, not be possible to stop all canvassing, any more than it has been possible to stop all corruption; but it would be possible to reduce it to infinitesimal proportions. (4) The personal liberty of the voter is more seriously threatened by the opportunities for intimidation which canvassing offers than would that of the candidate be by prohibition. (5) Canvassing is the great resource of "carpet-baggers," and prohibition would be some handicap to professional politicians. (6) The distinction between "conversation" and "canvassing," in the case of a petition, could be satisfactorily dealt with by the election judges, just as they now dispose of questions of "agency." (7) Canvassers devote most of their energies to ignorant voters and to "wobblers"; and thus these classes, which otherwise vote but little, often become a decisive factor in an election.

CAPITAL PUNISHMENT: its abolition.

Pro : (1) Capital Punishment brutalizes the public, as well as the officials who have to carry it out, thus tending to destroy all notions of the sanctity of human life. (2) Capital Punishment is no deterrent, and by some criminals is less feared than penal servitude for life. A large proportion of the murders committed are due to influences over which no deterrent can avail—drink, jealousy, etc.; whilst but few murderers actually pay the extreme penalty of the law. (3) Capital Punishment, being irrevocable, is too extreme a measure; with a wrong verdict and the sentence carried out, the mistake cannot be rectified. (4) Since it is largely accidental whether the victim of a murderous assault dies or recovers, the sentence depends upon chance. It is illogical that identical crimes may incur different penalties. (5) Capital Punishment, because irrevocable, induces juries to decline to convict; and leads, on the slightest pretexts, to petitions for mercy to the Secretary of State, and to pleas of insanity, neither of which are desirable in the interests of justice. (6) Punishment ought to be reformatory, not vindictive. (7) Capital Punishment has already been abolished in several foreign countries without ill effect.

Con : (1) Since executions have been carried out in private (1866), Capital Punishment can no longer be said to brutalize the public; and by punishing the murderer with the extreme penalty it upholds the idea of the sanctity of human life. (2) It is the best deterrent possible, and prevents the commission of many a murder (*e.g.*, by a convict to effect his escape). (3) The death penalty is never carried out where there is the slightest question as to guilt. (4) The application of Capital Punishment ought to be extended rather than decreased. (Some) It is a weakness that some murderous attempts should be punishable with only penal servitude; where intent to murder is proved, the punishment of death ought to ensue. (5) Petitions are presented only when strong doubt exists, and such petitions have occasionally prevented mistakes. (6) Punishment cannot always be reformatory ; in the case of a murderer, it is better to get rid of such a pest than to attempt reformation. As a matter of fact, punishment should be neither reformatory nor vindictive, but preventive.

CATHEDRALS, NATIONALIZATION OF.

Pro : (1) Cathedrals, which were built with national money when all England held the same belief, are national monuments, and ought not, in the event of disestablishment, to be allowed to become the property of the disestablished Church, but should be retained as the property of the State for the good of the community.   (2) Owing to the intellectual inferiority of the Clergy, no object is attained by maintaining sinecures (such as the Chapters) for men who add little or nothing to the intellectual progress of the age.   (3) National heirlooms ought not to be handed over to the control of a sect.   (4) The old idea of the Cathedrals and Churches had as much of the secular as of the religious element in it, village feasts being held in the Parish Church in pre-Reformation times ; hence it would be no innovation if the great intellects of the day, who are at present debarred by their heterodoxy or lack of orders, were to enter the pulpits.   (5) Public bodies ought to manage our Cathedrals, though they should be limited to repairs (not restorations).   (6) The Rubric excluding laymen from the ministry was not passed until 1660.   (7) The surplus revenues of Cathedrals might be applied to the endowment of scientific research.

Con : (1) Cathedrals cannot be considered national monuments, since, although the whole nation contributed towards their construction, yet by seceding from the Church, Dissenters *ipso facto* relinquished all claim to an interest in them.   (2) The Clergy are certainly not falling out of the intellectual ranks, and compare favourably with the representatives of Dissent. Any deficiency in the number of great men within the Church is due to lack of great men in the country. The Chapters, too, are by no means always sinecures, since they are often united to the offices of diocesan canons, missioners, etc.   (3) The Church of England is not a sect, since the majority of Christian Englishmen subscribe to her communion.   (4) It would not improve our Cathedrals to turn them into Halls of Science, and such a proceeding would offend the religious instincts of Churchmen and Dissenters alike.   (5) A public body would be utterly unfitted to manage a Cathedral or to carry out the necessary repairs with a due reverence for the past.   (6) The holding of livings by laymen was the outcome of a scandalous condition of affairs in Church and State, when sinecures abounded, children commanded fleets, etc.

CATHOLIC UNIVERSITY FOR IRELAND, A.

Pro : (1) Protestants have got a University in Trinity College, Dublin, which cannot be used by Catholics, who, since they form the majority of the Irish people, should have a University of their own.   (2) The Queen's Colleges were founded, not in accordance with what the Irish want, but with what they ought to want. The colleges should have been denominational.

Con : (1) Education ought to be non-sectarian ; and if Catholics want a University of their own they ought to pay for it themselves. Why should Protestants pay for an education which they cannot endure ?   (2) State education in Ireland ought to aim at minimizing religious differences, and bringing the different sects together.

CELIBACY OF PRIESTS (ROMAN CATHOLIC).

Pro : (1) Celibacy has been pronounced by Christ Himself and by the consensus of Christendom to be the highest state in which a man can live. (2) No great desire exists among the Catholic clergy for a relaxation of the rule.   (3) A priest is of full age when he takes the oath, and knows his own mind ; few ever regret their vows, and every priest worthy of his office receives aid by Divine Grace, which enables him to rejoice in the surrender of his life. **(4)** It is most undesirable to revoke so excellent a discipline. **(5)** A married priesthood would not help the cause of Reunion in England; many advanced Anglicans voluntarily undertake the vow of celibacy. **(6)** A celibate priesthood has never been found to produce the evil results attributed to it. Priests break their vows of celibacy no more than married clergy break their matrimonial vows, also undertaken for life and at about the same age. An unmarried priesthood is alone able to devote itself absolutely to the interests of its Church. **(7)** The Greek and Russian Churches forbid marriage in the case of Bishops; while the Russian Pope is no pattern of virtue.

Con: **(1)** St. Paul recommended a Bishop to marry, and it is certain that many of the Apostles were married. **(2)** A great desire to marry exists among many members of the Catholic clergy. **(3)** At the age of 21 to 25 no one can be said to be of a proper age to decide on such a question for life. The celibate state is unnatural, and the prohibition of marriage casts a slur on one of the most holy of relationships. **(4)** The rule, being one of discipline, can be revoked at any time by the authorities of the Church. **(5)** A married clergy would help Reunion in England. Celibacy constitutes a strong objection to the Roman Church on the part of Englishmen, who object to an unmarried man discussing the most intimate questions with their wives and daughters. **(6)** The whole history of celibate priesthoods is a protest against the system, the number of priests who have really broken their vows being greatly in excess of those who marry and leave the Church. **(7)** The Greek Churches in communion with Rome have always encouraged marriage among the parish clergy.

CHANNEL TUNNEL.

Pro: **(1)** The Tunnel would facilitate communication between England and the Continent, and improve the relations between England and France. It would save time and increase comfort. **(2)** It would not endanger England, since Dover would command the English entrance to the Tunnel with a battery of artillery. **(3)** The passage of any considerable surprise army would be impossible, as its approach could not fail to become known to us in ample time. **(4)** It would always be possible to flood the Tunnel, and thus destroy an attacking force; but, even assuming a successful landing, we could at least cut off all means of retreat. **(5)** Even if Dover were seized, it could be held only by the power which had command of the sea. **(6)** The value of the Straits of Dover as a safeguard against invasion is much exaggerated. If we are supreme at sea, the danger from the Tunnel would be infinitesimal; if not, we must yield in any case.

Con: **(1)** The sea-passage is short, and the discomforts, themselves slight, are being yearly reduced. **(2)** The Tunnel would, according to the best military opinion, increase the risk of invasion; and Dover is no sufficient protection. **(3)** In the case of an intended invasion, war would not be openly declared; declaration of war is frequently made after the first blow. The risk of the successful passage of an army, however small, is far too serious to make it worth incurring. **(4)** If such a surprise army once reached Dover, it would be impossible to cut off its retreat, as it would hold the Tunnel. **(5)** It is quite imaginable that England might lose her supremacy at sea. **(6)** It is wholly due to the Straits of Dover that we need so relatively small an army.

CHARITABLE RELIEF.

Pro: **(1)** Charity is a common and noble human emotion, which benefits the giver as much as the recipient of alms. It would be immoral, even were it possible, to eliminate the instinct. **(2)** Though rarely adequate, alms-giving is some alleviation of immediate distress; and the more it is encouraged the greater will the reduction in misery be. A giver of alms does what seems to him best, and cannot be held responsible for ultimate economic effects, which, moreover, are at present purely speculative, and the subject of widely different views. Even if charity be sometimes ill-applied, the fact of its having been given is a good, nor are the vicious always encouraged because assisted with the means of livelihood ; the withholding of alms often involves death, and who is to say that, even if present assistance does not result in good, the recipient, if kept alive, may not, by some other alms or influences, be subsequently led to adopt a good life ?   (3) The struggling poor, who may themselves at any time become indigent, regard charity as a possible last resort ; and, though they struggle against accepting it, do not look upon it with ill-favour, realizing that when a man has done his best he can do no more. Full inquiries into each individual case are usually impracticable ; moreover, too minute investigation degrades, and, in the case of the more self-respecting poor, leads them to postpone seeking assistance until, perhaps, it is too late to be of service.   (4) The fact that children are starving remains a fact whether we see them in the streets or not, and we should never object to have plain facts brought home to us. Abuses, no doubt, exist, but they are greatly exaggerated, in respect both of this and of the number of impostors.   (5) It is beyond doubt that many *bonâ fide* working families are at times thrown out of work through no fault of their own. It is cruel to attempt to dissuade the public from seeking to help them.

Con : (1) Indiscriminate alms-giving is the cause of vast mischief. It directly encourages vagrancy, deceit, and voluntary degradation ; it weakens self-reliance ; and, by thus demoralizing, helps the recipient on the downward course of professional poverty, resulting in absolute pauperism.   (2) It is never adequate, and ultimately increases rather than alleviates misery. If bestowed at all, it should at least be adequate, suitable, and administered with the utmost circumspection, a duty that no one can evade without grave responsibility.   (3) By being wholly chaotic, it creates a sense of injustice amongst the respectable poor, who quite properly resent premiums being given to improvidence whilst their own self-denial has to bear its honourable burdens. Private alms-giving (other than to, or through, recognized institutions) is wholly inexcusable.   (4) It is at times responsible for much cruelty to children, who, for the sake of gain, are taken into the streets as objects of compassion. Cripples are sometimes even manufactured. (5) Few beggars are *bonâ fide* workers suddenly thrown out of employment. In nearly every case where they have been workers at all there is something in the background, such as drunkenness, idleness, or legal crime.

CHARITY ORGANIZATION SOCIETY: methods and work.

Pro : (1) Charity, to be beneficial instead of harmful, must be administered in accordance with the principles of social economics. Current philanthropic opinion is no guide to scientific methods of administering relief, and one of the great dangers of the times is an epidemic of sentimental generalization. Organized charity, in the hands of experts, enables the charitable to rely on their gifts reaching the right quarters, and thus tends to increase charitable donations.   (2) The "unpopularity" of the C.O.S. (which is admitted) is really a tribute to the efficiency of its system ; scientific methods are always imperfectly understood by average, easy-going people, whose ideas are largely under the sway of their emotions. The more thorough the work of the Society is, the more "unpopular" it will become. (3) Close investigation is the first duty of all who seek to help the needy, and is the safeguard of the deserving, and the healthful horror of the idle, drunken, and vicious. The difficulties of these investigations have been increased of late by a somewhat new phenomenon—the over-sensitiveness of the poor, the result of an enlarged conception of their own case, a deeper realization of the happiness, or supposed happiness, of the rich, and a new belief that the one duty of society is to better the condition of the labour class. (4) Although not undertaking to find work for the poor, the C.O.S. frequently does so. The State affords indiscriminate charity; the Society does its best to regulate its charities according to deserts, where such charity will be likely to do permanent good, bearing in mind that the good of the poor as a class is of greater importance than the good of the individual, and that ultimate independence of *all* relief is the true end of charity. (5) The cases usually sent to the Society are those which the public finds itself unable to deal with, and wishes to get rid of. About half the total number of cases sent to the Society are assisted; and, if the good cases were sent by the public instead of only the bad ones, the proportion would be higher. The number assisted in a single year is about 10,000, each "case" representing a family of, say, 3 persons; in addition to this the Society has nearly 1000 pensioners, for whom it collects £10,000 annually; and it sends many hundreds yearly to convalescent homes. (6) The Council now consists mainly of responsible Hon. Secretaries, on whom the burden of local work chiefly rests, and of very active members of local committees. New workers rarely leave the Society from dissatisfaction with the practical work done. (7) The better administration of the Poor Law, for which end a competent and independent Commission should be appointed, and the wider practice of thrift, would be sufficient to meet the present problems of pauperism.

Con: (1) The distribution of charities through a Society has the great drawback that the personal element is wanting. Spontaneous charity does far more good than that which is the result of cold calculation on the part of a professional philanthropist, as it appeals by its very generosity to the better feelings of those relieved. All ostentatiously advertised schemes of relief, indeed, do more harm than good: they tend to create new members of the very class they profess to diminish. The C.O.S., moreover, shows a strong tendency to mere dogmatism, setting value on the expression of the principle of charity rather than on the principle itself. It makes a fetish of certain worn-out principles, and idolaters recognize no change. It thus in no sense represents the voice of the living, growing charity of the time. (2) The C.O.S. is extremely unpopular with both the general public and the poor, because it is so "cocksure" and rigid in its methods, so narrow in its sympathies, so Pharisaic in its judgments. (3) There is more "organization" than "charity" about the Society. It regards paupers almost exclusively from the policeman's point of view, running into purely detective work, which is better performed by Scotland Yard. Hence the really deserving poor are chary of making applications for relief. The inquiries necessitated by such a system are so protracted that their object may be beyond the need of charity by the time it arrives. *Bis dat qui cito dat.* (4) The C.O.S. does not profess to find work for a man, and helps only the deserving poor, taking upon itself to decide as to the exact measure of responsibility in misery. (5) It may be predicted that it will pronounce any case sent to it by the public as "undeserving of assistance." (6) The members of the Council are not personally familiar with the homes and needs of the poor. (7) The Society, whilst condemning outdoor relief, old age pensions, municipal relief works, etc., as forms of pauperization, offers no alternative suggestions, relying on the Poor Law and thrift. As a matter of fact, thrift may, under certain circumstances, be a crime, since a man's duty to his wife and children may exceed his duty to himself.

CHILD-LABOUR: "HALF-TIMERS."

Pro: (1) A certain amount of labour hurts no child, but assists his education by taking him away from mere book-work, whilst it affords him useful practical training. (2) Half-Time labour postpones the entry of a child into a factory on full time, and accustoms him gradually to the routine of factory life. (3) The wages earned by Half-Timers form a valuable addition to the family income.

Con : (1) The interest of future generations demands that children shall not be stunted in their physical or mental growth by premature toil. Under the influence of the factory, the child soon forgets all that he has learnt at school, and his physical development is retarded. Half-Time child-labour demoralizes parents, leading them to regard their children as mere money-earners. (2) It destroys the child's chance of obtaining a proper amount of recreation ; and at a time when his life should be bright, it is clouded over by the necessity of work. (3) The family does not reap much advantage from the earnings of a Half-Timer. Child-labour inevitably depresses men's wages, and thus men and children together may not earn more than the father was able to earn alone. (4) A father is encouraged in idleness by being able to obtain a contribution to his expenses from his children.

CHINESE, EXCLUSION OF (U.S.A. and Australia).

Pro : (1) The presence of the Chinese in America and Australia encourages sweating ; and since they regard themselves only as "sojourners in a foreign land," they hoard the money they earn and remit it to China, thus depleting the country of wealth. By allowing themselves to be sweated, and by working at a wage far below the market rate, they are the cause of the growth at once of enormous fortunes and of great poverty. (Some) There is no scarcity of native labour either in Australia or America. (2) They introduced opium-smoking and other forms of immorality. (3) Their exclusion is the only way out of the social and economical difficulties which they have created.

Con : (1) The Chinese are a very hard-working and economical race, and are willing to work under conditions which no Englishman or American would endure. In Australia (*e.g.*, Queensland) they can work in climates which are wholly unfitted for Europeans. (2) They are a law-abiding race, and add enormously to the material comfort of Americans and Australians. (3) The ill-treatment of those unfortunate people, who left their homes by invitation, was a disgrace to a republican country like the United States, and an eternal reproach to one that boasted of its democratic institutions like the Australian Colonies.

CHRISTENDOM, REUNION OF.

Pro : (1) The ideal of the Christian Reunion is not only desirable, but absolutely necessary, in order to enable the Churches to meet the attacks of scepticism and immorality, and to bring the spirit of Christ to bear on the social questions of our time. (2) All their minor and doctrinal differences, which are after all non-essentials, should be sunk, or natural allowances made for them, with a view to presenting a united front to the common foe. Without this, the power of the enemy will be vastly strengthened, what should be an obstacle becoming for him a powerful vantage-ground.

Con : (1) The ideal of Christian unity, however desirable, is not likely to be achieved for many generations. The proposals for unity put forward by the Church of Rome on the one side and by the Nonconformists on the other cannot be accepted by the Church of England, as they would undoubtedly tend to its disintegration. We can only patiently await God's appointed time, and meanwhile endeavour to calm the dissensions and heal the divisions within the Church of England herself. (2) The undenominational Christianity which would result from the sinking of doctrinal differences would be a colourless product, which none could accept—certainly not the Catholics, whose one condition is absolute submission to Rome.

CHRISTIAN SOCIALISM.

Pro: Christianity, or rather Christ's teaching, applies almost wholly to this world, and is more concerned with teaching us how to realize justice in this world than in informing us about the next. Many of the utterances in the Gospels which we take to refer to a future life, and the so-called doctrine of salvation, are really references to salvation in this life, through realizing that we are part of a larger organic humanity. The belief in the Fatherhood of God is a natural complement to that of the brotherhood of man as taught by the Socialists.

Con: There is no possible connection between Christianity and Socialism. Whereas Socialism recognizes that the chief aim of the individual is happiness in this life, Christianity, certainly that of Christ, teaches man that he cannot be happy here, but may be hereafter. Christianity makes this world a preparation for the next; Socialism, inverting this, makes this world the more important of the two, and teaches that the duty of man is towards the group or society of which he is a member, and that the concept of duty has been evolved by the competition of group against group—in other words, is essentially naturalistic.

CHRISTIANITY: its Divine Origin.

Pro: (1) The extraordinary influence which the personality of Christ has exercised over the subsequent course of the history of the world is a proof of the Divine origin of Christianity; how otherwise could this poor, uninstructed Child, born in an insignificant village, a member of a despised and conquered nation, coming into contact with the greatest empire the world had seen, at a time when Greece had put forward the finest fruits of her philosophy, not only become the leverage for the conversion of that empire in spite of the opposition of emperors, priests, and philosophers—in fact, all the greatest intellects of a time unique in the history of intellect—but prove the fitness of His teaching to meet the varied wants of men of all ages, races, and traditions! (2) To His followers the evidence must have been infinitely greater than can now be presented to the modern world; but it could have been only by Divine assistance, such as that given at Pentecost, that poor, ignorant fishermen could have appealed to the Roman world. (3) The wonderful evidence Christianity has shown of its ability to assimilate new truths is itself a sufficient proof of its Divine origin.

Con: (1) Extraordinary as was the influence of Christ on the world, it can be fully accounted for on purely natural grounds. It came at a time when the older civilization of the classical world was breaking up; when Rome, having become the mistress of the world, was being gradually undermined by her luxury, when her free institutions adapted to a city had proved incompatible with the demands of a military empire, and her religion had melted before the wider conception of the brotherhood of man, as taught by the Stoic philosophy, when philosophy itself was being lost in mysticism, and the world was anxiously looking for some new religion. Christianity appropriated only what was already in the air, and brought with it no new truths, merely restating and popularizing old truths. Its success need cause no more surprise than that of Buddhism in ancient times, or the Salvation Army, Socialism, and other similar ethico-religious movements of our own time, since the movement was essentially democratic, and its Apostles were men with a mission to the humble, preaching the equality of man before God. What wonder, then, that when they came to poor men and slaves, teaching them that they were the equals of their masters, the movement spread! (2) The Roman world was already in a state of moral and intellectual decay (as is shown by her adoption of Egyptian and Oriental rites and superstitions), and, therefore, fell an easy victim to any doctrine which had the merit of novelty and persuasiveness. (3) Christianity has assimilated new truths only by abandoning, gradually and severally, many of its main positions.

CHRISTIANITY: is Dogma a necessity?

Dogma must not be confounded with Doctrine. Doctrines are mere opinions which the holder may alter as he acquires fresh knowledge; whereas Dogma is opinion in a fixed, unalterable form.

Pro: (1) Religious Truth need no more lose all life from being dogmatically expressed than the axioms of Euclid. (2) Christianity assumes that we can know Truth, if not absolutely, at least with sufficient clearness and certainty; and that the Truths expressed by its doctrines are absolute, because they have been revealed to us by God Himself in the person of Jesus Christ and in the Written Word. If Christ be not taken as the Son of God, and if some of His teaching be denied, the value of the rest is impaired. (3) However clear any book may be in expression, clever men will always be found ready to understand it in a sense different from its intention, and to read esoteric meanings into it.

Con: (1) Truth cannot be crystallized into a dogmatic form without losing all life. (2) Finite beings can never attain to the whole Truth; hence to lay down a proposition and say that it is unalterable is to place obstacles in the way of the attainment of Truth. (3) If the dogmas were expunged, Christ's Personality would assume a greater importance, and the beauty of His teaching stand out more clearly. Dogmas lead to the worship of the letter; whereas, as St. Paul said, "the letter killeth, but the spirit giveth life." If God has given us such a clear revelation, why is it that the most learned men have never been able to say what is precisely intended, but rather have held opposing views!

CHURCH ATTENDANCE BY NON-BELIEVERS: is it justifiable?

Pro: (1) Church or Chapel is the only means of moral and intellectual enlightenment open to the large classes in the country; by countenancing it the unbeliever can do little harm in comparison with the harm his abstention causes. In the former case he may more or less injure his feelings of consistency, in the latter he saves his consistency at the risk of inducing, by his example, others less educated to cut themselves off from their only source of spiritual light. (2) In any case attendance greatly enhances his power of influencing others for good. (3) No man in attending Church need assert his belief in her formularies.

Con: (1) Honesty ought to be the first principle in every man's life. (2) By countenancing what he believes to be untrue, or non-true, he is making it harder for others to proclaim what they believe to be the truth. The relative amount of good and harm done by the Church is not calculable, but the good can arise only where it is thoroughly believed in. Attendance by a non-believer injures his own consistency and impairs the value of truth in the minds of others. (3) Attendance practically implies some sort of adhesion to the doctrines promulgated.

CHURCHES, THE: are social problems within their sphere?

Pro: (1) There is no limit to the sphere of Christian teaching. Christ's gospel was essentially a social gospel; and, unless it is to degenerate into a mere effort for personal salvation, it cannot neglect social difficulties as they arise. (2) The clergy especially ought to do their utmost to extend the principles of Christianity into all our social relations. (3) Such extension would tend to moralize and generally to improve the tone of politics. (4) The Churches have always regarded the poor as within their special province.

Con: (1) Christianity was a gospel of personal salvation, and is not directly concerned with sociological problems or mundane prosperity. (2) The extension of Christianity to social problems involves the secularization of the pulpit, and therefore its diversion from its proper functions, producing strife where peace should reign. The clergy are not to be trusted on these topics; they are not political or social economists, and, as a class, may be said to lack judgment and a sense of proportion. (3) It would deprive us of the one common meeting-ground in which we are free from politics. (4) The Churches have entirely failed to solve, if not aggravated, the problems of poverty, which have now to be dealt with on a strictly economic basis.

CIVIL SERVICE (ENGLAND).

Pro: (1) The present system works satisfactorily, and produces a conscientious and hard-working, if somewhat narrow-minded, body of officials. (2) Promotion by seniority is just, and makes the Service popular. (3) Any other system of promotion would open the door to nepotism and private malice; there would be no security of tenure for clerks, and a consequent loss of independence of spirit. (4) If the Civil Service were still a closed Service, opportunities would be given to a corrupt Minister to exert political influence by his appointments, and our permanent officials would no longer exist, but come in and go out with each Ministry. (5) Men of exceptional talent are quickly noticed in the Service, and means of extraordinary promotion are found for them (*e.g.* private secretaryships).

Con: (1) The present system tends to make the officials apathetic, or to convert them into mere machines. (2) Promotion by seniority, irrespective of qualification, deprives men of all stimulus to exertion. Were their promotion to depend on their work, better results would be shown. (3) Although promotion according to excellence might easily lead to abuse, such a result, considering the power of the modern press, would not be likely to ensue. At present there is absolutely no means of getting rid of a conscientious but incapable official. It would be better, therefore, to run the risk of nepotism, since the most able officials would have practical security of tenure. (4) A new Ministry would not change the Civil Servants on accession, since they alone are able to inform them as to the state of public affairs. (5) Under the present system, men of exceptional talent rise only by ordinary promotion, or by private influence.

CIVIL SERVICE (INDIA): Appointment of Natives.

Pro: (1) Indians already hold a few of the higher appointments, judicial and otherwise, in which the very highest qualities are required, and they have not shown themselves deficient in either judgment or administrative ability. English civilians will always hold the majority of these posts, and all that is asked is that opportunities for entering the service, by examinations simultaneously in London and in India, should be extended. (2) The Bengali Babu is vigorous and intellectual, and the impartiality of those holding judicial posts has never been impugned. Moreover, there is no evidence that they are inferior to or less popular with the natives than the Anglo-Indian. (3) Bengali Babus have already held very high civil appointments most successfully, even in the Sikh States.

Con: (1) The English are the dominant race in India, and it is of the greatest importance that all high administrative posts, especially those which require nerve and impartiality, should remain in their hands. (2) The Bengali Babu is sensuous and lazy, and strict impartiality is foreign to his nature. Glaring instances of gross injustice on the part of native judges are on record, and the natives themselves have lost all confidence in them, if they ever had any. By the finer Indian races (*e.g.* the Sikhs) the Bengali Babu is despised, and they consider the appointment of Babus to judicial posts a sign of weakness on the part of England. (3) (Some) There are enough native judges in India already, and their appointments have proved only qualified successes.

CIVILIZATION (EUROPEAN) IN SAVAGE LANDS.

Pro: (1) In the interests of the world at large the dissemination of the admittedly highest type of civilization is desirable. (2) So far from a higher civilization acting detrimentally on the lower, it confers inestimable benefits upon it. The vast masses of white savages who overwhelmed the Roman Empire were not exterminated, but, on the contrary, founded the nations which now dominate the world. Civilization has not killed out all low barbarians, *e.g.* the negroes (*cf.* those of the West Indies and the Southern States of the Union with the negroes of the Niger and the Congo); and often increases the efficiency of semi-civilized races (*e.g.* the Japanese). (3) Our accounts of the progress of civilization amongst barbarians come only from the superior race, which instinctively dislikes imitations of itself (*e.g.* we class men of the most diverse intellectual standings under the generic term of "Babu"). (4) The effects of the imposition of an alien civilization cannot be observed in a few years, centuries being required for a higher civilization to stamp itself deeply on a lower. In the transitional stages the inferior race is apt to appear bewildered, and hence advance is not noticed; external changes (such as dress unsuited alike to the climate and figures of its wearers) are at once perceived, whereas change in ideas and ideals is not so evident. We know, however, that such change is proceeding in India, and even in Egypt, where the higher civilization is of quite recent introduction. (5) The higher civilization produces the suspension of chronic terror by means of just administration of equitable laws; under low civilization terror in all its forms plays a large part in daily life: a benefit which, even if it stood alone, would furnish its justification.

Con: (1) In the interests of the "savage" or semi-civilized races, European culture is frequently a very qualified benefit and often a disaster. (2) No arguments can be drawn as to Civilization in Savage Lands from Savages in Civilized Lands; the two are not on the same footing, and cannot be used as examples to support each other. The imposition of a higher civilization upon a lower involves so great a pressure upon the brain that it either destroys the race subjected to it or positively lowers its intellectual capacity; savages usually perish under the burden of European education (*e.g.* Polynesians), or become utterly demoralized, often knaves (N.-American Indians); whilst semi-civilized races become positive fools (Arabs of Egypt), or mere "blotting-pads of civilization" (many Asiatic races). (3) The adverse reports by Europeans as to the advancement of savage races, arising from contact with European civilization, are in the main trustworthy, proving that it has not penetrated more than skin-deep (*teste* the violent native opposition to Lord Lansdowne's Child-Marriage Act, India, of 1893). (4) The developments of inferior civilizations proceed in a perfectly natural, and therefore effective, manner; success cannot attend external interference. Moreover, the introduction of our civilization always carries with it its attendant vices (alcohol, etc.), which appeal with peculiar force to the savage.

CODIFICATION OF THE LAW.

Pro: (1) The law is in a state of confusion; and, as everybody is "presumed to know the law," it is the duty of the State to express it clearly and simply. (2) If the law were clear there would be less litigation. The unscrupulous attorney, who is now at the bottom of much litigation, would disappear. (3) Both the Civil and the Criminal Law have been successfully codified by the Indian legislature, where the law is administered by judges who have had no special legal training.

Con: (1) Much has been already done by way of consolidating Statute Law. It is very doubtful whether a Civil Code and a Criminal Code would be intelligible to the layman. (2) Codification attempts to meet every case that may possibly arise, and in legal phraseology introduces the principles deduced from Case Law. A Code requires a trained legal mind for its right interpretation, and would in all probability tend rather to increase than reduce litigation, as each litigant would think he had found some points in his own favour. (3) It is a mistake to suppose that the Indian Codes can be or are successfully administered without a knowledge of the English Common Law, on which they are based. Their language is frequently obscure by reason of its brevity, and needs a specialist for its interpretation.

COLLECTIVISM (OR SOCIALISM).

The word Collectivism is taken to denote those theories which advocate the abolition or gradual extinction of all private property in lands, mines, capital, and the instruments of production generally, with the substitution in their stead of State Control, which may or may not be democratic. Collectivism (or Socialism) may in fact be said to be not incompatible with the extremest form of autocracy, though usually allied with a democratic form in the popular imagination. All reference to the principal doctrine associated with the name of Marx has been here omitted, because it appears that this has been abandoned by some of the leading English Socialists; and it has been attempted to give those arguments only that are essential and held by the whole school.

Pro: (1) The present competitive system gives the larger amount of the collective wealth or products of industry to those who "toil not, neither do they spin," but are enabled to levy a tax on the labour of others. The presence in the community of a large number of non-workers, living on the labour of others, entails extra work on the latter, who thus have to maintain them as well as themselves; and thus, whilst one class is demoralized by idleness, the other is crushed by excessive work. (2) While the rich are growing richer and more luxurious day by day, the poor are becoming proportionately poorer. The argument that the poor now have luxuries undreamt of by their fathers is not valid; this may be the case, and yet the fact be true that, of the total increase of the wealth of the country, the poor have received an altogether disproportionate share. As the smaller capitalists are gradually disappearing, owing to the action of fierce competition, the industry of the country tends to pass into the hands of a few large firms, and thus free competition is steadily inducing a condition under which there will ultimately be a few employers on the one side and a nation of slaves on the other. Investments on the Stock Exchange are all in favour of the large capitalist, who is able to get the best advice and manipulate the markets in the manner of American millionaires. (3) The creation of a great body of Unemployed, one of the most invariable accompaniments of Capitalism, is an essential product of its existence, since it forms the reserve on which the capitalist is able to fall back in case of a strike or when trade is very brisk. Collectivism, by abolishing the speculative or profit element in business, and by harmonizing manufactures with the wants of society, would abolish surplus production, and thus avoid the anomaly presented by the existence of a body of men in want of the bare necessities of life, which another body of men possesses in superabundance, and is unable to dispose of at a profit. (4) By making work obligatory on all men, Collectivism would reduce toil to a minimum for all alike, and thus give each individual leisure for self-improvement. (5) All men would be rewarded according to their work for the community; and while the remuneration would be sufficient to call forth the workers' best energies, the State would not allow them to keep their children in idleness on the results of their labour, nor would it permit them to accumulate claims, in the shape of interest, on the labour of the community. There is no reason to suppose that men, because deprived of the possibility of accumulating wealth, would refuse to give their best work. Under the present competitive system, some of the highest work (*e.g.* in scholarship, literature, science, politics) is done without thought of remuneration. Love of reputation would replace love of money. (6) (Some) Under Collectivism, where each member of society would be a worker, excess of population would not exist, since each new-comer would be an additional source of wealth to the community, not the reverse as now.

(7) The English, German, and French Post Offices are examples amongst many others of what a State can accomplish in Government administration on communistic lines.

Con : (1) It is not true that the present system allows the greater part of the wealth of the country to go to those who do not work. A large portion of the so-called unearned wealth of the rich is derived from money earned by them or their fathers, who, having elected to save instead of spend, have invested it, and are living on the interest thereof. It would be just as true to say that the labourer lives on the capitalist as that the capitalist lives on the labourer, since the former supplies the sinews of war with which the latter produces a commodity (neither could the capitalist exist without the labourer). Besides supplying the capital, the capitalist often directs production, furnishing the necessary ability which the labourer lacks. Indeed, most of the profits are the earnings of ability, and rightly belong to the "head" and not to the "hands." (2) The labourer has shared proportionately in the increase of wealth. Labour, though not entitled to it, has, in the opinion of the ablest statisticians, shared in a much greater degree than capital; besides which, the hours of labour are decreased, and the purchasing power of money is much greater than formerly. It is also untrue that there is a universal tendency to eliminate the small capitalist and business man; now, as formerly, there is always a good chance of success for a small business, when conducted ably and in accordance with the spirit of the age, since it will probably be better supervised in the hands of the actual owner than when trusted to salaried officials. Co-operative enterprize and Limited Liability Cos. also offer to small capitalists a field for profitable investment, and thus enable schemes to be developed which no private capital could undertake. The principal gambling, moreover, is not done in the shares of Companies which are on a sound basis; hence, while it is possible that the control of a speculative Company may be gained by methods similar to those of some American millionaires, this would be impossible in the case of a sound financial concern (*e.g.* an English Railway Co.). (3) The problem of the Unemployed would still exist under Collectivism, because it is as much a moral as an economic one. In every community idlers and black sheep will always be present, and Collectivism assumes an ideal state of society in which all men are equally good. Over-production, too, would also take place, since it is impossible to accurately gauge the future wants of the world. (4) Under Collectivism a leisured class would not exist ; and since we owe some of our noblest work in art, literature, and science to this class, culture and progress would decrease. It is hard to conceive that in a community of workers, where the majority were labourers, endowments for leisured toil would find a place. Were such endowments to exist, all would wish to enjoy them. Who, if not himself, should decide the trade or profession of each individual? (5) It is almost impossible to conceive how work is to be remunerated save on a competitive basis. Under Collectivism all kinds of work would have to be valued by reducing them to a common denomination, and that denomination could only be the amount of time spent in the production of commodities. Thus the value of painting a picture and ploughing a field would be gauged by the time spent in obtaining the results, and Collectivism would be possible only if all men were not only equally good, but also equally gifted. One of the chief incentives to labour would be removed if parents were deprived of the wish and ability to provide for their children's advancement. (6) Present over-population is due to the recklessness of parents; Collectivism would increase this evil, since no responsibility would attach to the production of children. Though for a short time work might be found for all, and the unemployed class disappear, yet the same tension, due to unrestricted production of children, would recur, and they would again become a source of poverty instead of wealth. (7) The English Post Office is in no sense, save that it belongs to the State, a socialistic institution.

It is merely a large business worked for a profit, and its employés are sweated as much as in a private concern. It cannot be argued that because the State successfully transacts the business of carrying letters, it would therefore succeed in managing the whole business of the country. (Some) The English Post Office is a model of bad management (*See* POST OFFICE).

COMMON-LANDS, ENCLOSURE OF.

Pro : (1) The enclosure of Common-lands has been one of the greatest instruments whereby the land of England has been brought into a state of thorough cultivation, under which it is able to support far more people than would otherwise have been the case. The rights of the Lords of the Manor in Common-lands had been recognized by Parliament for more than 600 years under the Statute of Merton; and therefore for Parliament to virtually repeal this Act and abolish these rights without compensation, as done by the Common Law Amendment Act, 56 & 57 Vict. c. 57 (1893), was pure spoliation. (2) Except in the neighbourhood of large towns, where the inhabitants are, or ought to be, able to look after their own interests without the assistance of a special Act, Common rights are a matter between the Commoners and the Lord. In country districts there is no need for any open ground, and the people are most indifferent as to their rights, which indeed had lapsed by non-user. (3) There is no evidence to show that there ever was a time when the Lord of the Manor did not exist; nor is the commonly accepted theory of a primitive communism, on which the lord was a later graft, borne out by closer examination. (4) Labourer's wages have improved through the enclosure of Commons, and his standard of comfort has risen enormously. The growth of population has made it impossible to turn cattle out on Commons; cheap coal has superseded turf or gorse for fuel, and bracken and heather are no longer used for litter or thatching. (5) Near London the Commons afford ruffians ground on which to ply their trade (threatening passers-by with violence, especially at night, etc.). They also facilitate improper assignations. (6) Even where it may in the public interest be right to keep Common-lands open, and to put them into the hands of public bodies, compensation ought to be paid for all rights dispossessed. (7) No District Councils, in fact no public bodies, are fit to be entrusted with such wide powers.

Con : (1) The Statute of Merton (A.D. 1235) had been obsolete for many years when it was revived by the landlords to support a policy of spoliation. (2) In the neighbourhood of large towns Commons are especially necessary; and it is here that they have suffered more than anywhere else at the hands of the jerry-builder and the greed of the lord. Even in the country districts, now that England is so much enclosed, it is only right that open spaces should remain for the recreation of the people, bringing the very poorest into touch with nature. (3) The lord was, according to very eminent authorities, a later importation into a system of communistic village groups, whose members held the land belonging to the group in common, and the Common-lands are a relic of this previously existing state of society. (4) By the enclosure of the Common-lands, the labourers lost the right to feed cattle or sheep, and to dig turf, or cut gorse, bracken, or heather for fuel, litter, or thatching; and although these privileges are not of as much value as formerly, they received no compensation for them. In any case, the Commons formed a most acceptable recreation-ground, and the Common right was valued by adjoining landowners as a means of preventing lords from enclosing and encroaching on Common-land. (5) Cases of robbery, etc., on Commons near London are very rare, and might be altogether prevented by a more efficient police patrol. (6) The lord's "rights," which are very often mythical, ought to be carefully examined before compensation is paid. (7) Representative bodies (*e.g.* District Councils) should have power to take over and manage all Commons within their districts.

COMPENSATION TO PUBLICANS.

Pro: (1) The State has always recognized that where a man is for the public benefit deprived of his means of existence through no fault of his own, he ought to receive compensation (*e.g.* slave-owners received £20,000,000). (2) The State has recognized the drink traffic as legitimate. An enormous amount of capital has been invested in it, and the licence has always been regarded as renewable, subject only to good conduct. Many have entered the trade, and invested their savings in it on this assumption. A resolution has also been passed in the Commons that compensation should accompany non-renewal of a licence; and in assessing the value of a property for Death Duties the value of the individual interest is assessed on the supposition that the licence will continue to be renewed, as a legally vested interest. (3) All licences suddenly withdrawn without cause shown or compensation given would involve unwarrantable hardships. (4) It would be inequitable to apply the principle of taxing unearned increment to public-houses alone. (5) Brewers and distillers, as well as publicans, should receive compensation, if compensation be right in principle. (6) The estimate of the cost of compensation at £200,000,000 is greatly exaggerated. Only a small number of public-houses would be closed, and these, being the inferior, would cost much less.

Con: (1) The State has never recognized any claim of the publican for a renewal of his licence, which is granted yearly, in the interests, not of the individual, but of the public. The right of slave-owners was not subject to an annual licence, and the money was not given as compensation, but as a free gift. (2) To claim a vested interest in a licence is to give an artificial value to a privilege. It was decided by the House of Lords (1891) that there is no obligation on the authorities to give any reason for declining to renew a licence. (3) Compensation is unnecessary, because, by virtue of the monopoly derived from the limitation of licences, publicans have already had the equivalent of compensation in advance, and, like all monopolists, must take the risk of a monopoly being withdrawn. (4) The greater the number of public-houses suppressed, the larger the increase in value of the rest. Consequently, publicans as a class would not suffer, and if compensation is to be paid, it should be paid by those benefiting to those dispossessed. (5) The brewers and distillers, not the publicans, would reap the benefit of compensation, owing to the system of tied houses. (6) Compensation is financially impracticable. It would cost some £200,000,000.

CONSCRIPTION, MILITARY, FOR ENGLAND.

Pro: (1) The English army is ridiculously small compared with those of other nations; were war to break out our ships are very uncertain, and we should be at the mercy of any force that could effect a landing. (*See* CHANNEL TUNNEL.) (2) The discipline of universal drill is very good for a nation, and creates habits of order and loyalty, which are the greatest safeguards for society against revolution. (3) The hardships are much exaggerated. In Germany only sons of widows, etc., are exempt; drill interferes very little with their capacity for other work, as is shown by the position of Germany in the commercial world. Society has great claims on the individual, since it is only owing to his life in an organized State, and to the labours of those who preceded him, that civilized life is possible to him; hence it is only fair that, in return, he should make some sacrifices for *his* successors. (4) The English Volunteers and Militia are useless, because the officers are incompetent. Whatever the men are, the officers must be professional soldiers, as the problems of tactics are intricate, and require a man's whole time to be mastered. (5) Conscription makes the people themselves very averse to war.

Con: (1) As long as England holds the sea, her army is of no consequence; if she loses that, she must in any case surrender. (*See* CHANNEL TUNNEL.) (2) The military system develops bullying in the officers and servility in the men. Nowhere is Socialism more rampant than in Germany. (3) The hardships of military service fall very heavily on the poor, who lose much time by it. Germany has made great strides, but the progress would have been much greater had it not been hampered by Conscription. (4) Our Volunteers form a perfectly adequate means of defence, and will be more so when the reforms lately put in practice have had effect. (Some) Service for a certain number of years in the Volunteer force for a certain period of the year might be made a condition of receiving Government technical education, etc., so as to raise the number of Volunteers; and (Some) A small pay might be given, which would give the Government a claim on the men, and enable it to insist on efficiency. (5) Armed peace, with its crushing taxation and periodical panics, is almost as bad as war.

CONSTITUTION, A WRITTEN, FOR ENGLAND.

Pro: (1) A Written Constitution would put a barrier in the way of hasty change, and, though unable to delay change, would give time for reflection. (2) It would clearly define the rights and duties of the State and the individual, and save much friction and doubt. (3) It is consistent with the growth of Constitutions if left open to amendment; all most recent Constitutions expressly provide for it.

Con: (1) Constitutions grow; they are not made. A Written Constitution would eliminate the advantage possessed by the flexible machinery of our present Constitution. It would have to be more or less a compromise, and hence uncertain in its interpretation and working. It would not prevent ill-considered change, but only irritate people and cause them to be unreasonable. (2) However skilfully and elaborately a Constitution might be drawn up, a most important part would still remain which is too fluctuating and indefinite to be capable of being fixed by words. (3) It is always hard to amend a Written Constitution; in America, where this is disallowed, it reduced the country to civil war.

CONTAGIOUS DISEASES ACT (WOMEN).

Pro: (1) The Act affords a sure preventive against the transmission of disease; and such protection, not only for the soldiers but for the women, has been found necessary in all the countries of Continental Europe. Since the repeal, venereal diseases have enormously increased. The Act was supported by all who had any working knowledge of the subject. (2) Individuals must, if necessary, be sacrificed for the good of the whole, and whatever the harm is done by occasional abuse of power, would be more than compensated by the immunity from disease on the part of the whole community, especially the succeeding generation. (3) Since soldiers cannot marry, the State should take care that their life be accompanied by as little evils as possible. It is the only way to keep the army at its maximum efficiency. (4) The powers given to the police were no more arbitrary than those given them to deal with any other contagious disease. Moreover, it provided cures gratis. (5) It tended to preserve public decency in the streets.

Con: (1) The Act afforded no security against disease, which might be contracted and spread between the inspections. Commissioners came to the conclusion that it had been perfectly useless. (2) The State ought not to countenance vice on any pretext whatever; nor ought mere utilitarian considerations to weigh against the degradation of women, or to shield men from the results of their vice. (3) To be really effective, the Act should have included also the inspection of men. (4) The powers given to the police were far more arbitrary than under any other Acts, and are inequitable because directed against one class. It enabled the police to bring false charges against and thus to ruin any woman against whom they had a grudge. (5) The Act made it impossible for a woman to take up an honest life again.

CONTRACTING-OUT CLAUSE: Employers' Liability Bill.

Pro: All legislation which interferes with freedom of contract should be avoided. Parties should be at liberty to contract out of the Act. It frequently happens that there is a mutual insurance scheme which is more beneficial to the workman than is the Act.

Con: The employer and workman, in making a contract of service, are not on equal terms, and the workman should be protected against himself. Permissive legislation is always a mistake, as the stronger side never fails to get the advantage. In any case, the State should be satisfied as to the nature of the insurance scheme before allowing an employer to escape his liability under the Act. The chief object of the Act is not to provide compensation, but to guard against an employer's carelessness as to the lives of his employés.

CO-OPERATION: can it supersede Capitalism?

Pro: (1) Co-operation, by substituting for the self-interest of an individual or a group of individuals the self-interest of the whole community of workers, puts each worker in a position to be, in a sense, his own master, and secures a higher standard of work than mere wage-labour commands, the whole proceeds of the work going into his own pocket. (2) The commercial policy is regulated by the advice of those immediately concerned in its success. (3) It places the producer in direct contact with the consumer, and thus saves the expenses of a middleman, *pro tanto* reducing the costs of production. (4) It increases the efficiency and decreases the cost of supervision, as each worker, in his own interests, supervises his neighbours' work gratuitously. (5) It eliminates the possibility of strikes. (6) Where tried, it has proved very successful; there is no reason why it should not be generally adopted.

Con: (1) By freedom of contract and Trades Unionism, the worker has already secured fair wages and equitable conditions of work. (2) Under Capitalism, the commercial policy is regulated by a single expert individual or small group of individuals, whether owner or board of directors; and thus a uniformity and continuity of policy are better secured than under the former. (3) Under Co-operative management the profits hitherto made by the Capitalist would be absorbed in financing the undertaking, as capital, which is not owned by the labour class, would be just as requisite then as now. (4) Mutual spying is scarcely a habit to be encouraged. A highly-salaried manager or managers would be needed, and the workers would grudge, if not decline, to pay high salaries to a few of their own body for doing what they would consider perfunctory work, which each would consider himself capable of. (5) Strikes have occurred in Co-operative establishments. (6) Merely distributive Co-operation has been successful; but Co-operation on a productive basis has been a pronounced failure. Private Stores are equally successful in mere distribution.

CO-OPERATION: is it better than State Socialism?

Pro: (1) Voluntary Co-operation, as opposed to State Socialism, seeks to make self-help the basis of social reform. By banding men together for a common end, it teaches them self-reliance and gives them independence. (2) Whereas Socialism is a distant and impracticable ideal, Co-operation has become a fact. (3) Whilst Socialism would depose the Capitalist only to exalt the State, thus leaving the worker as dependent as before, Co-operation would make him his own master, and render such abuses as "sweating" impossible. (4) Co-operation, unlike Socialism, does not aim at the expropriation of vested interests; it defrauds no man; neither does it cripple the nation with any scheme of wholesale compensation.

Con: (1) Co-operation benefits only a small portion of the working class, and thus tends to create an aristocracy of labour. It is useful only as training men to work together, and thus fitting them for the fuller realization of the same principle under Socialism. (2) Socialism is as easily realizable as universal Co-operation. (3) Co-operation simply leads to competing societies, instead of competing firms. Many Co-operative societies "sweat" their employés as cruelly as private employers. (4) It does not touch evils like the land monopoly, by which the mass of the workers are defrauded of the results of their labour.

CORPORAL PUNISHMENT IN SCHOOLS.

Pro: (1) Corporal Punishment for certain offences is most effective, because it is prompt, and appeals to all natures. (2) When inflicted justly and without anger, it chastens rather than brutalizes the master, and is not resented by the pupil; moreover, in most schools it is (and in all schools should be) resorted to only as a final punishment. (3) An occasional hasty cuff is soon forgotten by the pupil, and accustoms him to the hardships of real life. (4) It is impossible to always "make the punishment suit the crime." (5) Corporal Punishment often takes the place of long impositions, which deprive boys of proper recreation and tend to deaden the intellect.

Con: (1) Corporal Punishment is inefficient. It does not act as a deterrent on a hardened boy, while it is a perpetual and living horror to a sensitive nature. (2) It brutalizes master and pupil alike, and is simply a survival of barbarism. (3) Where it exists, the master becomes habituated to lifting his hand against his pupils, and the mutual good feeling that ought to exist between them is impossible. Corporal Punishment is not easily forgotten; nor does it accustom the recipient to the hardships of life. If so, he ought to be caned daily. (4) It saves the master much trouble, and is, therefore, often inflicted irrespective of the harm done to the pupil. (5) The *ennui* of impositions is resented by the majority of boys, and are, therefore, adequate.

CREMATION.

Pro: (1) Cremation is the most sanitary and cleanly mode of disposing of the dead. The epidemic earthworm is well known to have occasionally spread infection. (2) It can be so accomplished as to avoid wounding the feelings of surviving friends; under any circumstances, destruction by fire cannot be considered as more unbecoming than destruction by worms, the former doing rapidly what decay does slowly. The contortions of the body during the process (which lasts only two hours, and which gives off no odour) need not be witnessed. (3) It is a very ancient practice. (4) It eliminates all chance of premature burial, arising from trance, etc.—a by no means unimportant fact, as recent discoveries have shown; (we have it, moreover, on eminent medical authority, that it is impossible to be certain that a man is dead before actual decay is visible). (5) The objection that cremation destroys all evidence as to cause of death could be met by a stricter system of medical certificates. (6) The crowded condition of our cemeteries is a danger and a disgrace. Perishable coffins would go only a short way towards remedying this evil.

Con: (1) The tradition of nearly all nations is in favour of a reverent mode of treating the dead (Worship of the Dead has even been a widespread cult). Earth sepulture is alike commanded by the Synagogue and the Christian Church. (2) Cremation violates our best and tenderest emotions; we could never reconcile ourselves to submitting the bodies of those we loved to the flames, accompanied by the terrible contortions they suffer; and the fumes given off are noxious. (3) The practice was a late introduction in the Roman Empire to prevent bodies from being disinterred. It was forbidden by the Holy Roman Inquisition. (**4**) Premature burial can be rendered impossible by puncturing the heart of assumed corpses before burial. (**5**) Cremation destroys all evidences of the causes of death, rendering detection of murder impossible. (**6**) The substitution of perishable for imperishable coffins would meet the difficulty of overcrowding in cemeteries.

CRIMINAL APPEAL.

Pro: (**1**) *Humanum est errare*, and Judges and Magistrates are not exempt from this law. They will act with greater care if they know there is an Appellate Court above them. (**2**) A humane Judge will be glad to feel that, should he err, his error may be rectified. (**3**) In cases of life and death, at the very least, it is necessary that there should be an Appellate or a Revisionary Court.

Con: (**1**) *Interest reipublicæ ut sit finis litium* applies to criminal as well as to civil cases. Where is the right of appeal to stop? Is the convicted person to pay the costs? If so, the rich only benefit. (**2**) Magistrates and Judges are chosen with great care, and their responsibility should not be lessened by allowing them to think that their errors of judgment will be corrected. (**3**) If either were really necessary, a Revisionary Court would be preferable in capital cases; but it would involve great expense, and take up much time. Appellate and Revisionary Courts may be necessary in India, where the Judges and Magistrates are not trained lawyers; but even there the tendency, based on wide experience, is to increase the power and responsibility of the Court of First Instance.

DEATH DUTIES (ENGLISH), GRADUATED.

Pro: (**1**) Death Duties are as little felt as any form of taxation, since they are paid at a time when, having just inherited property, a man is well able to yield part of it to the State. (**2**) They no more act as a check on industry than other taxation. (**3**) They are a most fruitful source of revenue, and less open to evasion than the income tax. (**4**) Taxation should fall proportionately more heavily on the very rich, who have a much larger surplus *pro rata* after paying for the necessaries of life than poorer people; and the common sense of Englishmen would prevent this policy from being carried too far. (**5**) Real estate should not escape more lightly than personal; previously the taxation of it was ludicrously out of proportion. One injustice does not remedy another; and even if it could be proved that real estate bore the major part of local taxation, which it would be hard to do in the case, say, of the Westminster and Bedford Estates in London, it would be an argument rather for remedying this evil than for allowing it to weigh in the case of the Death Duties. (**6**) The State has the right to settle on what terms property shall be inherited, and has long imposed a tax based on the relationship between testator and heir. (**7**) Unlimited bequest encourages the growth of an idle class living on the industry of their progenitors, and themselves adding nothing to the wealth of the community. (**8**) The State may be described as a sleeping partner in the business of each citizen, without whose aid and protection it would be impossible to transact business or accumulate wealth; when the partnership is dissolved, the State, as sleeping partner, is entitled to a share in the capital. (**9**) Death Duties enable the State to tax property which otherwise would escape all taxation. (**10**) An increase of direct taxation in the shape of income tax and Death Duties lightens the enormous share of indirect taxation paid by the working-class. (**11**) The increase in the Death Duties can always be met by insuring properties to the extent of the duties. (**12**) The Duties may press hardly in some particular cases (*e.g.* widows); but this might be specially provided for, and some hardship is unavoidable in any scheme of reconstruction. (**13**) Any sacrifice is worth making, especially to our richer classes, in order to maintain the supremacy and independence of Great Britain.

Con: **(1)** Since Death Duties have to be paid in cash as a lump sum, they are much more severely felt than, say, income tax, which is paid annually in smaller amounts. This is especially the case with large landed estates, which cannot be suddenly realized, or partly realized, to meet the Duties, as can be done in the case of stocks and shares. **(2)** Death Duties are a great discouragement to all habits of thrift among the people, since a man objects to save money part of which will not benefit his heir, but be absorbed by the State. **(3)** The increase in Death Duties has led to such evasion (*i.e.* by gifts during life, etc.) as to actually diminish the amount received by the Treasury from this source. **(4)** Taxation should be arranged so as to fall on each man according to his means, and in strict proportion to their actual amount; otherwise, there is no guarantee against extravagance on the part of the State; the great mass of the people would countenance extravagance, if they could throw most of the expense on a few rich men. **(5)** Real Estate and Personal Estate are held on absolutely different bases. In addition to being much harder to realize, Real Estate already bears the chief part of the local taxation of the country. **(6)** There is no analogy between the case of a graduated Death Duty on amount and that on kinship, since the latter is designed to maintain the integrity of the family, which absolute freedom of bequest has a tendency to impair. **(7)** A leisured class so-called is the only means of maintaining the culture of the nation, and much good work is done by this class which could not be done so efficiently or cheaply by any other. **(8)** Even if the State does secure a man in the enjoyment of his property, she gets paid for so doing; otherwise, if she is to share in the profits, there is no reason why she should not participate also in the losses. **(9)** All property bears indirectly its due share of taxation. **(10)** Indirect taxation is much the easiest way of raising revenue, and enables the working-classes to pay their fair share towards the expenses of administration—no small consideration, when these very classes virtually dictate how the money is to be spent. **(11)** It is not always possible to insure properties, except at a very high premium, against Death Duties; moreover, the Government taxes such insurances. **(12)** The Duties press very hardly in the case of a widow inheriting property from her husband, or in that of a man receiving a small legacy from a large estate, etc. **(13)** It is not equitable to throw the brunt of the expenditure on the navy on a particular class in the community; and the sacrifice entailed on the landlords involves far heavier sacrifices on servants, etc., thrown out of employment.

DECEASED WIFE'S SISTER.

Pro: **(1)** The Deceased Wife's Sister is much the best and most natural guardian to her sister's children; and is often so appointed on the wife's death-bed. **(2)** The mere fact of marriage being prohibited would not prevent scandal, should the sister-in-law live in the house with her brother-in-law after the wife was dead. The world has never regarded the relations between the two as it does that between brother and sister. **(3)** Since these marriages have been forbidden only during the present century, having been duly recognized previously, society looks very leniently on them; and, as the law is constantly broken, it would be as well to repeal it. The law is, moreover, very hard on the children of these second marriages, if there happen to be any. **(4)** The law in regard to death duties treats the sister-in-law as a stranger; why should the marriage law treat her differently? **(5)** There is much more reason why the law should prohibit marriages between first cousins, than between a man and his sister-in-law. Relations by marriage cannot be considered as on the same footing as those by blood. **(6)** The Popes have many times allowed men to marry their Deceased Wife's Sister, and even his Deceased Brother's Wife. **(7)** It is legal in our Colonies and in most other countries. **(8)** The laws of the Church must conform with, not dictate to the State. **(9)** It is allowed by the law of Moses.

Con: (1) If a man could marry his sister-in-law, all brotherly feeling towards her would be destroyed, especially where she lived with her married sister; and it would create jealousy. (2) It would render it impossible for the sister-in-law to live in the same house with her brother-in-law after the death of his wife, unless she were willing to marry him; and hence the children would be deprived of the care of the one person best able to look after them. (3) The law must be obeyed, and it is no harder on the children of such a marriage than of any irregular unions. The fact that people have broken the law is no argument for its repeal. (4) The law, though it taxes bequests from a brother-in-law to a sister-in-law at the same rate as a bequest to a stranger (10 per cent.), puts bequests from a sister-in-law to a brother-in-law (3 per cent.) on the same basis as to a brother or sister. (5) There is no reason why marriages between first-cousins should be prohibited; they are on a totally different footing from all other kinds. Relations by marriage have always been considered as blood relations. (6) The views of Popes, who have always been lax towards kings, are not a criterion for English law-making. (7) England has certainly no reason to follow the marriage laws of her Colonies or other States. (8) It would produce a divergence between the law of the Church and that of the State, which would be most disastrous for both. (9) It is forbidden by the law of Moses and the Christian Church.

DECIMAL SYSTEM, THE.

Pro: (1) The present system of weights and measures is quite unintelligible to foreigners with whom we wish to extend our trade, greatly handicapping British industry. (2) The time required for learning our complicated system is much greater than that needed for the Decimal System. (3) Change must always involve some hardships, but this change has been effected without difficulty in every other country, and Englishmen are not more stupid than others. Although Decimal coinage, weights, and measures may be used, there is no possible objection to such vulgar fractions as $\frac{1}{2}$, $\frac{1}{3}$, $\frac{1}{4}$, etc., being employed also when convenient. (4) Though the Duodecimal System may be theoretically best, yet because its adoption would involve a change in the notation of the whole world, it is impracticable. One might go on for ever inventing numbers which are theoretically the best; if 12, why not 16 or 18? The advantages, however, are small compared with those of keeping the present system of notation intact, and unifying our standards accordingly. (5) Every civilized nation in the world except Great Britain and some of her Dependencies has a Decimal coinage, and the metric weights and measures have been adopted in all European countries except Russia and Great Britain, and in all the South-American States, as well as in Japan. (6) There is no necessity why our units of measurement should correspond with terrestrial measurements. The standard metre has been determined with the greatest scientific accuracy, and facsimiles of it have been supplied to nearly all civilized countries. (7) Scientists use decimals because they are obliged to use the quickest and simplest means, and even in commercial life, strong as habit is, decimal divisions are being increasingly resorted to (in machine shops, etc.). (8) The Metric System should—with a few years' grace—be made compulsory, in order to avoid the confusion incident to a double system. The change must cause inconvenience, but it would be best to make the transitional period as short as possible. In Germany, Austria, etc., from two to three years proved to be amply sufficient.

Con: (1) The difficulties of our weights and measures are much exaggerated. (2) The aim of education is to train the mind rather than to teach facts. (3) The change would involve enormous hardships on the poor, who could never understand it. (4) Though the Decimal System has been adopted, there are advantages possessed by 12 which 10 has not, e.g. 12

divides by 3 and 4 and 6 as well as by 2 ; 10 divides only by 5 and 2. The change would be comparatively simple ; it would involve only a small alteration in our counting to make calculation by groups of twelve similar to that by groups of ten. **(5)** The metric measures do not correspond with terrestrial measurements, though originally intended to do so. **(6)** Even where the Decimal System has been adopted, it is constantly being departed from (*e.g.* in Stock Exchanges, etc.), showing that it is not convenient. **(8)** It would be a mistake to make a compulsory change. If the change is desirable, to make it optional would be quite enough, allowing a universal change to be gradually effected.

DEGENERATION.

Pro: **(1)** The degeneracy which of recent years has been so noticeable a feature in the more cultured classes of Western Europe is unmistakably evidenced by the literature (including journalism) and art (including music and the drama) of the day. In both spheres the cult of the morbid and abnormal has usurped the place of healthy and beautiful standards and ideals. **(2)** The tendency is further witnessed in other departments, especially that of mental and physical health. The number of lunatics and weak-minded has greatly increased ; and disease, if not more prevalent than ever, is taking new forms, mainly nervous (*e.g.* neuritis, hysteria). Physique is also deteriorating. **(3)** Moral health also is retrograding, as our criminal statistics show. **(4)** Modern degeneracy has a parallel in the decay which overtook the Roman Empire, and is accompanied by very similar symptoms. **(5)** The causes for this decadence are to be sought in (*a*) the unhealthy lives now led by nearly all members of the community, owing to the severer struggle for existence arising from over-population ; (*b*) the higher standards of comfort, amounting to luxury, demanded by all classes ; (*c*) the democratization and consequent vulgarization of a large part of life, arising from the newly-sprung half-educated masses ; (*d*) the increasing use of stimulants, and especially sedatives, by an ever-widening class.

Con: **(1)** There is no evidence of true degeneracy, such as has been alleged, in contemporary literature and art. Much of what is new, and most of what shocks the æsthetic and moral canons of an older generation, are merely indications of a new and better era ; and such outcries as the present one have always arisen when men brought up in one era of thought come to adversely criticize the *Zeit-geist* of a succeeding age. **(2)** The *absolute* increase in lunacy may be admitted, but its alleged *relative* growth is not yet proved. Beyond mere printed statistics, we have to consider their ratio to an ever-growing population, and how far increased medical knowledge and greater precautions against lunatics bear upon them. *Per contra*, the renewed interest and the energy displayed in modern athletic games are indications of physical well-being. **(4)** No true analogy as to modern degeneracy can be drawn from Imperial Rome, as there is no parallelism between the concomitant circumstances. A great historian has said that the chief use of history is to dispel such analogies. **(5)** The influences to which the alleged decadence is attributed are no doubt unhealthy, but they are merely temporary ; and their importance for the higher life of the cultured classes is much exaggerated. Certainly in *some* directions the taste of the middle class has improved, particularly in that of artistic decoration of the home ; and the Pre-Raphaelite movement, though not of quite modern origin, never flourished so vigorously as at present.

DISARMAMENT, INTERNATIONAL.

Pro: **(1)** There is no reason why the chief European Powers should not agree to reduce their armaments to reasonable dimensions. **(2)** The expenses of armaments are almost insupportable ; and as international rivalry herein increases, the burden will reduce many States to a condition of bankruptcy. **(3)** Armaments are a standing provocation to war,

Con: (1) No such international agreement is possible. It would place those States which have spent much time and money on their armaments on an equality with their inferiors. On the other hand, a proposal to maintain the *status quo* would not be accepted by any nation which has aspirations. Besides, how could such agreements be enforced, or infringements punished? (2) However heavy the burden of preparation for war may be, the sacrifice is well made, as the price paid for national independence. (3) Armaments are a standing preventive of war; the stronger a nation is, the less the temptation to attack it.

DISENDOWMENT OF THE CHURCH OF ENGLAND.

Pro: (1) The Church being the State Church, its property is held subject to the welfare of the nation. (Some) The phrase Church Property is misleading if it means that the Church can exercize proprietary rights over it. The Church cannot hold property. She is not herself a Corporation, though composed of a number of corporations, in which the property is vested, and not in the Church. (2) Tithes were at first voluntary; but according to Dr. Stubbs, Bp. of Oxford, in A.D. 787 it was made "imperative by the legatine councils held in England, which being attended and confirmed by the kings and earldomen, had the authority of the witenagemotes. From that time it was enforced by not infrequent legislation." (3) The State has always exercized rights of ownership over what is called Church Property. It has taken some of it away, and applied it to secular uses. It has reduced the enormous incomes of Bishops, Deans, and Chapters in past days, and has suppressed bishoprics, deaneries, and canonries altogether. It has altered clerical incomes, abolished many clerical pluralities, and compelled clerical residence, just as it has regulated the Army and Naval and Civil Service. But it does not interfere in that way with the property in possession of Dissenters, because it is not State Property. (4) The Clergy do not receive the revenues for their own benefit, but in return for certain services. They are public functionaries, who are remunerated, not by salaries paid by the Treasury out of taxes, but by incomes arising from public property set apart for their benefit. (5) The State cannot be guilty of "robbery" in turning the national property to national purposes. The only possible robbery of public property is its transfer to private uses. In varying the particular object to which it is applied there may be folly, but not spoliation. (6) Tithes would continue to be paid, but to the State and for unsectarian purposes. The present generation of Clergymen would continue to receive their present incomes, but the next generation would be supported by those who desired their services. (7) The Church when endowed was the Church of the whole nation. Now only a portion of the nation attends its services, while large numbers provide places of worship for themselves. (8) The fact that every inhabitant of the country may claim the offices of the Church of England and the services of her Clergy is a proof that the Church is supported by national, and not private, funds; for, if the State did not support the Church, it would have no right to impose such an obligation upon it. As a matter of fact, however, the State Clergy cannot possibly minister to the wants of the entire population. Large numbers do not want their services, and, if they did, they could not have them. (9) Disendowment would be a great boon to the Church, for it would stimulate the now latent generosity of her richer members. Though the Church contains by far a greater proportion of very rich men than any other religious body, yet her members subscribe on an average less than those of any other religious denomination, considering in many cases that when they have paid Tithe they have done all that can be expected of them. (10) The future of Cathedrals and Parish Churches can be best settled when the proposal is brought forward. No doubt life interests would be fully respected. (11) Many of the Endowments of the Church come to her from pre-

Reformation times, and were left for specific purposes (such as prayers for the souls of the faithful), while they have been applied for others. If at the Reformation, why not now?

Con: (1) With the exception of a grant of £1,000,000 as a thanks-offering for the return of peace, and another of £500,000 for building churches, the State has given nothing towards the building of churches, etc. The property of the Church comes from the voluntary gifts of her members at various periods of her history, and is not national property. (2) Tithe is part of the rent paid sometimes to the clergyman, sometimes to a lay tithe-owner instead of to the landowner. Private individuals first voluntarily charged their land with it, and then the State recognized its legality, and provided a way of enforcing the payment, exactly as the payment of money due to Dissenters on their Endowments is enforced. (3) Parliament can confiscate any property; but might does not make right. (4) If the Clergy are public servants, why does not a charge for their maintenance appear in the National Budget? As a matter of fact, the inequalities in the incomes, the anomalies in the respective sizes of parishes, in methods of patronage, prove that Parliament did not endow the Church, but that individuals did. (5) The State would not be justified in applying money or buildings consecrated to God to secular uses. (6) If it did not abolish Tithe, Disendowment would benefit nobody, and would do harm to provincial trade by removing some of their best customers, the clergy. (7) The great majority of the nation are members of the Church; if not, why do the Dissenters object to a religious census? Dissenters, by leaving the Church, voluntarily abnegated all right to share in her Endowments. (8) The fact that the Church and her ministers are at the service of all parishioners is a great boon to the poor. The Church has made enormous strides of late years, and is well able to cope with any emergency that may arise. Any member of the community may obtain the services of her clergy if he need them. (9) Disendowment would give the Church such great power that she would be dangerous. On the basis of compensation paid to the Irish Church, she would be left with a property worth some £90,000,000. (10) The question of the possession of Cathedrals and Churches must always be fatal to any scheme, since there is a very strong feeling against national monuments becoming the property of a sect, or being applied to secular purposes. (11) The Endowments taken by the State at the Reformation were chiefly those of the monasteries, for which act ample justification exists, when we remember that the monasteries considered they owed obedience to Rome rather than the king; other Endowments taken were such as had been left for superstitious purposes, and consequently were no longer serving a useful purpose. (Some) Two wrongs can never make a right. The Endowments of the Church have largely accrued to her since the Reformation, and are not affected by the foregoing considerations.

DISESTABLISHMENT OF THE CHURCH OF ENGLAND.

Pro: (1) The Union between Church and State is undesirable, both Church and State being essentially different, in that the State has to deal with the individual as a member of society and in his relations to the world, whilst the Church looks on him as an individual with a soul to save, and from the point of view of his relations to his Maker. (2) So far from spiritualizing the State, the State has dragged the Church down to its own level, and breathed into her a spirit of worldly prudence, fatal to the spiritual mission of the Church. It is certain, for example, that the Bishops and the Clergy are, largely from this connection with the Throne, kept from denouncing evils which, in the interests of society, it is not wise to pass over. (3) The fact that she is Established renders all efforts on the part of the Church to reform herself nugatory. Parliament alone has the power to alter either the rites or ceremonies of the Church, though it is recognized that Parliament, consisting as it does of men of all denominations, is not a fit body to entrust with the doctrine or discipline of the Church. The part of the 20th Article, on the Church's "power to decree rites or ceremonies and authority in controversies of faith," was not inserted in Convocation, nor was it sanctioned by Parliament when the Articles were ratified in 1571; it was added by command of the Queen, in the exercize of her supremacy. In 1562 Convocation was instructed to revise the Articles of the Church, and to submit their work to the deliberation of Parliament. They obeyed, and when their work was completed they "humbly offered their suppliant little book containing their petitions to Parliament," which had no authority till it was approved by Queen and Parliament In 1539 the Act 31 Henry VIII. c. 14 imposed upon the Church the "Six Articles," containing certain doctrinal propositions "for abolishing diversity of opinion concerning Christian Religion." **(4)** A truly National Church was possible only when there was real uniformity in religious matters The Church has ceased to represent English life and learning. **(5)** The Church is so far under the power of the State, that the State, not the Church, appoints her chief officers, *i.e.* the Bishops and Archbishops, who are not even selected by the Crown, but by the Prime Minister. Similarly, the Lord Chancellor has a large number of livings in his gift. Now the Prime Minister may be of any religious persuasion—he may even be an atheist—and the Lord Chancellor anything but a Roman Catholic. Further, Parliament creates Bishoprics, and has created several in the last 40 years, and without her consent no See can be made. It is curious that the Church herself was apparently unconscious of any Apostolic Descent for 300 years, if she has it. **(6)** No one supposes that all Churches can be made equal by Parliament; but Parliament ought not to add artificial inequalities to those which are necessary. Religious Equality does not mean equality of sects, but equal treatment of all sects. **(7)** The Church, from the strife between her various parties, and by the consciousness of the anomalous nature of her position (which involves, as Dean Stanley showed, the acceptance by her Clergy of contradictory propositions), is unable to be very strict in her insistence on the rigid adherence of her Clergy to the literal interpretation of her formularies. Nevertheless, ever since she was founded, she has persecuted, as far as she has been able; and the Acts of Uniformity, etc., the cruelties of Laud, Sheldon, and others, alike testify to the spirit which has animated her. Dissenters object to a religious census on the ground that it forms an unjust and absolutely incorrect method of arriving at the convictions of the majority, since all those who are too indifferent to go to chapel, even atheists, are entered as Church members, and any census based on the congregations are absurd, as, when it was known that a census was to be taken, all those who had not been to church for years would be pressed to go for the purpose of the census. **(8)** Church Reform bears a different meaning in the mouth of each party in the Church, and there is no point on which they can agree. **(9)** The Parish Clergy, especially in country districts, frequently neglect their poorer parishioners altogether. **(10)** Even though the services of the Church are gratuitous, many poor, especially in rural districts, are Dissenters, and prefer to pay, that they may worship God in their own way. The Clergyman is usually far too closely identified, in the popular imagination, with the landowning class to have any real influence over the workers. **(11)** The charities of the Church, largely bound up as they are with church attendance, etc., and to which they are made to serve as baits, are the cause of widespread pauperization and demoralization. Charity, to do good, must be distributed according to merit. **(12)** By Act of Parliament (26 Henry VIII. c. 1), Henry VIII. was made "the only Supreme Head on earth of the Church of England." The changes of Elizabeth were wrought in the teeth of the Bishops, who opposed them bitterly in the House of Lords. **(13)** So far from being at any period independent of Rome, Rome always was appealed to in such cases as a disputed appointment to a vacant see; *e.g.*, Magna Charta was signed by the Pope's representative (Master Pandulph), and so could hardly have been directed against Rome. (*See* ANGLICAN CHURCH.) (**14**) The recent Church Discipline Act makes clergy dependent on a partizan Bishop by enabling him to get rid of old or incompetent incumbents. Incompetent might easily prove a wide term. (**15**) Disestablishment has made the Church of Ireland stronger than ever, and, according to her Bishops, she was never more prosperous than now. (**16**) The Bishops are among the most bigoted and obstructive members of the House of Lords. (*See* BISHOPS.) (**17**) Dissenters know that in a religious census all indifferents and even some of the weaker brethren among themselves would be classed as in the Church of England. No census can give any criterion of the real religious convictions of the majority.

Con : (**1**) Religion is one of the chief elements in national life, and the State cannot remain indifferent as to whether her people hold religious principles or not. Every nation is bound to have a national religion, and to teach it to the people. (Some) If the State provides secular education to her people, why should she not also provide religious ? (**2**) It is the duty of the Church to bring a moral element into our political and social life. Her connection with the State secures the members of her ministry against undue pressure from the Government, since they practically hold office for life, and are not dependent for livelihood on the favour of either princes or people. (**3**) Parliament cannot alter a single word in the Creeds, or modify a single doctrine. The Prayer Book was drawn up by the Church, and not by the State; it is incorporated in the Act of Uniformity as a sign of its acceptance by the nation. The XXXIX. Articles were agreed upon by the Clergy in Convocation. They were accepted, not made, by Parliament. The State Services which used to appear in the Prayer Book were bound up with it by order of the monarch, just as Tate and Brady's Psalms were, and were removed at Queen Victoria's command. They never had the least authority beyond the respect due to the expressed wish of the Sovereign, and certainly were not inserted or removed by Parliament. (**4**) At no time in her history has the Church been more popular, or more remarkable for her intellectual life and activity, than now. (**5**) The Supremacy of the Crown is an assertion of the supreme right of the civil power to the ultimate decision in all matters concerning the internal discipline of the State, and was a protest in the beginning against the arbitrary claim of the Bishops of Rome to interfere in the concerns of the kingdom. The Sovereign does not make Bishops, but merely allocates them to particular posts, and in this acts as hereditary representative of the nation, the choice being limited to ordained priests of over 30 years of age. The Prime Minister's share being merely advisory, it follows that the Sovereign is by no means bound to take his advice. Parliament only sanctions the erection of a see, but it is by the act of consecration as conveyed through a consecrated Bishop that Bishops are "made." (**6**) Religious Equality would forbid the State to recognize the barest Theism under penalty of insulting the atheists; if these people were ignored, the next question would be where to draw the line. (**7**) The Church has long been noted for allowing her Clergy to teach what they think right so long as they adhere to the main doctrines of Christianity and to the practices laid down in the Prayer Book. Thus it is much rarer in the Church than among Dissenting communities that a man is tried for heresy. (**8**) It is only to be expected that some scandals should occur, but they are very rare, and could be easily avoided by giving the Bishops power to remove unfit Clergymen from their posts. (Some) Were a greater voice in the management of the Church given to the laity, and the Clergy forbidden to alter the services without consulting their parishioners, much strife would be avoided. (**9**) There would be no one in the parish, such as there is now, whom the poor would have a right to call upon to perform services and to minister in the Church; no one to visit the sick, to bring the Gospel to the ignorant and careless, and to pray with the dying. **(10)** By Disestablishment, the very poor would be cut off from their only means of spiritual life. Whereas now the Church is open to all parishioners, this would be no longer the case, since both Church and Minister would be open (save as a favour) only to those who could afford to subscribe. **(11)** The charities of the Church are, especially in the only country districts, the great resource of the poor against want and starvation. **(12)** Many Acts and Charters recognize the Church, but none creates it. The common phrase "as by law established" does not mean first established, that is, planted or created, but recognized by the nation. **(13)** The Church of Rome never was established in England; the National Church was always called the Church of England. As an example of her independence, when King John endeavoured to bring her under Papal Dominion, the Barons, with the Archbishop of Canterbury at their head, resisted, and compelled him to sign Magna Charta. **(14)** Disestablishment would rob the Clergyman of his independence, and reduce him to a position of much greater dependence on the wishes of his congregation, especially the richer members. Thus they would no longer be able to denounce injustice, but would have to "cut their coat according to their cloth." **(15)** Disestablishment has been a failure in Ireland, and so far from having brought people any nearer to religious reunion, as was anticipated, has divided them more than ever. **(16)** The Bishops are among the few members of the House of Lords who sit by merit and not by birth. (*See* BISHOPS.) **(17)** If the Dissenters are the more numerous body, as they claim, why did they refuse a religious census? **(18)** As the Church of England grows weaker, so will the Church of Rome grow stronger; and if the Protestant succession to the throne were abolished, the Crown might again become Catholic, and England thus lose the liberty which the Reformation conferred on her. **(19)** (Some) If Disestablishment were effected, large bodies of wavering Anglicans would join the Church of Rome, and others drift into Free-thought, and ultimately Atheism.

DISESTABLISHMENT OF THE CHURCH OF SCOTLAND.

Pro: **(1)** The Church does not include the majority of the people, but is only one of three rival organizations of nearly equal strength. **(2)** The Establishment forms the great barrier to the reunion of the three. **(3)** The State Church is unable to cope with the religious needs of Scotland, and in the number neither of her churches nor of her adherents can she pretend to serve any more than a fraction of the population. In the Highlands nearly all the very poor belong to the Free Church. **(4)** The State Church holds funds given to a United Church. **(5)** The Church was also endowed to care for the poor and promote education, both of which are now managed by the nation. **(6)** The progress of the Free Church shows that Disendowment would be a gain rather than a loss to the Church, by the enthusiasm which it would call forth in her members.

Con: **(1)** The Church of Scotland has made enormous progress, and is far larger than any of the Churches in Scotland. **(2)** Reunion would not be helped by inflicting injustice on the Church. **(3)** No one Church approaches the Established Church in the number of her churches or communicants. **(4)** By seceding, the Dissenters lost all claim to the Church funds. **(5)** The sum which would be realized by Disendowment would afford small help to the rates. **(6)** Disestablishment would leave the country parishes in many cases without a resident minister. **(7)** By taking away the national recognition of religion, the State would cease to be Christian in any official sense. **(8)** Disestablishment has proved most unpopular in Scotland. **(9)** The richer classes would more than ever become Episcopalian, and a chasm would be created between the rich and the poor.

DISESTABLISHMENT OF THE CHURCH IN WALES.

Pro: (1) The Welsh Church, so called, is an alien Church, out of sympathy with the great mass of people. Frequently her Clergy even now do not speak Welsh, and are entirely out of touch with the national sentiment. (2) The Welsh are almost unanimous for Disestablishment, and nearly all Welsh M.P.'s are pledged to support it; in spite of the recent political reaction, only one or two seats changed. (3) There is ample precedent for dealing with Wales separately; she has already been separately legislated for in educational and temperance matters; and, holding passionately to their race traditions, as the Welsh do, it would be absurd on our part to ignore their nationality. (4) There is every reason for drawing a distinction between the Welsh and the English Churches; whereas the English is popular, and there is no desire to see her disestablished, the positions are exactly reversed as regards the Welsh Church. (5) The Welsh Church is pre-eminently the Church of the upper classes, not of the poor. (6) Even now, the manner in which the Established Clergy perform their duties is very bad and perfunctory. (7) The Church in Wales is not advancing faster than the Nonconformists; the progress of the Church is much more than equalled by that of Dissent. (8) Disestablishment and Disendowment would not only induce the laity to give more generously than they do to an Established Church, but, by removing a cause of bitterness, would render the task of the Church in attempting to retrieve her lost position among the people easier. (9) If Disestablishment would deprive many parishes of a resident minister, it shows how slight a hold the Church has on the people; as a matter of fact, the Nonconformist chapels, as Archbishop Tait says, are to be seen "in every village and on every hill-side"; and wherever there is a Nonconformist chapel, there also are to be found religious agencies of all kinds at work, whether there be a minister resident or not.

Con: (1) The Church of Wales is the true representative of the Ancient British Church, and is amongst the oldest representatives of Christianity in Great Britain. At the present time her Clergy, with few exceptions, know Welsh, and are regaining their position. (2) The great hatred of the Welsh people to the National Church is largely an affair of the past, though sedulously maintained by the Nonconformist Clergy, who dread the loss of influence. The parliamentary voting at the last election showed a diminution in the strength of the party in favour of Disestablishment. (3) Wales is not a separate nation, nor ought the idea to be encouraged by the passing of special legislation in her favour. (4) There is no reason for treating the Welsh dioceses differently from the rest of the English Church. Disestablishment should be a national, not a local, concern; if not, why not allow each parish to decide for itself? (5) The Welsh Church, like the English, is the Church of the very poor, and to disendow her would be to rob them. (6) Even if in the past the Clergy failed to perform their duties worthily, this has almost entirely ceased to be the case. (7) As the Church increases in the number and the devotion of her people daily, Nonconformity recedes, and it will not be long before the former becomes the Church of the majority. (8) Disendowment would cripple the Church in poor districts, where pew rents cannot be charged. It is no justification for doing an injustice to the Church to say that it will stir up wealthy members, who have already been heavily drawn on for Church building, etc., and could hardly contribute more in the present depressed state of industry. Disestablishment in Ireland has utterly failed to soften religious differences—in the present case it would only have the effect of leaving the Church people disaffected. (9) Disendowment would rob many parishes of a resident minister, and thus the people would lose their only source of spiritual comfort at all important moments of their lives. For this would be substituted the occasional visits of a peripatetic Nonconformist minister or a missionary priest, neither of them at all equal to the services of a resident, who knows the history of all of them.

DISTRESS FOR RENT, ABOLITION OF LAW OF.

Pro: (1) The law, by giving the landlord a priority of claim over other creditors, infringes the principle of freedom of contract. (2) The landlord loses neither interest (rent) nor principal. (3) The law of Distress impairs a tenant's credit. (4) It makes the landlord careless as to the character of his tenant, and deters the latter from improving the property. (5) If it were abolished, no landlord would allow arrears of rent to accrue (a great benefit).

Con: (1) Abolition of the law of Distress would still further reduce the value of land, and thereby check the investment of capital, and it would be necessary to allow immediate right of re-entry to prevent the landlord from being placed in a less favourable position than ordinary creditors. (2) A landlord only *lends* his property, and there is no question of his losing his principal. If he had no priority, he would have either to demand his rents in advance, or to raise them, in order to cover the additional risk. Other creditors can stop their credit at any moment, or insist on cash; the landlord is bound by contract. In case of bankruptcy, a landlord may not only lose his rent, but find his property depreciated in addition. (3) Loss of credit is set off by the credit the tenant obtains from the landlord. (4) Landlords would have to demand security, and would not accept men without capital as tenants—yet these often prove the best tenants. (5) The allowance of arrears of rent is often of great value to a tenant, especially in bad times.

DIVORCE.

Pro: (1) Though marriage was held to be indissoluble, yet in practice this has never held good, and some device has always been found to circumvent the difficulty, e.g. in the Roman Church the Pope has always had the power to dissolve marriage, provided it has not been consummated, a plea which has been visibly strained in many cases. In England, before the passing of the Divorce Act, a lengthy process had in each case to be gone through; thus, though Divorce was possible to the rich, the poor had to live together though one was unworthy, to live apart, or to live in sin with another. (Some) Marriage is a purely civil contract, and should be so treated in law and in practice. (2) It has always been held that adultery on the part of the woman dissolves marriage. To make adultery a crime is impossible in the present state of public opinion. (3) Divorce for adultery was allowed by Christ; there is no difference between the Greek word ἀπολύω (I put away) and Divorce. This doctrine was taught by a great many of the Fathers; and the Council at Arles has been reported in two diametrically opposite senses. (4) The denial of Divorce has never acted as a deterrent to adultery, and were the law very tyrannical on this point, public opinion would become most lax in regard to breaches of it. (5) The publicity and shame of the Divorce Court must always act as a very powerful deterrent. (6) (Some) Any evil effects which reports of Divorce cases might have on the public mind might be met by hearing such cases *in camerâ*. (*See* IN CAMERÂ.) (7) The home would be broken up far more by the knowledge on the part of the children as to the conduct and estrangement of their parents than by any proceedings in the Divorce Court. (8) Divorce has not produced the evil results in England that were predicted, although it has been introduced for many years. (9) Since the Clergy are public officers, and by the Articles the Queen is declared to be the supreme authority in Church and State, they are not entitled to say on what terms people shall be married in Church.

Further, the church belongs to the parishioners, who are entitled to have a voice in its conduct. It is inconsistent and wrong on the part of the Clergy to drive such people to the Registrar's Office, or leave them to continue in a sinful relation.

Con: (1) In the marriage ceremony no mention is made of possible Divorce ; each party swears solemnly to the other "for better, for worse, till death do us part." Though the State and the Church may have erred, there is no reason for doing so again. (2) If adultery be held to dissolve marriage, it would lead to relative promiscuity, since either party might remarry many times. Adultery ought to be made a crime, rather than release should be given to either party. (3) Even if Christ allowed Divorce for adultery, He never allowed remarriage, which was expressly forbidden by the Church at the Council of Arles. (4) The knowledge that they are not allowed to separate and remarry will always tend to induce husbands and wives to minimize differences which they might otherwise magnify into occasions for separation. The risk of an agreement between the two, that each should allow full liberty to the other, is not one of which the law can take account, but against which public opinion may be expected to express itself very strongly. (5) The publicity of Divorce Court proceedings is very deleterious to the morals of the people at large. (6) The trial of cases *in camerâ* would not prevent the publication of accounts of the trial, fictitious or otherwise, in low publications, with such fulness as the editor, guided only by considerations of profit and the fear of prosecution, might care to insert. Otherwise, the fact of its being held *in camerâ* would eliminate all fear of exposure. (*See* IN CAMERÂ.) (7) Nothing can be worse for children than the actual legal separation of their parents. The ideal home cannot exist in the absence of either of the parents, both being still alive. (8) Divorce has been most disastrous in America, where each concession has only led to further concessions, as it always does. (9) The State ought not to oblige the clergy to lend their churches for sacrilegious purposes, such as remarriage of divorced persons, since the Registrar's Office is always open to those who desire to marry in defiance of the Church's laws.

DIVORCE FOR WOMEN: should the "cruelty" condition be eliminated?

Pro: (1) There is no logical reason why any difference should be made between men and women in the matter of Divorce ; and, since the sin is equal, the penalties should be the same. (2) The law of Scotland allows Divorce on equal terms, with satisfactory results. (3) The Law Courts, fully endorsed by public opinion, twist almost any unkind action of an unfaithful husband into legal "cruelty," thus neutralizing the original intention of the law. Why, then, retain a law which is so often being stultified in practice?

Con: (1) Where the physical conditions are so different, equity demands a differential treatment of each sex. Penalties should be preventive, not retributive. If a man break his marriage vows, the consequences are far less harmful or wide-reaching ; he is not the child-bearer, and his sin does not affect the status of the home, whilst the wife's destroys it. (2) Scotland stands almost alone in her law as to this point. (3) A stricter view of Divorce will have to prevail in the near future, unless society is to become utterly immoral.

DOCKS (LONDON), MUNICIPALIZATION OF.

Pro: (1) The Docks would be better managed if under public control, and worked for the public good, than is the case at present, worked as they are for private profit. (2) Such policy has succeeded at Liverpool and Glasgow, where the circumstances are similar to those of London. (3) Public Trusts have proved themselves quite as ready to provide for the growth of commerce as private enterprize, which has generally thought more about its profits than the public convenience. (**4**) The purchase of the Docks would ultimately be remunerative monetarily, and, in the meantime, by the convenience it would afford. (**5**) No monopoly should be under private control. (**6**) The authorities could improve the status of the Dock Labourer, and would, while abolishing casual labour, substitute a permanent staff.

Con : (**1**) Private enterprize has already secured very good management, which is always better if in the hands of those who are directly interested in the success of the undertaking. (**2**) The fact that Municipalization has been successful in Glasgow and Liverpool is not a sufficient argument for London, since the circumstances are different. (**3**) Private enterprize has always shown itself quite as ready as municipal authorities to provide accommodation for the public, notably at Tilbury, where, in anticipation of a public demand, the Docks were constructed some years before they were wanted. (**4**) Private Docks do not, and have not for some time past, paid much (if any) interest to their shareholders, nor is it likely that they will pay any better under public management. The purchase money would be extremely heavy, and would raise rates. (**5**) A monopoly in private hands, if strictly regulated, is always likely to manage its affairs with public spirit, since it is at any time liable to lose its property. (**6**) Public control would always render public bodies open to the suspicion of undue influences, *e.g.* the Dock Labour vote.

DRAMA, THE: should it discuss social questions?

Pro : (**1**) The dramatist's field covers the whole life of man ; and social questions, arising as they do from a conflict between the individual and his surroundings, afford excellent material for the drama. Some of the greatest playwrights (*e.g.* Shakspere, Goethe) have freely touched on social questions. (**2**) If discussion proves the relativity of morality, let us by all means admit that morals are only relative. (**3**) Representation helps to enlighten its subject-matter. (**4**) The drama should be an important educative means, and the investigation of social problems is a far higher pursuit than is mere amusement.

Con : (**1**) The discussion of social questions on the stage before mixed audiences of all ages, sexes, and degrees of culture is bad for (*a*) public morals and (*b*) public education, since it leads either to (*a*) the open discussion and dissection of subjects which are much better treated by serious students in private, or (*b*) the omission or partial neglect of those aspects of social questions which alone give them importance, thus destroying the artistic and hence educative value of the representations. (**2**) It impairs the idea of the absoluteness of morality. (**3**) It leads to a mere superficial knowledge of many things characteristic of an age of hurry, but valueless. (**4**) The drama ought to be bright, healthy, and amusing.

DRINK, FREE TRADE IN.

Pro : (**1**) The limited competition now prevailing has greatly improved the state of our public-houses. Under absolutely Free Trade, brewers and others would be induced to spend still greater sums, and thus further improve the condition of the houses. (**2**) The licensing system has created a monopoly. (**3**) It gives the police a ready opportunity of levying blackmail on offending publicans.

Con : (**1**) Free Trade in Drink has already been tried, and its abuse led to the present laws. (**2**) Licences for trades which are by their nature peculiarly liable to abuse are very necessary. (**3**) Blackmailing policemen can readily be detected and punished by a proper system of supervision.

DUELLING.

Pro : (**1**) Many offences which the law cannot touch are yet offences against the stability of society, and it is desirable that they should not go unpunished. They are well dealt with by Duel. (2) Duelling, by making men more careful in speech, tends to put down slander and scandal. (3) It discourages the foolish idea of the value of human life as such, and shows that life is valuable only in so far as it is honourably lived. (4) Right is might by duelling, as elsewhere, and the consciousness of being in the right is always itself an element of strength.

Con : (1) It is not desirable that an individual should take into his own hands to punish what the law does not recognize as an offence. (2) Duelling creates a class of men who are always glad of an excuse for a quarrel. (3) It depreciates the idea of the essential value of human life. (4) It gives the advantage to the most practised, often for that very reason the guilty, man.

EDUCATION, MIXED.

Pro : (1) The mixing of the sexes in education being an economy, was formerly widely practised in Scotland, and is still in vogue at the Universities and University Colleges. (2) The feminine mind gains in strength when put through the curriculum given to boys and men. (3) Competition is greater between the sexes than between rivals of the same sex, and a higher standard of achievement is obtained. (4) Constant intercourse between the sexes leads to a more perfect development of character, and diminishes shyness. (5) Marriages so made are of the safest kind, inasmuch as both parties have an intimate and not a merely social knowledge of each other. (6) The presence of the opposite sex is often a wholesome restraint in a well-ordered institution. The heads of institutions in which women and girls reside are aware that one of the dangers of a conventual existence is the tendency that a woman may have to a hysterical passion for some member of her own sex. This does not occur in a morbid form under freer conditions. (7) The presence of women in colleges and universities raises the tone of those institutions.

Con : (1) In some subjects teachers find the joint presence of both sexes embarrassing. (2) (Some) It is undesirable to give strength to the feminine mind, inasmuch as domestic and social duties can be equally well, if not better, performed without it. Moreover, it would be possible (though it is not frequently done) to give women the same curriculum as men without educating them side by side in the same institute. (3) Competition is objectionable in any form, and should be discountenanced. (4) In institutions where the discipline is bad and the tone is low, both sexes are apt to lose in freshness and modesty, and very serious evils may ensue. (5) Attachments regulated by parents are more likely to be suitable from a worldly point of view than those formed under chance conditions. (6) It is undesirable that at a time when the whole energy of students should be given to mental development, they should be distracted by the presence of members of the opposite sex. (7) The presence of women in colleges and universities, whilst possibly raising their tone in some directions, tends to frivolity.

EDUCATION, MORAL.

Pro : (1) The moral instruction now given in elementary schools is made a part of religious instruction, with the Bible as a text-book ; hence (a) morality is based upon supernatural sanctions not understood by the child, and connected with tenets, such as the Incarnation, Atonement, Regeneration, which are unsuited to the capacities of children ; (b) morality is made to take a secondary place ; (c) portions of Biblical history suggest a morality unfit for children. (2) A distinct injury to the moral sense is produced by teaching stories of miracles as if they were reports of actual events ; while, in secular instruction, children are taught that the world is governed by laws which are not subject to miraculous interference. (3) Morality is the highest concern of life, and should be based on the needs of human nature, and not on supernatural injunction. Children should be led to see how the relations of the family and the community demand moral conduct, without the necessity for appealing to lower motives, such as fear of hell, or hope of heaven. (4) Since morality is a human, more than it is a Christian, Jewish, Mohammedan, or Buddhist subject, it should be illustrated from the histories and literatures of many nations, not exclusively from the Bible. (5) Morality being the subject of highest importance, its teaching should be founded on a definite science of conduct. (*See* ETHICS.) (6) Ethics should form an essential part of the training of teachers.

Con: (1) (*a*) Morality based on religious sanctions is more easily impressed on children than morality without such sanctions. (*b*) Right living depends largely on right thinking, and no attempt should be made to separate them. (*c*) The portions of Biblical history unfitted for the study of children should be omitted. When older, they will understand that the teaching of morality has been progressive, and that their rule of life is to be that of the Gospel. (2) Theists claim, not less than others, that the universe is governed by laws "not subject to miraculous interference," *i.e.* that the sequence of cause and effect is constant. But they hold that this is perfectly consistent with the existence of a Personal God, acting freely in the world, according to His laws. And Christians believe that the miracles of the Gospels were actual events, the outward sign of an adequate cause, working in full accordance with law. To omit teaching the miracles would be to teach part of the truth only. (3) A morality based only on the needs of human nature becomes more mechanical as it becomes more perfect, until at last it has no value to the conscience. Morality, as the outcome of the love of God, at once becomes the highest concern of life, and should be impressed on the child by every available argument. That it is the Divine command stands first. The Christian cannot admit that it appeals to a "lower motive." That it is his duty to his neighbour comes next; and the hope of Heaven and fear of retribution, though they may rank among "lower motives" as being of a personal nature, are powerful in their operation, and were frequently appealed to by the Founder of Christianity. (4) Morality may well be illustrated by examples taken from secular history. (5-6) A systematic study of Ethics would probably be useful, if over-worked teachers could find time for it, and did not allow it to obscure the fact that morality rests primarily on the Divine Command.

EDUCATION, RELIGIOUS: must it be dogmatic?

Pro: (1) The Christian Religion includes certain necessary truths, *e.g.* the doctrines of the Incarnation and the Atonement; unless it include this *minima* of belief, it becomes meaningless, and sinks into a colourless sentimentalism, tending to ultimate scepticism. (2) While the vast majority of her subjects, though differing on minor matters of discipline, hold all essential beliefs in common, the State cannot take on herself the responsibility of ignoring the nature of the religious teaching supplied by her schools. (3) Parents have a right to know exactly the nature of the religious teaching given to their children, so that they may be certain that doctrines of which they disapprove are not being instilled. (4) It is necessary for the teacher to himself be a believer to impart sound knowledge of the doctrines he inculcates. Teachers who "change their opinions" on such essential matters lose authority with the young. (5) The "Conscience Clause" enables parents to withdraw their children from all religious instruction, if desired. (6) The State provides secular education; why not also religious education?

Con: (1) Christ recognized no such hard and fast dogmas as are said to be an essential part of Christianity. The permanent element in Christianity is its morality, which it is quite possible to impart to children without forcing on them doctrines which, even if not erroneous, are not intelligible to them. (2) As comprizing subjects belonging to all religious denominations, it is unfair on the part of the State to expend national moneys on any particular religious section. (3) Under undogmatic religious teaching, parents can be just as certain as to the nature of instruction provided as under any other system. If more definite teaching be desired, the school instruction can always be supplemented outside the school. It can never be so great a hardship that children should be taught too little, as that they should be taught too much. (4) Under dogmatic education, a teacher who is not a member of the Anglican Church, or even a believer, would have either to teach what he himself does not, wholly or in part, believe, or else to resign his post. This would be specially hard on teachers whose religious opinions underwent change as their knowledge and experience increased. (5) The so-called definite teaching forces parents who disapprove of only part of it to withdraw their children from all religious instruction whatsoever, and place them in the same category as infidels and secularists. (6) Practical agreement as to the ends of secular education has been arrived at ; but there is no possibility of unanimity in regard to religious instruction, which should therefore not be provided by the State.

EDUCATION, STATE.

Pro : (1) Ignorance constitutes a national danger which it is the duty of the State to guard against. (2) The assumption by the State of the responsibilities of Elementary Education became necessary, because Voluntary Systems failed to provide an adequate number of schools. (3) Education develops the dormant talents of the nation. In order that England may maintain her position in the world, it is absolutely necessary that all her citizens should be educated.

Con : (1) Elementary State Education destroys local and parental responsibility. (2) No work is so good as voluntary work. Much that was good has been lost by the partial suppression of voluntary agencies. (3) The Voluntary System, if it had been allowed to develop on natural lines, would eventually have undertaken the education of the whole nation.

EDUCATION, STATE: COMPULSORY.

Pro : (1) State Education would be useless if non-compulsory. (2) Compulsory Education makes it impossible for parents to wholly sacrifice the interests of their children to their own selfish ends, and prevents premature work of children in factories. (3) Under Compulsory Education opportunities for future self-culture are provided, since every child is instructed in the rudiments of learning.

Con : (1) Compulsory Education encourages the idea that school is the only place where knowledge is imparted ; whereas what a child learns in the daily work of, say, a factory, is of much greater real value to him. (2) It is only right that children should earn something towards their own maintenance, and factory work does them no harm. (3) Compulsory Education teaches them enough to be able to read " penny dreadfuls " and other injurious literature, but creates no desire for higher knowledge.

EDUCATION, STATE: FREE.

Pro : (1) As Education is compulsory it ought to be free, since the State, by depriving parents of the labour of their children, entails great sacrifices on them. (2) The fees were a great burden on the resources of hardworking people, since the parents indirectly pay towards the expenses of State Education, partly through rates and taxes (to which again, either directly or indirectly, they contribute), partly through their loss of the profits accruing from the labour of their children. (3) An enormous waste of time was involved in the collection of school fees and their arrears ; owing to the involved state of the law, these, when collected, formed only a very small item towards the total cost, and were scarcely worth enforcing. (4) All parents are at liberty to avail themselves of the opportunity offered them. Moreover, the education of future generations is a matter in which all citizens are interested, and there is no hardship in calling on all to contribute towards that end.

Con : (1) Free Education reduces parental responsibility. (2) Payment of school fees made no ultimate difference to the parents, as these fees formed an element in raising wages proportionately. (3) However small the payment, and however insignificant the total collected, the fact of contribution on the part of the parent kept up the idea of the parent's responsibility. The law as to recovery of school fees and arrears might be simplified. (4) It is unjust to make those who do not send their children to school, or who have no children to send, pay for the education of others. (5) Free Education creates a difficulty with the Voluntary Schools, since either Board Schools must be started where Voluntary Schools already exist, or the taxpayers have to contribute to a school over which they have no control.

EDUCATION: VOLUNTARY SCHOOLS.

Pro: (1) The demands of the Education Department have grown so enormously within the last few years, and are rapidly becoming so serious a drain upon the resources of the Voluntary Schools, that if the demands (as they with absolute certainty will) grow in the future as they have in the past, the Voluntary Schools will be extinguished altogether, unless the Government gives them an increased grant. (2) The fact that they were setting up a dual educational system was recognized as no disadvantage by the framers of the Act of 1870, since it was seen that it would be folly to ignore bodies which had been and still were doing such excellent work as the National Society and other religious bodies. (3) It would be an unnecessary expense were the Voluntary Schools abolished, since nearly two-thirds of the elementary school buildings in the country are owned by religious corporations. The adoption of a universal system of School Boards would mean that in each of these cases sites would have to be bought and new schools built, unless, indeed, the managers chose to hand them over voluntarily (which neither their inclination nor their trust deeds would probably allow them to do), or unless the State took them, which would be confiscation. (4) Board Schools are more extravagant than Voluntary Schools, and education in the former costs about three times as much per child to the ratepayer as education in the latter costs to the subscriber. The same applies to the cost of building Board Schools, which is always much greater than is the cost of a similar accommodation in Voluntary Schools. (5) Board Schools are always open to a sudden change of policy consequent on an election, which is very bad for the discipline of the school. (6) Board School teachers are at the mercy of the electors, often ignorant parents ; and, especially in country places, have to keep them pacified. (7) The personal supervision of the clergyman and one or two working managers is apt to be more efficient than that of any Board, however well meaning, since the former is sure to be so freer from regulation, etc. (8) Voluntary Schools secure religious teaching of a definite kind to large numbers of children, whilst Board Schools put it in the background, and encroach on the time which ought to be given solely to religious teaching. (9) Parents can withdraw their children from the religious education under the "Conscience Clause," if they disapprove of the teaching. In Voluntary Schools they know the nature of the education which will be given, of which they cannot feel sure in a Board School. (10) The Church enjoys no monopoly of education anywhere. When the majority of the parishioners demand it, a Board School will be at once set up ; it is also open for a minority to establish a school of their own, provided that they can meet the demands of the Department. (11) Board Schools, having practically unlimited command of money, have been able to compete unfairly with the Voluntary Schools in respect of teachers' salaries, buildings, etc., in which many School Boards have displayed uncalled-for extravagance in order chiefly to cut out the Voluntary Schools; on the other hand, Board Schools in country districts have often shown a tendency to cut down the teachers' salaries unduly. (12) The managers of Voluntary Schools should not be compelled to allow them to be used for political and other meetings, which may be antagonistic to the best interests of the Church or society. Nor is there any reason to suppose that the members of a School Board would be any more tolerant than the parson or the squire. (13) Every year each school is examined by a Government Inspector, to whom all the audited accounts have to be submitted, every bill and voucher to be produced, and the greatest care taken to see that not one penny of the pence or the grant goes to anything except secular instruction. (14) (Some) No objection would be raised to the ratepayers being represented on the board of management, provided that they had no power to alter the denominational character of the school. (15) Voluntary Schools are as efficient as Board Schools, at least in the large towns; if the average is shown by statistics to be lower when the whole country is considered, this will be fully accounted for when it is remembered that the Voluntary Schools are almost universal in country districts, which fact naturally damages their average. (16) The Voluntary Schools provide and pay for the religious instruction given, with the attendant expenses of diocesan inspection, etc. (17) The fact that it is a matter of comparative difficulty to dismiss a teacher always tells against the discipline of the Board School, and leads to such breaches of discipline as the attempt of the teachers to intimidate the London School Board into submission to their wishes. (18) Since the religious belief or disbelief of a teacher must colour his whole teaching, it can never be a matter of indifference to parents who wish to see their children brought up with a sound grounding in the essentials of Christian belief and practice.

Con : (1) The duty of the State is to secure a thoroughly efficient system of National Education, not to allow education to be subordinated to the interests of any ecclesiastical sect or organization. (2) The perpetuation of the Denominational Schools is due to no thought-out policy on the part of the framers of the present educational system; it is the outcome of that spirit of compromize which has so often stultified our national policy, and has reduced our educational system to a battle-field between two contending theories. (3) The State has contributed very largely to the building of Denominational Schools in the past, and pays by far the greater part of the charge for maintaining them now, so that the State would be fully justified in doing what she liked in the matter of taking them over with or without the consent of the managers. As a matter of fact, the Denominational Schools are often so inadequate to meet the demands on them, that it is doubtful whether they ought not in any case to be rebuilt. The Act of 1870 overrides any provision of any trust deed which would otherwise prevent schools from being handed over to a School Board. (4) Board Schools are not more expensive to build than Voluntary. For the cost of the latter no official statistics exist, excepting the limited number which received a building grant between the years 1870 and 1882, and tables exist showing the cost of all the schools that received building grants from 1839 onward. (*Ann. Rept. of Educ. Dept.* 1894-5, p. xxv.) But these figures are no guide whatever to the present cost of these schools, because the value of the sites, often given gratuitously, is not included, and the statistics refer only to a small proportion of the existing schools, all built when the Department was content with a far lower standard of structural suitability than now; whereas the statistics of the Board Schools include (*a*) amount of loan sanctioned, which "is generally somewhat in excess of the sum eventually spent"; (*b*) cost of sites, "which in the case of the numerous Board Schools in London and in large towns is often very considerable"; (*c*) cost of laboratories, workshops laundries, cooking kitchen, School Board offices, etc. **(5)** Voluntary Schools are open to sudden fluctuations with the appointment of new managers, or a new clergyman. **(6)** The head teacher in a Church of England School must please the clergyman and his wife, as well as do justice to the scholars; and there is generally no effective committee of management to protect the teacher from unjust treatment. **(7)** The supervision of the clergy and lay managers is too often a *quantité négligeable*, if we may judge from the published complaints of diocesan inspectors, etc. **(8)** The most eminent dignitaries of the Church have confessed themselves completely satisfied with the nature of the teaching given in the Board Schools; whilst Voluntary Schools have often been accused by diocesan inspectors and others of trenching on or even ignoring the time allotted to religious instruction. **(9)** There is less need in Board Schools than in Denominational Schools for making use of the "Conscience Clause," since the religious instruction is Biblical, and not limited by the doctrines of any particular Church. **(10)** The Church enjoys a monopoly of education in rural districts. It is idle to talk of a minority of agricultural labourers (most of whom hold their cottages on very short periods) establishing Schools, as, even if they could raise the money, they must obtain the consent of some landowner, most of whom are Churchmen, to grant land. Moreover, there is not much chance of obtaining a School Board in face of the opposition of the powers that be, viz., the squire, the parson, and the farmer. **(11)** The Board Schools, as is quite right, try to obtain the best teachers, considering this to be the truest economy, since they are able to make the best of the children; and if some Boards are unduly economical in their ideas as to salary, even they must follow the market price. The Inspector will bring pressure on them to keep the school up to the mark, and they can always command the necessary funds. **(12)** Where there is a School Board the people have a room of their own in which to meet for various public purposes. Since schools are maintained by the public, there is no reason why a few gentlemen should be able to forbid the use of them for purposes of public discussion, when they are not wanted for any other purpose. **(13)** Managers are required to sign a form declaring that the salaries paid by them to the teachers are for services performed in the day school only; and yet they demand many other services as conditions of employment. The Roman Catholic bishops issued a manifesto declaring that teachers in Catholic Schools must also undertake Sunday duties. **(14)** If the public are to pay the expenses of Denominational Schools, unlimited public control is essential. **(15)** Neither in large towns nor in small places could the Voluntary Schools bear comparison with the Board Schools for efficiency. In the 24 largest towns a Parliamentary return, for the year ending Aug. 1891, shows that the Board Schools were better attended, better taught, and earned larger grants than the schools under denominational management in the same towns. In the Voluntary Schools the average grant was 18s. 0¾d., that in the Board Schools 19s. 1¼d. per head. Further evidence of the greater efficiency of Board Schools is found in the number of schools reported by the Inspector to be "excellent," as compared with the total number of schools in those towns. **(16)** At present the people are finding nearly all the money for Denominational Schools, and have but little control over the spending of it. In some places, out of an income of over £200, not more than £10 or £15 comes from voluntary subscriptions. In many Voluntary Schools there are no subscriptions, and the managers make a profit out of the grants and parents' fees, and so pay nothing for the privilege of disseminating their peculiar views. Moreover, the teachers are largely required to perform duties extraneous to day schools without additional remuneration, and their failure to perform these duties to the satisfaction of the clergyman often entails dismissal. Thus public funds are employed for parochial purposes, and the money paid for education sometimes used to provide organists and Sunday-school teachers,

(17) Under a Board School, discussion must always precede the dismissal of a teacher, which practically secures a teacher against arbitrary dismissal, such as he is liable to under a Voluntary School Committee, when the clergyman often has the sole management; thus a Board attracts a better class of man. (18) A School Board is not likely to insist on other qualifications besides efficiency in teaching (*e.g.* religious orthodoxy); and more likely to recognize that a policy of tests is likely to lead to hypocrisy. (19) Religious hatred is softened by bringing children of different denominations under one common religious teaching.

EGYPT, EVACUATION OF.

Pro : (1) England's word was openly and spontaneously pledged to the European powers at the commencement of operations by the British forces, and the pledge has been repeatedly renewed by successive Governments. It cannot be denied that order has been re-established; and England must redeem her pledge, at whatever cost. (2) The continued occupation is a barrier to good relations with Turkey, the suzerain power, whose friendship ought to be most valuable to us, and with France, the most deeply interested of European powers in the political status of Egypt, whose hostility is provoked by a flagrant breach of faith. (3) The occupation confers no direct advantages on England. On the contrary, the British troops stationed in Egypt diminish *pro tanto* the effective fighting strength of the home army. At the beginning of a war, the British fleet would, in all probability, evacuate the Mediterranean, when our regiments would have to be either considerably reinforced or withdrawn. Their exposed and isolated position would invite an attack on the country, which might otherwise be spared the horrors of war. (4) Native public opinion both in the upper educated circles, including the Khedive and Egyptian officials, and among the lower classes, is strongly opposed to the British occupation.

Con : (1) It is admitted that order has been established in Egypt. The spirit of the pledge was that the British troops should be withdrawn so soon as the ordinary state of things called into life under the control of our forces has acquired stability independently of their presence. That is far from being the case. What at present safeguards the good administration of the country is the presence of British officials. These elements of stability would disappear altogether on the withdrawal of our troops; while the machinery of government would fall to pieces, and the country relapse into the state of anarchy which used to be its normal condition. It is England's duty to uphold the good government which is her creation, until it can be trusted to stand alone. (2) This view of the pledge given by England is shared by the majority of the European powers. Their attitude in Egypt is based on the recognition of the correctness of England's attitude. (*a*) The hostility of the Sultan of Turkey arises from his complete misconception as to the reality of his suzerain powers. Egypt is agreed with all civilized Europe that the Turk shall never again rule in Egypt. This attitude of the Porte need not be a permanent source of estrangement, as may be seen from the French occupation of Tunis, which was a Turkish province, and over which the Sultan claimed, and even now claims, similar rights to those which he claims over Egypt; a fact, nevertheless, which does not prevent him from regarding France as his ally, when it suits his purpose. (*b*) It is assumed by some that Egypt is the chief cause of France's hostility to England. This may be allowed so far that having invited England to co-operate in pacifying Egypt, France was foolish enough to withdraw, leaving England master of the field, which, being a disadvantage of her own creation, is naturally a sore subject, leading her to see in it another instance of "Albion's perfidy." The real cause, however, is the natural antagonism of the two countries, the outcome of a procession of causes traceable back through centuries. Wherever, owing to diversity of national and traditional aims the great interests of two States clash, friction, and, in the end, war ensue; but the hatred is the effect and not the cause of the clashing of interests. Egypt merely offers France a convenient means of showing her ill-will. France might, perhaps, be conciliated for a time by England's withdrawal; for she wants to hold Egypt herself. As a rule of conduct for nations, however, a system of concessions must fail in its object, for the reason that long before the hunger for concessions is appeased nothing will be left to concede. Our evacuation of Egypt would not make France less aggressive in Siam, on the Niger, or in Newfoundland. The sincerity of France's wish for our departure is further much discounted by the fact that an enormous proportion of Egyptian bonds are held by Frenchmen, the payment of dividends on which the British occupation alone guarantees; and so far is this recognized in France, that whenever there is talk of our evacuation, a quasi-panic on the Paris Bourse occurs. (3) It is not England's policy to seek exclusive advantages for herself in foreign lands. The doors of her Empire are open to every stranger that comes in peace; if the expansion of her influence implies sacrifice, that cannot be a reason for shrinking from duties felt to be real. British predominance in Egypt confers, not on England alone, but on the whole civilized world, the inestimable advantage of securing a firm government at one of the most important points in the highways of international commerce. As for the position of our garrison in Egypt, strategy shows that so long as we command the seas, nobody can attack Egypt; should our command of the sea be lost to a hostile power, the Empire could not be saved by the additional resources of a few battalions. (4) Native opinion in Egypt is not hostile to British occupation as such. The difficulty lies in its indeterminate character; no real confidence can be given to an authority which never ceases to proclaim its intention of departing to-morrow. Once clearly understood that England means to stay to see good government firmly rooted, and little more will be heard of native opposition; for, like most Orientals, the Egyptian, unable to provide good government for himself, but appreciating its value, willingly accepts a stronger authority whose rule secures peace and works justice. The late Khedive was a staunch supporter of his English protectors. Discontented Pashas and quasi-educated natives, whose intellectual pabulum is the literature of the local French press (admittedly the most contemptible in the world), do not express the feelings of the people, even though they shout loudest.

EIGHT HOURS' DAY, A LEGAL.

Pro: (1) The long hours worked by the working-classes to-day are bad for the race—physically, intellectually, and morally—leaving them little or no leisure for self-culture, recreation, or political education, and, while sapping their vitality, robs them of all inclination for other than the baser pleasures. (2) Modern factory labour is so monotonous, that it cannot be prolonged beyond a certain point without injury to the worker and diminution in the value of his work. (3) The nominally short hours in some industries are counterbalanced by the fact that "over-time" is habitually worked, as in the dockyards. Moreover, habitual "over-time" inevitably tends to reduce the scale of wages, and ultimately to raise the hours. (4) Trade Union effort can mean only a strike; and then can benefit only a few of the better trades. Moreover, a voluntary agreement can rarely be enforced, and if broken by one, must be broken by all the parties concerned. (5) While individual employers have introduced, and will from time to time introduce, the Eight Hours' Day, most employers are too much ruled by the force of routine to venture on a change, even when shown to be advantageous. (6) The law would protect the majority of workers from the selfishness of the minority. (7) Wise legislation increases the independence of the working-classes, *teste* the result of Factory legislation. (8) There is no Freedom of Contract between an employer and one of his "hands"; the former has a large market to select from, and can afford to bide his time; the latter is unable to pick and choose on what terms he shall work. **(9)** The conditions under which adult labour works have often been interfered with by Acts of Parliament, which are admitted to have acted beneficially, *e.g.* the Factory Acts, Truck Acts, Mines Regulation Acts, etc. **(10)** Trustworthy statistics from employers who have had enormous experience of the relative capacities of the working-classes in all parts of the world, prove that all improvements in their condition, whether by way of better food or greater leisure, have increased their efficiency to an extent more than commensurate with the increased cost. **(11)** Diminution in hours might tell against small industrial concerns; but this would be an advantage, as large establishments can work under much better sanitary and economic conditions. **(12)** An international agreement is not necessary, as nations do not benefit in any way by the longer hours; *e.g.* the hours worked in England and the United States are short compared with those in Russia, yet the latter do not cut out the former. **(13)** (Some) An international agreement is possible and desirable. **(14)** Capital (*e.g.* plant, etc.) cannot be transferred from one country to another; nor can capital be rapidly realized. (Some) England suffers from being over-capitalized; and our great insurance companies and banks find it hard to invest their money. **(15)** Since any legislation on hours would be piecemeal, trade would have time to accommodate itself, and no panics would occur. **(16)** An Eight Hours' Day, by raising the standard of comfort, would, according to economics, tend to keep population within reasonable bounds (Some) By decreasing production, the Eight Hours' Day would afford occupation to the large body of Unemployed, and thus tend to raise wages all round. **(17)** The Eight Hours' Day ought to apply to all Government employés, and all in the employment of railways and other national monopoly undertakings. It is, in the interests of the public, urgently imperative in the case of signal-men and others holding similar positions. **(18)** (Some) Mining (*a*) being a dangerous and hard occupation, calls for special legislation to ensure the worker the needful rest. (*b*) Most coal miners work more than eight hours a day, more especially the boys. (*c*) The Eight Hours' Day was acquired by the Northumberland and Durham miners as the result of an arrangement of the shifts, by which men work only seven and a half hours on an average, whilst boys work much longer. Their opposition to a legal Eight Hours' Day is based on selfish motives, and with a callous disregard of overwork of boys. The vast majority of miners, however, are in favour of a legal restriction of the hours. (*d*) An Eight Hours' Day would be more easily introduced experimentally into the mining industry than into any other. **(19)** "Trade Option," so called, whereby each trade would be allowed to settle its own hours of work, would not be open to the same objections as a universal scheme. **(20)** "Local Trade Option," so called, whereby each trade in each locality would be allowed to settle its own hours without interference, would obviate all difficulties. **(21)** (Some) An Eight Hours' Day might be temporarily introduced on a small scale as an experiment.

Con: **(1)** He who works hardest, almost regardless of the stratum of society to which he belongs, is the man who finds most time for self-improvement. Culture must emanate from a desire on the part of the individual to improve himself and his surroundings. Further spare time for most working men would mean merely more opportunity for drinking, etc. **(2)** The monotony of work is no greater now than formerly, and is inevitable in certain trades, which consequently offer higher wages. **(3)** Why should not a man work "over-time," and so obtain extra comforts for his family? **(4)** Hours of labour and similar matters are better left to private arrangement between employers and employed, as each party knows his own interests better than any Government Department can. Trade Unionism has proved quite sufficiently strong to secure an Eight Hours' Day where it has been needed. No extra legislation is necessary to protect employers and employés against unscrupulous rivals, since it is their duty to see that their opponents are bound by a written agreement to observe any compact entered into, and to prosecute them for fraud in case of non-observance. (5) Employers know their own business best, and may be left to choose their own lines of policy. (6) To coerce the minority in the interests of the majority is to infringe those principles of freedom which have allowed the individual to become the arbiter of his own destiny. (7) Over-legislation tends to sap the independence of the individual, and to make him look to Acts of Parliament, rather than rely on his own efforts, for his social well-being. (8) The employer, though nominally free to make his own bargains, is actually as little free with regard either to time or price as his own "hands," owing to the effects of competition and the necessity to obtain orders. A good workman can always make reasonable terms with an employer. (9) The Truck Acts, etc., were framed mainly with the idea of preventing fraud or removing inducements to crime. (10) The fact that previous reductions in hours have not been accompanied by lessened or inferior output, does not justify the conclusion that further reductions will turn out the same way; so the argument might be forced to a *reductio ad absurdum*, by urging that the largest production would ensue when men ceased to work altogether. (11) To crush small employers by an Act of Parliament would be a gross act of injustice. (12) International competition is already rendering the position of our leading industries very precarious, owing to the advantages conferred on our rivals by lower wages and longer hours. (13) An international agreement on such a question is wholly out of the range of practical politics. (14) Were our capitalists induced to gradually invest their surplus moneys abroad, British industries would necessarily suffer. (15) The growing feeling of distrust engendered by the tendency to encroach on the rights of capital, would cause a want of confidence which would have disastrous results. (16) Under the present conditions, any improvement in the state of the working-classes would be attended by a rise in the relative numbers of the population, thus making all improvement merely temporary. Especially would this be the case were the present Unemployed to be called into employment. If an Eight Hours' Day has the effect of decreasing production, it must either lower wages or increase costs of production, and hence prices, thus stultifying itself by a greatly decreased consumption. (17) There is no reason why Government or railway employés should be benefited at the expense of the rest of the community, since such benefits must be paid for out of taxation or out of the pockets of the travelling public. (18) Coal mining (a) is no more dangerous or unpleasant than many other industries (*e.g.* the chemical). (b) An Eight Hours' Day already practically exists in the mining world. (c) Less than an Eight Hours' Day has already been gained by the Northern miners, through negotiation with the owners; and they not unnaturally object to any unnecessary legislation in the matter. The boys are not overworked. (d) Coal mining suffers from foreign competition almost as much as any other great industry; and anything that increased the cost of production would have serious effects. (19) Under a scheme of "Trade Option" it would be impossible to say what constitutes a trade, or who are its members; moreover, many men belong to more than one trade. This scheme would place most arbitrary power in the hands of the Trade Union officials. (20) "Local Trade Option" would be open to even more serious objections, since it would expose employers not only to foreign competition, but also to that of employers of other districts. (21) Experiments by way of an Eight Hours' Day would either be very expensive, or be carried out on too small a scale to be a criterion of universal adoption.

ELECTIONS, SIMULTANEOUS.

Pro: (1) By leaving the fixture of the polling day to the Returning Officer, often a partizan, the law makes it possible for him to select a day advantageous to one political party; large classes may thus be disfranchised (*e.g.* costermongers, who cannot leave their barrows on Saturday). (2) Under Simultaneous Elections, the likelihood of an election falling on a market-day would not be great, and even then would not involve any great disturbance of trade. Moreover, elections occur rarely. (3) By diminishing the period of uncertainty between two Parliaments, simultaneity of elections would benefit trade enormously. (4) Under Simultaneous Elections, the great influence which the earlier elections have over the later would be avoided; and electors would not be tempted, as now, to vote with the winning side. (5) They would, to a large extent, abolish plural voting. (6) Elections are now so quietly carried out, that there is no need for extra police. (7) It would be easy enough to get Returning Officers, etc., from the district. At present a few firms of solicitors have the whole business in their hands for three or four constituencies, and naturally arrange the election to suit themselves.

Con: (1) The poll-day is fixed, as a rule, only after consultation with both candidations or their representatives, and not with regard to party considerations. (2) If all elections were simultaneous they would occasionally fall on a market-day. The only day of the week equally convenient to all is Sunday, which is out of the question. (3) The gains to trade would be scarcely worth consideration. (4) The influence of earlier over later elections acts beneficially, by tending to give the party in power the greater majority, thus strengthening the Government. (5) Simultaneous Elections would scarcely diminish plural voting, least of all in London, where it is most common. (6) It would be impossible to get the extra police required at elections. (7) It would be impossible to provide sufficient election officers, etc.

ELGIN MARBLES: ought they to be restored to Greece?

Pro: (1) The climate is an ideal one at Athens, whereas the soot in London is deadly to the Marbles, which already show signs of deterioration. (2) In Athens they would be far safer from fire, situated on a height above the town. (3) Athens is the centre of Greek life, and the Acropolis the one great national monument, bound up with their past; these masterpieces of their greatest sculptors ought to be restored to them. (4) Their great beauty can be fully appreciated only in their natural surroundings, where they could be seen as a whole, not fragmentarily. Many students go to Athens.

Con: (1) The Marbles are a national trophy, and are priceless. The Modern Greeks are not the descendants of the ancient Greeks. (2) The Acropolis has been bombarded many times, and is most insecure. The Marbles were brought to England to keep them from the French, and to prevent their destruction; and during the 60 years that they have been here, no deteriorations due to climate are apparent. (3) If the Marbles ought to be restored to Greece, many other similar collections ought to be given back to other countries. (4) Though not in their natural surroundings, the Marbles are suitably housed here, and more people profit by their being in the greatest city of the world than if in Athens. There would also be the additional risk of another sea voyage.

EMPLOYERS' LIABILITY: "COMMON EMPLOYMENT."

Pro: (1) The judicial interpretation of the Factory Acts, now abolished, whereby it was laid down as an axiom that no workman can claim damages from an employer for injuries inflicted by the carelessness of a fellow-workman, caused great hardship to an injured workman who was not responsible for his own injury. (2) There is no reason why the employer should not be held as liable in the case of his own servants as in that of a stranger. The former is very often as little able to protect himself as the latter.

Con: (1) Workmen, knowing that employers are liable, are much less careful to protect themselves from injuries, and perhaps even seek them for the sake of compensation. (2) An employer cannot reasonably be held responsible for injuries arising from causes wholly beyond his control. Employés, like everybody else, including their masters, must look after their own safety.

ENGLAND: why is she unpopular as a nation?

Pro: (1) England is naturally unpopular because she is successful—where other nations have failed—in the fields of Colonial and commercial enterprize. (2) England cannot form alliances in the same way as other powers, since there is no power whose interests do not in some way clash with hers. (3) England has been forced to continue her Colonial expansion by the action of other powers, who deliberately and aggressively entered into fields which she had previously occupied alone; the charge of bullying made against England was merely a device on the part of those powers to create a strong feeling against her, and to force her hand. (Some) Much of the abuse which England has received has been from powers who had every desire to court her alliance, but saw no other means of obtaining it save by threats. Otherwise it is incredible that Germany would have risked war with England for the sake of some worthless colonies in Africa. (4) France having withdrawn her troops from Egypt at the last moment, and now discovering her mistake, is angry with England, because she declines to give up the country to the anarchy from which years of patient labour have rescued it, that France may, through the occupation of Egypt, reach a position which might enable her to overthrow the maritime supremacy of England. As regards the promise to withdraw, it is sufficient to say that the obstacles have proved far greater than could possibly have been anticipated. (5) The Command of the Sea is absolutely necessary to Great Britain. While to others it is merely a question of vanity, to England her very existence is at stake; herself an island, she depends on foreign countries for food, and has huge Colonial possessions to defend.

Con: (1) England is unpopular because of the cant and hypocrisy which are so characteristic of her in all her dealings with foreign nations. While professing goodwill to mankind in general, she never fails to profit by their misfortunes. (2) England's foreign policy is so confused and vacillating that no nation dare trust her as an ally. England's true foreign policy would be to come to terms with those powers whose interests coincide with her own, and form alliances, so that wherever those mutual interests are attacked, both powers would be ready to defend them. (3) England is naturally unpopular on account of the "dog in the manger" policy she has always pursued in Africa, where, while trying to forbid other nations to occupy territory, she has refused to do so herself. (4) France considers that England has behaved very badly in refusing to withdraw from Egypt when, according to the terms of a solemn promise given by Mr. Gladstone and renewed by Lord Salisbury, she was bound to do so. France claims that the circumstances have not changed, and that, order being restored, England is bound to retire. It must be remembered that England recognized France's right to occupy Tunis, so there can be no counter-claim here. (5) The claim to the Command of the Sea is one that can be allowed by no other power, and is needlessly provocative.

ENTAIL, ABOLITION OF THE LAW OF.

Pro: (1) The law of Entail is the mainstay of the aristocracy, and its abolition would be a step in the progress of democracy. (2) The law protects a class, and class protection is politically bad. Moreover, it protects the profligate from the results of his own folly. (3) It would be an unqualified good to the nation if all the profligate land-owners were effaced. (4) The law weakens parental control, since it makes the eldest son independent of his father. (5) It tempts eldest sons to anticipate their inheritances; and is a great hardship on younger sons. (6) Any legislation that would increase the number of land-owners, and would diminish absenteeism, would be desirable. (7) The chief result of the law is the creation of a few very large estates, which is politically dangerous. (8) The law places an artificial value on land, since properties which would in the natural course be purchasable disappear from the market. (9) It leads to the mortgage of estates in order to provide jointures, and thus handicaps the whole property. (10) Under the law the holder, having only a life interest in a property, is apt to mismanage it; and, as he has only the income and not the capital, is unable to spend as much on the land as is often required. (11) England is the only country in which the law obtains. (12) If it is true that rents are lower on entailed than on unentailed properties, it is because the land has deteriorated by bad farming.

Con: (1) An ancient aristocracy is a source of strength to every country, and an attempt to undermine its strength should not be sanctioned. (2) Any alteration in the law of Entail would practically revolutionize the present system of society. The spendthrift would not be less profligate if he had entire control of a property. The law protects a son from the follies of his father, and preserves the great families. (3) If the middle class were to obtain possession of the land, great harm would be done, as they have no traditions to maintain, and do not realize the responsibilities attaching to land. (4) From earliest youth an eldest son has the good of the land at heart. Were Entail abolished, the good relations between squire and tenant would disappear, the village would cease to be proud of its "family," and the pride of the nation, "the landed gentry," would become extinct. (5) The spendthrift eldest son would be a spendthrift under any circumstances, and post-obits are not unknown. The alleged hardship to the younger sons is often more sentimental than real. (6) All property is unequally divided—land not more so than other. If Entail were abolished, land would change hands, and the only result would be that it would accumulate in the hands of another class; hence absenteeism would not be less prevalent than now. (7) The existence of large estates is a good; on these alone is a uniform system of agricultural policy pursued. The alleged political danger arising from large estates is nullified by the Ballot and the Corrupt Practices Act. (8) That there is no "free trade in land" enhances its value as an investment. (9) Mortgages, raised for suitable purposes, are a convenience, and it is financially sound that an estate should provide itself with the means of its own improvement. (10) Under the law of Entail an owner cannot treat his capital as if it were income, and estates are better cared for, except in a few exceptional cases, since the interests of the tenant for life and his successor are not antagonistic. (11) Farmers prefer entailed estates, as the rents are lower and the tenure more secure. (12) It is impossible to argue from one country to another.

EQUALITY, RELIGIOUS.

Pro: (1) The truth or error of speculative questions is no concern of the State; at the most, interference by the State is justifiable only when the doctrines held by a sect are bound up with social *practices* which are inconsistent with the welfare of the community (*e.g.* Mormonism). (2) The denial of Religious Equality induced the Spanish Government to establish the

Inquisition, enforcing orthodoxy at the cost of the mental life of Spain. (3) Where a Government (*e.g.* the Indian) rules over peoples of varying creeds, she can maintain her sway only by preserving religious neutrality.

Con : (1) The State cannot remain indifferent to the truth of religion without virtually establishing atheism. Creeds cannot be separated from their social consequences ; and where the conclusions of a creed loosen social ties, the State must interfere to prevent its propagation. Where opposing doctrines are regarded by the State as equally valid, the value of truth must be lowered, and indifference to all creeds follows. (2) The recognition by the State of one creed as true need not lead her to persecute the others. (3) The Indian Government, though tolerant, discourages all *practices* inconsistent with Christianity.

EQUALITY, SOCIAL.

Pro : (1) Most social differences are largely the result of surroundings and education. (2) The recognition of Inequality leads to snobbery and the worship of wealth, rank, intellect, athletic powers, etc. The undue respect paid to the so-called intellectual professions leads to the disparagement of equally necessary social functions, and to an undue specialization of labour, with the concomitant evil of unequally developed mental and physical powers. (3) Special gifts are endowments of nature, and are not due to personal merits ; hence there is no reason why intellect alone should be singled out for honour. Popular education is lessening the inequalities of the classes ; and as long as undue honour is paid to intellectual labour, the evils of social Inequality become only more accentuated, and the prejudice against manual labour increased, to the injury of the vitality of the nation. Great moral and physical benefits would accrue if all would work with their hands as well as heads. (4) Though this union of different kinds of labour in each individual may not be possible under the present organization of society, it is a condition nevertheless to which we are rapidly being driven ; and some alteration will become necessary, since, though learning is being accumulated, it is only the few who are affected by it, whilst opposed to them stand the masses, no less ignorant than they are numerically strong.

Con : (1) Social differences spring from more than mere differences in surroundings. They are inherent in men ; they often occur among children of the same family and with the same environment. (2) Some incentive, such as social reputation or honour, is needed to evoke the best energies of genius ; while respect shown to an unworthy object degrades a man, it raises him when he acknowledges the superiority of intellect, and pays to it its due meed of honour. To intellectual work has always been accorded the greatest respect. It is intellect that distinguishes man from the brute. (3) Great excellence in any one department of knowledge can be obtained only by specialization, and demands undivided attention. The time, therefore, that is not devoted to special work should be spent, not in another kind of work, but in recreation. (4) We can deal with society only as it is, not as it should be. Intellect will always rule the world ; even popular movements are directed by it.

ETHICAL MOVEMENT, THE.

Pro : (1) The grounds on which allegiance to the Good Life has been habitually claimed by the Churches in the past no longer retain their hold on large classes of people. Under these circumstances, there is a danger of moral obligations appearing, to those who have mistaken the alleged grounds for the real ones, to be of less binding application. (2) It is therefore a pressing need of the day to make it clear wherein the true significance of Right Living consists. (3) This involves, in the first place, the endeavour to set forth in popular lectures and classes the relations between the lives of individuals and the permanent well-being of society; and further implies the attempt to show on theoretic grounds that social well-being is an object in itself worth striving for, and one which we may hope to further by the consistent endeavour to purify and enrich life. (4) To secure that a beginning be made towards the realization of these ends, Societies should be formed, consisting of men and women of all shades of opinion, whose one bond of union shall be the belief that "the Good Life has a claim upon us in virtue of its supreme worth to humanity," and that by their union it is possible to assist individual and social efforts after it.

Con: (1) Allegiance to the Good Life is an essential doctrine of all the creeds within Christianity, and, indeed, of every religion. The scepticism and doubt of to-day are attributable to apparent but passing causes, such as the rapid growth of scientific knowledge, which, when properly assimilated, will not be found to be at variance with the teachings of the Churches. (2) Christianity has always, and never more strongly than now, laid stress on the significance of the Moral Life. (3) Sociology alone is a wholly insufficient basis for morality, in that it makes no direct appeal to the religious instinct. Scriptural authority is an essential sanction to any theory of practical Ethics, and supplies the life-blood to its teachings. Abstract Ethics cannot be reduced to a scientific method, if the will be free, since by that very fact an incalculable element is introduced; whilst, if the will be not free, Ethics, being based on the doctrine of human responsibility, becomes impossible. Few people, for instance, agree as to what is meant by the word "goodness." (4) The fact that the only bond of union between the lecturers and members of Ethical Societies is so slight a one, and a common article of belief to all civilized beings, is a source of great weakness; until the Societies have established an "Ethical Creed," they can hope for no extensive influence or support, still less to supplant any existing Churches.

ETHICS AS AN EXPERIMENTAL SCIENCE.

Pro: (1) In every other field of knowledge progress has been attained only by abandoning purely theoretical speculation in favour of direct observation of facts; similar results may be expected from similar methods in Ethical investigations. (2) It is not necessary that, before starting on our inquiries, we should solve deep metaphysical problems (*e.g.* Freedom of Will) which have for centuries been the theme of controversy and the despair of philosophers; we should rather attempt to ascertain our facts first, and draw our inferences afterwards. (3) While it may be admitted that widely different views as to the basis, province, and aim of Ethics exist, it must also be allowed that differences as wide-spread existed in all ancient theories concerning the physical realm (*teste* the hopeless divergence of views on physical matters in the classic world). (4) As the Science of Social Health, Ethics should be based on an accurate observation of the laws which govern it, just as in hygiene we look for the laws which govern physical health. Neither hygiene nor medicine loses much of its force from the fact that it is based on experiment. Why should Ethics?

Con: (1) Ethics cannot be reduced to an exact science as physics or even biology can, since its subject-matter is of a totally different nature, not susceptible of the same accurate treatment. The science of Ethics consists not so much in the collection of facts as of judgments upon facts, towards which mere facts offer little help. (2) The solution of the problem of Freedom of Will lies at the root of all ethical questions; without having a clear idea of what we think on the subject we cannot decide on any ethical question. Responsibility is the very keynote of Ethics. (3) The subject of Ethics has been under discussion by the best thinkers for more than 2000 years, and we are no nearer a solution. Is it likely that a collection of facts, however large, will help us? (4) If merely the science of Social Health,

Ethics would miss its most important factor, viz., the individual and his duty to himself; and would tend to substitute an unwilling conformity to the dicta of society for the willing service of a free man.

EXAMINATIONS, COMPETITIVE.

Pro: (1) Under the Competitive Examination system, appointments, scholarships, etc., are open to all, and, in the case of the Civil Service, instead of being subject to nepotism, as formerly, are an object of honourable ambition. The examination *must* be competitive, and not merely qualifying; otherwise the same evils as before will arise. (2) According to the testimony of many leading physicians, the health of students is not suffering from over-work at school or college. (3) The effect of Competitive Examinations on young persons is healthy; thousands are encouraged to try their metal against their compeers; and even the dullest are urged to exert themselves. (4) The vast majority of the leading educationists (Head Masters of Public and Board Schools and Inspectors of Schools) favour Competition, considering it the only practical means of testing efficiency and awarding prizes, which are a direct incentive to learning. (5) Teachers are no more to be trusted to "audit their own accounts" than other people. (6) The examiners select the candidates able to make use of their knowledge to the best advantage—itself as desirable a qualification for Government service as is actual learning.

Con: (1) Competitive Examinations, at any rate for the Civil Service, ought to be reduced to a minimum, a year of probation being substituted for the final examination. (Some) Qualifying Examinations should replace Competitive. (2) The present system is a great danger to the health, physical and moral, of youth; every year some valuable young lives are lost by overstrain. (3) It morally depresses both teacher and pupil, by deliberately setting itself to take a sordid view of education. Many brilliant prizemen have lived their mental life before they are five-and-twenty. (4) Educationists are biassed judges; the vast majority of others well able to form an independent opinion are in favour of modification of the Competitive System, which cramps school education and leads to over-specialization. The clever are overtaught, whilst the stupid, who need most teaching, are neglected. (5) Examination is a useful instrument in the hands of a teacher to test his own work; but it necessarily exerts a fatal influence when made of such importance that teachers simply conform to an external standard. (Some) Examinations by strangers test nothing; in Germany it has been found that the teacher is best qualified to know the merits of his pupils, and compulsory publication of papers secures against abuse. (6) All examinations should aim at discovering general intelligence.

EXPERIMENTAL, THE, IN POLITICS.

Pro: (1) In political, as in every other science, the only means we have of testing the value of a theory is by experience. As regards politics, complex as are the materials and momentous as are the results, it is yet possible by making experiments on a small scale to draw satisfactory conclusions, without endangering the fabric of society. For instance, an Eight Hours' Day might be tried for a few years, farm colonies for the unemployed, etc. (2) Costly as such experiments might be, they would not be so expensive as if measures were taken without such first test.

Con: (1) When dealing with phenomena so complex as those of human society, it is almost impossible to draw correct conclusions from even the simplest experiments, since we can never tell how far they are affected by disturbing influences. In ordinary science, experiments are often rendered untrustworthy by such influences, but such experiments can be repeated: whereas in politics the number of our experiments must be comparatively limited; and in taking into account the experience of foreign countries we are largely ignorant of the special circumstances peculiar to them. Political experimentation would keep society in a perpetual state of unrest, and would tempt statesmen to undertake wild schemes for social amelioration without properly weighing the effects they were likely to have. Many experiments could be carried out only on a very large scale and over many years. (2) The costs of such experiments would be enormous, and it would be almost impossible to go back to the *status quo ante* without great friction.

FAGGING AT SCHOOLS.

Pro : (1) Fagging instils into the minds of boys when they first go to school habits of discipline and respect for their elders. (2) It induces in older boys a feeling of responsibility, and urges them to set a good example. (3) Very little bullying results from Fagging. Such as there is, is found amongst those boys who have not yet quite reached the position of having their own fags. (4) A boy having a fag allows no other boy to bully that fag. In any school where there are both big and little boys, some sort of fagging is sure to exist, and it is better that this should be regulated, and the big boys made responsible. (5) Fagging acts as an inducement to boys to rise as quickly as possible in the school, in order to avoid fagging, and to themselves obtain fags. (6) Public opinion and the traditions of the school prevent abuse.

Con : (1) Fagging impairs the feeling of self-respect in the smaller boys, and encourages in them an admiration for false ideals. (2) It makes the bigger boys lazy, self-assertive, and tyrannical. (3) It encourages bullying amongst all classes, and though checked by the bigger boys, the spirit remains. There is nothing to check the big boys themselves from being bullies. (4) It is the duty of the masters to supervize the conduct of the boys out of school-hours ; this duty should not be relegated to the elder boys. (5) If freedom from the obligation to fag is sufficient to induce lazy boys to work, its hardships must be very considerable. (6) Public opinion in a school means the private opinion of the head boys, and consequently fluctuates considerably.

FAIR TRADE (RECIPROCITY) v. FREE TRADE.

Pro : (1) Fair Trade is not Protection. The blessings of Free Trade are admitted by all ; but, without retaliation, it is impossible to force other nations to adopt it. (Some) Free Trade should be maintained for all raw materials, with a duty imposed on all manufactured articles. England's one chance of retaining her supremacy lies in becoming the workshop of the world. (2) Free Trade, to be equitable, must be universal, which is not the case now. England has opened her ports to all nations, but no nations have opened their ports to her ; hence our manufacturers cannot place their goods on foreign markets at rates which compete with local industries, whilst foreign countries compete freely here. (3) Partial Free Trade benefits protected countries ; hence England damages herself for the good of others. (4) The export trade of foreign countries has lately increased proportionately more than ours ; and while, as a result of their Protective duties, our exports to them decline, their imports to us increase. (5) Free Trade is leading to the destruction of all our industries ; which, once lost, could never be revived, as other countries would have obtained our markets ; the ruin of England would result. (6) England does not import only necessary articles. Foreign countries, owing to lower wages, compete with us in our own markets in goods which we can manufacture satisfactorily ourselves. (7) Without Reciprocity real Free Trade does not exist. If the exports of those countries which protect their industries against us were taxed, we could force them to adopt Free Trade ; or continue to tax them as long as they remained recalcitrant. (8) The consumer and producer are so closely connected that any injury to the trade of the latter at once reacts on to the former; in slackness of trade it is the consumer who is most affected, since his livelihood depends on the producer; hence any action that revives trade would increase the prosperity of all. **(9)** Even if the price of commodities rose, the consumer would in the long run be a gainer, since the greater portion of the import duties would be paid by the foreigner, and there would be a corresponding diminution in taxation. Moreover, absolute beggary would stare the majority of consumers in the face if our manufacturers were ruined. **(10)** The distribution of wealth in England is becoming more and more unequal, the rich growing richer, and the poor poorer, while the converse is the case in protected countries. **(11)** Free Trade is not the real cause of the increase in our wealth, which is due to the extension of railways, telegraphs, improvements in machinery, etc. France and the United States are examples of prosperity under the Protective System. **(12)** If we adopted Fair Trade, and imposed duties on the imports of foreign commodities, we should be able to negotiate fairer Commercial Treaties, and eventually should "buy in the cheapest market and sell in the dearest." **(13)** Our imports are largely in excess of our exports. Consequently, we must be living on our capital, and such action leads to bankruptcy. **(14)** Absolute Free Trade does not obtain even in England, and there is no reason why Protective duties should not be extended to other articles of commerce. **(15)** Our policy of Free Trade is resented by some of our Colonies, who, finding that they cannot compete with English manufactures, have been compelled to impose high Protective duties. **(16)** (Some) We ought to establish absolute Free Trade with our Colonies, and Reciprocity with the rest of the world. This policy would make Imperial Federation possible. **(17)** England is the only Free Trade country in the world. **(18)** Fair Trade, by making us independent of foreign nations, and encouraging our own industries, would strengthen us in time of war.

Con: **(1)** Fair Trade is only Protection in another form, since every import duty would protect some industry. **(2)** Obstacles in the way of trade are bad; hence any freeing of markets is better than none, and partial Free Trade is of great benefit to England. **(3)** England imports goods for her own benefit, not for that of others. **(4)** The gradual decline of our export trade is to be deplored; its resuscitation is not to be sought in a Protective tariff, which would only raise the price of commodities, and thus increase distress. **(5)** England successfully competes with foreigners in foreign markets; the remedy for the present depression in trade is not Fair Trade, but fresh markets and expansion of Empire. **(6)** If foreigners are able to successfully compete with us at home, it only proves that our costs of production are too high. If Fair Trade were adopted, Protection to be equitable must be extended to all articles of industry—a suicidal policy for a country that depends on imports for necessaries of life. **(7)** Even if the principle of Reciprocity were adopted, it could not be carried out, since we are bound by Commercial Treaties and by the "most favoured nation clause" for many years to come. **(8)** Any prospective revival of trade and consequent increase of wages to the consumer from the action of Fair Trade would be more than neutralized by the immediate rise in the price of all commodities, and we should be worse off than we are now. Protection can be repelled only by more Free Trade. **(9)** The majority of the consumers, the working-classes, would not be benefited by any reduction in taxation; and any action that raised the price of the necessaries of life would be an unmitigated evil. **(10)** Though it may be true that the poor are daily becoming poorer, it is undeniable that under Free Trade they are much better off than when Protection obtained. The more equal distribution of wealth in Protectionist countries is due to other causes. **(11)** The increase in the wealth of England is not due to the extension of railways, etc., but to the abolition of Protective duties. For many years before the adoption of Free Trade, our trade was almost at a standstill. Moreover, Protectionist countries are passing through a severer period of depression than we are. The United States are not an example of prosperity under Protection, since America is self-supporting; and other causes are at work in the case of France.   (12) It is only under Free Trade that we can "buy in the cheapest market and sell in the dearest."   (13) Though our imports exceed our exports, we have a large market for our goods at home, and we are not living on our capital.   (Some) It is not true that our imports far exceed our exports to Foreign Protective countries—only with France is this the case; with other countries the balance is largely in our favour.   (14) Commodities are now taxed only for the sake of revenue.   The aim of all English financial legislation is to remove duties, not to impose them.   (15) The very fact that our Colonies protect themselves against our manufactures, proves that England is able to produce more cheaply than others. Protection would merely mean an increase in the cost of production, to the detriment of the home consumer.   (17) England's partial Free Trade is of the greatest possible benefit to her. If America adopted Free Trade, she would be able to successfully compete with us in nearly all our markets.   (18) It would be very difficult for Custom-house officials to carry out any scheme of Fair Trade, which would probably lead to goods being sent to England through some free port (as in the case of French brandy, where potato spirit went from Hamburg to Bordeaux, to return to England with the Bordeaux marks as "old brandy").

FAIR WAGES CLAUSE IN PUBLIC CONTRACTS.

Pro: (1) State and Municipal Authorities ought, both in the labour they directly employ and in all contracts they give out, to stipulate that men in their service be paid the full Trade Union rate of wages, and that their hours shall not exceed eight *per diem*.   (2) By doing so the State would be acting as a model for employers, and would attract the best men into her service. It would be paradoxical and illogical for the State to pass, for instance, an Eight Hours' Law, while she herself is a sinner.

Con: (1) Public bodies, in the interests of taxpayers should carry out the work entrusted to them as economically as possible. To pay higher wages, and to work men less hours than the market, would be tantamount to being generous at the expense of the public. This would depress industry, and create a favoured class at the expense of the rest.   (2) If the State were to raise wages throughout the district beyond the amount which employers could afford, it would merely result in the employment of fewer hands.

FARM COLONIES FOR THE UNEMPLOYED.

Pro: (1) The establishment of Farm Colonies would provide healthy employment to many.   (2) Our country districts are being depopulated, and land is going out of cultivation; hence Farm Colonies would be a great benefit.   (3) Hadleigh Farm, amongst others of the same kind, has been a great success morally, if not financially, and it has helped many to emigrate.

Con: (1) The enormous cost of buying land is a great difficulty in the way of establishing Farm Colonies, apart from the total unfitness and incapacity of the Unemployed for agricultural work.   (3) No Farm Colony has ever really been a financial success, and finding work for the Unemployed is too large a scheme for charity. (*See* UNEMPLOYED.)

FASHION IN DRESS: is it an evil?

Pro: (1) Changes of Fashion are the result of a craving for variety, which indicates a morbid taste that should not be encouraged.   (2) Whatever is good in design and workmanship should be permanent. Under the influence of Fashion, designs aim at variety rather than excellence of work.

manship, which is superfluous in a merely temporary article. (**3**) Fashion, by keeping its devotees in leading strings, tends to deprive them of whatever power of original design they may possess. (**4**) The designs dictated by Fashion are often ill-adapted to the needs and surroundings of the individual (*e.g.* the hat of the factory-girl). (**5**) Fashion in dress does not take into account the primary considerations of health and utility, *e.g.* people wear symmetrical boots although the foot is unsymmetrical, distort their waists, etc. (**6**) A study of the Fashions diverts the mind from better objects. (**7**) Without Fashion we should have greater individuality of taste, and more variety of appearance. (**8**) A scarcity-value is given for things of the newest design by people who wish to be fashionable. This is an economical mischief. (**9**) Changes of Fashion lead to rapid alternations of over-work and idleness in industrial centres. Hands that have been employed in one kind of work are unable to take up work of a totally different nature. Moreover, temporary industrial activity fosters early marriages and a larger increase of population than can be maintained; consequently, when the tide of Fashion recedes, a large number of parents are left out of work, with young families on their hands.

Con : (**1**) Within certain limits variety is wholesome, and the mind is refreshed by changes of Fashion. (**2**) A fashionable design is not of necessity a bad design, and articles which have been in use many years, and by virtue of the excellence of their workmanship have withstood the wear and tear of time, become less fresh and wholesome than the more lightly-made temporary articles. (**3**) If people designed their own articles they would often be of worse design than that imposed on them by Fashion. In the vast majority of cases, the taste of the individual is below even that of the leaders of Fashion. (**4**) If the individual is foolish enough to adopt unsuitable designs, she (or he) would probably do so under any *régime*. (**5**) There is no reason why Fashion in dress should not take into account considerations of health and utility. The late Mr. Worth was too great an artist to do otherwise; he designed dresses for the individual, not for society. (**6**) It is often an immense saving of time and trouble to find things ready-made to a given fashionable pattern; few people have time to give to the design of original costume. (**7**) Fashion imposes greater uniformity on individual taste, greater variety on society. (**8**) Poor people can often buy superior articles at less than the cost of production, because they are no longer fashionable. The wealthy and leisured classes thus contribute a share to the pleasures of the poorer classes. (**9**) Alternations of industry and idleness take place at industrial centres quite independently of Fashion. Moreover, a loss of trade to one centre involves an increase of trade to another; so that the community as a whole does not suffer from the changes of locality for industrial activity.

FEDERAL GOVERNMENT IN GREAT BRITAIN AND IRELAND.

Pro : (**1**) A careful analysis of the causes which have led to the breakdown of the Parliamentary machine, as exhibited in the frequent failure of governments to pass any important legislation except after frequent and exasperating delay, leads to the conclusion, arrived at by so strong an opponent to change as Lord Salisbury, that decentralization or devolution of some of the powers of Parliament to local bodies is the only means by which the present state of affairs can be remedied. (**2**) An examination of the records of Bills passed by the House of Commons since the date of the two Unions, will show that the wants of both Scotland and Ireland have been almost habitually subordinated, whilst England has always received the lion's share of attention. (**3**) Ireland has long groaned under the evil of this state of things, and, having seen the reason, has demanded liberty to manage her own affairs. Scotland also, feeling the same evil, but for a long time ignorant of its cause, has now awakened; and most of the Scotch Members of the House of Commons are united in favour of a separate legislature for Scotland. Meanwhile the English Members also, finding they cannot get all they require, lay the blame on the fact, as they say, though without truth, that Ireland receives too much attention: the truth being, that we are trying to govern an essentially Federal State with the constitution of a United State. (4.) To adopt a Federal System is not to revoke or in any way tamper with the main principles of the Union, since the Federal Government would retain its supremacy, and would merely delegate certain of its powers to bodies better able to perform them. (5) There can be no doubt that the desire for National Independence among the Irish is wholly due to England's injustice, past and present. Were England to give due heed to Ireland's wrongs, and endow her with such powers of self-government as were consistent with the honour and safety of the United Kingdom, at the same time clearly showing her that no more would be conceded, there is every reason to conclude that Ireland would soon settle down. An Irish National Party with wants unsatisfied would be quite as dangerous as a discontented Irish Parliament, and, while far more likely to be discontented, would be as well able to treat with a foreign foe, because no foreign Government that would treat with a subordinate Parliament would refuse to treat with a National Party. This, of course, on the supposition that the Imperial Parliament retained in its own hands the power of tax-collecting. (6) The contention that Members are elected, not to look after the interests of their respective countries, but as representatives of the whole, is rendered absurd, considering that by far the greater portion of the legislation passed by the House of Commons is purely local, which by its very nature does not require such treatment, the consequence of which is that, by a system of mutual accommodation, the minority in one country can impose its will upon the majority in the other, with the help of outside Members who know nothing of the real merits of the case, and whose constituents will not be submitted to the law. (7) The fact that by this Measures are delayed, and often have to be dropped, is in no way a good thing, since it does not make the supporters of a Measure reasonable, or induce them to again weigh over the *pros* and *cons*, such as would be the case were they able to discuss and hear it criticized in the House of Commons. Rather does the delay irritate them, and turn them into unreasoning and fanatical partizans, who lose all sense of proportion, and can see the value of nothing but the one Measure they wish to pass. It also encourages log-rolling, where one Member or group of Members supporting the Bill vote for another, in order to secure the votes of the others for their own Bill. (8) By getting rid of the merely local business, Parliament would be free to undertake the task which it is elected to perform, viz., to supervize the estimates, and would also bring the influence of the people to bear on the policy of the Government. The evils of popular interference in matters which they do not understand would be much less were the popular control more continuous, and less apt to be diverted by side issues. The chief mischief of popular interference lies with those who allow absurd statements to go uncontradicted, and who, by making foreign policy a mystery, do not hide their hand from other nations, but only make it possible for their own nation to be led hither and thither by the demagogue. Supposing, however, that the prediction proved true, that all interest passed away from the Parliamentary Election, it is surely much worse that people who have no interest in foreign policy in and for themselves should be practically stimulated to influence them by endowing a body of men, who were elected because of their attitude on home and local questions, with supreme power on foreign and colonial.

Con: (1) It is certain that if every Member is to insist on his right to speak on all possible occasions (and this is the state of affairs towards which we seem to be drifting), no matter how little business Parliament has to do, it will never be done. (2) The statistics relied on to prove the fact that England has monopolized the attention of Parliament are absolutely valueless, since they tell us nothing of the character of the legislation or the time it has taken to pass. One really well-drafted Bill, or even if not well-drafted, a Revolutionary Land Bill might prove that Ireland had received more attention than ten or even twenty Bills for England would prove. Also debates of a merely local interest are apt to involve a large principle, *e.g.* the liberty of the subject. (3) Whatever injustice may have been done to Ireland in the past, there can be no reasonable doubt that she has received more than her due share of attention of late years; and as a proof of this, nothing is more remarkable than the growing indifference of the people to all political agitations, in spite of the attempts of interested agitators here and in America to stir up bad blood. Parliament has always shown itself willing to meet all reasonable demands of the Scotch Members; and there is every hope that, by the extended use of the Committee System, and possibly the excision of one or two of the unnecessary stages, the present burden may be removed. (4) The removal of all local matters would be a deadly blow at the unity of the Kingdom, for not even the warmest advocate of the Federal System can say that Foreign, Indian, or even Naval affairs would be enough to rouse the enthusiasm of the electors. National interest would therefore concentrate on the local Parliaments. This would be further accentuated by the fact, for example, that while England is Conservative, Scotland is Radical; and Scottish Radicalism would be very angry if it received a check from the Federal Government, and would at once demand separation. (5) The demand for Home Rule, as far as Ireland is concerned, can be clearly shown to be based on the desire for separation, a desire which has been sedulously maintained by the enemies of England in the United States and elsewhere, and which desire would be aided, rather than checked, by the creation of a Local Parliament, which, though enough to focus national discontent, would not and could not be allowed to possess sufficient powers to gratify the national pride. An Irish Parliament would be inclined, should England find herself in difficulties, to make capital for Ireland by a secret alliance with her enemies. In any case England, however anxious she may be to atone for the past, must yet be guided by considerations of political expediency and national safety. (6) Hitherto the Members of the Imperial Parliament, not as representing the interests of England, Scotland, and Ireland separately, but as Members of an Imperial Parliament, are bound on every occasion to look at the subject discussed as it affects the interests of the whole; and this prevailed till quite recently with the English and Scottish Members, for while Scotsmen have from 1832 been for the most part Radicals, they have never been sectional Radicals; and, as a matter of fact, no English Cabinet has been formed on the idea that there was any necessity to represent proportionately the different nationalities. (7) Whatever the effects of delay may be on the partizans of any Measure, it is certain that, as far as the nation at large is concerned, the effect is to prevent a large amount of positively mischievous legislation; while the fact that the partizans become fanatics is more apt to tell against than in favour of their chances with the great mass of cool, thinking men and women; for instance, we may see how much temperance legislation has been delayed by the action of its fanatical supporters. The House of Lords is probably the best check on log-rolling, since the country, as it showed at the last election, will always back it up when it represents the best interests of the nation, against the effects of groups to destroy it. (8) Parliament, if deprived of the greater portion of the work it has been elected to do, would be tempted to interfere unduly with the executive, and with the worst possible results. • The evils of Parliamentary control arise largely from the fact that it is impossible for the Foreign Secretary to say all that he knows, or, in other words, to adequately defend his own acts. The outcry against secret diplomacy can be upheld by no one who considers the magnitude of the issues, or how far a Minister is bound to weigh his words, for fear of committing his country to a course of policy which maturer reflection will show to be false.

FREE LIBRARIES.

Pro : (1) Free Libraries will stimulate an appetite for reading, and thus become a valuable educational institution. (2) They form a sort of club to many poor people, and are thus an important counter-attraction to the public-house. It is always possible to prevent abuse of the reading-room. (3) They form a good means of keeping up the influences of school. Newspaper and novel reading will create a taste for higher literature; and *good* novels (to which Free Libraries as a rule are and always should be limited) are themselves an education; moreover, it is always possible to gradually put a restriction on fiction. Although much standard literature may now be bought at nominal prices, the poor have no comfortable homes in which to read. (4) The Library rate is never high.

Con : (1) There is no more reason why literature should be supplied free to the people than any other amusement. (2) The Free Public Library is often used as merely a warm shelter for the needy, no pretence of reading being made; half the "readers" are sometimes asleep, to the great discomfort of their neighbours. (3) Apart from newspapers and magazines, novels, mostly trashy and sensational, are the only works considerably read, while serious standard literature is all but neglected. Moreover, the time allowed for reading is, and must be, too short for any work requiring thought. Novel reading as a habit, like dram-drinking, debauches the taste. Further, the abundance of cheap editions of the best standard literature renders Free Libraries an unnecessary addition to the rates. (4) Free Libraries would become an enormous burden if a really large section of the public took to study. The latest books would have to be bought, and large buildings provided. The reason why the rate is at present low is that so few people use the Libraries.

FREE LUXURIES FOR THE POOR.

Pro : (1) Whilst the poor must maintain themselves and their families by their own exertions, the State, or private charity, should provide them with those luxuries which alone make life worth living, and which, being possible, are therefore expedient. (2) This field for direct assistance is almost boundless, and consists of two main divisions, the one concerned with the means of cleanliness and self-respect, the other with more positive pleasures. The former is in various ways partially provided for; the latter is almost wholly neglected, being regarded as a pure extra, of small importance from a public point of view. For most natures, however, excitement in some form or another is an essential, more truly a condition of happiness than even personal cleanliness; and to substitute a refined excitement for a coarse one would be a universal boon. (3) The provision of such happiness is of all public charities the easiest to secure, since it is not fraught with the dangers which attach to other forms of aid. (*See* CHARITY.) It would be the surest means of closing the public-house. (4) The capacity for enjoying good art, whether graphic, musical, or dramatic, involves neither education nor refinement, but is implanted in nearly all Englishmen, though many pass from the cradle to the grave without discovering its existence.

Con : (1) Luxuries, in common with all means of maintaining or enjoying life, must be provided by the people for themselves, if independence of character is to be gained. All forms of external, whether State or private, assistance are demoralizing, though the provision of luxuries is perhaps the least injurious. (2) Even were education not necessary for the enjoyment of refined pleasures, the drudgery and squalor to which fate first condemns and then adapts the poor, would disqualify them for their appreciation,

(3) The music-hall is the only counter-attraction to the public-house; and the lower the hall, the greater its success. (4) Capacity for the higher enjoyments implies elevation of mind, of habits, and of material conditions; unsensational æstheticism can have no chance, except through the slow machinery of Board Schools, Temperance Movements, and Improved Dwellings. That comfort must precede a love of beauty is evidenced by the small attendance of the really poor at East-End Picture Exhibitions and Concerts.

FREE MEALS AT BOARD SCHOOLS.

Pro: (1) Attendance at school being compulsory, it is a necessary corollary that sufficient food should be given to necessitous children to render their education effective. Starving children cannot learn, and brain-work added to empty stomachs leads to ill-health. Apart from the question of humanity, education that is only partially effective is bad economy. (2) Where Free Meals have been introduced, schools have greatly benefited, both intellectually and physically. (3) Where abuses of the privilege of Free Meals exist, they can readily be checked by teachers. (4) The poor find difficulty in providing their children with proper and sufficient food. Even were it true (which it is not) that the money thus saved them would only be spent in drink, why should the children's education suffer for their parents' sins?

Con: (1) The provision of food for their children is the first duty of parents. The State should compel parents not only to send their children to school, but to send them sufficiently fed. (2) Free Meals are morally harmful to the children, leading them to rely on charitable assistance. (3) The knowledge possessed by teachers of the circumstances of the parents of each child is not sufficient to form a safe basis for selection. (4) It reduces the responsibilities of marriage, thereby increasing the number of improvident marriages. If help is absolutely necessary, it were much better given privately to the family as a whole. (*See* CHARITY.) (5) Free Meals would eventually reduce the rate of wages earned by the poor, whose bare necessities are in the end always the measure of their earnings.

FREE SHELTERS AND REFUGES.

Refuges and Shelters are of two kinds: (a) Free caravansaries where free shelter and some food are indiscriminately given, for varying periods, without inquiry or organized effort towards permanently helping. (b) Institutions where, in addition to food and shelter being provided, inquiry is made into the antecedents of applicants, and attempts are made to permanently assist by finding them, or inciting them to find, employment. The so-called Shelters and Refuges, such as General Booth's, where a charge, however small, is made for either food or lodging, do not come within the scope of this article. They form part of the question of Cheap Lodging Houses.

Pro: (1) Individuals may find themselves without the wherewithal to obtain a night's lodging, and yet shun the social stigma attaching to the Casual Ward and the Workhouse: temporary help may be of great service here, for when once a person has fallen as low as the Casual Ward, self-respect vanishes—a calamity which a little help might have obviated. (2) Workhouse rules are so rigid, and the labour test in Casual Wards frequently enforced so harshly, that inmates are kept to their allotted task until it is too late in the morning for them to seek work successfully; the result is chronic return to the Casual Ward. (3) When private charity relieves ratepayers of the expense of supporting the indigent, ratepayers should be grateful. (4) More personal influence and care can be bestowed on waifs in a private Institution; and it is a Christian duty to mitigate their privations more than State Institutions can with their prison-like discipline. (5) Those who have fallen behind in the struggle of life, may often, by a little sympathy and skilled counsel, be put in the way of finding suitable work, who, unaided, would become a permanent burden to the community. (6) Refuges and Shelters, where inquiry is made (unlike indiscriminate Institutions), besides saving many on the verge of destitution, become a positive deterrent from imposture, by demonstrating the different treatment meted out to the loafer and to the genuine case. (7) There is great advantage in personal contact between rich and poor when dealing with such cases, supplying to charitable workers a good training, and helping to inculcate in them the spirit of true citizenship.

Con: (1) If sometimes deserving people find their way to Free Refuges who would otherwise drift into the Casual Ward, this good is more than counterbalanced by the opportunity they give to loafers to avoid the wholesome discipline of the Poor Law. People of real grit come through the Poor Law ordeal unharmed, and find their proper level afterwards. Refuges of all sorts positively sap independence, and cause people to give up the struggle for existence sooner than if only the Casual Ward and Workhouse lay before them. (2) The rules in the better regulated Casual Wards are so relaxed that, where individuals are eager to get work, they are able to do so. If the place is pleasant, it is an inducement to those who have been there to return again. (3) The ratepayer makes provision for the destitute in his Poor Rate, and is wasting his money in attracting them from a well-regulated Institution to one managed by less responsible and less experienced authorities. (4) Private philanthropy is apt to be "faddy," sentimental, and unpractical, and tends to encourage pauperism and hypocrisy. Many such Institutions, after the first burst of charitable impulse which started them, fall under the management of well-paid officials, over whom no efficient control is exercised. Some Institutions lack in cleanliness; and the discipline necessary for dealing with the destitute class is in nine cases out of ten more kindly and Christian than the temporary housing and feeding of a few, who are afterwards turned adrift in no better condition than before. (5) Those in search of employment could have the same kindly interest brought to bear in their behalf, without being housed and fed by private charity. (6) Shelters and Refuges which hold out prospects of finding employment attract unemployed from outside districts, and unduly burden the district with a surplusage of destitute. (7) All genuinely intentioned efforts devoted to the organized private investigation of cases, or to housing and feeding, would be better bestowed by the philanthropist in doing his duty as a citizen on a Board of Guardians, etc., and in trying to level up State Institutions to his charitable ideals. Individual interest between helper and helped could be as well brought to bear in Workhouse and Ward as in an atmosphere where impulsive, irresponsible kindliness is apt to result in ill-considered action, rather than in judicious and effective methods.

FREE SOUP KITCHENS, CLOTHING, COALS, ETC.

Pro: (1) Free Soup Kitchens, Clothing (including blankets), Coals, Refuges, etc., are a perfectly legitimate form of relief, so long as they are administered with discrimination. (2) They often relieve unmerited distress arising from economic causes over which workers have no immediate control, and prevent utter collapse of deserving families by enabling them to tide over difficult periods. (3) They are not sufficiently accessible to attract any considerable number of outside poor to centres with which they are not directly connected. (4) Tenants (if there were any) who pay increased rents for tenements, owing to their neighbourhood to centres of relief, would soon learn that they were being imposed upon; and the relief granted is not widespread enough to have any influence on wages. (5) Such slight theoretical harm as may be done by these charities is often eliminated by nominal charges being made. In any case the evils are more than counterbalanced by the good. A State, still less its richer members, can never regulate their entire conduct by abstract economic laws, one of which, moreover, is the humanitarian instinct, which will always have a controlling influence on human affairs.

Con: (1) Soup Kitchens and all similar forms of charity are economic errors, directly encouraging pauperism and removing incentives to industry. (*See* CHARITY.) Clothing and other gifts with a commercial value are as often as not at once pawned or sold. (2) They are at best merely a temporary expedient, the benefit of which is more than counterbalanced by their lasting injurious effects. (3) They directly encourage vagrancy and hypocrisy, and increase the concentration of indigent poor in cities. (4) They raise rents, since neighbourhood to a Soup Kitchen is held out as an advantage; and they lower wages, which, in the case of unskilled labour, are ultimately measured by the bare necessities of life. (5) The harm is mitigated, but not removed, by small charges being made. No system that is not entirely self-supporting can in the long run be of any real benefit.

GAMBLING IN COMMERCE, SUPPRESSION OF.

Pro: (1) Commercial Gambling disturbs the markets and greatly handicaps legitimate business. (2) It causes great fluctuations in prices, and gives rise to fraudulent transactions in non-existent goods. (3) It creates an army of parasites on commerce, who absorb a very large part of its legitimate gains. (4) Trade is already so depressed, owing to a combination of inevitable causes, that all unnecessary elements of risk are evils.

Con: (1) Speculation is, in varying degrees, an inevitable concomitant of commerce. (2) It does not create, but is created by, fluctuations in prices; and helps to repair the balance of good and bad years. (3) Middlemen are an essential factor in commerce. They are often the chief capitalists and distributors. (4) Commercial Speculation cannot be prevented by legislation without its being so wide as to be a great hindrance to trade.

GAMBLING, MORALITY OF.

Pro: (1) Speculation is the essence of commerce. There is no difference between gambling on the Stock Exchange and on the turf; and gambling is sure to arise wherever a risky element exists in a business. (2) The love of sport, of which gambling is an inevitable accompaniment, is an important national trait. (3) Where a man can afford to gamble, no harm is done. If he cannot, there is no necessity for him to follow the example of those who can. Similar logic would deprive every man of every luxury, on the ground that his poorer neighbours might be tempted.

Con: (1) No one can pretend that pure gambling is in any way a *bonâ fide* element in trade. (2) It is the ruin of true sport. (3) It enables a man to get that to which he is not entitled. A man either can afford to gamble, in which case he is setting a bad example, or he cannot, when he is wasting other people's money. Gambling is a prolific source of crime.

GAMBLING, LEGAL SUPPRESSION OF.

Pro: (1) Gambling ought to be suppressed by law, since it leads clerks, etc., to steal money from their employers to pay their losses. The greater the facilities for betting, the more it is indulged in, and though the law cannot perhaps prohibit it altogether, it can keep it within narrow bounds. (2) The law cannot refuse to recognize any widespread incentive to crime. Many who would not yield to any other inducement to steal, do so in this case; they rely on winning, and regard the theft as merely a temporary loan.

Con: (1) The law could be only carried out unequally; it would be absurd to abolish say Tattersall's, an action which would result in the creation of secret betting-places, placing a great temptation in the way of the police to levy blackmail. All trade is gambling in some shape or degree, especially stockbroking and insurance. (2) It is absurd to attribute much petty larceny to gambling; a man who would be tempted to steal in order to gamble would steal for other purposes. It is not proposed that the Sumptuary Laws should be reintroduced.

GAME LAWS, ABOLITION OF.

Pro : (1) Game cannot be called property in the ordinary sense of the term, since the owner's rights in it are dependent on its territorial movements. (2) The Game Laws involve great expense, since they protect rights that are difficult to defend. (3) They create an artificial right, not founded on Natural Law. (4) They introduce another uncertain element into farming, since the destruction to crops due to game cannot be estimated; it is unjust to refuse the farmer both protection and the right to protect himself. (5) Game rights, if granted, should be taxed as ordinary property. (6) If landlords visit their estates only for the sake of sport, they are of little service to the country, since they forget that property has its duties as well as its privileges. (7) Game might be protected in the same way as song-birds.

Con : (1) Game is property just as much as is any other product of the soil. (2) A law of trespass would be required if the Game Laws were repealed. (3) Natural Law, apart from actual law and as applied to the relations of human beings, is a meaningless phrase. (4) A tenant is compensated for any loss caused to him by game. (5) Game rights are already taxed in the shape of Game Licenses. (6) Game and the prospect of sport attract landlords to their country seats, and thus help to maintain the feudal relation between landlord and tenant. (7) If the Game Laws were repealed all game would be exterminated, and a valuable means of relaxation would disappear.

GAS SUPPLY, MUNICIPALIZATION OF.

Pro : (1) Gas has become indispensable in our towns for lighting and cooking, and, notwithstanding the increase in the use of electric light, Gas will not be superseded by Electricity. It should therefore be municipalized. (2) It could be manufactured more cheaply and its quality improved, if undertaken by the Municipality. (3) The duties of a Municipality cannot be absolutely defined. Where it is believed that it can produce any necessary of life cheaper and better than a Company, it ought to undertake these duties. Every monopoly should be publicly, rather than privately worked. (4) Municipal bodies are quite as good business managers as the directors of a large Company, who as often as not are in the hands of their manager.

Con : (1) Electric lighting is being so largely adopted that it would be unwise for the Municipality to undertake a declining industry; moreover, an interest in Gas would influence a Municipality to check the progress of Electric lighting. (2) Municipal Gas would probably be more expensively produced, less well supplied, and stereotyped in quality. (3) Municipalities have already enough on their hands, and hitherto they have not been free from the suspicion of jobbery. As long as a private monopoly is not abused, there is no reason why it should be disturbed in possession. (4) The business of a large Company is usually well managed, since it is subject to the control and criticism of a body of interested members.

GIBRALTAR : should it be ceded to Spain?

Pro : (1) Gibraltar is of very little use as a harbour, containing no dockyard. In the event of England being at war, the harbour would be open to the fire of the Spanish guns, and no fleet could rest there safely. (2) England has no reason to remain in the Mediterranean; her position there is sufficient to call forth an attack on the part of allied powers, which she would be unable to meet. (3) It would be better to exchange Gibraltar for Minorca; (Some) for the Canary Islands. (4) The possession of Gibraltar brings us the hostility of Spain. (5) In any case, it would be right to give up what we have unjustly taken.

Con: (1) England is already preparing to build a dockyard at Gibraltar. (2) It is essential that England should maintain her command of the sea, to do which she must hold the Mediterranean, and as long as she is there she must have ports, coaling stations, and dockyards, in case of war. (3) Gibraltar may not be as good as Minorca, but since it is an impossibility for us to get that, Gibraltar must be kept. (4) To give up Gibraltar would not bring us the friendship of Spain, who would regard the restitution only as her due, whilst it would lower England's prestige in the eyes of Europe. (5) Gibraltar is a national trophy, secured by the bravery of our soldiers; if we were to give back what we have taken in the past, England would soon be stripped of all her best possessions.

GOTHENBURG SYSTEM: should England adopt it?

Pro: (1) The proposal that Town or County Councils should take over the retail trade in alcohol would involve no confiscation of vested interests, as full compensation would be given. (2) It would not seek to abolish the use, but only the abuse, of alcoholic drinking. (3) It would sell nothing but good liquors. (4) It would reduce intemperance and crime, since the vendors would have no interests in the sale of the drinks. (5) Public-houses would by it become converted into eating-houses. (6) It has proved very successful in Sweden.

Con: (1) Compensation to the publicans would be a ruinous policy, and is unnecessary. (2) It would be wrong for the municipality to in any way be connected with the sale of alcohol. (3) The municipal authorities would be tempted to make up for the enormous outlay which the policy would involve by selling adulterated liquors. There is no evidence that the working-classes would buy drinks of good quality; they ask for quantity, not quality. (4) The municipal authorities would have the same temptation to make profits as the publicans have. (5) If there were not already sufficient eating-houses, others would soon be started. (6) Success in Sweden does not guarantee success in England. Moreover, it still has to be shown that the system has been really successful in Sweden.

GREEK, COMPULSORY, AT THE UNIVERSITIES.

Pro: (1) A knowledge of Greek is indispensable to a well-educated man, and no effort should be spared to spread it. For philological, philosophical, and belletristic purposes it is essential, and no comparative studies of learned subjects can be prosecuted without it. The inadequate stock of Greek acquired by the average passman is no reason why the subject should be abolished as a necessary study, but only an argument that it should be better taught. (2) The effort to acquire it is itself an education, far more valuable than a knowledge of facts, which are often soon forgotten; moreover, the study of Greek is not incompatible with that of other subjects. (3) It is for the Universities to hold up a certain necessary standard of education, not to hunt for popularity. There are plenty of technical colleges and similar institutions where "modern" and scientific education is well cared for; and our old Universities at least should be retained for the highest culture.

Con: (1) Greek, if of value, will hold its own naturally, and compulsion should be unnecessary; the study of it ought not to be forced on those who have no aptitude or inclination for it. Moreover, the vast majority of students remain absolutely unaffected by the beauty of the language. There are many instances showing that Greek is not indispensable to a highly-educated, cultured man. (2) It takes up much time which might be spent more profitably. (3) Many boys at some Public Schools never learn Greek. Are they to be thereby prevented from going to the Universities? The Universities ought to be as catholic as possible.

GROUND VALUES, TAXATION OF.

Pro: (1) The owner, partly by law, partly by agreement, is able to throw the payment of all rates on to the shoulders of the occupier. (2) The would-be tenant very rarely takes rates and taxes into consideration; to him the house is worth so much a year, and as competition has fixed this already high, any amount that the landlord pays in rates will hardly induce him to offer more. The fact that landlords have had to pay Landlord's Property Tax, though levied in the first instance from the tenant, has had no appreciable influence on rent. (3) When many of the existing contracts were made it could not have been foreseen by either party that rates would rise to anything like their present height, so as the circumstances have materially altered since the contracts were signed, Parliament is justified in interfering. (4) Since not only the occupier but all the various interests which come between occupier and ground landlord, including the latter, benefit to a certain degree by even the most ephemeral rates (*e.g.* lighting), and in a greater degree proportionately as the objects for which the rates were raised become of a more permanent nature (*e.g.* paving), each of the various interests should contribute towards rates. (5) Since owners are enabled to draw an enormous profit from the numbers and industry of their fellow-citizens, it is only fair that they should also contribute towards their burdens. (6) The occupier is, under the present system, taxed on the improvements put by him into his landlord's property. (Some) Saving requires no encouragement. (7) Inasmuch as the municipal authorities are bound to pay off within 50 or 60 years all debts contracted for works of permanent value, the greater part of the burden in these cases falls on the occupier, while the landlord receives the ultimate benefit. (8) In consequence of the undue severity with which the present system of raising rates presses on occupiers, there is a strong opposition on their part to any measures of improvement; thus much necessary work has to be put on one side owing to the opposition of ratepayers. (9) The law ought not to allow one class of the community to contract itself out of its responsibilities; even if owners were poor, which as a rule they are not, it would not exonerate them from their civic duties. (10) If any taxation that may be thrown on landlords will fall on tenants, it is not easy to see why the landlords should oppose this tax.

Con: (1) Since the occupier agreed to pay all rates, there is no injustice in his having to pay them. Why should the State be asked to interfere so long as the rates are secured from the property? (2) Rent is generally a matter of keen bargain, and there is no doubt that if the occupier knew that he was going to be free from certain charges, he would be disposed to pay more. (3) Had the rates fallen instead of risen, the tenant would have been the last person to have tendered a higher rental. Parliament should never interfere with the sanctity of contract. (4) It would be absolutely impossible to estimate from the rental, etc., what interest each of the various owners or tenants has in a particular property; even ground-rents are often arbitrarily allotted between areas of the same value, and there are many other considerations in the agreements between the various middlemen and their tenants and sub-tenants. (5) Ground Values are only one out of many forms of investment which have become appreciated; and it would be impossible to get at all other forms of appreciated property. The cost of levying taxes in this manner would also be very heavy, rendering them hardly worth the trouble of collecting. (6) The tenant in the interim has the use not only of the improvements he himself puts into the property, but also of whatever increased value and convenience may accrue. To tax the landlord on his reversionary interest in any public improvement would be to tax capital during the lifetime of its owner—a practice contrary to the first principles of finance, as discouraging the habit of saving, and the accumulation of wealth by the people. (8) The fact that the burdens of taxation fall on occupiers makes them more keen to keep municipal expenditure in check, which curbs undue extravagance. (9) The ground landlord does indirectly pay rates. Ground-rents are largely held by a class of poor people, who would feel any extra taxation very heavily. (10) Such a tax would upset existing contracts, and thus cause great inconvenience and distrust generally; while, in future, contracts would not benefit the tenant at all.

HOSPITALS, NATIONALIZATION OF.

Pro: (1) Over most of our public Hospitals there is neither public control nor responsibility to the public; the Governors, though nominally elected by the subscribers, are practically elected amongst themselves. (2) As these institutions are supported almost entirely by public subscriptions, and as that public is largely interested in their good management, it is most important that full information should be in their hands. (3) The great Hospitals of the Metropolis and other large cities are practically managed by the medical staff. At a meeting of the Hospitals Association, held on 23rd April, 1884, Mr. Timothy Holmes said "the chief use of Hospitals was that they should teach practitioners of medicine and surgery." In an oration at the Mansion House by the President of the Medical Soc. of London (reported in the *Lancet*, 16th June, 1886, p. 1250) it was avowed that "the greatest use of Hospitals is to promote the advancement of medical science." It is dangerous to the community to entrust the whole care and responsibility of the Hospitals to the class which claims that firstly a Hospital should be a place for medical education, and only secondarily for the relief of suffering. (4) The municipalization of Hospitals would allow of their better organization, and abolish the inevitable waste of money and energy engendered by the competition between the various Hospitals, and between these and the infirmaries and dispensaries. Co-operation would enable many improvements to be effected in all departments. (5) Hospitals are now scattered over the Metropolis, without due regard to local needs. (6) The public authorities already very successfully manage a large number of Hospitals. (7) The care of the sick is too important an element to be left to the chance vagaries of charity; and the money spent on the appeals to the public makes the present method costly in the extreme. (8) There seems no reason why under municipalization the doctors should not be as willing as at present to give their services. Supposing this were not so, it would be better to pay them high prices than to allow them to work gratuitously in return for a free hand in experimenting on patients.

Con: (1) The committee on Hospital management, in a Report issued in 1892 came to the conclusion that the Hospitals were on the whole well and economically managed. (2) The public, by means of the Saturday Committee, have very efficient control. (3) It is inevitable that the Hospitals should be under the control of the medical men, and it is only right that this should be so, as they alone have the necessary knowledge. The Governors, however, have very extensive powers to check abuses, and while certain organs of the Press have only been too ready to take up charges against the medical staff, not one of these charges has been proved. (Some) Neither medicine nor surgery has been to any extent advanced by the practice afforded in parish infirmaries, county asylums, or similar institutions; and a free hand must be permitted to doctors if medical science is to progress. (4) The competition between Hospitals promises their efficiency and prevents stagnation. (6) Hospitals being no longer charities, the ratepayers would claim the right to medical treatment, and many who now pay for medical advice and operations would flock to the Hospitals, thus helping towards their cost. (7) Municipalization of the Hospitals would paralyze the charitable motives which at present support them. The expenses of maintenance would soon fall entirely on the rates, and the increased demands on the parish exchequer would be enormous.   (8) Under Municipalization the professional staff would have to be paid, and it would not be possible to secure the co-operation of the best men, unless at such cost as would entail a still further demand on the public purse.

HUSBAND AND WIFE AS WITNESSES.

Pro: (1) Husbands and Wives should be admitted as witnesses for and against each other; the question of credibility rests with Judge or Jury. (2) One or the other is frequently the only person who knows the real facts; and to preclude such evidence is unfair either to the prisoner or to the prosecutor.

Con: (1) Can means must; and this would destroy the sanctity of the marriage tie, and very often lead to perjury.   (2) A Jury would give very little credit to what the Wife said in favour of her Husband, or *vice versâ*, but exaggerate every little admission against the accused.

IMMIGRATION OF DESTITUTE ALIENS, RESTRICTION OF.

Pro: (1) England already has a population too large for her resources. In encouraging emigration while allowing immigration, we get rid of some of our finest specimens of men, only to fill their places with foreigners of an inferior type. The Jews always remain a foreign race, speaking a foreign tongue, and, as a class, though law-abiding, are unscrupulous, and frequently uncleanly.   (2) Every other country has found it necessary to check indiscriminate immigration—even America and our Colonies. At times immigrating foreigners have been refused by the American authorities and sent on here.   (3) The aliens who come have nothing to recommend them, nothing to teach us, except the capacity of working for a minimum wage. Free asylum to all refugees is a fine sentiment, but a Government must make its own people its first consideration.   (4) England could check immigration as easily as America.   (5) There is great danger that wholesale Jewish immigration may some day cause anti-Semitic agitation in England. (6) The statistics as to immigration in the Government reports are most incomplete, and are whittled down in the most arbitrary manner.

Con: (1) The numbers of immigrants have been vastly over-estimated; *e.g.* it has been usual to class as immigrants all those who re-booked at once to America; besides which, many proceed to America after a short stay here. The Jews are a most law-abiding race, and soon assimilate themselves to English habits and language, and become Englishmen in every sense. (2) England has always afforded an asylum for those fleeing from persecution, religious or political.   (3) There has been no displacement of English labour owing to foreign immigration, the sphere of the Jews' influence being perfectly well defined; and it is found that the latter have really established a new trade, viz., the manufacture of ready-made clothes and boots, in which they have enabled London to hold her own against provincial and foreign manufacturers. Moreover, the Jews, though they work for low wages at first, demand the market rate as soon as they have learnt their trade.   (4) It would be very difficult to check the immigration of aliens, inasmuch as many pass through Dover and other ports, where no attempt is made to estimate second-class passengers. Immigration laws can hardly be said to have succeeded in America, if we can judge from the fact that there is always a demand that the law should be made more rigid.   (6) The statistics are most carefully compiled from all available information of the railway companies and others.   (7) Restriction would damage our transport trade, which at present gains enormously from the large numbers of aliens that pass through England to America.

IMMORALITY: should it be a bar to public life?

Pro: (1) The State should do all it can to uphold the sanctity of the marriage tie, and, by debarring delinquents from public office and dignity, it could do much in this direction. (2) A man who has been guilty of gross duplicity is not to be trusted with the conduct of public affairs. (3) Public opinion is, as a whole, strongly in favour of maintaining purity in the private life of public men at all costs; and (Some) men who are known to be impure, even if not convicted in a law court, should be excluded.

Con: (1) The State has already repealed all laws in punishment of breaches of the marriage contract, and any attempt in the way of fresh control would be retrogressive. (2) Some of the greatest statesmen have been men of notoriously immoral (private) lives. The State cannot afford to do without the services of the best men, regardless of their private morality, which has no necessary connection with the conscientious fulfilment of public duties. (3) State interference would tend to exalt the Seventh at the expense of all the other Commandments. It would be dangerous to act on mere hearsay.

IMMORTALITY OF THE INDIVIDUAL.

Pro: (1) The universality of the belief in Immortality amongst nations of all degrees of civilization is evidence for the fact. (2) Our inability to conceive ourselves as ceasing to exist shows that we shall continue to live. (3) A future life is necessary for the redress of the inequalities of this world. Man's powers take such a long time to develop that it would be a great waste if, while they were still in their prime or had not even reached it, they were cut off for ever. (4) The strong desire we feel to be reunited to those we love implies that there must be some foundation for the craving. (5) (Some) The phenomena of Spiritualism and the wide-spread belief, lately revived among us, of the possibility of communicating with the departed, are evidences of Immortality. (*See* PSYCHICAL RESEARCH.) (6) Whatever other theory be true, it is certain that the materialism which asserted that thought was a secretion of the brain is dead; and now eminent men of science can only declare their entire inability to explain how it is possible to pass from matter to thought. It is quite reasonable to hold that thought might under certain circumstances be independent of matter, as thought-transference shows. (7) Our inability to explain how the belief arose, and the utter failure of all hypotheses raised for this purpose by eminent philosophers, point towards the truth of the belief.

Con: (1) The universality of a belief is no argument for its truth, *teste* the once commonly-believed doctrine of the revolution of the sun round the earth. (2) A mysterious *ego*, which survives after the body has disappeared, is an inconceivable hypothesis. (3) It is quite possible that we may have another life in which the evils of this world may be redressed, without being immortal. (4) The fact that we desire a thing is no proof that we shall get it, and in this case, it may be added, we do not all desire the same thing. (*See* IMMORTALITY: ITS VALUE.) (5) The results obtained by Spritualism are of very doubtful value, and *prove* nothing at all. If the existence of a so-called ghost had been proved (which it never has), the value of its evidence would be much discounted when we remember that, according to Spiritualists, ghosts often tell lies, so that it could not give us trustworthy information as to whether it is immortal. (*See* PSYCHICAL RESEARCH.) (6) Science, it is true, has never been able to bridge the chasm between thought and things, but between brain and thought the connection is proved to be very close; and without brain we are unable to conceive of thought any more than we can conceive of sight without an eye. (7) The origin of the belief is perfectly easy to account for on some such theory as Herbert Spencer's dream theory.

IMMORTALITY OF THE INDIVIDUAL: its value.

Pro: (1) It gives a deeper value and meaning to life, since it shows us that life does not end here; that the friendships we have made, the habits we have formed, the knowledge we have gathered, will cling to us, for good or evil, to the end of time. (2) Without belief in a future state, man would have no incentive to live or to act except for selfish motives. Social influence could bear only on his public acts, and not always on these; for society, especially a society without any definite convictions, is apt to be very tolerant, even on matters of social practice. No merely social sanction, moreover, can ever attain anything like the power possessed by trust in the perfect justice of the world, a justice which will reveal itself in a final act of moral retribution. It is also a great source of consolation to think that we shall be reunited to those we love.

Con: (1) Belief in Immortality and Future Retribution tends to draw men's attention away from this world and its duties. Such great teachers as Moses and Buddha ignored it. (2) If men believed that our life here was our only life, they would be much more considerate to those they loved, since there would be no possibility of hereafter atoning for any lack of tenderness here. Is not the desire to be reunited to the dead ones we love based on the impossible wish to have them as they were? Are we quite sure our friends would be the same to us, if, as is said, passions, whether good or bad, have no place in Heaven? What would be the case if passions still retain their force, say, with those who had been married more than once. (3) Is not an immortality such as we get through our children and our children's children sufficient? And is it not an infinitely more important one, involving us in duties far higher than those of merely personal salvation?

IMPERIAL FEDERATION, BRITISH.

Pro: (1) Imperial Federation is a perfectly feasible ideal. It is impossible, indeed unnecessary, to form a cut-and-dried plan at the present moment, as indeed has been the case with all the great Federations. While the general principle was agreed upon, it was not till the last moment, and after much argument and compromize, that the United States, the Dominion of Canada, and the German Empire have been formed. (2) It would bind the Empire together, and make it practically impregnable against any foreign combination. As it is, the Colonies gain enormously from their connection with a world-wide Empire, and are secured against aggression on the part of any other European Power—no unimportant matter, in view of the Colonial activity recently displayed by our continental rivals. None of our Colonies are now independent of European politics. The closer the connection, the greater the advantages derived from it. (3) The fact that the American Colonies broke away from us is no reason why our other Colonies should follow their example; the United States had a stong bond of union among themselves, and cause of hatred to us; they left us in order to escape religious oppression, which was absent in the other Colonies; further, they had no reason to fear any other European Power. (4) Though the Colonies contribute towards Imperial Defence, it is only a very small proportion of the whole cost, thus reducing the Colonies to the condition of paupers on Britain's bounty: this can hardly be otherwise so long as they have no voice in the Imperial expenditure. (5) The Colonies should be enabled to state their opinions on questions of peace and war; at present they might find themselves involved in war without their consent having been asked. (6) Distance is no bar to union in days of steam and electric telegraph; only 100 years ago people prophesied that the American Union was too large and scattered to hold together, yet it has done so in spite even of a gigantic war. (7) The idea of Federation is very popular in most of the Colonies, and, though it is impossible to forecast what precise form it would take, it is certain that questions of Fair Trade, India, etc., would be easy to solve. India need not be worse governed by such an assembly than by the House of Commons. (Some) As the British Empire contains within itself all climates, and grows all kinds of produce, having among other things some of the finest wheat land in the world in Canada, it would be better to encourage trade between the various portions of the Empire by trade tariffs. (8) Federation would be a great help towards maintaining the peace of the world. (9) (Some) The United States might be asked to join such a Union. Indeed, they would be much more likely to join a strong Federation than a weak one (in such a case the word "Imperial" would be omitted). The old indifference of the States to European politics is a theory impossible to maintain in practice—witness their interference in Armenia, and again in Asiatic politics. (10) There is no reason why Imperial Federation should necessitate a written Constitution, as what was necessary could be done by Act of Parliament admitting the Colonies to a share in the Imperial Council. (11) Imperial Federation would not take away from the Colonies any powers which they now possess, but would add to them those from which they are at present cut off, viz., a voice in deciding the foreign affairs of the Empire.

Con: (1) No workable scheme, especially as regards tariffs, has so far been put forward. (2) The great danger to the different sections of the Empire arises from their connection with Great Britain, and similarly Great Britain is endangered by her connection with her Colonies, *e.g.* Canada is quite a possible *casus belli* with the United States. Distant Colonies must always be a source of weakness to a country, which could really help them but little in time of war, whilst they necessitate the maintenance of a very large navy: for our Colonies themselves, there can be little object in a policy which keeps them within range of European complications. (3) The Colonies are practically independent already, and have had sufficient experience, from the manner in which the Colonial Office has mismanaged their affairs, not to wish to return to the yoke again under any such specious forms as Imperial Federation. (4) The Colonies would not pay more for an Imperial Defence from which they derive little benefit, seeing that, whatever it is worth, they now get it for next to nothing. (5) They would have very little control over their representatives, who again might easily be out-voted by other Colonies on a question of vital interest to them. (6) Distances may be comparatively short; but it is not easy to see how countries whose interests are so absolutely divergent could be united. The expense would prevent frequent reference by a representative to his constituents; and whilst posts work quickly, the world moves more quickly still, nor is it easy to consult by telegram. There is no analogy between any known Federation and the British Empire so called. (7) Federation is not really wanted by the majority of our Colonies, which are more and more inclined to independence. In so far as the connection with the Mother Country is favoured at all, it is because it enables the Colonies to borrow British money easily and at low rates—a distinctly demoralizing influence, which corrupts Colonial finance. India could not be excluded from any Federation scheme, nor has any scheme been devised by which she could be represented. (8) Imperial Federation would constitute a standing menace to the peace of the world. (9) America does not want to belong to any world-wide Empire, the idea of Empire being foreign to her spirit. American politicians are not in the least concerned in European politics, and do not want to be so. (10) It would necessitate a written constitution. (*See* CONSTITUTION, A WRITTEN.)

IN CAMERÂ PROCEEDINGS.

Pro: (1) The publication of disgusting details in judicial proceedings is against public policy, as it tends to deprave the young and ignorant. (2) It would materially assist in the detection of crime if the law were to compel certain specified investigations to be held *in camerâ*, as persons would come forward who would not do so otherwise.

Con: (1) Publicity acts as a deterrent, and the respectable Press treats such matters judiciously. Moreover, trial *in camerâ* would not prevent newspaper reports. (*See* DIVORCE, Con 6.) Secrecy is apt to engender a feeling that justice has not been done. (2) Trial *in camerâ* would be likely to lead to blackmailing.

INCOME TAX, A PROGRESSIVE.

Pro: (1) Taxation should be arranged so as to fall most heavily on those who possess the largest available surplus over their immediate wants. While hard to draw a definite line of demarcation between wants that are immediate and wants that are secondary, it may be said generally that only those wants are of prime importance which are shared by all men alike (a sufficiency of food, clothing, and shelter): when secured, other wants successively arise, but they are of secondary importance, the gratification of each further want yielding a diminishing amount of satisfaction. (2) Increased taxation of the richer classes would tend to reduce the number of their servants, and would *pro tanto* be beneficial, since the community in no way benefits by large numbers kept in idleness, or virtual idleness, for mere purposes of ostentation, degrading to both master and man, because creating an entirely false relation between them. (3) By English law, incomes below a certain amount are exempted from the tax, and the principle of a Progressive Income Tax is thus established. (4) As bad legislation in the past, as well as in the present, is largely responsible for the inequalities of fortune which are such a bad feature of modern society, the State should do her best to readjust them by taxing the rich in a higher ratio than the poor. (5) The protection by the State of a rich man's property costs more than its fair proportion, since the owner is in no way able to look after it himself; he should therefore pay at a higher rate for the extra protection he receives. (6) The poor man contributes a much larger proportion of his income in the shape of indirect taxation than the rich man; and the richer a man is, the greater does this disproportion become. (7) The State has a right to raise money in such manner as is least felt by the majority of the people. (8) It is desirable to tax saving rather than consumption, since the over-saving of the rich, accompanied by the under-consumption of the poor, is responsible for the present glut in all markets. (9) It would be possible to raise the tax by levying Income Tax (as done in Prussia) on the lump sum of a man's income, instead of through the sources of income, such as Joint Stock Companies. (10) The State should draw a distinction between incomes which are earned and those which are not earned; taxing the latter proportionately more heavily than the former, if only for the reason that between an income say of £1000 a year from money invested, and £1000 a year from money earned, there is a difference; the latter, depending as it does on the individual, may be cut off at any moment, and consequently a considerable proportion of it has to be set aside every year as a provision for the future, thus reducing its net value; the former represents a net income, which is to all intents and purposes perpetual.

Con: (1) Taxation should be so arranged as to take from every member an amount strictly proportionate to the benefit he receives under the protection of the State, and ought therefore to be arranged in a strictly arithmetical proportion to the income of each man. It is not possible to distinguish between immediate and secondary wants, for they differ widely with different individuals; what to one man is a necessity of life is to another a pure luxury. (2) A Progressive Income Tax would be a great hardship to local shopkeepers, domestic servants, etc., since the first economies effected would be to cut down entertainments and to dismiss servants. (3) The fact that incomes below a certain sum are exempt from taxation is due to a desire on the part of the Legislature to relieve the poor, not to penalize wealth. (4) It is impossible to decide such questions as how most large fortunes have been made. (5) To guard a rich man's property costs proportionately less than a poor man's, since the rich man, though perhaps doing but little personally, has many servants of his own to look after the property. (6) It is impossible to gauge the actual proportion between the respective contributions of the various classes towards indirect taxation; but it is the duty of the State to remedy each inequality on its own merits, though not by creating a fresh inequality in another direction: two wrongs can never make one right. (7) If the State is allowed to throw the whole increased expenditure on the rich, a great check to extravagance on the part of the Government will have been removed. (8) By taxing the rich man at too high a rate, the State would offer a premium to thriftlessness. (9) Under the present system, the Income Tax is to a large extent self-collecting—an important advantage, which would disappear were the tax levied on the whole income instead of on its constituent parts, which latter method would open the door still wider to evasion. (10) No distinction can be drawn between earned and unearned incomes. Such a policy would greatly discourage thrift. Moreover, the State already does as much as can be expected, by exempting from taxation any moneys paid as Insurance premiums.

INCREASED ARMAMENTS, THE DANGER OF.

Pro: (1) Every year witnesses an alarming increase in the sum of money set apart for so-called defensive purposes. Every year the Ministers say that the sum they ask is absolutely necessary to put the Navy in a state of absolute safety against attack, only to show the next year that it has been absolutely inefficient. Under these circumstances, the question is, How are these growing demands to be met or checked, short of national bankruptcy? (2) The policy of expecting our fleet to rival those of any two other powers is folly; apart from the expense, we see its futility in the fact that for every ship we add Russia and France add one too. (3) The sole danger, at any rate the chief danger, that threatens our commerce lies in the arrogant manner in which we ignore the wishes of other powers, and break our most sacred promises (*e.g.* Egypt). (4) At the present rate of naval expenditure bankruptcy is an infinitely greater danger to us than war. (5) While our trade has hardly risen 15 per cent. in twenty-five years, our expenditure for defence purposes has swollen 100 per cent.; in which case it becomes a question how far our commerce is worth defending at such a cost. (6) The maxim that "If you want peace, you must prepare for war," is false. The expenditure requisite for guarding against all possible risks is out of all proportion to the benefit; moreover, every nation, especially a great one, must run some risks. (7) It is inconceivable, when we consider the difficulty of establishing a perfect blockade in one or two harbours for even the biggest fleet in the world, that England, with her harbours scattered all round the coast, should ever be blockaded, or that it should be possible, in these days of swift steaming, for steamers with corn to be unable to run a blockade.

Con: (1) England's fleet must conform to necessity, and in estimating its requisite size we must consider the work it may be called upon to perform. To France and Russia a navy is more or less a luxury; to England it means her very existence. No price is too heavy to pay for national independence. (2) We must either have a decided superiority in ships to enable us to rely on defeating any hostile combination, or we must effect the same end by alliances with those powers whose interests are identical with our own, so that, in the event of any of those interests being threatened, we can rely on the aid of that particular power. But it must be clearly understood that a policy of isolation, while conferring advantages, must be paid for. At present our understanding with Italy enables us to act with the certainty that we shall not be attacked by Russia or France; but some years hence the Italian Navy will have become antiquated, and it is our chance now to make our Navy so strong that we shall be able to overcome any hostile combination which then may be brought against us. (3) The arrogance of England is a myth, invented by the foreign Press. In all recent disputes England, so far from bullying, has shown too great willingness to abandon her undoubted rights. The accusation for greed for territory comes from nowhere with more vehemence than from Germany, who during the past twelve years has added as much, or nearly as much, to her Empire as England in the same period—largely at England's expense. (4) Our commerce means our food. Were it possible to deport a large part of our population, so as to reduce it to such an extent that we could live on home-grown wheat, it might be possible to reduce our navy; but not till then. The Armenian question alone shows how impossible it is to be always on good terms with our neighbours; further, no nation which reserves to itself the right to denounce injustice and persecution, as we denounced the Russian Government for their treatment of the Jews, can afford to be without the means of defending itself against pressure from the government criticised. (6) The argument that "If you want peace, you must prepare for war," is proved true by the every-day experience of us all as individuals. (7) The risks from a blockade are too great for England not to strain every nerve to avert them.

INDEPENDENT LABOUR PARTY v. THE LIBERAL PARTY.

Pro: (1) The economic and social evils of the time call for a bolder and more clearly thought-out programme than is offered by the Liberal Party. The only policy that can suffice is that of the Socialist Party, which, in so far as it is immediately practical, receives the support of the Independent Labour Party, which recognizes, however, that in the main the Socialist programme represents the ideal to be worked for, rather than the immediately practical course. (2) The Liberal Party theoretically welcomes Labour Members, but in practice has always tabooed them, save when they have forced their way into the House of Commons, when it has generally succeeded in "converting" them. (3) The Liberal Party is too much under the control of its richer members to be really free to act effectually on industrial questions. The National Liberal Federation is admittedly non-representative of the Party. (4) Labour Members are required to check the predominance of lawyers and capitalists in the House of Commons. (5) A small and united party with a well-planned programme would be much stronger than one which, being divided on principle as the Liberal Party is, would be unable to form a clear idea of what they stand for. (6) The principles of Liberalism are dead; with a few exceptions, the reforms which the historic party fought for have been achieved. As regards the House of Lords, the Liberals can hardly be called consistent assailants, seeing that they add members of their own party to that House on every possible occasion.

Con: (1) The social evils of our time can only gradually be cured. Violent changes promote only reaction, or, being ill-considered, create fresh evils. The Independent Labour Party is by itself powerless: it can at best only contribute to the success of the Tories. The Socialists offer a programme which, by the violence of the changes it calls for, is opposed to the common-sense of Englishmen. (2) The Liberal Party has encouraged Labour Members; but it has always left individual constituencies free to choose their own candidates. (3) The richer members have no control over the Party (*teste* the Death Duties, and the Party Programme generally) The Party lost ground through attacking vested interests. (4) All classes must be represented, not the Labour classes alone. As a rule, educated men are the best representatives. Successful revolutions have generally been led by members of the classes, acting in the interests of the masses. (5) The Democratic Party must be united if it is to succeed at all. Compromize is inevitable in politics, and the Liberal, like all other Parties, is more or less a compromize, though on matters of minor importance only. (6) Liberalism is not dead. As long as the House of Lords stands it has still much to do; and the present House of Commons shows how little truth there is in the saying that "the Old Toryism is dead."

INDIA: CHILD-MARRIAGES IN, PROHIBITION OF.

Pro: (1) Child-Marriage inflicted great physical harm on small children, since the marriage was generally consummated before the girl had reached the age of puberty. The disparity in ages between man and wife was often enormous, and marriages were not marriages of choice but of arrangement. It also exposed the girl or woman to involuntary lifelong widowhood. (2) By making marriages with children under the age of twelve illegal, Government acted wisely, and were as justified in suppressing the custom as they were in forbidding suttee, human self-immolation at the procession of the Juggernaut Car, and other abominable ceremonies. (3) Although England in 1858 entered into a compact not to disturb native customs, she is justified in abolishing such an evil institution as Child-Marriage.

Con: (1) The evil of Child-Marriages was much exaggerated. The marriage was seldom consummated before the child had reached the age of puberty, and the disparity in the ages of the couple did no more harm than it does in Europe. Considering the position of women in India, parents are much more likely to choose a suitable husband for their daughters than the latter are for themselves, and there are fewer unhappy marriages there than in the West. The wife translated to her husband's home long before the marriage was consummated, grew to love him, and centred all her interests in him. (2) The prohibition has excited much discontent among the Hindu population, and is likely to make English rule still more unpopular than it already is. (3) The English Government solemnly declared in 1858 that she would in no way interfere with any religious ceremonies observed by the natives, and by prohibiting Child-Marriages she has broken her faith.

INDIA: HOME RULE.

Pro: (1) Were India granted a larger measure of self-government, all ill-judged interference on the part of the House of Commons in Indian local affairs would receive its death-blow. (2) Englishmen rarely understand the natives; and those who have never been in India are entirely out of sympathy with them, completely failing to realize the Indian attitude of mind; thus injustice is done more through ignorance than ill-will. (3) (Some) The native Princes would rule their fellow-countrymen better than any English officials, and the Indian Government would at once secure the loyalty of both rajahs and people by such liberal action.

Con: (1) As long as England holds India, India must be subject to the Home Government and to the will of Parliament. Any measure of Home Rule would be the beginning of the end of English rule in India. (2) Except as united under the rule of England, there cannot be said to be an Indian nation. The peoples of India are as distinct as ever they were (witness the recent cow-killing riots); and it is only by our remaining supreme in India that law and order can be maintained. The English Government is the protector of the poor cultivator from the oppression of the zemindars (landowners); and if the rajahs were again given free control, it would be the signal for the revival of all the tyrannous pre-Mutiny acts. (3) The English Government has always availed itself of the services of the rajahs where possible, and it would be absurd to introduce what has never been really demanded.

INDIAN DEFENCE: is Retrenchment possible?

Pro: (1) Russia is not likely to attempt the invasion of India at present, and our best policy is to show to the world that we do not fear such a contingency. (2) By allowing Russia to take Constantinople, which no interest of England prompts us to prevent, provided sufficient care be taken to preserve the independence of the Balkan States, England would secure Russia's friendship in Central Asia. (3) The best defence of India exists in the lofty ranges of mountains and other obstacles that nature has placed in the way of an invading army. (4) A modern army would find invasion a very different matter from what it was to the old invading tribes, whose transport was no difficulty. (5) Previous conquests were possible because the invaders met with virtually no opposition from natives weakened by mutual strife, whereas now they are strong and united. (6) The policy of annexing wild regions pursued during the last few years is very expensive, and, in view of the depleted Indian treasury, reckless, since it necessitates extra taxation on an overtaxed people, directly fomenting discontent. When useful public works are being stopped for want of funds, a very strong case ought to be made out before we undertake fresh expeditions of this sort. (7) We ought to leave the tribes beyond our borders to settle their own disputes; it does not matter to us whether one robber chief is replaced by another or not. (8) It is enough for us to punish acts of depredation without annexing a worthless country, e.g. Chitral. Annexation irritates the tribes, who set a very high value on independence. (9) The natives would be grateful for full independence, and would feel bound to help us against the Russians, knowing that with the supremacy of Britain was bound up their sole chance of independence. (10) Annexation conveys to the natives the impression that we feel our position not to be so strong as that of the Russians; and our only hope of keeping our hold on the Indian people is by making them believe in our strength. (11) Russia is encouraged in her ambitions by our apprehensive attitude. (12) Russia would not have gained much if she had occupied Chitral, nor been much nearer the invasion of India, as any officers would have been shut in during the winter with little to eat, and cut off from all reinforcements. (13) We cannot afford to occupy Chitral as it is, and to carry out the policy of retention would need a very large force there. (14) The Chitral Road makes the approach of Russia infinitely easier; and while we rely on native assistance to keep it open, our policy embitters the natives by reminding them of their loss of independence. (15) The retention of Chitral contravenes the line of policy laid down for us by the great Indian statesmen in the past; though, while details of policy alter, the principles remain true.

Con: (1) Even if Russia is not likely to attempt an invasion of India at present, it is none the less advisable to ignore no steps which put India in a position of still greater safety. (2) If such a step as allowing Russia to take Constantinople were against British interests, we should be very foolish to tolerate it on Russia's bare promise not to cross a certain boundary-line in Asia, a promise already given to us; additional promises would afford no additional security. On the other hand, if it is not our business to prevent her, there is no reason why we should demand futile terms for allowing her to take the step. (3) That the Himalayas are no sufficient barrier to Russia's advance is proved by similar obstacles she has elsewhere overcome. (4) India has always been invaded by way of the mountain passes, and it is futile to say that such an invasion is impossible. Moreover, the Russian soldier carries more than two days' rations, which materially reduces the necessary baggage. (5) The possibility of Indian discontent, culminating simultaneously with a Russian invasion, is always open, and would render our position absolutely untenable. (6) Our security in India is worth almost any sacrifice. Considering all things, India is very lightly taxed;

certain large classes of the population escape all taxation (7) If we do not interfere with the native tribes, they will interfere with us, giving an excuse, by virtue of raids on Russian territory, for a policy of aggression on Russia's part.   (8) Punitive expeditions not followed by annexation cost an enormous sum in the end, since they have to be repeated *ad infinitum*, or until annexation. They irritate the natives, and fail to inspire them with respect for us; annexation establishes the *Pax Britannica*, and secures us the obedience of the natives.   (9) As professional warriors, the border tribes do not settle down to peaceful pursuits, and are equally ready to fight either for or against us; had we left them alone, Russian intrigue would have won them over to her side.   (10) All military authorities agree that we should have to meet an invading force outside India, because, among other reasons, the danger of an Indian rising would be increased tenfold if we waited till the Russians had shown their prowess in subduing the Hill Tribes. (11) Russia knows our weak places as well as we do, and would be greatly encouraged by seeing our officials pursue a policy of "masterly inactivity." (12) Russia might easily have sent to Chitral in the summer a small body of 500 men, who would have spread sedition through the country, and thus done us immense harm.   (13) The policy of retaining Chitral with a small force, just large enough to prevent Russia from occupying it, may be the means of saving India vast expenditure on ousting the Russians, who, in our absence, would be sure to occupy Chitral.   (14) We must have a line of communication with our troops, and the Chitral Road will not be harder to keep open than the Khyber Pass, the inhabitants of which, though infinitely more warlike than the Chitralis, have given no trouble. The futility of relying on the wild nature of the country for extra aid was shown by the late expedition to Chitral, and the ease with which the ground was covered by our troops.   (15) The public policy of a nation can never be conducted on absolute principles holding good for all time, but must be modified to meet the requirements of each age.

INDIVIDUALISM.

Pro: (1) Government exists for the sole purpose of defending the lives and the property of citizens; all other duties (*e.g.* the control of education, of the Post Office, etc.) should be left to the initiative of individuals, since the fewer duties a State undertakes the better she fulfils them. By their very nature, Government offices and State undertakings, even in the simplest matters, are never so well or so economically managed as, and are more governed by routine and red tape than, a private business run for profit. (2) As Government has to rely on taxation, the more duties it undertakes the more heavily do they weigh on the taxpayer, thus depressing industry whilst restricting the field of private enterprize. Whereas the capitalist pays for his own mistakes, the Government official throws the costs on taxation.   (3) Where the Government (*e.g.* in the Post Office) works an institution for profit, it lays an indirect tax on industry, raising money by illegitimate means.   (4) History is one standing protest against the folly of over-legislation, undertaken with the most excellent motives, as most of such legislation was. The best legislative work of this century is that which has freed us from the legislative enactments of previous centuries. (5) The more we increase the number of indictable offences, the more (to a large extent unnecessary) criminals we create, and the more blackmailing and corruption we render possible. It is easy to pass Factory Acts, but useless unless they are carried out; and it is notorious that, though possibly direct corruption may not exist in the case of Inspectors, indirect corruption probably does.   (6) The more Government undertakes, the more it checks that wholesome spirit of self-help which has already carried the English-speaking races to the foremost position in the world. Our Colonial Empire has been entirely won for us by the energy of individuals, in despite of the blunders of various Governments. (7) Government interference tends to preserve the less fit members of society against the workings of natural selection, and thus to lower the general standard of society. (8) The rule of the majority will not be any better than that of the king or of the aristocracy.

Con: (1) Private enterprize may be preferable to an over-centralized State department, yet the case is different if, by a judicious system of decentralization, we substitute for the central body a local authority anxious to maintain its credit against that of its neighbours. In this case it is more probable that public control could be wisely exercized over many things which are still left in the hands of private enterprize, especially when by private enterprize we mean public companies managed by salaried officials. In all branches of trade which are of the nature of a monopoly (such as the gas supply in big towns), competition has proved an impossible policy, sometimes defeating itself by the companies coming to mutual understandings. (2) The return to the individuals in the shape of increased protection against disease, avoidable accidents to the person and danger to property, is out of all proportion to the increase in the rates and taxes, which in their turn have not grown proportionately to the increase in the wealth of the country. (3) The State must raise money in the manner that causes least inconvenience to her subjects. (4) All the errors made by the State are noted, whilst those of private enterprize are never heard of. (5) It would be quite easy to protect society against the corruption of officials. When once a measure has become law, it is for the individual to obey it; society cannot delay useful legislation because a few men may break the law. (6) Good legislation may be an addition to the freedom of the subject rather than the reverse, and by freeing men from tyranny of other kinds increase their capacity for self-help. (7) There is no reason why society should not adopt some beneficent measure of artificial selection, instead of following the crude workings of natural selection; natural selection among men, in the absence of government, would not lead to the survival of the fittest, but to that of the strongest or most cunning. (8) Democracy is an expression of that larger life through which alone each citizen becomes conscious of himself as an individual, and which secures him his rights as such. At any rate, if oppression exist, "every man is his own oppressor." (J. R. Lowell.)

INFALLIBILITY, PAPAL.

The General Council of the Vatican (1870) claims Infallibility for the Roman Pontiff for the time being, not merely for the line of Pontiffs. It does not assert that he is free from sin, nor that his conduct is always prudent: but only that he is free from error when teaching ex cathedrâ. Four conditions must be fulfilled by the Pontiff: (1) he must teach as Pope, not in his private capacity; (2) on faith or morals (only); (3) with the intention of settling a controversy, not merely of giving advice or instruction; (4) intending to address the whole Church, although in form he may speak to one only.

Pro: (1) The doctrine is implied in the terms of reconciliation arranged between the Eastern and the Western Churches, under Pope Hormisdas (A.D. 520), at the Second Council of Lyons (1274), and at the Council of Florence (1439); in other words, it has been accepted by the whole Church. (2) The Scriptural basis of the doctrine is found in the texts where St. Peter is made the Rock on which the Church is built (Matt. xvi. 18); that where he is bidden confirm his brethren (Luke xxii. 32); and that where he is charged to feed the sheep and lambs of Christ (John xxi. 15-17). If Peter taught falsehood, the Rock would be shaken, the brethren misled, and the sheep poisoned. (3) Christ, in conferring these prerogatives on St. Peter, did not intend that they should cease with the death of that Apostle, but that they should form an essential constitution of all time; and, if this be granted, they certainly reside nowhere but in the Roman See, for no claim is made to them elsewhere. (4) Popes Zosimus, Boniface, St. Leo the Great, and others claimed the prerogative, and no outcry was made against the claim as a novelty. Rome was constantly consulted on disputed points of doctrine, even when the Pontiff was not a man of personal weight; communion with Rome was the test of orthodoxy; the voice of Rome was regarded as the voice of the Church; and Rome was the supreme judge of heresies. (5) While in form and wording the doctrine may be called novel and non-scriptural, it is not true that it is so in substance. Reason has been given showing it to be old and scriptural; the same objection was raised when the Council of Nicæa (325) put forth the creed containing the word Consubstantial; but almost all Christians admit that the Council was right. (6) Though many writers who might have been expected to refer to the doctrine do not do so, neither do they refer to Councils which they undoubtedly recognized. (7) The doctrine is not based on the forged decretals; rather the decretals were the outcome of the wide-spread belief of the Church at the time in the doctrine; the doctrine is, as a matter of fact, far older than they are, while St. Thomas Aquinas, for instance, expressly bases his belief in the doctrine on the texts of Scripture, not on the evidence afforded by the forged documents. (8) The Infallibility of the Pope does not render General Councils of the Church unnecessary; for the moral weight of the authority of the collected episcopate facilitates the arrangement of business of all kinds; when Councils examined Papal letters on dogmatic subjects, they did so that the bishops might be able individually to testify that the doctrine of the letter was in agreement with the tradition of the Church throughout the world. (9) It is untrue that any of the Popes have taught error *ex cathedrâ*; *e.g.* Pope Honorius was condemned, not for teaching heresy, but for want of vigour in repressing it; moreover, the letter on which his condemnation was based does not contain any heretical definition intended to bind the whole Church, and therefore was not *ex cathedrâ*. In the same way all the other alleged cases of heresy taught *ex cathedrâ* on the part of Popes break down on examination.

Con : (1) There is no evidence that the doctrine of Papal Infallibility was heard of during the 1300 years after the foundation of the Church. (2) St. Peter received no privileges which were not equally bestowed on the other Apostles collectively (John xx. 21–23); and so far from being one whose lead was acknowledged in any way (Luke xxii. 31–32), he was the one of whom it was foretold that he would deny his Lord; and he is bidden, when this necessary repentance has taken place, to support by his newly-revived zeal his yet unfallen brethren, lest they should sin as he had sinned. To fortify them by a confession of his own weakness is not akin to exercizing authority over them. The exclusive claims on behalf of St. Peter are not compatible with John xxi. 20–22. (3) No word is said by Christ to indicate any special privileges to the *successors* of St. Peter, even if they belonged to St. Peter himself. (4) The fact that Bishops and Patriarchs consulted the Pope does not prove him to have been considered infallible by them. (5) The doctrine can be found in no part of the Bible, nor can it be proved that St. Peter ever held the See of Rome. (7) If the false decretals were superfluous, why was it thought necessary to write them, and attribute them to an earlier period? (8) If the Pope obtains Divine Assistance to decide on questions of faith and morals, that is all that is necessary. A General Council is surely not needed to lend moral weight to one who is Divinely guided. (9) The Sixth Œcumenical Council (680) condemned and excommunicated Pope Honorius (625–638) "as a heretic monothelite, who, with the aid of the old Serpent, had scattered deadly error." This anathema was solemnly repeated by the Seventh and Eighth Councils, and even by the Popes themselves, who, down to the 11th century, in a solemn oath at their accession, endorsed the Sixth Œcumenical Council, and pronounced "an eternal anathema" on the authors of the monothelite heresy, together with Pope Honorius, "because he had given aid and comfort to the perverse doctrines of the heretics." The three Councils which condemned Honorius had the approval of the Popes Agatho and Hadrian I. and II.

themselves. The latter, which was written by him as Pope, in reply to a request from the patriarch Sergius that he would sum up a controversy, ends up, "These things your fraternity will preach with us, as we preach them in unanimity with you." Either the Pope was wrong on a point where the Divine Assistance might have been expected to direct him, or the Councils and the succeeding Popes were wrong in condemning him for promulgating heresy.

INSURANCE OF CHILDREN.

Pro: (1) If the Insurance of Adults is desirable, why not that of Children? (2) The danger of child-murder, for the sake of obtaining Insurance moneys, is greatly reduced by the fact that Insurance Companies always make the strictest investigations, which acts as a deterrent to possible murderers. (3) Statistics do not warrant the conclusion that Child-Insurance often leads to child-murder. In any case, however, statistics might be expected to show a fairly high ratio of deaths among insured children, owing to the fact that it would be chiefly weakly children who would be insured. (4) Child-Insurance encourages thrift amongst the poor. It at any rate enables them to give their children a decent burial, instead of relying on the parish.

Con: (1) If the Insurance of Children were as little dangerous as that of adults, nothing could be urged against it. (2) The inducement to child-murder for the sake of obtaining Insurance money is much greater in the case of children than of adults, who can protect themselves. It would be small comfort to know that a criminal parent did not receive the Insurance money. Deterrents from crime are of course desirable, but it is better still to eliminate all possibility of inducement. (3) Statistics show that Child-Insurance frequently leads to child-murder. (4) The burial of deceased children can be as well provided for by a Burial Club as by Insurance.

INTER-IMPERIAL COMMUNICATION.

Pro: (1) Great Britain ought to contribute to the establishment of a line of steamers uniting her with Canada; these would join the Canadian and Pacific Railway, and complete the communication with the existing line of steamers connecting Canada with India, Australia, and other British colonies. She ought also to contribute towards establishing telegraphic communication on the same lines, including even the African colonies. She would thus have communication with the colonies which would not be open to the world, and which would not be liable to interruption in time of war. The line of communication would not be dependent on the railway through Maine, U.S.A., since the latter is only one of three alternate routes, the other two of which pass completely through Canadian soil. (2) It would be much the quickest and shortest route by which to despatch soldiers to India, etc., and would be less liable to interruption than a route passing through Suez. By the use of snow-sheds, the Canadian Pacific Railway has been kept almost entirely free from obstruction. American interference would not be likely to be attempted, as it would not only be unjustifiable, but also a breach of the peace. (3) The Canadian and Pacific Railway has opened out a most fertile tract of country; and, though it has not yet paid, it is likely to be well worth its cost, owing to the extra security it gives to the country.

Con: (1) The Canadian and Pacific Railway is open to great interruption at certain periods of the year, while steamers between England and Canada would be in constant danger from icebergs; and the line of telegraphic communication would always be open to interruption from the United States. Moreover, the railway at one part actually passes through Maine, U.S.A. (2) It is not the quickest route to India, or, rather, that part of India where troops would be required in case of an invasion; and it would always be liable to interruption. The Americans have announced that they will not allow it to be used for this purpose. (3) The Canadian and Pacific Railway has been a most ruinous speculation; and, owing to the large tracts of desert through which it passes, is not likely ever to be remunerative.

INTERNATIONALISM.

Pro: (1) Every day makes it more apparent that the struggle of the future will be between classes and not between nations. (2) All the nations of Western Europe have the same industrial problems to face. A great deal may be expected from International Miners' Congresses and others of a cosmopolitan character. (3) The means of communication, the telegraph, the press, and commerce, all tend to bring nations closer together.

Con: (1) National rivalries become more and more accentuated; they do not diminish in vigour. (2) Though each country has more or less similar problems to solve, each has its own way of looking at them. At the Miners' Congress the various delegates voted largely by nations. (3) Internationalism is utterly unpractical, and will probably remain so for many years to come, inasmuch as the States are at very different stages of development, and each nation has a large stock of traditions, which it will take a long time to uproot.

INTERNATIONAL MONEY.

Pro: (1) International money would facilitate the important work of the statistician. (2) It would enormously facilitate trade. In many places the value of the national money is not certainly known, and it is only those with special knowledge who can venture to trade with such countries. (3) It would expedite exchange, and render unnecessary the melting of coin into bullion for exchange purposes. It would be more convenient for tourists, and increase their number, and would exterminate the crowd of bullion-dealers, etc., who live by the difficulties of interchange. (4) If based on a Decimal System, it would involve no difficulties to the less educated. (*See* DECIMAL NOTATION.) (5) The standard of coins could be settled by international agreement. Any Power not adopting this system could easily be dealt with by the other Powers, by refusing to recognize its coinage as equal payment.

Con: (1) The statistician has to suit his methods to his facts. (2) Trade would be greatly disturbed and considerable expense incurred by a new system, for which there is very little need. (3) No travellers would stay at home on account of the trivial difficulties attaching to ignorance of foreign money systems. (4) The Decimal System is not needed. (*See* DECIMAL NOTATION.) (5) It would be difficult to ensure that all Governments should coin up to the required standard, and, following Gresham's law, any such inferior coins would work good coin out of circulation. (6) In the present state of national feeling on the Continent, European States would not change their present money systems.

INTESTACY, ABOLITION OF THE LAW OF.

Pro: (1) It is unjust that the law, making a distinction between real and personal property, should leave the real property to the eldest son exclusively, whilst the personal property is equally divided amongst the children. (2) Where there is a large personal estate, no great hardship is done; but where the estate consists mainly or wholly of real property, great injustice ensues, as the younger children are thereby made dependent on the eldest son. It is the duty of the law to seek to interpret the wishes of an intestate, and it ought to assume that it is unnatural for a man to desire so unequal a provision of his property.

Con: (1) Much inconvenience, and, in many cases, great pecuniary loss to an estate would occur if the Court of Chancery were to order the division of real estate. The law now protects the best interests of the family *qua* family. (2) If the father had made a will, he would probably have bequeathed the real property to his eldest son, in order to ensure the continuance of the family. Scarcely anyone having real property dies in ignorance of the law.

IRELAND:
ABOLITION OF THE LORD LIEUTENANCY.

Pro: (1) The Lord Lieutenancy directly encourages the idea of Irish nationality as distinct from British. (2) The abolition of the post would largely contribute towards uniting the two peoples. (3) The appointment is viewed with great dislike by the majority of Irish, who regard it as a symbol of oppression, and would rejoice to see Dublin Castle and its associations abolished.

Con: (1) The Lord Lieutenancy maintains English predominance; (Some) It is desirable to retain it as a memorial of Irish nationality. (2) Its abolition would do nothing towards reconciling the mass of the people to English rule, and would be a great loss to trade in Dublin, since the more wealthy part of Irish society would gravitate to London, depriving Dublin of what little life it still possesses. (3) Many Lord Lieutenants have been Irishmen, and some have been very popular.

IRELAND: HOME RULE.

To keep the main question as clear as possible, the pros and cons as to the continued presence of the Irish members in the Imperial Parliament are given elsewhere. The question here dealt with is the advisability of establishing in Dublin an Irish Parliament, to manage purely local affairs on the lines laid down in the Home Rule Bill, 1893.

Pro: (1) The failure of the policy of the union is proved, since after more than 100 years of trial the union remains merely a "paper union" By keeping up a Lord Lieutenant, etc., in Dublin, and by legislating separately for Ireland, England has many times acknowledged the Irish nationality. (2) Ireland has been estranged from England by many years of misgovernment and injustice: her commerce was ruined in the interests of English manufacturers, her religion was trampled on, and she was treated as a conquered nation. (3) Even Grattan's Parliament, little as it represented the Irish nation, passed many good measures, and the Act of Union was passed only by barefaced jobbery. (4) The British Parliament has always ignored the Irish Question, till forced by the discontent of the Irish people to take some sort of action, when its invariable idea has been coercion on the one hand, or bribery in the shape of Land Acts, etc., on the other. Thus, all the so-called remedial legislation having been forced out of the English Parliament, Ireland has come to see that the only way to get her wrongs righted is to show England that her weakness is Ireland's opportunity. (5) Ireland is now a source of weakness to England, as the number of troops required draws heavily on our resources in time of peace, to say nothing of war; whereas a happy and contented Ireland would be a great source of strength. (6) Ireland can be conciliated only by Home Rule; mere Local Government without Home Rule would only give greater opportunity for the expression of the demand without the power of satisfying it. (7) (Some) The delegation of local business to Local Parliaments would relieve the Imperial Parliament, and give her time to attend to matters more properly within her sphere. (8) It is improbable that Ulster men will carry out their threats of forcible resistance to the Home Rule Bill, any more than they carried out the same threats in respect of the Disestablishment of the Irish Church. (9) When once Home Rule is granted, the National Party, having no longer a common aim, would probably break up into sections, and, so far from the Catholics persecuting the Protestants, the Protestants would be the stronger party. The antagonism would, however, not be between Protestants and Catholics (the return of votes in Belfast has shown that Protestants have already voted for Catholics)—the struggle would be changed from the religious to the industrial sphere. Home Rule, so far from meaning Rome Rule, would perhaps bring about an anti-clerical movement: ecclesiastical tyranny and political freedom are incompatible, as evidenced by the whole course of history. The Nationalist movement was not initially a Catholic movement; it was led by a Protestant, and arose in spite of the opposition of many Irish Bishops; the priests, in fact, have derived their power only by identifying themselves with National aspirations. (10) Where possible people should be allowed to rule themselves. A capacity for self-government is acquired only in the exercise of responsibility. It is not fair to charge against the movement crimes committed while the people were smarting under injustice. Responsibility is an essential condition of moral development. (11) The same power that created the Parliament could always recall it; and this consideration alone would moderate any tendency to excess. (12) Home Rule would not involve Separation, since all Foreign Affairs and Imperial matters would be beyond Irish jurisdiction. It would, on the contrary, be a first step towards Imperial Federation, one of the cardinal principles of which is the management by each member of the Federation of its own private affairs. (*See* FEDERALISM; IMPERIAL FEDERATION.) (13) The Federal principle has succeeded in Canada and in European countries (Austria-Hungary, Norway, Sweden, etc.); in cases where a legitimate demand of the kind has been refused (*e.g.* Holland's refusal of Home Rule to Belgium) it has resulted in absolute Separation. England has already granted the same or fuller powers to her Colonies, and has always sympathized with such demands (*e.g.* the Poles). (14) The English Colonies largely sympathize with Irish Home Rule; is it wise to ignore the opinions of a great part of the English race, especially when we wish to bind them more closely to us?

Con: (1) The policy of the Act of Union has been a success. There are two Irish nations; one of which (and that the more prosperous, if not the more numerous) detests the idea of separation from England, and dreads the rule of the numerical majority, which is their enemy as well as England's. (2) England has long since atoned for any injustice she may have done to Ireland. (3) Bad as was England's treatment of Ireland, it never equalled the severity of the Coercion Bills passed by an Irish Parliament. (4) Even if the Houses of Parliament have neglected Ireland in the past, and yielded only when forced to do so, all this is changed, and the Imperial Parliament has spent the greater part of many Sessions in the consideration of measures relating to Ireland. (5) The fact that Parliament has made mistakes in governing Ireland is no argument for abandoning the work. Where law and order are habitually set at defiance, they must be maintained at all costs, whether by "coercion" so-called or otherwise. The fact that England has weakly yielded to Irish disaffection before, is a strong reason why she should not do so again. (6) There is no reason to think that anything short of absolute Separation would satisfy the moving spirits in the Home Rule Movement—the Irish Americans. In the event of war, an Irish Parliament would afford a centre for Irish discontent. (7) Ulstermen strongly object to the Bill, and would regard it as a cruel desertion on the part of England. Property and Trade in Ireland are opposed to it. (8) The Nationalist party would not be contented with any Home Rule short of Separation; and so long as they are not contented, they will not break up into other parties. Except in Belfast, there are no materials for a struggle between Capital and Labour. Judging by the fate of Mr. Parnell, no anti-clerical movement would be very successful in Ireland. The Nationalist movement has always been backed by a powerful party among the Irish Priests. (9) The Irish have never shown any capacity for Home Rule, nor have their leaders been men who could be trusted with any sort of responsibility. (10) The gift could be recalled only by force of arms, and at the cost of great bloodshed.

It would mean the reconquest of Ireland. (**11**) It would materially weaken the Union, besides making it illogical not to give the same power to England, to Scotland, and to Wales. Imperial Federation is essentially different from Irish Home Rule, since it is meant to bind tighter the bond that has got loose, rather than loosen one that is still tight. (**12**) Federal Government has been a success in Austria only because of the direct influence of the Crown; in Norway and Sweden there is constant tension, and it caused a gigantic war in the United States. As regards England, the present system ensures local questions being discussed apart from local jealousies. (**13**) The Colonies would strongly object to any expression of opinion by the English Parliament on purely Colonial matters; and it is not easy to see why England should pay attention to their opinion on what is, after all, a matter of Home politics. The opinion of Colonial politicians is based upon a desire to pander to the Irish vote.

IRELAND: is she overtaxed?

Pro: (**1**) The Royal Commission appointed to examine into the financial relations decided, with but one dissentient voice, that Ireland now pays more than her fair share of taxation. Amongst the men who agreed to this were eminent financiers (**2**) Irishmen of all parties, including prominent Unionists, agree that the Government ought to remedy this injustice. (**3**) Ireland was recognized as a separate taxable entity in the Act of Union, and the proportion of her contribution fixed. So high was it that Ireland under the greatest pressure could never pay it. (**4**) The estimates as to the relative wealth and taxable capacity were made by very able financiers after long inquiry. (**5**) Indirect taxation, when imposed on an article which one section of the people use more than another, is always unjust. Whatever may be said of whiskey, there is no reason why the tax on tea, coffee, tobacco, etc., should not be reduced for Ireland. (**6**) The amount spent on Irish government is excessive, and might well be reduced to the great advantage of Ireland. In proportion to her poverty, she spends more on her government than any other small country, except Portugal. Ireland, moreover, has nothing to do with this expenditure, which is ordered by the Imperial Parliament. (Some) Ireland gets no equivalent as a purely agricultural country from the Imperial expenditure on the army, navy, etc., the benefit of which goes to England. (**7**) The taxes which Ireland does not pay and England does, are insignificant. (**8**) England might make a grant to Ireland for a certain number of years to enable her to develop her resources, and to atone for past injustice and over-taxation.

Con: (**1**) All the Commissioners were Irishmen or Home Rulers, excepting one, and he found that no grievance had been established. In matters of detail the malcontents differed greatly. (**2**) The Government cannot sacrifice England and Scotland even to please a temporary coalition of all the Irish Parties. (**3**) If Ireland be recognized as a separate taxable entity, why not Scotland, Wales, or the agricultural counties of England? Man for man, the people of Ireland pay no more than the English. The aim of the Union was to gradually unite the two systems. (**4**) The estimates as to the relative wealth of the two countries, largely based as they are on observations of untrained officials, are too untrustworthy for an estimate as to the taxable capacities of the two countries to be based on them. (**5**) The tax on whiskey, which forms a special part of the grievance, was imposed on moral rather than financial grounds. To exempt tea, etc., from taxation in Ireland would involve setting up an Irish custom-house, with all its hindrances to trade. The Irish suffer no more than poor people in England suffer from indirect taxation, which always falls somewhat more heavily on the poor, and forms a set-off to the Income Tax, from which they are exempt. People can always reduce their contribution to indirect taxation by drinking less whiskey, etc. (**6**) An Independent Ireland would, judging from the other small countries in Europe, probably spend as much. In any case she must pay for defence, and, as a separate nation, this would be much more costly than her contribution to the British fleet. An Independent Ireland would, moreover, always have a powerful neighbour to guard against. (7) Englishmen and Scotchmen pay taxes which the Irish do not pay; these alone in England amount to about £4,000,000 yearly. (8) Grants do more harm than good.

IRISH LAND ACTS.

Pro: (1) The State is justified in breaking through contracts made under circumstances which it deems to be unjust; especially in the case of Land, of which the State has always retained a theoretic ownership. (2) The Irish Land Question presented many points which justified exceptional treatment for Ireland; among other things, Ireland, unlike England, had no large manufacturing centres which drew the mass of the people off the land; but, on the contrary, the large population on the limited soil made the competition for land very keen, and the ignorance of the people enabled the landlord to exact his own terms, which were often very exorbitant. Free Trade in Irish land, in so far as it was inaugurated by the Sale of Encumbered Estates Act, was a failure, as Ireland was not advanced enough for it, and the new landlords who bought land at the time had all the vices and none of the virtues of the old landlords. (3) The Land Question is at the root of Irish discontent; hence it was sound policy, while putting down lawlessness, to remove the chief cause that led to it.

Con: (1) The State should do all it can to uphold the idea of the sacredness of contract and the rights of property. (2) It would have been better if, instead of pampering the Irish tenant and teaching him to look to the State for a solution of his difficulties, Government had encouraged him to effect his own salvation. The sale of encumbered estates effected all that was wanted to get clear of thriftless owners, or, at least, was a step in that direction, its purpose being to free the sale of land from undue fetters, and to make it negotiable as Consols. (3) The legislation passed under the influence of panic has necessitated numerous Acts attempting to set it right, which have, however, only made matters more involved.

IRISH MEMBERS: their exclusion from Imperial Parliament.

Pro: (1) The supremacy of the Imperial Parliament could be amply maintained by restriction placed on the Irish Parliament. (2) The sum paid by the Irish to the Imperial Exchequer would be fixed, and could be altered only by the consent of the Irish. (3) Their presence would be unfair to the other countries of the Union, especially England; and, if they were allowed to be occasionally present, it would destroy Parliamentary Government; the Government would one day be in a minority and the next in a majority, accordingly as the Irish members were present or not. (4) The Irish do not want representation in the Imperial Parliament.

Con: (1) The exclusion of Irish members would be tantamount to Separation. (2) Exclusion would be taxation without representation. (3) (Some) Irish members might be allowed to vote in the Imperial Parliament when matters concerning Ireland alone were under discussion. (4) Ireland is an integral part of the Empire; exclusion from Parliament would reduce her to the position of merely a tributary province. By narrowing her interests it would retard the political and moral development of the country.

IRISH MINISTRY OF AGRICULTURE, THE NEED FOR.

Pro: (1) A Joint Committee, comprising Irishmen of all shades of political opinion, after considering what measures could be taken on non-controversial lines to improve the condition of Ireland, came unanimously to the conclusion that in order to stimulate the development of the latent industrial resources of the country, to organize the forces, and spread knowledge of all kinds, a special Department should be created, presided over by a Minister responsible to Parliament. Great as has been the boon from the existing agencies (Fisheries Board, Congested Districts Board, etc.), what is wanted is to organize these various agencies, and carry still further the work they have begun. (2) It is not intended that the new Department shall in any way supplant private enterprise, but that it shall stimulate it. The experience of Europe (France, Germany, etc.) proves the immense boon the State can confer on agriculture and industry generally by the spread of knowledge of markets, of technical information, by supervising transport, aiding in the formation of people's banks, etc. In this way Würtemburg, from being a poor State, has become prosperous. (3) The conditions of Ireland are totally different from those of England. History shows us that the trade of Ireland was deliberately killed by England, whose manufacturers, at the close of last century, feared the possible competition of Ireland. Ireland has thus scarcely any industry save agriculture, and her population, being dependent on this, has suffered enormously from the repeal of the Corn Laws. It is only just that England should attempt to recompense Ireland for this injury. (The Northern industries never competed with the English, and consequently escaped destruction.) (4) The Chief Secretary is already overwhelmed with duties of all kinds, and his work would be more efficiently done were a special Department created to relieve him of the more specifically economic duties. (5) That the proposed Minister would change with every change of Ministry would be no evil, provided he had a strong permanent Secretary. The Department should be kept in touch with the farmers, etc., by means of an Agricultural Council meeting twice a year at least, elected by those concerned, at which meetings the Minister should be bound to attend. The India Council is non-elective, and not to the point.

Con: (1) No fresh Department created by Dublin Castle will be able to do anything for the amelioration of Ireland unless the Land Question is boldly attacked. The abolition of Castle government—not an extension of it, but the substitution of a local and representative government—is required, in order that the real grievances of Ireland may be removed. The great majority of the Irish Parliamentary Party were unrepresented on the Committee, which had no authority to speak for the Irish Nation. (2) Government Departments only cramp industry and impose fresh taxation. Private enterprise will, in Ireland as in England, prove finally the only mode of resuscitating Irish industries. (3) England has long ago made up to Ireland for any wrong she may have inflicted on her. The lack of industry is due to the sloth and improvidence of the Irish people; if not, why has the North of Ireland always flourished? (4) The Chief Secretary's Department is quite competent to undertake all the necessary work. (5) Ministers are in power too short a time to learn their business. Permanent Secretaries get hide-bound and out of touch with the people, whilst Councils are rarely listened to, *e.g.* the Indian Council in London is habitually ignored by the Secretary of State.

JOURNALISM: are signed articles desirable?

Pro: (1) With Signed Articles responsibility is transferred from the journal itself to the contributors personally, and the public is thus enabled to estimate at their true value the opinions expressed, discounting, if necessary, any known idiosyncrasies of writers. The abuse of the editorial "we" is notorious, a fictitious value being attached to it by the general public. (2) In the case of literary, scientific, and technical journals, articles, to be of any value, must be signed, since this renders "log-rolling" nugatory. (3)

Anonymity deprives the writer of all responsibility, and occasionally leads to political dishonesty, the same journalist contributing leading articles to papers of opposite political views. (4) Leading articles, if of joint composition, ought to be signed by all those co-operating.

Con: (1) Anonymity in journalism has the great advantage that the journal itself is responsible for its contents, enabling its editor to maintain a uniform standpoint and policy, expressing the views of a great party (political or religious), instead of merely bringing together a mass of heterogeneous opinion: for such a purpose an editorial "we" is infinitely stronger than any number of isolated "I's," even though indicating unanimity of views. (2) Anonymity enables critics to fearlessly express their real convictions, and excludes mutual recrimination, such as disgraces the French press. (3) The writers are almost always known; and this is a safeguard against irresponsibility. (4) Leading articles (which are sometimes the production of several writers) could not be signed.

JURY SYSTEM, THE.

Pro: (1) A man has a right to be tried by his peers, and twelve ordinary men are more likely to arrive at the truth than a single Judge, however capable. (2) The system has always worked well; and time-honoured institutions, more especially where originally established to prevent flagrant abuses, should not be abolished without sufficient reason. (3) A Jury is often better able to form a correct opinion as to facts connected with the daily life of the working classes than a Judge, who has only an academic knowledge. The Jury are likely to be freer from prejudices, and less hasty. (4) The process of explaining a case fully to a Jury often elucidates facts which would otherwise be overlooked. Knowledge is rarely complete until it has been clearly expressed.

Con: (1) An innocent man would, in nine cases out of ten, prefer to be tried by a Judge, rather than by a Jury, as he would be appealing to a higher order of intelligence. (Some) Juries are at the mercy of the Judges, and hence useless. (2) The system has not worked well recently. As a rule, one Juryman dominates the other eleven, and himself becomes practically the Judge; and many guilty persons have escaped punishment through fear of responsibility in the Jury, or by one obstinate Juryman. (3) A Jury is apt to be prejudiced, especially if the person tried is known to any of its members. They are liable to be influenced by public opinion, which is often wrong. (4) Appeals to the emotions very frequently influence a Jury, whilst a Judge simply weighs facts and administers law.

KINDERGARTEN SYSTEM, THE.

Pro: (1) A child's training should begin in the cradle, the aim of true education being to develop a child with the same scientific care as is employed for, say, a choice plant, its individualities being duly respected and considered. Note should be taken of the love of play and movement inborn in every healthy child, and these natural tendencies should be woven into the training it is to receive. (2) A child bears a "threefold relationship—to Nature, animate and inanimate; to Man; and to God"; and all claim equal attention at the teachers' hands. To attain due development, the child must first be brought into actual contact with nature (by gardening, tending animals, etc.). Through its love for dumb pets and plants, the child will grasp its duties to its fellow-men; and finally its religious feelings will be aroused by noticing the workings of God in and towards them. (3) Special attention should be given to the development of the senses, attainment of manual deftness being practically sought. (4) To carry out these principles many "Occupations" and six "Gifts" have been devised —all designed to give training and instruction; whilst affording pleasure to tiny pupils. "Action-songs" and gymnastic exercises are also introduced into the games, as also story-telling. No lesson lasts longer than from ten to twenty minutes. (5) Companionship is essential to children, and a great aid to the teacher.

Con: (1) The years usually spent by children in a Kindergarten (from 3 to 7) would be better spent at home, untrammelled by any set lessons. Herded together with others, a child's individuality cannot be so much respected as in a well-managed nursery. If, however, the child must be sent to school at three, it is better off in a Kindergarten than in an ordinary infant school. (2) Unless conducted by exceptionally gifted teachers, the Kindergarten system is so elaborate that it fails in its aims, deteriorating into mere play: exceptionally gifted teachers are rare under any system. (3) Too much attention is given to mere manual dexterity. This part of the system, even in the training of its teachers, is carried to the point of a fad. (4) The number of "Gifts" and "Occupations," combined with the short duration of each lesson, encourages restlessness, and an inability to give more than fleeting attention to any one subject, fostering a craving for constant change. (5) To throw very young children amongst numbers of others is rarely wise. Before any powers of discrimination are developed, they influence one another too much, often more for harm than good. Crowding young children together in rooms, moreover, leads to much illness. Frequent absence from school on this account is notoriously one reason why Kindergartens hardly ever pay.

LAND NATIONALIZATION.

Pro: (1) Land differs totally from all other kinds of property, inasmuch as its value is not the result of human labour, which alone constitutes a valid claim to property of any sort. (2) Land is limited in quantity, yet essential to all. (3) Land more and more passes into the hands of the few (a tendency which Free Trade in Land has enhanced rather than reduced), and the few thus acquire undue power. (4) It is not just that first occupation should convey a right to levy a perpetual tax on the labour of others. (5) The present system deprives the agricultural labourer of all interest in the Land which he cultivates, making him thriftless and careless. (6) The possession of Land places enormous power in the hands of those holding it, to influence the opinions, political and religious, of all who are in any way dependent on them. (7) Country districts are becoming more and more depopulated by the absence of all chance of employment, the small amount of cottage accommodation, and the difficulty even of obtaining a plot of Land as an allotment. (8) Rural depopulation leads to overcrowding in towns, and competition for work on the part of town wage-earners, resulting in reduced wages. (9) By overcrowding in cities, the vitality of the race is being sapped; the unhealthy lives of the people leading them more and more to rely on alcohol, tobacco, and other stimulants. (10) Private ownership has created a class of men who, by levying a tax on the labour of others, are able to live without themselves producing work of any kind; while many members of this class perform useful work as magistrates, etc., yet their remuneration is entirely disproportionate to its value. (11) One of the results of State ownership of Land would be that the art treasures, etc., now held by the lords of the soil, would tend to pass into the hands of the nation, and the enjoyment of them would be open to all. (12) Since the Land acquires the greater part of its financial value from (a) the growth of population, (b) the industry of man, this unearned increment should not pass into the hands of the few. (See BETTERMENT.) (13) The present system enables the landlord to appropriate, especially in large cities, improvements made by his tenant, and, when a tenancy is renewed, to charge him a higher rental on the strength of them. (14) Property in Land has led to abuses such as the Highland clearances (by which thousands of hard-working people have been ousted from their homes to make way for sheep and eventually for deer); to the Irish Land difficulty; and to the enclosure of Commons in England, by which the agricultural labourer has been deprived of a most useful grazing place, formerly free to him, for his cow. (*See* COMMON LANDS.) **(15)** Landlords long refused all requests on the part of labourers for Land for allotments, gardens, etc., and even now let them only at rentals equal to 3 or 4 times as much per acre as the farmer pays for his Land. **(16)** By the system of royalties and way-leaves charged by the owners of the Land, they have seriously handicapped English colliery-owners in their competition with the lessees of the State-owned mines in Germany, Spain, etc., where royalties do not exist. **(17)** Peasant proprietorship has proved absolutely ineffectual to improve the lot of the poor: it has rescued the peasant from the hands of the landlord merely to put him into the power of the money-lender. Neither has it solved the question of unearned increment, for why should the peasant proprietor reap where he has not sown, any more than the landlord? **(18)** The owners of Land, in large cities especially, have imposed the harshest terms on their tenants. **(19)** The present system has led to great waste by way of over-consumption of the mineral resources of the country, due to the landowner's desire to get money at all costs. **(20)** (Some) Though it would be a costly process to buy out the landlords, the investment would pay in the long run. **(21)** (Some) Notice could be given to landlords to quit at the end of, say, 100 years. This would be equitable to the landlords, who, if they sold, would get about 30 years' purchase, and on the part of the State it would be a net advantage, since it would involve no payments for compensation. Care could be taken by means of Acts of Parliament, etc., that landlords were prevented from abusing their powers meantime, by putting it into the hands of the Secretary of State to assume possession at once, with or without compensation, if he thought fit. **(22)** (Some) The State ought not to buy out the landlords, nor to confiscate their property; but she should, by a heavy graduated tax on rents, bring ultimately all rents into the National Treasury. **(23)** The State would manage the Land better than private landlords, in the same degree as large estates are better managed than small. The Commissioners of Woods and Forests, City Corporations, etc., manage large estates liberally and well; and the glare of publicity that is thrown upon the doings of a State department tends to keep it efficient. **(24)** The State or Municipal Authorities might be allowed to experiment on a small scale at first, and, if successful, to enlarge the sphere of their operations.

Con : **(1)** Land derives almost its whole value from the fact that it has been brought into cultivation. Where, for instance, can any distinction be drawn between the Land and the crops that grow on it? **(2)** All commodities are limited in quantity; and Land is no more necessary to the individual than food or clothing. There is plenty of unoccupied country still left in the world. **(3)** The estates of large landowners are, as a rule, far more generously managed than those of small owners. Being more open to criticism, large owners are also less harsh to their tenants. **(4)** A man should pay for the privilege of entering into the results of others' labours: whether in a lump sum or in the form of rent is a small matter. If a man be not allowed this right of property in Land which he himself or his ancestors have cultivated or paid for, no one is likely hereafter to invest his labour or money in Land, **(5)** Merely to transfer Land from the hands of landlords to the State would not increase the labourer's interest in the land. **(6)** Few landlords now attempt to control the opinions of their tenants; whereas if the land were concentrated in the hands of the State it would afford numerous opportunities for fraud on the part of venial officials and politicians. **(7)** The depopulation of the countryside results from far deeper causes than mere inability to obtain allotments, one of the chief being that, owing to the rapid spread of education, a craving has arisen on the part of the rural population for a fuller and more varied life than the countryside affords. **(8)** The chief cause of overcrowding is the large surplus population, aggravated by the constant influx of pauper aliens. (*See* IMMIGRATION.)   **(9)** The evil effects of cities on the vitality of a race are much exaggerated. Statistics show that the death-rate in London is exceptionally low, whilst the sports so freely indulged in by the townsman greatly promote his bodily health. **(10)** The existence of a leisured class is necessary for the maintenance of the art and culture of the nation. The services rendered by the landed gentry are numerous, and, on the whole, efficiently and economically performed. **(11)** Art collections in public buildings have not the same refining influence that they have in private houses, where each object is more individualized, and in more appropriate surroundings. As owned at present, they are in many cases thrown open to the public at stated times, and thus the influence they exercize is diffused over the whole country, instead of being limited to London or other cities. Moreover, when dispersed, art collections, or their chief treasures, more often go to America than not.   **(12)** If the landlord gains by a large population on his land, he loses heavily by its migration. If the community were to tax him for unearned gains, it ought in like manner to compensate him for unearned loss. (*See* BETTERMENT.)   **(13)** The question of tenants' improvements and repairs is one that should be agreed upon before a lease is entered into. Should the tenant undertake repairs, he already gets in all cases a *quid pro quo* in the form of a reduced rental. **(14)** Public opinion is the best safeguard against abuse of power by landlords; and though hardships have, no doubt, been inflicted in the past, it is with the needs of the day that we have to deal. All transitions in the social and industrial worlds are necessarily accompanied by hardships.   **(15)** Landlords are obliged to charge more for an allotment than for a farm, since (*a*) the expenses of rent collecting are heavier; (*b*) while the farmer takes the Land as it is, bad Land being often intermixed with good, the allotment-holder takes only a choice plot; (*c*) the expenses of subdivision and the chance of the less desirable plots remaining untenanted must be covered. Labourers are eager for allotments at the present rent, which proves that they find them profitable.   **(16)** Royalties, way-leaves, etc., simply represent the price a lessee is willing to pay for a well-situated in preference to a less-favoured mine. They do not affect the price of coal; were they abolished, the lessees would be better off, but not the nation. In Spain and Germany, where the State owns the minerals, it is a usual practice for a lessee not to work the mine himself, but to sub-lease it.   **(17)** Peasant proprietorship, by making a man master of his own holding, frees him from all outside interference. There is no class so free or so thrifty as the French peasant proprietors, by whose savings France was enabled to pay the enormous war indemnity of 1871. A government tenant, on the other hand, being always harassed by the red tape of a Department, would rarely be able to make the most of his Land.   **(18)** Landlords, as a rule, impose only such terms as are intended to guard their property against abuse. (*See* LEASEHOLD ENFRANCHISEMENT.) **(19)** The State would not be likely to use minerals more carefully than present owners, nor is there any evidence that they have been wasted. They are limited in quantity, and will therefore be exhausted in time; but some efficient substitute will no doubt have been discovered before then.   **(20)** To buy out landlords at a fair price would cripple the resources of the nation for many years, and, moreover, create an idle class, without responsibilities. **(21)** It would be most unjust on landlords if the State were suddenly to change a permanent interest into a merely temporary one. The Land represents the landlord's capital and the rent his interest: by this proposal the State would allow him interest for a limited period, but would confiscate his capital. The extent of the confiscation can be seen if we compare the relative prices paid for a leasehold for 100 years and for a freehold. It would lead the landowners to get all they could out of the land during their limited tenure. (22) There is no essential difference between a high income tax on rent, and confiscation. Taxation has hitherto been imposed to provide for necessities; to apply it to the purpose of reducing inequalities in wealth, or abolishing a particular class of property, is to change its whole nature. (23) Land would not be better managed in public than in private hands; certainly, the management of Crown Lands and of the estates of City Corporations or Hospitals does not justify such an assumption. (24) To allow local authorities or the State herself to experiment in Land-holding would be very costly, and quite inconclusive, since, as soon as they became sole owners without rivalry or criticism, their energy would flag, and their management deteriorate.

LEASEHOLD ENFRANCHISEMENT.

Pro: (1) All property is held subject to the will of the people, as expressed through the State, and is subject to its conformity with the highest interests of the community at large. (2) The ownership of the land on which London and other large towns are built, being concentrated in a few hands, constitutes a monopoly, which is further accentuated when it is remembered how relatively small a proportion of that land is available for residential purposes. (3) Most men are bound to live in a particular locality, and there can therefore be no "freedom of contract" between them and the ground landlord. (4) The State has already interfered with freedom of contract in the case of Railway Companies requiring land, when it compels the landlord to sell at a fair price. (5) The concentration of the land in so few hands is a danger to the rights of property generally; for the more widely property is distributed, the safer will it be against the attacks of Nationalizers, etc. (6) Leasehold Enfranchisement involves no confiscation of property, since a fair price would be paid. (7) The landlord taxes his tenants on improvements they have made by fines, increased rents, etc., which are very hard on shopkeepers who work up a business in a district, which they are consequently obliged to live in, or lose their money. (8) The Leasehold system, by rendering the tenure of the builder a limited one, induces him to fix his rentals high in order to compensate himself for his risk. (9) The present system enables the landlord to place any restrictions he may see fit on the liberty of his tenants, and often prevents them from making improvements. The local authorities have power already (and if not sufficient they could easily get enlarged powers) to prevent a purchaser from making himself a nuisance, or depreciating the property of his neighbours. (10) By announcing improvements as going to be made at the end of, say, 20 years, the landlord checks all improvements in the meantime by the tenant. (11) The Leasehold system encourages jerry-building, because no builder has any interest in erecting a house that will last beyond his term. (12) It has led to the system of leases on lives, which effectually bars all improvements by the tenant. (13) The tenant, being unable to buy his freehold, is unwilling to improve his landlord's property, so that the present system tends to let houses fall out of repair at the end of the lease. The contrary would be the case if the house became the own property of the tenant. It would lead to the formation of societies, whereby workmen would be enabled to buy their own houses; and in any case, since purchase would be at the option of the tenant, he would not buy the house unless he could afford it. (14) A man would be able to borrow money more easily on a freehold than on a leasehold; hence, there would be no difficulty about the purchase. (15) The Leasehold system encourages overcrowding, by bringing into existence a class of middlemen, who, in certain districts, buy the "fag ends" of leases; and, having converted them into lodgings, make a profit out of overcrowding. As building land is much more valuable than agricultural land, owners would always be glad to use land for the former purpose, which fact would ensure a sufficient supply of houses, and tend to keep rents at a low level. **(16)** The Leasehold system, which is of comparatively modern date, scarcely exists outside England, and here only in certain parts of the country. **(17)** Leasehold Enfranchisement to be effective must include existing leases. **(18)** It would not prevent the nationalization of the land, etc.: in fact, it would be a first step towards it.

Con : **(1)** Though the State has power to confiscate the property of any of its members without compensation, she would be very foolish to do so, for she would thereby strike a blow at the sanctity of property, without which no industry is possible. A very clear case must be made out to show that the public interest demands that she should take land; and full compensation must be paid for all rights dispossessed. **(2)** The land on which London and other large towns are built is in no sense a monopoly. **(3)** Since no man is bound to live in any particular locality, perfect freedom of contract exists between tenant and landlord. **(4)** State interference is justified in requiring landlords to sell their land to the Railway Companies at a fair price, for this is obviously in the public interest; though even here injustice is often done (as when a railway is constructed to go through a particular part of an estate to the great injury of the rest). Leasehold Enfranchisement breaks through a free contract in order to benefit a certain limited class of men. **(5)** Nothing would be so dangerous to the rights of property as ill-advised interference with them on the part of the Legislature, since it would always form a bad precedent. **(6)** There is no security nor provision that the landlord under Leasehold Enfranchisement would get true compensation. For instance, where the landlord is obliged to sell to the Railway, the latter ought to pay him a price over and above the market price, in consideration of the compulsory element in the bargain. But this is not allowed for in the case of Leasehold Enfranchisement, nor is any allowance to be made for the fact that the property may be broken up, and its value seriously impaired, by the sale of a particular lot; nor for the uncertainty such a power would introduce into the relations between landlord and tenant, since the tenant, being allowed to buy at any time, would choose the moment most convenient to himself, and might thus involve the landlord in considerable loss. **(7)** The tenant when he takes a house does so with his eyes open, and on terms which he knows perfectly well. Where the tenant gets a house at a low rent, on an improving lease, it is only right that the landlord should get some *quid pro quo* for having been kept so long out of his money. **(8)** Both the rent which the tenant pays to the house owner and the rent which the latter pays to the ground landlord are fixed by the law of supply and demand. **(9)** The restrictions contained in leases are generally such as will prevent the tenant from making himself a nuisance to his neighbours. **(10)** The present landlords can carry out improvements on a large scale, which would be impossible in the case of small freeholders. **(11)** The great landlords impose stringent regulations for the prevention of jerry-building, which is consequently all but unknown on large estates. **(12)** Even if the leaseholder could buy his freehold, he often could not do anything more; hence the repairs would not be nearly so well done as under a leasehold. Since the working man is rarely able to take his house for a longer period than a year, it is not likely he would benefit by the proposed change. **(14)** The general sense of insecurity which Leasehold Enfranchisement would effect, would be fatal to any chance a man might have of borrowing money on his freehold. **(15)** How little overcrowding has to do with the Leasehold system is proved by the experience of the American cities, where, though leaseholds are almost unknown, overcrowding is as great an evil as in London. Though the speculative middleman is tempted to buy "fag ends" of leases, in order to make money by overcrowding, even then he is meeting a public need and providing extra accommodation for working men. Leasehold Enfranchisement, on the other hand, by depriving landlords of all incentive to turn their land into building sites, would accentuate the existing evil by rendering it impossible to acquire sufficient house accommodation for the needs of a growing population. **(16)** The Leasehold system has been devised to meet the wants of the people of London and other large towns; so that the experience of a whole continent is of no great value, unless its wants are shown to be identical. **(17)** To make Leasehold Enfranchisement retrospective would simply be a transfer of the property of one man into the pockets of another, and would favour one party to a contract at the expense of the other. **(18)** It would be a distinctly reactionary measure, and, if it succeeded, would create a large class of men who were opposed to all reform whatsoever.

LEGAL EDUCATION, REFORM OF.

Pro : **(1)** Apart from the complete fusion of the two branches of the profession, which to many seems undesirable, there is no reason why the Legal Education of barristers and solicitors should not, up to a certain point, be the same. At present there is a want of breadth in the system of Legal Education as managed by the Inns of Court and the Incorporated Law Society. (The Lord Chief Justice proposes a School of Law in which the Inns of Court, the Incorporated Law Society, and the Universities should be represented.) **(2)** The above would provide for the theoretical part of the Education. For the practical, an apprenticeship should be rendered compulsory to barristers, as it now is for solicitors.

Con : **(1)** The chief requirements for a barrister are those which cannot be taught in any school—a wide experience of men, and tact in dealing with them. Quite as much law can be picked up under the present system as is necessary for a barrister starting in his profession: experience alone can do the rest. **(2)** A compulsory apprenticeship is unnecessary. As a matter of fact, a young barrister starts by "devilling" for some senior barrister in good practice.

LIBERTY OF OPINION, SPEECH, AND WORSHIP.

Pro : **(1)** The faculty of rational Speech, which distinguishes man from the lower animals, keeps society together, and enables the individual to work out the purposes of his life. While Speech is the medium of the Thoughts, the manner in which the mind works, and in which the various passions, affections and desires are communicated from one to another, lies altogether beyond the domain of the law. Thought, therefore, must, by its nature, be free; and Speech, which is only the vehicle of Thought, should be equally free. Liberty of Public Worship, of Public Meeting, of Petition to the Crown and to Parliament, of publishing Parliamentary Debates and proceedings of the Law Courts, and commenting on all matters of *bonâ fide* public interest, follow logically; and the extension of Freedom of Thought to the creation of property in Thought, resulting in the establishment of copyright, patent right, and eventually trademark, is a natural and proper development. A policy of Repression, were it even generally possible in this country and in these days, would either increase the dangers of discontent by driving it underground, as it has in the past, or stifle all progress and vigour in the nation (*teste* Spain). Where resorted to, Repression has tended to martyrize the object of its attack, sometimes having even created public sympathy for a perfectly worthless or even base cause. **(2)** Free criticism is the life of institutions, and keeps them from stagnating. There is no reason why the practice of Tolerance on our part should imply doubt as to the validity of our position. A period of unrest always precedes a period of the greatest progress, since it forces men out of the old grooves, and gives development a chance of free action. **(3)** Practically it does not much matter to the State what a man's theological creed may be, so long as he obeys the laws and his practice does not interfere with an equal freedom on the part of others. (4) By Repression, the State may be suppressing the publication of a new truth, and in so doing would inflict a great injury on humanity. (5) Licence can always be checked. (*See* BLASPHEMY.)

Con : (1) The State has to look to the education of her people, and is fully justified in suppressing (within reason) such pernicious teachings as are likely to inflict a national injury. With adequate measures, vigorously enforced, the State could generally stamp out such evils, and thus protect the majority of her people from moral, as she does from physical poison. (2) Free criticism often leads to reckless criticism, which creates false impressions in the minds of the unintelligent, who are always more open to moboratory than to true reasoning. A feeling of unrest, occasionally leading to most dangerous upheavals, may be the result. Moreover, open discussion informs foreign Powers of our schemes, and frequently enables a criminal to escape. (3) The great endeavour of life should be to attain Truth, or at least to get as near to it as we can : it is impossible that we can seriously tolerate what we believe, or know, to be false. Undue Tolerance leads to a despairing scepticism of ever attaining the Truth ; and scepticism results in the abandonment of all intellectual and moral effort. (4) The State has to deal with what is true now, not with what may be true hereafter ; and to allow the unrestrained spread of what is false teaching for to-day, even though it may, under altered conditions, become true teaching for some future day, is bad statesmanship, because over-speculative.

LIFE : is it worth living?

Pro: (1) The ideal state for men which thinkers of all ages have approximately identically imagined, may, as the social and humane instincts develop, become a reality, and is already partially accomplished. Even if individual life ceases with the death of the body, the life on this earth, though it may not afford the supreme happiness which the future life is believed by some to offer, is of positive value, and the absorption of the individual into and loss of his identity in the absolute is, rightly appreciated, nothing to cause us consternation or grief. The co-existence of Omnipotent Benevolence with evil is no contradiction, as is so commonly asserted. The statement absolutely ignores the hypothesis of development : in so far as good gradually supplants evil, in so far as life gradually rises from lower to higher forms, is the change not good ? and what contradiction is involved in its not fulfilling itself in the space of a few thousand years ? (2) Happiness is most surely found by those not seeking it. Fulfilment of the daily duties of life, and a due recognition and cultivation of the social instincts, are themselves a substantive happiness, the achievement of which is independent of external conditions. (3) The good of the whole should be our standpoint. At any rate, there are extremes at which pain ceases to be commensurable with pleasure.

Con : (1) It is impossible to be habitually happy without being virtuous; and with religion morality is rapidly decaying. (Some) Since the impossibility of personal immortality is assured, and the present iniquitous distribution of good and evil (which is itself a contradiction of Omnipotent Benevolence) therefore final, the immediate extinction of the human race is desirable. (2) It is terribly possible to be virtuous without being happy. Moreover, where the cause of grief is the sundering of affections, the pain is keen in proportion to the strength of those very elements in life which, in view of the general sum of happiness, have proved themselves the best worth emphasizing and encouraging ; so that a paralogism is presented whereby the individual's life in a society seems stultified. (3) No happiness is possible where the consciousness of so much misery around us is present to all of us. Even a happy average would be no consolation, for no one would create a million happy lives at the expense of one hopelessly unhappy one. We all rejoice when a sufferer obtains unconsciousness in sleep, whilst it never occurs to us to pity the temporary unconsciousness of a happy person.

LIVERY COMPANIES (LONDON): THEIR ABOLITION.

Pro: (1) The Livery Companies, like many other ancient public institutions, which in the old days survived from generation to generation without inquiry or challenge, should be abolished, and their funds devoted to public objects. (2) They have practically ceased to perform the trade functions for which they were originally established, and are no longer what they profess to be—representatives, guardians, and promoters of trade interests. Such few duties as still remain to them are either neglected or fulfilled in a perfunctory manner. (3) The Guilds are an essential part of the Corporation of London: up to a quite recent date membership of one of the Guilds was a condition of Freedom of the City. Hence they are public rather than private bodies. (4) Their wealth is enormous; and, if managed by public officials, would afford great relief to the general taxation of London, in addition to continuing the support now given for education and other public objects. (5) The enormous amount of property held by the Livery Companies in mortmain and exempt in perpetuity from succession duty, as well as the large fees paid to members of the Courts for attendances (by some of the Companies), cause a great loss to the Imperial revenue. (6) Though the sums contributed by the Companies towards education and charities are large, they are reduced by the extravagant sums yearly spent on feasts, balls, salaries, fees, etc. (7) The Companies do not publish their accounts, and are privately managed by an irresponsible body. Even under the Royal Commission (1880) some of them refused to give full information, whilst a few declined to give any at all. (8) The Royal Commission of Inquiry (1880), comprising the Duke of Bedford, Lords Coleridge and Sherbrooke, the Earl of Derby, Sir R. A. Cross, and others, almost unanimously reported in favour of the appropriation for public purposes of the funds.

Con: (1) The Livery Companies are part and parcel of a grand municipal machinery, which is invisible, and ought to be indissoluble. Throughout their whole history they have maintained the honour of the City, holding aloof from dubious enterprises, and excluding from their society thousands of conspicuous City figures whose methods have been questionable. (2) Their main object has always been, not trade, but charity and alms; and their history shows that their early freedom from molestation was due to their comparative insignificance, political and financial. As time has gone on, and their resources have, by wise foresight and pious bequests, expanded, such Companies as have survived the widespread ruin following the Civil War, the troubles in Ireland, and the Great Fire, have returned to their original work, helping their less fortunate brethren, and maintaining the Company for the benefit of the rising generation in the trade. (Some) Even if some of the original trade functions of the Companies have, by process of time, lapsed, there are many others to which they can, and do, devote their funds and energies. (3) The fact that membership of a Company was an essential condition of Freedom of the City is no evidence that they are public bodies. (4) The property of the Companies is their own, in part absolutely, in part as trustees. In the latter capacity they keep the funds distinct from their general funds, and deal with them according to the terms of the trusts. A considerable part of their corporate income is, moreover, annually devoted to the augmentation or extension of the trusts. No gain would accrue either to the nation or to existing or future beneficiaries by the trust estates being taken over by the Government. The alienation of their trust estates would not affect their integrity or their title to their acquired and absolute property, while it might in some leading instances form a source of advantage to them and of loss to the public. (5) The charge that the Companies by their constitution intercept a large sum which should be available for succession duty, was met in 1884 by the imposition of a Corporate Tax of 5 per cent., which yields the exchequer several thousands a year. By their charters the Companies were expressly entitled to hold in mortmain; and this Corporate Tax is itself inequitable. In any case, this charge can apply only to their corporate property, since their trust estates are purely eleemosynary, and it is all the less valid in that a fair proportion of the annual receipts passes to members, and thus becomes liable to taxation (and the greater the proportion, the greater the amount taxed); if it were not so, it is within the competence of the Companies to at any time dissolve themselves, so far as their corporate property is concerned, and to divide the assets. (6) The expenditure by the Companies on their feasts, etc., is ridiculously exaggerated. A certain expenditure in this way is desirable, as a bond of fellowship which connects trades, classes and families, and as almost the only survival of Old English hospitality, which is not limited to the municipal bodies, but from time to time extended to almost every member of English society of note. If their property were applied to the relief of taxation it would hardly make any difference. (7) When the Commission called for their accounts, they were, with a very few exceptions, handed in under protest. (8) The five Reports (1884-85) of the Royal Commission, though containing some recommendations for reform, were on the whole very favourable to the Companies, showing that their property was wisely and generously administered, very largely in the interests of the public. No Government has founded on the Reports any proposal to Parliament, nor has any step been taken, beyond the slight redistribution of administrative powers under the County Council system.

LOCAL OPTION.

Pro: (1) The present system works very badly. No body is better fitted to deal with the question than the Town and County Councils, who, being representative local bodies, know the wants of the localities much better than licensing magistrates. (2) Where evils exist, the liberty of the minority must give way to the interests of the community as a whole; moreover, if individual houses were closed, it would only happen by the vote of the local majority. The number of houses open is far in excess of the public wants. (3) The question of temperance is one of the most important questions of the day, and the more it bears upon local elections the better. (4) Municipal authorities are well fitted to deal with questions of public morals; and the more pernicious the trade, the greater is the need for its control by the Municipality. (5) Compensation might have to (Some, should not) be given.

Con: (1) The present system on the whole works well; the licensing magistrates administer the law ably and impartially. (2) Local Option would be an infringement of the rights of the subject, and lead to the arbitrary and unnecessary closure of many public houses. (3) It would introduce a new element into municipal elections, and often be the issue upon which elections would turn. (4) (Some) Municipal authorities ought to have no concern in liquor licensing, as it would give them an interest in a trade which is demoralizing. (5) Compensation would have to be given, which would either be ruinous, or lead Municipalities to allow houses to remain open, thus nullifying the measure.

LOCAL VETO.

Pro: (1) Power should be given to the ratepayers of every locality to elect whether they should tolerate the sale of intoxicants in their midst or not, because they best know their own interests. (2) It would relieve municipal authorities of the work proposed to be handed over to them under Local Option. (3) It is fully in accord with democratic principles, and has been found to work well in Maine, U.S.A.

Con: (1) The drink question is not a local one: the needs of *bonâ fide* travellers by road or rail have to be considered. It is a question for the State, and not for local opinion. Under no circumstances would Local Veto be successful; it would either operate only in those districts where, owing to the natural sobriety, it was unnecessary, or lead to the formation of drinking clubs. (2) Local Veto would cause strife and tyranny. (3) Its alleged success in Maine is no criterion for England.

LONDON SELF-GOVERNMENT.

Pro: (1) The Local Government Act, while for the first time giving London outside the City a truly representative government, has encompassed that body with such restrictions as to render it comparatively helpless. (2) London being more than a county (in fact, a city), her governing body should possess powers such as are proper to her importance and dignity, instead of only such as belong to a County Council. Birmingham and other large provincial towns possess the fullest powers of self-government. (3) The London County Council has already done good work in the improvement of the town and the removal of abuses. Those members of the Council who complain most about its over-activity are the men who do least. (4) The Council is at a great disadvantage in promoting a Bill in the Commons, and absolutely at the mercy of the party in power so far as raising loans, etc., is concerned. (5) The fact that the Imperial Government is partly responsible for the government of London complicates the issues, and, while it subjects London to great neglect, disturbs the government of the country on a purely local issue. (6) The persistent refusal to grant Home Rule to London accounts for the apathy of Londoners in local affairs. (7) Control by the ratepayers is the best guarantee for economy and efficiency. (8) Greater danger is likely to arise from unsolved social problems than from any extension of the powers possessed by the local governing body in London. (9) The fact that London is denied self-government is sufficient to make the Council favour that party which promises them enlarged powers.

Con: (1) The Local Government Act is quite sufficient for its purpose. (2) As the capital of the Empire, London cannot be put on the same footing as the provincial towns; the actions of the Leeds or Birmingham Town Councils affect only their inhabitants, those of a similar body in London would affect the very existence of the Empire. (3) The County Council already has sufficient powers—too much, in fact, for any public body to properly exercize. Already it takes up the greater part of its members' time, and is, in consequence, becoming more and more the playground of the professional politician. (4) The mere fact that the Council has to pass its Bills for loans, etc., through Parliament is a check to needless expenditure and jobbery, and forces the promoters to consider their proposals carefully. (5) London issues are often more than local issues; and Parliamentary control is essential. (6) Londoners do not really want Home Rule. (7) Control by the ratepayers did not keep the Metropolitan Board of Works from the grossest corruption. (8) A powerful local body in London would, under certain circumstances, be a great menace to the power of the Imperial Government. (9) The County Council has hitherto allowed itself to become the instrument of a powerful party, much in the same way as has the Municipality of New York.

LONDON, UNIFICATION OF.

Pro: (1) It is a great anomaly that London, though the greatest city in the Empire, should have no central government, exercizing such powers as are possessed by all our great provincial towns. As a great town, London requires town and not county management. (2) The City Corporation alone among the greater municipal institutions of the country was left absolutely unreformed by the Municipal Corporations Act, 1835. (**3**) The City has only gradually come to mean the comparatively small portion of London which it now represents, and at one time it claimed a vast jurisdiction over Westminster and the surrounding country. (**4**) The City fails to attract the services of even the best men within her own borders, while the County Council draws men from all ranks of society into municipal administration. (**5**) The Commissioners in making a report (1837) upon the relations of the City to the other parts of London, allowed that they were unable to discover any circumstance justifying the distinction of the small area within the municipal boundary from the rest, except that, in fact, it was, and had long been, so distinguished; as regards the plan for creating municipalities in other parts of London, they said that it would multiply and perpetuate an evil. (**6**) A Commission appointed in 1894 to consider how the amalgamation could best be achieved produced a scheme which showed not only that it was desirable, but how it could best be accomplished. (**7**) Sufficient power has been delegated to the vestries by the Local Government Act, 1894, to counteract any tendency to over-centralization, though it is possible to grant such further powers to them as may seem desirable, provided that the central body, the new Corporation, approves. (**8**) The same objections to amalgamation were raised in the case of Liverpool and other large towns (1835), when the area under the control of the Corporation of London had become narrowed down to a comparatively small proportion of the total area covered by those towns; yet the reform was carried, to the ultimate satisfaction of all parties concerned; and the tendency now is to still further enlarge the municipal area. (**9**) The Lord Mayor, as representing the whole of London, instead of only a small portion of it, would not be less able to maintain the great traditions of his office. (**10**) A single central administration would be able to do certain duties much more economically than they can be done by the present authorities, and could manage the markets, docks, water supply, etc. (**11**) The Corporation accounts are disgracefully mismanaged: while they ought to show a very large surplus, they barely pay their way.

Con: (**1**) As the capital of the Empire, London cannot be treated in the same manner as Manchester, Liverpool, or other smaller towns. (**2**) London government was not reformed by the Municipal Corporations Act, because London was already then enjoying a truly representative government. (**3**) The City, as it is, represents the wealth and commerce of the greatest commercial city in the world. (**4**) Though not so conspicuous as the County Council, the City Council is composed of able men, who do their work quietly but efficiently. (**5**) The Commissioners of 1837 were dealing with a London which was totally different from the London of to-day, with its various and complex problems. (**6**) The field of the enquiry instituted in 1893 was too limited in scope to be a real criterion; and instead of seriously investigating how far amalgamation was desirable, the Commissioners assumed its necessity, and proceeded to draw up plans for its execution. The City representatives, finding that they could not obtain a fair hearing, withdrew. (**7**) It is certainly desirable to further strengthen the local bodies, to reward those who serve on them by municipal titles, and to give each district a municipal government of its own. (**9**) There is no reason why the old City with its ancient traditions should be stripped of its dignity in order to gratify the jealousy of the County Council. (**10**) The County Council has already far more work on its hands than it can efficiently manage, and it is undesirable to increase the opportunities for mismanagement and jobbery, or to establish in London such an institution as the Municipality of New York or Paris.

LORDS, HOUSE OF: ABOLITION OF.

Pro: (1) No institution ought to be allowed to exist unless it can be shown that it fulfils a useful purpose. (2) As an institution, the House of Lords is an anachronism, and out of sympathy with the democratic spirit of the times. It is the only Chamber of the kind in Europe. (3) While the House of Commons has been made more representative of the whole nation, the House of Lords has stood still; and thus the constitutions of the two Houses are entirely at variance. (4) It is a great anomaly that men who are not representative of the mass of the nation, or accountable to them, should have the power of obstructing the declared wishes of their representatives in the Commons. The anomalous character of this is further accentuated when it is borne in mind that the Lords sit in their House by hereditary right, and not by qualification. (5) The attendance of Peers is notoriously very small; in fact, a great many attend only to vote on party measures, or those affecting their private interests. (6) The House of Lords has become a mere party instrument in the hands of one man: while Liberal and Radical Bills are either summarily rejected or mutilated, practically the same measures, if introduced by a Conservative Government, are passed almost without discussion. (7) The House of Lords always has to give way in the end, and each occasion this occurs tends to bring the Lords into greater contempt than before. (8) It has often been responsible for withdrawing men from useful public service in the Commons to the cramped atmosphere of the Lords, and has thus ended many a promising man's political career. (9) It sometimes forces Governments to appoint inferior men to important posts, in order to obtain the requisite proportion of Peers. (10) The fact of a Minister being a member of the House of Lords renders him less amenable to criticism than if he were a member of the Lower House; this is especially felt where the Minister holds the position as Secretary of State for either the Colonial or some equally important department. (11) The House, to be a real bulwark against the over-hastiness of the Commons, should be reconstituted on an elective basis.

Con: (1) Any existing institution, especially if it can point to an ancient and honourable career, has, *ipso facto*, an argument for its continuance, unless better reasons can be shown to the contrary. (2) The House of Lords has grown up with and forms an integral portion of the British Constitution, and is consequently much more adapted to its purpose than any new Second Chamber could be. (3) It is thoroughly representative of the wealth and culture of the nation, and represents that aspect of the national life more fully than the Commons. (4) It is necessary to have some body to check the impulsiveness of the Commons. A body of men like our present House of Lords, who have enjoyed the very best education the country can give, and have in many cases wide experience of political and social life at home and abroad, are better qualified to give a ripe judgment on any proposed change than the "carpet-baggers" who happen to have commended themselves to the electors of some constituencies or other, and who form such a large element in the present House of Commons. (5) The attendance of Peers is always very full when any important measure is to be discussed, which is more than can be said for the Commons, where the debates on many important subjects (*e.g.* Indian) have long been famous for the small number of members taking part in them. (6) The fact that the Lords delay Radical measures is an argument in their favour rather than otherwise; and Conservative Governments never propose very revolutionary changes. The wisdom of the Upper House in rejecting measures of this sort, which would otherwise have become law, at the 1895 election met with the most cordial expression of approval ever vouchsafed of late years by the democracy. (7) The Upper House has always yielded to any really decided wish of the nation. (8) It has ensured the continued service to the nation of men who, for various reasons, would be unable to face a contested election, but whose experience entitles them to a voice in the national councils; if it were abolished, the only result would be to fill the House of Commons with Peers, and we should thus practically lose our House of Commons. (9) The obligation to take so many Ministers from the House of Lords is no worse in its effect on the status of Ministers than a similar provision with regard to the Commons. In fact, it opens the door for Ministers to raise a specially able man to the peerage, in order to secure his services as a Minister. (10) It would be quite possible to arrange that Ministers should be able to speak and answer questions in either House, though not able to vote. The House of Commons already has the power to summon strangers to address it on particular points: hence the power is already there when Parliament and the Government shall agree to inaugurate it. (11) If the House of Lords were put on an elective basis, there would be constant deadlocks between the two Houses; whereas now the Peers are very careful to avoid conflicts with the Commons.

MAGISTRATES, STIPENDIARY.

Pro: (1) The workman is worthy of his hire; and unpaid services are not often worth much, and are, moreover, sometimes interested. Under the present system, the unpaid Magistrate is dependent for his knowledge of the law on his clerk, who, however, gives his opinion without any responsibility: such division of knowledge and of responsibility is bad in principle. (2) The county benches are often filled with landlords, whose great idea is to maintain the Game Laws at all cost, and whose sentences under those laws are disproportionately heavy. (3) A reform of the magisterial system being inevitable, it would be better to have a professional man, who has had an education and knows his work, than a working man, whom it is proposed to appoint with a view to counteract the class prejudices of the magisterial bench. (4) A professional Magistrate would at least be as independent as County Court Judges, and might do his work in the same way—by a circuit system.

Con: (1) The change would involve a great addition to the rates or the taxes, according as the expenses came out of the Imperial or Local exchequer. The Magistrate is advised by his clerk, who, being a lawyer of experience, is able to keep him right on points of law, which the Magistrate is able to apply from the point of view of common sense, and with entire freedom from professional bias. (2) The public always hears the bad side of the magisterial bench, never the good. So far from applying the Game Laws with undue severity, the Magistrates are most reluctant to put them in force: the poacher is very often a thoroughly bad character, whose offences against the Game Laws are only an incident in his life of crime. As a matter of fact, the Magistrates are no more arbitrary in their decisions than Her Majesty's Judges. (3) No reform is required, as the present system works very well. (4) The Stipendiary Magistrate would not be indifferent to considerations of the same sort as the landlord, or independent of social influence. As long as the Game Laws exist, they must be enforced; and, being difficult to enforce, the penalty must naturally be greater.

MANHOOD SUFFRAGE.

Pro: (1) Every male adult member of the community has a right to share in its government, unless he has proved his unfitness by being a pauper, a lunatic, or a criminal. (2) The more representative of every class in the community a Government becomes, the stronger it is. (3) Every class has its own way of regarding political problems, and consequently each is able to add something to the discussion of a question. (4) Manhood Suffrage would be the logical completion of Parliamentary Reform, and would leave nothing more to be agitated for in that direction. (5) Those whom the present scheme would principally include would not be a really new class, but merely the younger generation, who are among the most intelligent members of the community. (6) All are equally interested in good government; and political power, when vested in a fresh class, has a tendency to create a sense of responsibility in that class. (7) It would be better to grant Manhood Suffrage freely than wait till it is forced from us. (8) Electoral rights should represent persons, not property. (9) Manhood Suffrage would abolish the anomalies of the present system, and lead to the adoption of the doctrine of "One Man One Vote" as the guiding principle of a democratic government. (10) Manhood Suffrage has been adopted in Germany, France, and other European countries, as well as in America and our self-governing Colonies.

Con: (1) No *right* to the Suffrage exists in any section of the community. (2) The House of Commons already fully represents all sections of the community, and, as a matter of fact, Universal Suffrage would disfranchize all but the lowest (and most numerous) classes in the community. (3) The better-educated classes have a much wider outlook, and are better able to consider problems apart from class considerations, than uneducated men. (4) The Suffrage is cast quite low enough already. The argument that it should be extended in order that nothing more might be left for the working-classes to ask for is based on a fallacy: the vote ought to be granted to a class solely on the grounds of its fitness to use it rightly. (5) Those newly enfranchized under the Manhood Suffrage would naturally be the least-educated section of the community, or, if young men, be too liable to be carried away by their emotions, owing to lack of experience, to be of much value as voters. (6) The richer a man is, the greater his stake in the prosperity of the country. However well the previous extensions of the Suffrage may have turned out, it does not follow that this further extension would prove an equal success. (7) The change is not wanted by any large section of the community. (8) It is only fair that property should be represented, in view of the numerous schemes for confiscating all forms of it in the interests of the "have nots." (9) It would involve a redistribution of seats, especially in Ireland. (10) Manhood Suffrage, where introduced, has by no means proved an unqualified success.

MARKETS, LONDON: MUNICIPALIZATION OF.

Pro: (1) London is very badly served in the matter of Markets, both as regards their quality and their number. (2) The Markets, such as they are, are regarded as a source of income to one or two wealthy private monopolists and the City Corporation, rather than as supplying the needs of the population. (3) The mere right to hold a Market, which was granted by the Crown to certain individuals, has been construed by the lawyers into a specific declaration of a right to prohibit all other Markets within a distance of 3 miles. In one case this monopoly right was used to prevent the erection of a Market in a crowded district of the East End, which happened to be just within 3 miles of Spitalfields Market. (4) Since there is no Market authority in London, there is no power to see that sufficient accommodation is provided. Other towns have control in this respect, and most have their own Markets. (5) Markets, being a monopoly, are run on purely self-seeking lines, the sole idea being to maintain prices; with which end in view, good food (notably fish) is sometimes destroyed. (6) It would pay the London ratepayers to buy out the present owners at a fair compensation. (7) Londoners want Markets for their own sole use; Markets for the supply of the whole kingdom do not satisfy their requirements.

Con: (1) The number of London Markets is already sufficient; with the exception of Covent Garden, which suffers from being cramped in all round, the accommodation is as good as that of most provincial towns. (2) There is no evidence to show that the London County Council, or any other public body, would regard the Markets in any other light than that of a source of revenue and relief to taxation. (3) A monopoly was probably implied in the concession of the right to hold a Market, since it would not have been of much value otherwise. At any rate, the monopoly has since been recognized by the law. (4) If the public authorities were to own the Markets, they would be as loth to enlarge the accommodation as are individual owners, and would probably ignore the recommendations of any inspector. If inspectors were appointed while the Markets were in private hands, owners and lessees would make it worth their while to ignore any lack of accommodation. (5) The Markets must to a certain degree be a monopoly, whether private or public, as was proved by the failure of Columbia Market. In any case, it is probable that middlemen will more or less monopolize the Markets, wherever situated, as the general public have neither the time nor the inclination to buy at Markets, seeing that, by paying a very little more, they can have goods delivered at their doors. (6) The owners of the Market rights could be bought out only at very great cost, which under public working would probably be unremunerative. (7) The London Markets supply all England, therefore it would be unjust to treat them as if they concerned London only. Fish, for instance, is supplied by the Billingsgate dealers even for Parisian consumption.

MARRIAGE LAWS, REFORM OF.

Pro: (1) The custody of the wife's person should not be given to the husband. She should be a free agent, having authority equal to his. (2) The exclusive control and guardianship of the children of the marriage, at any rate during their earlier years, should be vested in the mother, who is their natural protector. (3) A wife's earnings should be her own absolutely: she should not be compelled to support an indigent husband. (4) There is no reason why, in cases of intestacy, a widower should inherit the whole property of his deceased wife, whilst a widow takes only a portion of the property of a deceased husband. (5) Women should not lose their maiden names in marriage. The Belgian system of joint names for married people might be advantageously adopted. (6) The whole system by which the legal existence of the wife is, to a large extent, suspended during marriage, is based on an entirely false conception of the wife's relation to her husband. (7) Many of the best women now decline to marry under the existing laws; and this will become increasingly the case as women get more and more emancipated.

Con: (1) Though the husband and wife are practically one, it is necessary that there should be one Head of the Family. The husband is necessarily the prominent partner, since he is, as a rule, though perhaps less often now than formerly, the bread-winner. The husband's legal control over his wife's movements is nowadays nominal rather than real. In the Jackson Habeas Corpus (1891) decision it was found that the husband could not confine the wife against her will in his house. (2) The father is responsible to society and the State for the upbringing of the children, and their control is therefore properly vested in him. On good reason being shown that the father is not a proper guardian for the children, the Court of Chancery can transfer the custody to the mother (Taylor case, 1876-77), and the age of the child may be taken into account. (3) It is right that a wife should be compelled to maintain an indigent husband, just as he under similar circumstances must support her. (5) The husband may adopt his wife's maiden name if he pleases; nor would such a course be without precedent. The system of joint names, if universally adopted, would be decidedly troublesome: it is, however, sometimes advantageously adopted now (*e.g* where the wife has earned a reputation). (6) Few men would be likely to submit themselves to the proposed new laws, which would lead to the increased frequency of irregular unions.

MIDDLEMAN, ELIMINATION OF.

Pro: (1) If the Middleman be eliminated, the Workman will, in the form of higher wages, get his fair share of the profits of trade. (2) At present the Middleman (distributor) makes a higher profit than the Manufacturer (producer). The Consumer would also gain by dealing direct with the Manufacturer.

Con: (1) The Manufacturer has already begun to do a retail as well as a wholesale business (*e.g.* the Farmers' Supply Association, the West of England Cloth Manufactory, with their many shops). But it does not materially affect the Workman's wages. (2) In many cases the Manufacturer has neither the time nor the money to do a retail business; and the Middleman often supplies the capital (*teste* the large drapery and furniture businesses in London). The Middleman also saves much trouble to the Consumer, as he collects under one roof the products of many Manufacturers. The useful function which the Middleman plays in modern society is proved by the failure of so many of the societies which have been started to supersede him.

MILITARY COUNCIL, THE NEW.

Pro: (1) The office of Commander-in-Chief had become too onerous for one man, the mania for centralization having become so vast that no one man could acquire the requisite knowledge. Over-responsibility amounts to no responsibility. (2) Decentralization was required; and, to effect this, it was considered desirable that officers with well-defined duties should be appointed to preside over the various departments of military organization, etc., forming a Council presided over by the Commander-in-Chief, whose duties were also defined. This Council, not the Commander-in-Chief, was to have the command, under the Secretary of State for War, of the army. (3) The War Secretary, being responsible to Parliament, must have real power over the army, and it must be open to him to get what advice he wishes from other members of the Council, irrespective of the Commander-in-Chief: otherwise, a deadly blow will be struck at our system of Cabinet and Parliamentary Government.

Con: (1) Under a well-managed system, and with good officers under the Commander-in-Chief, centralization is no evil but good. The Chief ought to confine himself to general aspects, leaving details in the hands of experienced subordinates. In war there is much more work than in peace, yet it is not found that good Commanders wish to be helped. (2) No Military Council could work well. It is impossible to define departments very clearly; and how could the Secretary of State, the ultimate arbiter, decide between his various advisers, or, after a disaster has occurred, determine in whose department the responsibility lay? (3) The War Secretary has such multifarious duties that it is hardly possible that he would be able to command the army, as the proposed scheme would mean, even if he were a soldier. It would be better that the Cabinet should undergo modification than that England should find herself helpless in times of war.

MINORITIES, RIGHTS OF.

Pro: (1) All great movements owe their origin to a small body of men, or even a single man. The great mass of mankind has nearly always been in the wrong. (2) The Government ought to represent all shades of opinion; and to effect this, care should be taken that influential Minorities should receive an adequate share of representation. (3) Representative Governments should approach as near to the ideal as possible.

Con: (1) The opinion of the majority may not always be right; but its unanimous verdict is of considerable value, and affords a good enough working principle for a Government. (2) The rights of the Minority may be turned into a power to obstruct the will of the nation, rendering government impossible. The greatest safeguard of the Minority is the right to turn their minority into a majority, a fact that tends to keep the majority from abusing its power or laying itself open to the charge of so doing. To require unanimity would be to hand rule over to the most obstinate. Government, to be effectual, rests on the approval of the great mass of the governed. (3) No perfect system of representation can be devised.

MONARCHY v. REPUBLICANISM.

Pro Monarchy: (1) Monarchical government keeps the head of the State above party politics; the monarch is thus not associated in the minds of the people with the man who but a few months before resorted to all sorts of means for gaining their votes. (2) A monarch's education is devoted to making him a capable ruler, whilst from his earliest years he has mixed with those who have made their mark in the world: he thus starts where they leave off, and so gets every chance of acquiring insight into the meaning of current events. (3) Whereas Prime Ministers change, monarchs remain in office; thus a continuity of policy is kept up, whilst many a new minister owes much, especially in foreign affairs, to the advice of the monarch. (4) The intermarriages of monarchs of different countries tend in the direction of peace. (5) The monarch has to maintain the traditions of a noble line of ancestors; there can hardly be a better influence. (6) Monarchy gives the nation a *locus standi* among the Powers, which is not possessed by a Republic. (7) It separates the ornamental from the executive branches of the Government, and, while not impairing the value of the latter, emphasizes the importance of the former, as can rarely be done in a Republic; for nothing tends so much to raise the State in the minds of certain of its subjects who are often not susceptible to other kinds of influence, as grandeur and display. (8) It is only right that the Head of the State should not be outdone in wealth by his subjects (as is the case in America). Republics waste far more in other ways. (9) Republics have always been subject to corruption on the part of their officials, who "make hay whilst the sun shines." (10) Under a Monarchy there is often more real liberty than under a Republic, since no hereditary monarch dares act so arbitrarily as the President of a Republic. (11) In no country is there more talk of the Democracy, and less effective control by it over the working of government, than the United States: in no country is the popular control more real than in a nominally monarchical country like the British Empire. (12) In a Republic snobbery of birth tends to become snobbery of wealth, an even more repellent form, especially when masquerading under the catch phrases of Liberty, etc.

Pro Republicanism: (1) Republicanism not only brings the Head of the State into direct relations with the people, but also gives the people the feeling that they themselves are the Government, that the State is subservient to their interests and wishes, not something above and opposed to them. (2) A Monarch ought to be a better ruler than a President; but though the art of ruling may be born in a man, it is rarely bequeathed to his successors (*e.g.* Charlemagne, Marcus Aurelius). Unless a man is himself great, he is not likely to learn much from mere intercourse with great men. (3) Monarchs have little influence on the guidance of current politics (*e.g.* Queen Victoria was not able to restrain a complete reversal of foreign policy in 1880). The Prime Minister in England is the virtual Sovereign in fact if not in name, while the needful continuity is supplied by the permanent officials. (4) When national interests clash, war is likely to result, and no consanguinity between Monarchs can prevent it; nor will any Government act contrary to its interests on account of such considerations. (5) The Monarch has the traditions of a very varied line of ancestors, some good, some bad, to look up to, and it depends on himself which he imitates. Similarly, the President of a Republic can keep before him a high ideal of the greatness of his nation, equally as strong an incentive to him, if a great man, as any line of ancestors. (6) The fact that it may not be possible for the President of a great Republic to be present on certain ceremonial occasions is a small matter, with no influence on the actual position of a nation. (7) A Republic does not aim at impressing itself on the mob by the magnificence of its displays, but seeks to win the esteem of its better members by the more real qualities of good administration. (8) A Republic holds out an ideal of simplicity of living in its President, and, so far from entering into competition with the more luxurious members of the community, tries to form a contrast to extravagance and ostentation. (9) Republics have no more suffered from corruption than have Monarchies, absolute or otherwise. (10) Such liberty as is secured by the fact that the Head of the State dare not exercise his rightful legal powers can hardly be described as worth much. It is a great advantage that the Head of the State should be a reality, not a mere figurehead. (11) There is no reason why the forms of Democracy should not be joined to the reality, though it may be allowed that this is not true of the United States; but any other nation adopting a Republic would know what pitfalls to avoid. (Some) The present state of affairs in America is due to the influence on American politics of the *laissez-faire* traditions of the 18th century, and to the consequent desire to give a free hand to property of all kinds, which has resulted in an *imperium in imperio* of an appalling character. (12) A Republic tends to discourage snobbery of all sorts; and though among certain classes in America snobbery is as rampant as ever, among the great masses of the people there is a strong feeling of the dignity of manhood.

MONOGAMY, LEGAL.

Pro: (1) As the lifelong union of one man and one woman is the basis on which our whole social system is built, the law should do all it can to enforce such union, and not leave it to the chance inclinations of individuals. Marriage has never been recognized by any State as merely an ordinary contract. (2) Legal Monogamy makes the parents jointly responsible for the maintenance of their children; nor is it in the smallest degree probable that society could hold together which allowed indiscriminate intercourse with the right of throwing the maintenance of children on to the common funds. The State would at least be compelled to adopt some method of limiting its numbers, and of deciding questions of parenthood, which would be demoralizing to the self-respect of its members, and not so efficacious as the responsibility of parents. (3) Monogamy is necessary to the existence of the family as a social unit, which, under the name of Home, has, in the vast majority of cases, an influence attainable by no system of communal life. It brings an indefinable sense of mutual sympathy and interdependence between parents and children; it teaches the child morality in a concrete, personal form (the only manner in which it can be understood by a child, who can appreciate the word "mother" or "father" when such terms as humanity or society convey no meaning). Though the ideal Home is not always, or perhaps often, realized, the ideal should be maintained, or, rather, insisted on more strongly. (4) It puts woman and man on an equal footing, as separately imperfect but unitedly perfect, each making up for the other's defects. It gives woman an individuality, and elevates her to a true companionship with man. (5) The fact that Monogamy is lifelong makes both parties smooth over differences which otherwise they might magnify into opportunities for separation, whereby "free unions" so-called would easily slip into promiscuity. (6) Monogamy has been the rule amongst all the most progressive nations of the earth, and its relaxation was, in the case of the Roman Empire, one of the earliest symptoms of decay.

Con: (1) In cases where a marriage is happy, there is no reason why the law should interfere; where it is not happy the law ought not to bind two people together who find themselves unsuited. It is absurd that the law, whilst enforcing a lifelong union, should refuse to sanction one for 10 or 20 years, or any other forms of marriage, such as polygamy, provided always that no deception is practised. (2) There is no reason why power should not be given to the State to place some effective restraint on the right of individuals to bring forth children; she might even refuse to be responsible for more than a certain number, and, while taking care of the others, charge the parents for their education and maintenance. (In order to check the multiplication of the unfit, the State should have a right to say what individuals are competent to become parents.) (Some) Under a proper organization of society there would be no fear of over-population, as the extra members would be an addition to the wealth-producing capacities of the community. (3) Where parents quarrel it would be better for the children if the home did not exist. Under a system of "free unions" it would be possible for the parents, if fit, to exercize an influence over their children; but if they were unfit, it would be absurd to force on them a duty of which they are not capable. (4) So far from Monogamy tending to elevate woman, it frequently degrades her into the position of a domestic slave. (5) Under "free unions" each party would be more considerate of the other, as the bond of union might be broken at the option of either. (6) It is not necessarily true that, because Monogamy has been the rule among all so-called progressive nations, it always should be so, or that some other system may not denote an even higher stage of civilization. Conclusions cannot be drawn from the decline of the Roman Empire as to the conditions of the 19th century.

MUNICIPAL DWELLINGS FOR THE POOR.

Pro: (1) Municipal authorities should set an example of what Dwellings of the Poor might be, by providing good, cheap houses, discouraging jerry-building, etc. (2) The authorities would be as anxious to adopt improvements as private builders are. (3) A Municipal scheme for providing Dwellings for the Poor has been adopted in Glasgow and other large towns with great success. (4) The state of the slums in our great cities is a crying scandal as well as a danger to health; if the authorities are to insist on proper sanitary precautions, they may just as well rebuild the houses. (5) There is no reason why the authorities should let the houses at a loss; at any rate, even if the dislodged class did not go to them, though they need be very little if at all higher in rent than the slum rents, it would be worth the expense, if only to have cleared away the slums. The lowest class will probably only be reached by reflex action. (Some) The authorities ought to let them at cost price. (6) The authorities would be able to guard against overcrowding, and to insist on sufficient sanitary precautions. (7) The work is too large to be left altogether to private philanthropy.

Con: (1) No public body can build as cheaply as private enterprise; moreover, municipal building would discourage not only builders, but also philanthropists. (2) The tendency of public authorities is to stereotype particular plans, and to hinder improvements: competition avoids these evils. (3) Municipal building has so far proved very expensive, often costing double the amount of the original estimates. (4) The unsatisfactory state of the slums will remedy itself in time, by more sanitary requirements being exacted. (5) Unless tenements are let at cost price or less, they cannot possibly benefit the lowest class, for whom they are intended. It would merely mean that the dispossessed inhabitants would move on to the dwellings abandoned by the class above them, which they would soon reduce to the status of a slum, or go to swell the numbers in the few remaining slums. (7) Private philanthropists, like the late Mr. Peabody, have through their executors been able to do so much, and are likely to do so much more, that it is unnecessary for the State to interfere and throw further expenses on the swollen rates.

NATIONAL PARTY IN POLITICS, A.

Pro: (1) A National Party would invite the best qualified men into the service of their country. (2) The national welfare would supply just as efficient a bond of union as the present party cries. (3) A National Party would supply continuity in the administration of the affairs of the country and in her political aims. (4) It would do away with all the false party cries which do so much to obscure the issues.

Con: (1) A so-called National Party would be entirely illusory; it would soon either split up into two or more sections, or its members would return to their previous parties. (2) The welfare of the nation is obviously not sufficient as a basis for a new party, as each individual would be found to mean something totally different by it. (3) The mere fact of the existence of a party implies that it is united by a common bond, and that on most questions its members hold essentially the same views.

NAVAL ADVISER, A: is such an officer necessary?

Pro: (1) To keep the naval forces up to an efficient standard, a Naval officer should be appointed to advise the Cabinet on all questions concerning the Navy; this officer should give his advice in the form of a Report, stating what fleets would be brought against us in the event of a war, calculating the possible combinations of Powers, with their respective fleets and probable plan of campaign, together with the force necessary to meet them, and the course he proposes should be followed. This officer ought to be he who, in case of war, would take over the command of the Fleet, and who, for the purposes of his Report, would be able to get all the information he required, and be allowed to consult whom he thought fit. By this means the nation would feel that its Government was in the position to know the real state of the Navy. (2) The nation would be saved periodical panics about the Navy, which, instead of being strengthened to meet popular clamour, would be maintained in a scientific manner, with due regard to the real requirements.

Con: (1) The appointment of such an officer would place the supreme power in the hands of a man who was not himself responsible to Parliament, and would be a death-blow to our system of Cabinet Government. (2) Exorbitant financial demands for Navy purposes might be made by such an officer, who would not himself be responsible for raising the money, and who would have the power to threaten to resign if his demands were not met. Thus he could either force the Government to undertake expenditure which they did not feel justifiable; or the Government, by being constantly compelled to change their chief officer, would demoralize the Navy.

NAVAL RESERVE.

Pro: (1) All experts are agreed that the manning of the Navy falls short of the number required. This constitutes a great danger, and cannot be neglected. Experience tells us that the official views as expressed by the First Lord of the Admiralty are untrustworthy, and the Naval Lords are powerless against the Treasury and the Civil Lords. So far from our Navy being strong enough to fight Germany, Russia, and France, we have not nearly enough ships to carry out an effective blockade against Russia and France alone, which in the opinion of all our ablest officers we should, in the case of war, have to do to secure the command of the sea. Nowadays population is not the question, but trained seamen; and the nation which has most of these will hold out against the others. (2) The question of expense is not one which we can allow to weigh in the balance when the question of our Naval supremacy—which to England is the *sine qua non* of her existence—is at stake. Moreover, as we already have a Naval Reserve, it is a foolish policy to go on paying for an absolutely inadequate force, the greater part of which is still more inefficient by lack of knowledge or experience. While it takes almost as many years now as it took days in the olden time to make a sailor, the great majority of our Naval Reserve are trained on land only for a few months in the year with obsolete weapons. (3) A Government which brought forward a liberal programme for the Navy would always get support. (4) England remains the only country without an efficient Naval Reserve, though sea-power is a far greater necessity to England than to any other country. To France and Germany it is only a means of gratifying ambition.

Con: (1) If our Naval Reserve falls short, this is an argument for not increasing our ships till we can man them. Otherwise our Navy is amply sufficient, being equal to those of France, Russia, Germany, and one other small power combined. The question of manning must, however, depend in the long run on population, and here we are far behind France and Russia; hence our pretensions to have a Navy at least equal to those two powers are idle. A small efficient force is better than a large inefficient one, and any increase on our part is followed by a corresponding increase of our rivals' fleets. Our sea pretensions are a great source of weakness to us, as every other power suspects us in consequence. (Some) It is almost universally held in the Navy (according to a leading official expert) that, were war to break out, the number of merchant ships, etc., laid up would more than make up for any deficiency in the men by the number of men thus set free to serve. Whereas the Naval Officers were the keenest supporters of the agitation ten years ago, to-day they are quite satisfied; and it is from outsiders (politicians, etc.) that the demand for a still larger Navy now comes. The Naval Lords can use their power to threaten to resign *en masse* if they find themselves outvoiced on an important occasion; but they never do, showing that it is quite unnecessary, as they know that were they to follow this expedient, no Government, no Chancellor of the Exchequer would nowadays face the opprobrium of stinting the Navy to the danger of the nation. (2) Every pound of unproductive expenditure handicaps us as a nation of traders in the international competition which is now becoming so fierce. Industrial, not Naval "supremacy," is the *sine qua non* of England's existence. If the present Naval Reserve is so much in arrears as to knowledge and experience, we had better improve it before extending it. (3) Popular enthusiasm even about the Navy is apt to be intermittent in nature, and to be put in the background by other questions, thus giving an opportunity to cheese-paring Chancellors of the Exchequer—especially would this be the case were the present Government to spend a great deal on the Navy, as then the Chancellor of the Exchequer would be aided by a reaction in public opinion; as it is, public opinion is somewhat in advance of the Government, and thus every proposal the latter makes is eagerly passed; but were the Government to presume on this, a reaction would set in. (Some) If the country knew the real facts of the appalling and still-increasing waste of money on armaments, they would not allow it any longer. (4) It is a piece of arrogance and a gratuitous insult to say that to France and Germany the fleet is "only a means of gratifying ambition." The arguments for Continental Navies are not precisely the same as for our own (in regard to protection of food-supplies, for instance), but they are quite as strong. These countries are very much more threatened by invasion than we are, and they must, or think they must, protect their coast-line as well as their land frontiers. Both France and Germany also have extensive colonies, and the Englishman does not generally regard colonies as "only a means of gratifying ambition."

OFFICIAL EXPENSES OF PARLIAMENTARY CANDIDATES.

Pro: (1) By making the Member pay the official expenses of his election the State is imposing a property qualification, thus debarring men from the House on the score of poverty, a special hardship on Labour Candidates. (2) As the State has devised the registration of machinery, etc., for its own purposes, the cost of it should not be thrown on the Candidate. These expenses are further increased by the greater facilities for voting, and consequently the greater number of persons on the register. (3) The Second Ballot would be a useful check on frivolous Candidates; or each Candidate might be obliged to pay a certain deposit, which might be liable to forfeiture if he did not gain more than a fixed percentage of the votes recorded. (4) Abroad these expenses are paid by the State, and in our Municipal elections from the rates, with no evil results. (5) The Candidate has no check over the sum demanded of him, and often has to pay for what he himself never sanctioned: this would be impossible were the charges met out of the public purse. (6) (Some) Mere exemption from the Returning Officer's charges would not encourage the adventurer, who is more deterred by the cost of sitting as a Member than by merely standing as a Candidate. (7) It would not lower the independence of the Candidate.

Con: (1) The official expenses are very light; no man has been prevented from standing by them, who would not have been deterred by the expenses of sitting as a Member. (2) It is only common-sense that a Candidate should bear the expenses of his own election. (3) Payment of official expenses would encourage frivolous Candidates; and Second Ballots would only aggravate the evil, while a system of deposits would amount to a property qualification. (4) Neither abroad nor in our various Municipal contests are frivolous Candidates unknown. (5) The charges are fixed by Act of Parliament, so that they cannot be very high. (6) Exemption of any kind would lower the tone of Members of Parliament. (7) It would sap the independence of the Candidate.

OFFICIAL EXPENSES, PARLIAMENTARY: ought they to be a local charge?

Pro: (1) Since the district chooses the Member, it ought to pay the cost of his election. (2) In Municipal elections the cost is paid out of the rates. (3) Ratepayers and electors are almost identical; whereas many who have no vote are taxpayers. (4) Local payment of expenses would discourage contests, and thus lead to the same Member being chosen time after time. (5) If the ratepayers had to pay the cost of elections, they would be very careful to see how such costs were incurred.

Con: (1) The Member represents not only the interests of his own district, but also those of the nation at large. (2) There is no analogy between Municipal and Parliamentary elections; one is purely local, the other Imperial. (3) Many ratepayers, especially women, peers, etc., are not electors. (4) Local payment would be disastrous if it discouraged contests and Parliamentary Elections, since it would check discussion on questions of the day, such as a general election always causes. (5) A by-election would involve a double charge to the constituency if charges were paid out of the rates, whereas if they were paid out of Imperial taxation the charge would be uniform. (6) Control by the Exchequer would defeat the ends of those who were interested in increasing the expenditure.

OLD-AGE PENSIONS.

Pro: (1) The number of paupers in a country depends on the conditions of trade, rather than on the degree of strictness with which poor-relief is granted; nor can we count too much on the experience of a few parishes which have tried a more rigid method of poor-relief, or argue that because rigour has answered in a few cases it will be equally successful in all. (2) One marked feature in the statistics of poor-relief is the relatively large number of aged assisted. (3) The present system of poor-relief, since it makes no attempt to distinguish between the deserving and the undeserving, is inadequate to meet the case of those who, through no fault of their own, find themselves, after a life of toil, without the means of subsistence in their old age. (4) The earnings of the greater portion of the working classes do not suffice to enable them to save much towards their old age, while any saving that they can make is often at the expense of their own and of their children's health. Thus it is questionable whether such saving as is exhibited, for instance, by the French peasant proprietor is not deleterious to the vitality of the race. (5) (Some) As a national policy, saving is ruinous, and saving on the part of all members of the community would, by checking consumption and increasing available capital, lead to general overproduction and stagnation in all branches of industry. (6) The fact that the poor man is never certain of being able to save enough to keep him in his old age will outweigh any sacrifice of present gratifications for such a doubtful future, especially when he remembers that, however hard he may toil and save all his life, if he apply for parochial relief, the authorities will, as a *sine qua non*, demand that he give up his savings, and he will thus find himself no better off than the man who has never saved at all; whilst, if he were assured of a small pension, barely enough to maintain him, say after sixty, and allowed to enjoy this concurrently with the interest of his savings, he would have every incentive to save, in order to secure extra comforts—a much more potent motive for saving against old age than the fear of starvation. (7) If a poor man does save, it is extremely hard for him to know how to invest his money safely; nor has he any moneyed friends to advise him. Moreover, the number of Friendly Societies that become bankrupt cannot be ignored. (8) State Pensions would help the Friendly Societies, by relieving them of the need to provide for their older members, a very heavy charge, and one of the chief causes of the financial weakness of many. (9) The Friendly Societies cannot make satisfactory provision for pensions in old age; therefore their opposition is not justified. (10) The Friendly Societies help only those who are already inclined to thrift; they do nothing for those who are not. (11) The problem of poverty would be much more easy of solution if it were not mixed up with the problem of the aged. (12) Old-Age Pensions would not be likely to lower wages, since they would not be sufficient to tempt a man to relax his efforts to save. (13) Although large numbers of the working classes earn larger wages, owing to the influence of Trade Unions, the strain is greater on their systems by virtue of the different conditions under which they work, and thus they are sooner worn out. The rules of most Unions being very strict against any relaxation of the minimum, employers often find themselves obliged to dismiss their older men, who, in consequence, find it very hard to get work at all. (14) The aged worker is as entitled to a Pension as the soldier or the Civil Servant, and any objection which applies to Old-Age Pensions, as regards the age limit, applies equally to deferred pay of all kinds. (15) The present system of outdoor relief possesses all the disadvantages without any of the advantages of a scheme of Old-Age Pensions. (16) Under the present constitution of society it is almost inevitable that the thrifty should have to pay for the extravagant and the vicious, unless society is prepared to allow the latter to die of starvation; further, any measure directed against the idle must, under the present administration of the poor-law, also apply to a large extent to the unfortunate. (17) It is better that the cost of the aged poor should be thrown on the nation, than that they should be absolutely dependent on their children. (18) (Some) As it would be impossible to discriminate between the deserving and the undeserving poor, it would be better to give Pensions to all alike. Why should this demoralize the poor any more than it demoralizes a man to come into money? (19) The manifest injustice of a strict administration of the poor-law is likely to do much harm by leading to a reaction in favour of a lax system of outdoor relief.

Con: (1) The number of paupers depends largely on the degree of strictness with which the poor-law is administered. All the Unions in which a more rigorous administration has been tried have told the same tale; nor is it to be expected that where men find they do not benefit by thrift, that they will be thrifty. (2) The stricter administration of the poor-law, by diminishing the number of able-bodied paupers, brings into greater prominence the number of the aged in receipt of relief. (3) The poor-law exists for the relief of destitution, not for the purpose of awarding praise or blame to a man for his past life; as a matter of fact, however, relief is made as unpleasant as possible so as to deter persons from applying for it. (4) Almost every man is, at some time of his life, able to put aside money to provide against adversity, old age, and sickness. The savings of her peasantry enabled France to pay the huge war indemnity demanded by Germany after the Franco-German War (1870-71). (7) Members of Friendly Societies, etc., hardly ever seek parish relief; and while the money that a man has himself saved forms an inducement to him to save more, that acquired without effort makes him wish to get more in the same manner, but will not be a sufficient impetus to urge him to save more. (8) Old-Age Pensions would ruin the Friendly Societies; who would subscribe when he can get all he is likely to want gratis? The difficulties of the Friendly Societies have been due rather to the pressure of the sick than to the old-age fund. (9) Though the Friendly Societies have only lately started the Old-Age Pensions, they have already been very successful in this direction; and the settlement of the whole question might advantageously be left to them. (10) It is impossible to make people thrifty by promising them a subsistence after a certain age. (11) Why should the aged be rewarded in preference to the sick, the infirm, or even the genuine unemployed? (12) Old-Age Pensions would tend to lower wages, since a man in search of work, who felt that his old age was provided for, would be inclined to work at a lower rate than otherwise—in fact, would, under stress of competition, present the capitalist with the equivalent of his Pension. (14) There is no analogy between an employé of the State in the army, navy, or Civil Service, part of whose pay is given to him in the form of a retiring Pension, and an ordinary working-man. (15) Old-Age Pensions would constitute a form of outdoor relief more pernicious than outdoor relief itself. (16) It is not right that any scheme should deliberately throw on the thrifty and well-to-do the burden of maintaining the idle and extravagant. (17) It always has been recognized as the duty of children to maintain their aged parents. (18) An indiscriminate gift of money to all above a certain age, say sixty-five, would demoralize the nation. (19) (Some) It would be better to try the effects of a somewhat less rigid administration of outdoor relief, than to plunge into extravagant schemes like that of Old-Age Pensions.

ONE MAN ONE VOTE.

Pro: (1) Plural Voting on the part of one man is inconsistent with the principles of democratic government. (2) Parliament ought to represent men, not property or localities. (3) All members of the community have an equal right to be heard on questions of government. The poor man has in reality a greater interest in the good government of the country than the rich; bad legislation may partially depreciate the property of the one, but may reduce the other to absolute penury. (4) The present system is not even based on the amount of property held, but simply on its situation—whether it happens to be in one place or scattered over several constituencies.

(5) Plural Voting frequently allows residents to be out-voted by non-residents, and thus tends to make the former apathetic in the discharge of their municipal and national duties. (6) It has led to many evils, such as the creation of faggot votes, the purchase of a vote (often made in the case of those attaching to the City Livery Companies), etc. (7) The principle of One Man One Vote would greatly simplify the register of voters, and would be no harder to carry out than in the case of a man who has numerous plots of scattered property in the same electoral division. Each man would be asked if he possessed a vote in any other constituency, and in which constituency he meant to exercise his right, while strict penalties would be attached to any attempt at deceit. (8) The change advocated would lead to the abolition of the University Vote, which is not, as is contended, used in the interests of learning, but is practically bought, and used for a strictly party purpose. (9) It would not destroy any man's electoral qualifications, but take away unjust privileges. (10) The adoption of Simultaneous Election (*see* ELECTIONS, SIMULTANEOUS) would not avoid this, since the abuse is most aggravated in London constituencies. (11) Plural Voting is not allowed in the County Council, Town Council, or the School Board elections.

Con: (1) It is quite possible to apply a general principle, like that of Democracy, in too detailed a manner. (2) Parliament should represent all classes in the community fairly, and it is only right that if a man has interests in several places he should have a vote for each. (3) A rich man has a larger stake in the government of the country than a poor man. A man who has shown his capacity to manage a large property is *ipso facto* better fitted to share in the government of the country than a man who has not. (4) The question of Plural Voting is absolutely insignificant, since the number of Plural Voters is very small, and of those about 45 per cent. never use their privilege. (7) It would make registration a much more difficult operation, by introducing disturbing factors, such as a resident in London coming into possession of a small farm in Cornwall or taking a place in the country. It would entail correspondence between the various agents, to see that the same man had not declared his intention to vote in several constituencies. (8) The abolition of the University Vote would deprive learning and culture, as such, of all voice in the management of the affairs of the nation, or in looking after their University interests. (9) By reducing the cultured few to the level of the ignorant masses, the change advocated would practically destroy the influence of culture. (10) Simultaneous Elections would do all that is required to abolish any grievance in respect of Plural Voting.

OPIUM TRADE IN THE EAST, SUPPRESSION OF THE.

Pro: (1) Opium being at once a valuable drug and a poison, its use ought to be confined to purely medical purposes, as is the case in England; nor ought its sale to be countenanced by the Indian Government for any other purpose. (2) It has been asserted by some of the most eminent medical men, European as well as native, that Opium is absolutely useless as a prophylactic against malarial fever: this is further accentuated by the admitted fact that those doctors who defend its qualifications in this respect do not use Opium for the purpose. It may further be remarked that in the very districts where malarial fever most abounds, the use of Opium is forbidden, while its consumption is often greatest where malarial fever is totally absent, and the climate most healthy. (3) If the action of the drug is beneficent, why does the Indian Government put any obstacles in the way of a more extended use of it, *i.e.* by keeping the price so high? Why does it not rather allow the price to be lowered? (4) The manner in which Opium has been forced on the Chinese Government is a disgrace to any professedly Christian Government and country. Though the professed object of the war may not have been to force Opium on China, yet the effect was the same; and there can be no reasonable doubt that the Indian Government tolerated smuggling when the importation of Opium was forbidden by the Chinese Government. (5) As far as we can discover, Opium appears to have been introduced into China by the East India Company, there being no evidence of its previous use there. (6) The use of Opium is not necessary to the Chinese; all their principal statesmen admit its evil effects, and would gladly prohibit its sale, were they certain that they would be allowed to do so by England. (7) There is no analogy between the use of alcohol in England and that of Opium in India and China; for (1) the effects are entirely different: a man may recover from the alcoholic habit, but rarely does from the Opium habit, which steadily grows upon him; (2) in England the great majority of the inhabitants use alcohol to some extent, Opium is used by only a small proportion of the Indians or Chinese. But even if an analogy did exist, the prevalence of one vice in England would be no argument for propagating another vice abroad. (8) The missionaries, who are among the few Europeans who really understand the Chinese and who speak the vernacular, unanimously condemn the use of Opium as in every way harmful to them. Similar testimony was given before the Commissioners by consuls, medical men, and English merchants. (9) Many merchants in India and China have testified that it is not wise to trust a man who uses Opium to the same degree as one who does not. (10) Any deficiency in the Indian revenue caused by the abolition of the Opium Trade England might undertake, in order to put an end to the immoral traffic with which her rule in the East is so closely connected. (11) So far from the prohibition causing dissatisfaction among the native States, it would in many cases do the reverse; some of the native princes actually desire prohibition, but under the present *régime* it would be impossible for a single State to prohibit the growth of opium, so long as the Indian Government allows it to be grown on its own territory. (12) There would be no need for the Indian Government to compensate the native growers: she has never recognized any right on the part of the growers to a licence, but has given or withheld a licence as seemed fit. (13) The Indian Government has been obliged to raise the price paid on Opium, so as to induce the natives to grow it: this hardly looks as if they were so anxious to grow it or found it so remunerative as the Indian Government officials like to make out. (14) It has never been proved that the abolition of one vice tends to the increase of another, or that the use of Opium keeps that of alcohol in check. (15) The report of the Opium Commissioners was not unanimous: one member refused to sign, and two others, both natives, who did sign, made many important reservations; the report, too, ignored much of the evidence and garbled the rest, except where it made for a foregone conclusion. For example, the only witness from China quoted from among those examined in London was a man who did not appear in person, and who did not mention (nor is it mentioned in the report) that he had been a large importer of Opium, though, as a matter of fact, evidence had been given by consuls, medical men, missionaries, etc., on this very aspect of the Opium question. In short, the report, drawn up by the Secretary, a member of the Indian Government, constitutes a brief for the Indian Government, not an impartial statement of facts. (16) The suppression of Opium smoking was recommended by both native members of the Commission, and its practice was universally condemned as degrading by all the members of the Commission; while it was said by the majority of those competent to speak, that little or no discontent would be caused by prohibiting the habit.

Con: (1) There is no evidence to show that Opium, taken in moderation, has any of the ill effects attributed to it; many of the evils noted are due to the state of health of the smoker, and have nothing to do with the Opium habit. (2) Malarial fevers are not all of one kind; and, while it is almost certain that some kinds, varying largely according to locality, yield to Opium, others do not. Again, much of the evidence against the utility of Opium in cases of malarial fever is vitiated by the fact that the witnesses have been unable to distinguish between fevers which were, and those which were not, malarial. (4) The importation of Opium was not the cause of the war with China. (5) Opium was known in China long before the end of the fifteenth century, and was imported from India before any Europeans had arrived on the scene. (6) There is every reason to believe that among large classes of the population of China Opium is an absolute necessity. If the Chinese Government wished, it has been able, at any period, to put a stop to this traffic; and the fact that it has not taken any steps, in spite of declarations of responsible British Ministers to that effect, proves the absence of all sincerity on the part of the Chinese officials when they declare their wish to suppress the trade. (7) There is a strong analogy between the use of alcohol in England and that of Opium in the East. Each in its own way, whilst doing no positive harm, adds to the enjoyment of its consumers. (8) Missionaries are rarely competent to distinguish between evils arising from the use of Opium and those which do not; moreover, a large number of missionaries have refused to support the proposals of the anti-Opium party. (10) England is not likely to undertake to make up the heavy deficiency which the loss of the Opium revenue would cause to Indian finance. (11) There is much evidence to show that prohibition would create great dissatisfaction amongst large classes of Indians, who would consider that England was simply taking the step for her own benefit. Prohibition would render it very hard on the native States to raise their own revenue. (12) Compensation would have to be given in cases where men were deprived of their means of livelihood; the Home Government ought to meet this expense, and not force it on the impoverished Indian Government, even if it were not to make good to the latter the loss of revenue. (13) There is no evidence to prove that cultivators consider themselves bound to continue the cultivation of the poppy. The evidence, indeed, goes the other way; as a matter of fact, Opium, being by far the most remunerative crop, is eagerly taken up by the ryot in preference to any other. (14) There is much evidence to show that the prohibition of Opium would lead to an increased consumption of alcohol, in itself a much more serious evil, in India; in fact, the native Commissioners on the Royal Commission, while expressing their fear that to prohibit Opium would have this effect, suggested that alcohol was already an evil in India which it would be well to check. (15) The Opium Commission, a body made up of representatives of all parties interested, after a long inquiry, came to the all but unanimous conclusion that it would be unwise to interfere with the cultivation of the poppy or the sales of Opium. Amongst the Commissioners who signed this report, and who in the main agreed, were an Indian Prince and another native gentleman, neither of whom would be likely to be hoodwinked by, or predisposed in favour of, the Indian Government, whilst the solitary exception was a man without any special knowledge of India or of medicine. Further, the Commission was, on its journey through India, accompanied by a representative of the Anti-Opium Society, who was there to see that his Society's views should be impressed on the Commission with sufficient clearness. (16) Any intended measures to put down Opium smoking would have to be most inquisitorial, and, as such, would be deeply resented by all classes. (17) The Indian Government undertook to control the Opium industry more with a view to secure the purity of the drug, than with any idea of raising revenue.

OUTDOOR RELIEF: should it be encouraged?

Pro: (1) The fact that Outdoor Relief is open to abuse is no argument for its total abolition, but only for greater care in its administration; to refuse such relief is merely a confession of inability to wisely administer it. (2) For a person to be obliged to go into the workhouse almost inevitably pauperises him, rendering it impossible for him to rise out of the "slough of despond" into which he has fallen; whilst Outdoor Relief may enable him to pull through bad times, and set him on his feet again. (3) Excessive rigour in the administration of the poor-law is apt to lead to reaction in favour of a more indiscriminate method, in which prudence is cast to the winds. (4) A distinction can and ought to be made between the deserving poor and the professional pauper; and to force them into the same company is to demoralize the former, and excuse the latter, in the eyes of the public. (5) Indoor and Outdoor Relief are so interdependent, that the increase of one, instead of leading, as might be expected, to an increase in the total amount of poverty relieved, by reducing the other, leaves the total practically unaltered. (6) The refusal of Outdoor Relief means the break-up of the home, a terrible ordeal for an old couple who have lived together happily for years, which should not be lightly inflicted in a society professedly resting on the basis of the family. (7) A diminution of the numbers relieved affords no real test of the decrease of poverty; undue severity so far deters men and women from entering the workhouse, that sometimes they die from starvation rather than submit to the humiliation. These cases are as a rule deserving, and are just those for which the poor-law is designed. (8) Undue severity only drives poverty from one parish to another; it does not diminish it. (9) The fact that a man, on accepting Indoor Relief, has to sacrifice all his earnings, *pro tanto* discourages thrift amongst the working classes; for among large classes of the community it is impossible that they should save during their short working life enough money to maintain them without aid in their old age. (10) It is not impossible to combine Outdoor Relief with encouragement of thrift. (11) Outdoor Relief, when given after careful investigation, tends to raise rather than to depress wages. (12) "Once a pauper, always a pauper" is the general rule with Indoor Relief, which is thus much more costly and less effectual than Outdoor Relief. (13) To saddle the relief of the worst cases of poverty and hardship on private charity, is to throw on a small section of the community what ought to be shared by all. (14) The poor have in many cases themselves contributed largely to the rates, and relief ought therefore to be treated in some degree as insurance money which has already been paid. (15) The problems relating to Poor Relief are not now the same as they were fifty years ago, when the present poor-law came into force; the present poor-law has revolutionized the state of society; and we now have new problems to face, which we can satisfactorily do only by means of new and improved methods. (16) Widows with children ought to be granted Outdoor Relief, and not be forced into the workhouse, which results in the whole family becoming paupers, and possibly criminals. Widows are often left badly off, their past circumstances having precluded their saving; nor is it right to leave them to depend on the charity of friends and relations, while the fact of the guardians taking one, or at the most two, of their children is scarcely any help at all.

Con: (1) Outdoor Relief is open to abuses which no care in administration can prevent, and the refusal to grant it is a sign rather of strength than of weakness in the Board. (2) The workhouses now do classify their inmates, so that it is not necessary for respectable people to associate with those whose manners and conversation are bad. (3) The fact that rigorous administration of the poor-law may cause a reaction is no argument against it; where a stringent administration has been tried, it has proved an unqualified success. (4) It is impossible for the poor-law authorities to make any distinction between deserving and undeserving cases. The distinction must be reserved for voluntary associations, such as the Charity Organization Society, etc. (5) That lax administration of Outdoor Relief leads to an increase in the number of applicants for Indoor Relief has been the opinion of all competent observers for many years. (6) It would be a disastrous policy to allow paupers, while living on the parish, to add to the population; though aged couples are no longer parted, nor children divided from their parents in well-managed workhouses. (7) It is inevitable that individual cases of hardship should arise under a strict system of poor relief; but the advantages of maintaining a consistent rule more than outweigh this evil. A large portion of the deaths from starvation occur among those who are actually in receipt of Outdoor Relief at the time. (8) When a more strict administration of the poor-law obtains, it will deter people from going from one workhouse or one parish to another. (9) It would be impossible to allow men to regard poor relief as a supplement to the amount they receive from Friendly Societies, etc., since it is a *sine qua non* of poor relief that the recipient of it should occupy a worse position under it than the worst paid labourer not dependent on the rates. If the labourer could supplement his income in this way, he would merely put less money into the keeping of his Friendly Society. (10) Outdoor Relief is the greatest obstacle to thrift extant; no man is likely to save if he can be just as well off without doing so. (11) Outdoor Relief must always tend to lower wages, since it acts as a bounty, enabling the recipient to sell his labour more cheaply than others can who are unassisted. (12) The granting of Outdoor Relief leads to Indoor Relief in almost all cases. (13) Charity is much more effective than the poor-law can be; it introduces a note of kindness and sympathy into its work in a manner which is impossible to a poor-law official. (14) Poor relief is not an insurance fund, it is a provision against destitution; the past payment of rates constitutes no real claim to it. (15) The fact that the poor-law, as amended fifty years ago, has wrought many improvements in the condition of society ought to encourage us in the belief that a continuation of the same policy will be even more successful in the future, and arouse a suspicion that a return to our previous policy would be disastrous. (16) Nothing could be more disastrous than giving permanent Outdoor Relief to widows with families; such relief cannot suffice to keep them, but will necessitate an increase, which will be earned at starvation wages. The refusal of Outdoor Relief rarely forces widows into the workhouse; it induces relations to assist who, whilst they would do nothing to save them from receiving relief, will provide funds to keep them "out of the House." Children brought up in workhouse schools are much more free from the pauper taint than children whose parents are in receipt of Outdoor Relief, and who, being insufficiently fed, take to vagrancy as a matter of course. Widows are often much better off than appears, nothing being harder to find out than the actual means they possess.

PARLIAMENT, MEMBERS OF: PAYMENT OF.

Pro: (1) That constituencies may secure as wide a choice of candidates as possible, it is desirable that no man should be deterred from standing for mere lack of means. (2) The non-payment of Members of Parliament is felt especially in the case of working-men candidates, and while a few rich unions are able to pay their own representatives' expenses, this does not hold good for the great mass of unorganized labour, which is consequently unrepresented, save in the persons of capitalists, lawyers, and others. (3) The Labour Members are universally acknowledged to be some of the most useful Members of the House of Commons. (4) The payment of the official expenses out of the public purse would not remove the disabilities of a poor man, for, if selected, the costs of maintaining himself as a Member form his main difficulty. (5) In order to get the best work, the nation must pay for the whole time of the best men. The duties of Parliament are growing so exigent, that it is becoming more and more impossible for a man to properly attend to his Parliamentary duties and earn his living at the same time. (6) Ministers are paid, in spite of the fact that the services of equally good (or the same) men could easily be obtained for these posts without remuneration; moreover, pensions are paid to ex-Ministers on application, though they do no more work for them than private Members do; no stigma attaches to them on this score, nor would it to paid Members. (7) The constituencies may be trusted to choose the best Members, whether paid or unpaid. Further, Members would not be under the same temptation to become "guinea-pigs" for Limited Companies, etc. (8) If a candidate were to offer to return the whole of his salary, if elected, to his constituency, in some form which would avoid the Corrupt Practices Act, he would by so doing be likely to lose as many votes as he would gain; so that Payment of Members could not in this way lead to a new form of bribery, as suggested. (9) Some of the most independent Members have been men who depended on their constituents for their means of livelihood. (10) The expenditure involved in Payment of Members would not be heavy. (11) In almost every other country and in most of our colonies Members of the Legislature are paid for their work; this was formerly the rule in England; the system broke down because the cost was charged on the constituency, not defrayed by the State. (12) Payment of Members would lead to a reduction in their number, and thus increase the efficiency of the House as a working body.

Con: (1) Good men are rarely debarred from entering the House of Commons on account of lack of means. (2) The number of working-men Members is increasing in the House in spite of their difficulties. Constituencies where unorganized Labour predominates have found means of providing funds for a Labour Member when they wanted one. (3) The few good existing Labour Members, the pick of their class, form no evidence as to the qualities of possible future Labour Members. (4) (Some) The payment of official expenses would remove all charges which the candidate ought himself to be obliged to pay. (5) Some of the best public work done for this country is performed gratuitously by the leisured class; and the influence possessed by the House of Commons is enormously enhanced by the fact that men do not enter it for gain, but make some financial sacrifice to do so. Payment of Members would encourage the growth of a class of professional politicians, already too numerous. (6) Ministers must give their whole time; Members give only their hours of leisure. (7) The salary would not be large enough to keep a man in luxury, hence he would be as much tempted as now to supplement it by becoming a "guinea-pig," or otherwise lending his name to financial schemes. (8) Payment of Members would encourage a new form of bribery, by enabling a rich man to pay back his salary in subscriptions to charities within his constituency, etc. (9) Payment would, with the majority of Members, tend to impair the independence of their judgment. (10) It would be a wholly unnecessary addition to taxation. (11) The tone of the British House of Commons is superior to that of every other Parliament, largely because the Members are unpaid. It is true that many get elected because membership is indirectly remunerative; but in so far as this is so it tends to lower the tone of the House.

PARLIAMENT, MEMBERS OF: should they be delegates instead of representatives?

Pro: (1) Theoretically every elector ought to vote by proxy on every question of government; the nearer the approach to this ideal, the more perfect is government likely to be. A Member, therefore, ought to represent his constituents in each vote he gives, and should accordingly consult them on every occasion where a vote is involved. (2) Members of Parliament are frequently elected on some special point of general policy; and, if they are otherwise at liberty to vote as they please, their constituents may be misrepresented on all other questions. (3) Constant appeals to constituencies would not be regarded as derogatory to the dignity of a Member, and, consequently, equally good men would offer themselves for election. (4) Under the present system the House of Commons, so far as all matters other than those before the electors at the time of the election are concerned, is dominated by the opinions of a few, whose general views are at variance with those of their constituents.

Con: (1) Members of Parliament are elected on broad issues only, and should therefore be left free in matters of detail, as it is impracticable for them to take the sense of their constituents on every point; even were this feasible, the constituents would not be capable of forming correct opinions on most of the questions that would be put before them. (2) Where new issues arise, it may chance that Members may misrepresent the majority of their constituents, but this cannot be avoided. (3) No man of independent spirit would be likely to consent to act as the mere mouthpiece of his constituents on all questions alike. It would destroy all interest in a political career. Further, should a vital difference of opinion arise between a Member and his electors, no redress on behalf of either party would be possible, for by resigning the Member would *pro tem.* disenfranchise his constituency, whilst, if he followed his instructions, he would vote against his conscience. (4) It is a good thing that the House of Commons should consist of a body of men of superior wisdom and training, who can take a broad view of State policy, and withstand sudden outbursts of popular feeling.

PARLIAMENTS, SHORTER.

Pro: (1) There are at present no means whereby the nation may give voice to its opinions save at a General Election. (2) The Septennial Act gives the majority in the House of Commons absolute power of office for the term of seven years. Thus the public, during that term, cannot call the Government to book for broken promises, etc. (3) The people ought to have a chance, before any new policy is adopted, particularly in foreign and colonial affairs, of expressing their opinions on the proposed change. (4) In these days of steam and electricity, public opinion very frequently changes, in view of a fuller knowledge and experience; thus, an increasing want of sympathy often arises between a constituency and its Member. (5) The Septennial Act was passed to ensure the stability of the House of Hanover for at least the first few years of its life. (6) Enormous changes in the *personnel* of an electorate take place every year; an opportunity of expressing their opinions should be given to new electors. (7) Members who intend to resign are apt to be lax in their attendance; thus, the more frequently Parliaments are elected, and they have to meet their constituents, the more assiduous will they be in their attendance. (8) A greater interest would be aroused in politics if General Elections were held more frequently. (9) The certainty of an early appeal to the country would make the Government more careful, and the Opposition stronger. (10) It would urge the House to pass measures as quickly as possible, consistent with efficiency; the best work of a Parliament is always done during the first period of its existence. (11) More frequent elections would tend to lessen the reaction that sets in when a Government is felt to have outstayed its mandate; in any case, it would give our Government a better position in the eyes of foreign countries, and force the latter to treat us more seriously. (12) More frequent elections would tend to retain old members. (13) If elections were more frequent, candidates would reduce their expenditure as much as possible. (14) More frequent elections would lead to a demand for the payment of Members and their expenses out of the rates. (15) Shorter

Parliaments would decrease the number of by-elections, and the excitement caused by a General Election. **(16)** The decrease of the duration would not actually affect their real duration; it would only make the date of dissolution more certain. **(17)** The present system gives the Government a very great advantage over the Opposition, since it can always dissolve at the moment which is most convenient to it. **(18)** In no other country is Parliament elected for so long a period as in England, and our own Municipal Elections are for three years only.

Con: **(1)** By-elections give frequent occasions on which the people may express their opinions. **(2)** No Government ever sits for more than five or six years; and, while theoretically irresponsible, no Government dare move or pass any measure in the teeth of violent opposition on the part of the electors. **(3)** Every Government must have a certain latitude in dealing with, *e.g.*, foreign affairs as they arise; for it is impossible that the Government should render public delicate matters. **(4)** Public opinion can make itself heard through public meetings, the press, etc., and the Government has every reason to keep in touch with the main body of the people. **(5)** The Septennial Act was introduced to meet the state of restlessness the country was reduced to by too frequent appeals to the constituencies. It has worked well. **(6)** It is probable that of the numbers who disappear from the electorate annually a large proportion reappear elsewhere. It is better, too, that a General Election should come in the natural course of events, and not be hurried on to meet the desire of new electors to exercise their powers. **(7)** Shorter Parliaments would make Members less independent than they are even now, and destroy their honesty. **(8)** Very frequent elections would lessen public interest in them. **(9)** Shorter Parliaments would weaken the independence of the Government, and thus constitute a serious danger to the policy of the nation. **(10)** They would lead to the passing of hsaty and ill-advised measures. A new Member takes some time to learn the work of the House; under the proposed measure he would no sooner have learnt this than he might be obliged to retire. **(11)** More frequent elections would keep politics in a constant flux, nor is there any reason to suppose that a Government resigning at the end of two or three years would fare any better at the hands of the electors than if it stayed on for five or six years, provided it retained its Parliamentary majority. Thus it is not probable that foreign politics would gain any increased stability from the measure. **(12)** Constituencies would be no more faithful to a three-year than a six-year Member; at any rate, the latter has a longer time in which to accomplish something. **(13)** Frequent elections would enormously increase the expenses of candidates. **(14)** It would be a very bad thing, if the increased expense led to the payment of Members or of the official expenses of an election out of the rates. **(15)** The country would be kept in a perpetual state of turmoil. **(17)** There is no adequate reason for the change. The uncertainty of dissolution under the present system is a distinct benefit, since it enables Ministers to choose a moment to dissolve when it can be done with least dislocation of the trade of the country. **(18)** Governments never abuse the powers which the right to dissolve at pleasure gives them; the number of Governments which are turned out on appeal to the country prove this.

PAROCHIAL BOARDS.

Pro: **(1)** With a view to increase the influence of the Church, Parochial Boards should be appointed by the parishioners, who should have power to share with the clergy in the administration of the parish. **(2)** The present system gives too much power to the clergyman, who is able to alienate his parishioners, and to change the usages of the Church and parish as his inclination may prompt him.

Con: **(1)** The clergyman has had a special training to fit him for his parochial work. It would, therefore, be both unwise and unfair to associate with him a body of men ignorant of Church polity, and possibly with few religious convictions. (2) Wisdom does not always lie in a multitude of counsellors; and a single trained mind is often needed for the successful solution of a parochial problem. Divided counsels create jealousies and paralyse work.

PARTY GOVERNMENT.

Pro: (1) Party Government has always been the rule, and has been a conspicuous success. (2) Party Government is almost inevitable; on almost every political question two attitudes are possible; and it is natural that those who have a large number of beliefs in common should agree to ignore minor differences, and combine to work for their common ends. (3) Criticism and opposition are necessary to keep Government up to the mark; and Party Government imposes a certain responsibility on the Opposition, since they know that they will, in all probability, have later on to face the same difficulties themselves. (4) The system secures the thorough discussion of all questions of public importance. (5) The fact that there are two great predominant parties in the English House of Commons prevents that Chamber from becoming, like the French Chamber of Deputies, a mere collection of heterogeneous groups, whose sole bond of union often lies in mere opposition to the Government, with the result that, no French Ministry being stable, firm government is impossible.

Con: (1) Party Government has put the government of this country into the hands of a small oligarchy, composed of the leaders on both sides, who, with a few exceptions, are chosen from a comparatively small circle of wealthy families. (2) On many questions there is only one possible "side"; yet Party Government, by creating a body whose duty it is to oppose all measures emanating from the Government of the day, has created an utterly false atmosphere in politics, obscuring the fact that unless both sides are wrong (which not infrequently happens), one side must be right. Party Government leads to an even worse abuse than this when it induces supporters of various measures to secure votes by voting for measures of which they themselves do not approve; every measure ought to be treated on its own merits. (3) Criticism is valuable; but opposition for form's sake is fruitless, and converts Parliamentary Government into little less than a farce. It employs the energies of some of our best statesmen in obstructing, not in aiding the Government. (4) The Party System does not even secure the thorough discussion of a question, nor is it probable that any speech, however great or convincing, would affect more than two or three votes. As long as the Government has a majority, its members and supporters are obliged to vote for it, even when they know they are in the wrong, while closure has really reduced debate in the House of Commons to a farce. (5) The present system stifles all independence of thought on the part of private members, and is turning the House of Commons into a mere reflex of the Government of the day.

PAUPER CHILDREN, BOARDING OUT OF.

Pro: (1) The family is a divine institution: therefore to place a child in a family is to bring it up in God's own way. (2) By being placed in a family, a child secures a father, mother, and perhaps brothers and sisters. (3) The child learns how to make itself useful; and, where there are younger children in the family, its stunted affections get developed. (4) The child has the advantage of moral and religious training, which it sees applied to the concerns of every-day life. (5) The child learns how to take care of itself, and gets some idea of the value of money, etc. (6) The system fits girls for domestic service by the work they perform in the cottage, and gives boys some knowledge of agricultural work. (7) The Boarding-out System takes away the children from the evils of a workhouse, and frees them from the pauper taint. **(8)** It is cheaper than any other system. **(9)** Boarding-out has been most successful, to judge by the small number who return to the workhouse; experience shows this to have been the case in all countries where the system has been tried. **(10)** The children are too closely under supervision for abuses to occur. **(11)** Situations and employment are found for the children by a Boarding-out Committee, or by the foster parents, without any trouble to the Guardians. **(12)** The abuses reported by the Local Government Board have all taken place outside the Union; Boarding-out within the control of the Union and under the Guardians' eyes is likely to be more successful. **(13)** Girls gain a knowledge of cottage life which will fit them for such a life when married. **(14)** Boarded-out pauper children turn out better than pauper children brought up under other systems. **(15)** Foster parents take them from their love of children, or the wish to do good; and become so deeply attached to them, that they cannot bear to part with them. **(16)** The advantages of Boarding-out are, in themselves, doubtful to the working classes. Deserting parents have been frequently known to claim their children when they have found it likely that they would be boarded-out beyond their own reach. **(17)** The system provides a home to which boys and girls can return when out of place after ceasing to be chargeable.

Con: **(1)** The true family is a divine institution; but no one contends that there is anything divine about foster mothers. Whether or not a child is brought up in "God's own way" depends entirely upon the character of the people under whose care it is placed. **(2)** Foster children are often ill-treated and neglected. Parents naturally prefer their own children to those of strangers, and rarely treat them alike. **(3)** Foster children are usually the drudges of the family, which is not likely to call out any of their higher qualities. **(4)** The quality of the moral and religious teaching given depends upon the character of the home. **(6)** Work in a cottage is no efficient training for work in a larger house, nor will cottagers give time to boarders when their own children require to be trained, nor are they often capable of systematic training. In the present state of agriculture, knowledge in this direction is of small use; it is impossible to find employment for more workers on the land. **(7)** The surroundings of a workhouse may be better than those of a cottage, especially if the cottager be in receipt of outdoor relief; nor is it possible in a village that the child's circumstances should not be known. **(8)** The cheapness of the system is no argument in its favour; the best system is always the cheapest in the end. **(9)** There are no complete statistics whereby to estimate the success of the system. Those published have been prepared either by those interested in the success of the scheme, or by those responsible for its administration. **(10)** The supervision is too intermittent to prevent all abuses. **(11)** Even where a Committee of ladies exists, they do not always find employment, especially for boys; and where no Committee exists, it depends on the Guardians. **(12)** Inspection must be made by experts to be efficient: this now only occurs in the case of those boarded-out beyond the Union. Were expert inspection extended to those boarded-out within the Union, as many cases of ill-treatment would probably be discovered as in the case of those boarded-out beyond the Union. **(14)** The Boarding-out System gets undue credit; only the pick of the children are boarded-out, and the Guardians are bound to take back from the Boarding-out Committee all those with whom the Committee cannot deal, on account of bad health, habits, or conduct: thus the workhouse becomes responsible for the failures of the Boarding-out system as well as its own. **(15)** Foster parents take children to profit by them, and are more attached to the payments than to the children. **(16)** The system induces parents to desert their children, that they may be otherwise provided for.

PEASANT PROPRIETORSHIP.

Pro: (1) Peasant Proprietorship encourages the growth of a sturdy, independent, and thrifty class of men, who are in every sense the backbone of a nation, and to whom, more than to anyone else, France owes it that she has been able to overcome the misfortunes of the Franco-German war. (2) Peasant Proprietors have, in many instances, by means of co-operation, been able to amass sufficient capital to carry out works of irrigation, etc., an undertaking supposed, on financial grounds, to be quite beyond their power. (3) The cultivation of small Peasant Properties has been carried to a great degree of perfection, and has in some cases made land, originally unfruitful, valuable. (4) The experience of most European countries, especially Germany, points to the creation of Peasant Properties as the surest method of keeping the labourers on the soil, thus helping to solve the social question. The presence of such a large body of conservative opinion must strengthen the hands of those who are upholding law and order as opposed to revolutionary changes. (5) The establishment of land banks would enable Peasant Proprietors to obtain credit, while leaving them independent of covenants. (6) It may be questioned whether the English resident landlord really has the refining influence attributed to him; for is not the Peasant Proprietor in France, Switzerland, or Germany vastly superior to the English labourer? (7) The great hope for Ireland lies in the creation of a body of Peasant Proprietors and the abolition of the present dual ownership. (8) The evils of subdivision are grossly exaggerated. Except in certain parts of Germany, they are non-existent, and even in those parts the evil is not very great. So far from the system tending to small families, in Germany the opposite effect has been observed. (9) The creation of a Peasant Proprietorship would undoubtedly tend to increase home consumption, as opposed to the consumption of imported goods. (10) The standard of living among Peasant Proprietors is unquestionably higher than that of our rustics: they put all profits into their own pockets, whilst the English rustic gains nothing.

Con: (1) Peasant Proprietorship establishes a class of men who, not having enough land to keep them in comfort, are miserable. Generally in the hands of the money-lenders, and without capital, their land is starved and improvements are impossible, interminable labour on the part of themselves and their families hardly enables them to live, and being shut out from all prospects of anything better, they grow up with an utterly sordid view of life. (2) What a few intelligent Peasant Proprietors may have been able to do by means of co-operation affords no sufficient evidence to enable us to decide that the same arrangement would be possible among a people less used to habits of mutual help. At any rate, the English system of big farms enables the tenant to devote his money entirely to agricultural purposes, such expenses as purchase money, cost of permanent improvements, etc., all falling on the landlord. (3) The English and Scotch farming systems have done more than any other to introduce scientific methods into agriculture. (4) France and other countries show that rural depopulation continues in spite of Peasant Proprietorship; it is caused by a longing, on the part of the people, for a wider, freer, and fuller life than the country can afford, rather than by a sense of the injustice of the land system. The political effect of a Peasant Proprietary would be to create a large body of men opposed to all reform. (5) The existing credit institutions afford all reasonable facilities for loans on a safe basis. Agriculture is notoriously uncertain—it being largely dependent on the weather—and credit cannot be granted on the same terms as are possible with other businesses. (6) The presence of the landlord has unquestionably a refining influence on a district, as may be seen by observing those estates where the Hall is shut up. For the richer classes to be brought into closer contact with their poorer neighbours helps to keep up social ties and to promote good feeling. (7) Ireland would lose a great deal more than is generally supposed were the landowners dispossessed, as they form the only people of light and leading fit to undertake public functions among an ignorant and superstitious peasantry. (8) Subdivision has been a great source of evil in France, which is now overcome by resorting to means which are even worse in their effects on the nation, viz., the voluntary limitation of the family. (9) A Peasant Proprietorship would be able to bring a strong influence to bear in favour of protection and a dear loaf in antagonism to the interests of the town workers, on whom England's prosperity depends. (10) The standard of living among Peasant Proprietors is very low, and is in no whit remedied by the fact that the savings are their own : they generally go to the usurer. (11) It would be almost impossible to introduce the system into Great Britain, where the existing system works very well, and has proved that it is adapted to the wants of the people.

POLICE, METROPOLITAN, AND POPULAR CONTROL.

Pro: (1) The Metropolitan Police are paid out of the local rates, and ought to be under the control of the ratepayers. (2) This is done in every other town of any importance in the United Kingdom. (3) The necessity for it was seen in the behaviour of the police, acting under instructions from the Home Secretary, as to the right of meeting in Trafalgar Square ; had they been under municipal control such a conflict would have been impossible ; that the Government was wrong was shown in that the succeeding Home Secretary revoked the policy in question, allowing meetings to be held in the Square. (4) (Some) A compromise might be effected by allowing a special force to guard the Government Offices, Houses of Parliament, Royal Palaces, etc.; whilst the Metropolitan Police, under the County Council, had control of the rest. Outlying districts (*e.g.* Croydon), now under the Metropolitan Police, might have their own force, and be absolved from contributing to the Metropolitan Force.

Con: (1) The preservation of order in London cannot be left to the vagaries of a popularly-elected body. (2) London stands on a different footing from other towns in the Kingdom. As the centre of the Empire, and containing the national buildings, public offices, etc., it belongs to the whole Empire, and not only to its inhabitants. (3) The case of Trafalgar Square illustrates the wisdom of keeping the police independent of elected bodies ; Trafalgar Square was the least fitted place in London for a large demonstration, since its space is confined and its traffic immense. The Government was justified in denying the right to a comparatively small number of agitators to obstruct the traffic and depreciate the property of the people in the neighbourhood. Had a popularly-elected body had control, it would not have shown the same firmness in quelling the riots. The succeeding Home Secretary put such restrictions on the use of the Square, that, whilst giving way nominally, in reality he kept up the *status quo ante.* (4) Great confusion of jurisdiction would ensue if the Government Offices were under one jurisdiction and the streets under another ; and great advantages exist in having a uniform system over a large area, so that the various policemen in the different districts can co-operate.

POPULATION, AND THE MEANS OF SUBSISTENCE.

Pro: (1) Men, animals, and plants all tend to multiply far beyond their actual requirements ; and any one species, if it were to increase unchecked, would soon cover the earth with its own kind, to the exclusion of every other. (2) Even if "Survival of the Fittest," brought about by this tendency of Population, has hitherto resulted in the progress of mankind, it does not necessarily follow that this will always be the case; civilization has been throughout a protest against the ruder methods of nature, and Natural Selection itself is wholly altered when it becomes a conscious process. The phrase "Survival of the Fittest" itself requires definition. (3) Competition does not produce the highest type of men, or the cleverest, but rather the most selfish and shrewd. (4) The higher the birth-rate among members of a certain class, the higher the death-rate; for where parents have not enough money to give their children sufficient food, the children will not be healthy. (5) Increase of Capital is a different thing from increase in the means of subsistence. (6) Emigration is a palliative, not a remedy; for, though large portions of the earth are still uninhabited, many are uninhabitable; the few remaining must soon be occupied at the present rate. (7) So long as we leave it to nature (*e.g.* pestilence) to correct surplus population, so long shall we be exposing ourselves to social misery. (8) The national benefits arising from small families with the possibilities of thrift, are clearly shown by the taxation France bears with equanimity.

Con : (1) No species has ever succeeded, or is ever likely to succeed, in monopolizing the whole earth; what is true of animals and plants is probably also true of mankind. (2) Society must be governed by the laws of social welfare; since the progress of the race has, under Natural Selection, hitherto been satisfactory, it would be folly to seek to interfere with it. (3) Competition is the best means for developing what is good in men. (4) Children of small families tend to be weakly and dependent, owing to the over-anxious attention received from the mother; they become healthy and independent in proportion to the size of the family. Numbers are of the highest importance to a military nation. (5) The average standard of life is higher to-day than it was some years ago, a proof that population has not increased faster than the means of subsistence during the present century. (6) Emigration will always relieve such temporary pressure as arises from industrial causes, and the vast tracts of land still unoccupied reduce the fear of over-population to the level of a mere chimera. It must be borne in mind also that England's foremost position among the nations is largely due to the fact that she has often had to search for fresh fields for emigration. (7) The surest indication of prosperity in a nation is a rapidly-increasing population, and the sign most dreaded by economists is a falling off in the birth-rate. Social distress must be dealt with by other means. (8) In France, in spite of the steady decrease in the population, poverty still exists. (9) The people most likely to adopt Malthusian principles are just those whose progeny is most likely to benefit their country.

POST OFFICE, THE, AS A PUBLIC MONOPOLY.

Pro : (1) The Post Office efficiently fulfils a very distinct public want. It supplies a uniform system of postage all over the kingdom; competition, while serving the big centres very efficiently, would neglect the agricultural districts, just as the Railway Companies expend all their energies on more or less useless competitions between the large towns. (2) Whereas in Railway parcel-carrying, goods which have to pass from one Company to another frequently get lost or delayed in transit, in the Post Office such losses or delays rarely occur. The Dead Letter Office is infinitely more conscientiously managed than it would be if in private hands. (3) If the Post Office were open to rivalry and run on competitive lines, the system would eventually result in a "pool," whereby the public would certainly not benefit. (4) The Post Office is all the better for not being too anxious to take up every novelty, regardless of profit. (5) The profit earned by the Post Office is a great relief to the overburdened taxpayer, and it is a very fair way of raising revenue, and one that is hardly felt at all. (6) Were it admitted that theoretically no profit should be earned by a public department, it would be impossible to work out the accounts to balance exactly. (7) The purchase of the telegraphs was right; and though too high a price may have been paid for them, yet the blame is due not to the system, but to the men who were responsible for the payments. (8) A Government department need not work a business of this sort badly, as may be seen from the German and French postal and telegraph systems.

Con: (1) The Post Office is derived from the worst traditions of the English Government, having been originally devised to provide an income for the then Duke of York. It is badly managed, and private enterprise would furnish a far more effective economical service, which would not neglect the country districts; Railway Companies always find it better to construct even an unprofitable line, rather than let a rival Company enter their district. (2) Losses and delays of railway parcels are much exaggerated. The Dead Letter Office spends an absurd amount of energy and intelligence on curious inquiries which would be better expended in other directions. (3) If the monopoly were abolished, the Post Office would have to rely on its merits, and the service be *pro tanto* improved. (4) The Post Office is opposed to reform; it took years of agitation to persuade it to adopt penny postage. The establishment of an Agricultural Parcels Post at low rates, to give farmers better communication with their markets, has not been undertaken even yet. While the Railway Companies carry their own letters for about one-thirty-sixth of a penny apiece, and make a profit on it, the Post Office charges the traditional penny. The Post Office by its monopoly has checked and thwarted the use of the telephone; and the excellent system of Boy Messengers has been crippled by the heavy sum which has to be paid to the Post Office authorities. (5) The present system puts it in the power of the Government to remove a part of the expenditure from the direct supervision of Parliament. (7) When the Post Office took over the Telegraphs these were paying very good dividends; but owing to the exorbitant price given, and to bad management since, it has proved a heavy loss to the Department. Again, as far as the Parcels Post is concerned, the price paid to the Railway Companies on account of carriage was so heavy that the Post Office finds it in many cases cheaper to revert to the old stage-coach method of despatching parcels by road. (8) A business of this sort is not suitable for management by a department of State.

PREMATURE BURIAL: are preventive means necessary?

Pro: (1) Owing to the absence, in most countries, of proper laws relative to the disposal of the dead, to hastiness of Burials during epidemics, to the uncertainty in the signs of death, as well as to the existence of certain morbid states that very closely counterfeit the appearances of death, the danger of Living Burial is a very real one. (2) Many hundreds of cases of Premature Burial are on record; and the recent discussion of the question in the press has added a large number of instances, and of cases of narrow escape by accidental good fortune. (3) The practices of embalming, autopsy, burial and cremation should be discouraged, until every possible source of doubt is removed. Sudden death is most uncommon, unless accompanied by great mutilation, or the injury of a vital part; and no evidence except decomposition is trustworthy, or should be so accepted. (4) The erection of mortuaries for all bodies in which decomposition has not yet commenced, should at once be undertaken; and a close examination by experts should be made the day previous to the funeral. (5) Failing the erection of mortuaries, the least that can be done is to insert in the coffin a bottle of chloroform with a leaky stopper, in all cases in which decomposition has not become unmistakably manifest, unless autopsy or embalming has been performed.

Con: (1) The present laws and regulations are quite sufficient. It may, doubtless, be true that a body may occasionally be prematurely buried; but this must be excessively rare, at any rate in Europe. The commonly accepted signs of death are admitted by all the best scientific men to be valid. (2) "Cases" got up by laymen are almost always untrustworthy, especially when they are sent to the newspapers, many of whose editors accept almost any sensational matter, regardless of its authenticity. (3) The practice of cremation should be encouraged, and the sooner it is universally adopted the better for all. (*See* CREMATION.) Assuming that some bodies are disposed of before death, cremation would, at any rate, prevent the risk of resuscitation after Burial. (4-5) The erection of mortuaries would be an unnecessary expense, since the whole scare about Premature Burial is nothing but a fad.

PRISON REFORM.

Pro: (1) Reformation of criminals is the duty of the State towards society. (2) Every prisoner should be individualized and given the special treatment adapted to develop him on the point on which he is weak, physically, intellectually, or morally. (3) Time must be given for the reformatory system to take effect. The cure is facilitated by the prisoner's co-operation, and often impossible without it. Therefore, power must be given to the Director of the prison to lengthen or shorten the term of incarceration. (4) The whole process of reformation should be educational in its widest sense; it should draw out every faculty of the body, mind, and soul. (5) (Lombroso and his school) Criminals may be divided into three classes: (*a*) Political Criminals; (*b*) Criminals by Passion; (*c*) Habitual Criminals. The last are by far the most numerous, and will be found to exhibit certain common characteristics, *e.g.* heads of an abnormal shape, liability to epilepsy, scrofula, sullenness, and other clearly-marked abnormal types. These facts point to the conclusion that Crime ought to be regarded as a disease, and treated medically, rather than in a punitive way. (6) The Elmira State Reformatory in New York, and the Convent Prison at Neudorf, near Vienna (where, owing to Austrian women being exempt from Capital Punishment, there are never less than 100 inmates), have been very successful in their humane methods of dealing with their inmates; and this system, or such modification of it as may be necessary for this country, might with advantage be introduced, at least as an experiment. (7) There is no reason why treatment should be made pleasant; but unpleasantness should not be sought for its own sake, reformation being the sole end in view.

Con: (1) The duty of the State is to the public, not to the individual or to the criminal class. (2) The whole reformatory system is a fad. It leads to the grossest hypocrisy on the part of the prisoner, whose sole object is to secure his release. (3) The reformatory system applied to prisons would be very costly. Why should we spend more on educating our criminals than our non-criminals, when money is needed for Primary Education? (4) Incorrigible offenders should be locked up for life, as dangerous to society. Other offenders should be treated with the utmost severity, to prevent a repetition of the offence, and as a warning to others. (5) The science of Criminology, as originally enunciated by Prof. Lombroso, is made up of theories and distorted facts. Many of the traits so loudly announced as criminal have no necessary connection with rime, and are constantly found in people who have shown no criminal tendencies at all. If true, however, it does not seem worth while to burden the ratepayers for the sake of a doubtful cure, when extermination would be the most efficacious remedy. In any case, the theory is a very dangerous one for a State to hold, and relaxes the idea of responsibility. (6) Elmira was long a byword, for the prisoners had a much better time of it inside than outside its walls, and New York State has now declined to support the institution. (7) Punishment must be to a certain extent retributive, to satisfy the wounded feelings of the community.

PROFESSIONALISM IN FOOTBALL (AND IN CRICKET).

Pro: (1) When it was found that Football drew large crowds of spectators, clubs began to charge entrance money; and players, often working men, saw no reason why they should not benefit. So clubs, although payment of players was illegal under the laws of the Association, began to pay their men according to the gate receipts. This was soon discovered, and after a struggle, professionalism was eventually legalized, entirely altering the character of the game. The modern professional is quite different from the secretly paid player of some years ago, who was an unqualified evil, professedly playing for sport whilst really almost living upon it. The modern professional, whilst still a lover of the game, sells his play openly, and is no worse than a mechanic or an actor. (2) Professionalism improves the quality and raises the standard in all sports. This has been specially true of Cricket, Racquets, Rowing, and Football, *e.g.* the theory of combination and "passing" in the Association game is the product of Northern professional Football, and has superseded the old individual "dribbling" game. It is natural that men who devote the best part of their lives to a sport, who make a scientific study of it, and physically train for it, should be useful as examples to amateurs. (3) It is also good for the professionals, as games have an ennobling influence on their devotees, and call forth many moral qualities. (4) Professionalism in Cricket is an unmixed benefit to the game; and a necessity, if first-class Cricket is to continue. There must be practice-bowlers, and men to coach schools and young players: and the game takes up so much time, that it is impossible to find enough amateurs to play in three-day matches, or get sufficient practice for first-class proficiency. Why not, therefore, professionalism in Football? (5) Football weekly attracts thousands of people, especially the poor, as spectators, and provides them with healthy and manly entertainment, instead of leaving them to seek their Saturday afternoon amusement in low places. This spectacular Football cannot be provided without professionals. (6) (Some) A compromise between professionalism and the amateurism which is said to be impossible for the working man may be found in the legislation of payment for broken time, but nothing else.

Con: (1) Professionalism in all games, but especially in Football, tends to lower their tone, by introducing into them a commercial element. Games are amateur by nature, and are ruined by being turned into trades. If professionals are necessary for coaching purposes, they should be debarred from playing in public, for it is in this relation that abuses and scandals arise. (Some) It would be better to have nominally no professionals, taking the chance of secret sins, than to have professionalism with its attendant League Matches, combinations, cup competitions, and the circus performance defined in the North as a "Friendly," with the result that genuine inter-club matches, which are not propped up by such additional supports, go to the wall, the game losing thereby. Association Football, since it has legalized professionalism, confirms the forecasts that were made of it. The ordinary amateur can scarcely get an Association game, except in London or the southern districts. He must either learn to play Rugby or give up all idea of keeping up the sport. Let us not also spoil Rugby Football, which so far is practically undamaged. (2) Games develop quite satisfactorily under amateurs. In Football "passing" must sooner or later have replaced "dribbling" in any case. (3) Professionalism in games has no ennobling influence on the players, but degrades. The one ground on which all might meet in friendly rivalry is turned into a commercial arena. So keen are professionals on winning, and so great is their stake, that they are often tempted to adopt unfair and dishonest practices. (4) Cricket as a profession is quite different from Football. A cricketer can get employment from eighteen or nineteen years of age till he is almost an old man, and can save money for his last years. A Football professional has a very short career. Some turn their transient reputations to good account. Many receive shops or public-houses, as bribes to transfer their allegiance from one club to another. (Some) Everyone can afford to play Football without receiving any payment beyond his out-of-pocket expenses. (5) Spectacular Football without professionalism is provided in the Rugby districts; were this not so, the people should be contented with such sport as they can get. (6) Payment for broken time would be merely the thin edge of the wedge eventuating in pure professionalism. The history of Association Football shows this.

PROFIT SHARING.

Pro: (1) The worker creates, to a large degree, the profits pocketed by the capitalist, and it is only right that he should be allowed a share in them. Though he cannot directly contribute to losses in bad years, he may do so indirectly by the establishment of a Reserve Fund, and by foregoing bonuses in good years. (2) Under the present system an employé has no interest in the success of a business, in the prevention of waste, or of damage to machinery. (3) Profit Sharing brings the capitalist and the worker together, and tends to prevent strikes. (4) It improves the quality, and leads to an increase in the quantity of the output. (5) It has, with a few exceptions, succeeded very well where tried. Had the two most noted English examples (Briggs & Co., Ld., and Fox, Head & Co., Ld.) not been turned into a means for defeating the Trade Unions, it is probable that their success would have been continuous.

Con: (1) As long as workers have no share in losses as well as in profits, any scheme for Profit Sharing amounts to charity on the part of the employer. The employé has no claim beyond the competitive value of his labour: it is a pure fallacy to argue that he does any work that contributes to earning the *profits* of a business. The controlling force in this respect is the employer, who, according as he uses his brains and his capital wisely or foolishly, will make a profit or a loss. (2) Profit sharing, when adopted, is merely a device on the employer's part to increase his own ultimate profits, by getting more efficient, and a larger amount of, work out of the men. (3) It is a mere palliative of evils inherent in our present industrial system, and does not touch the real sources of mischief. (4) Profit sharing is apt to injure the health of the workmen, by inducing overwork, and to demoralize them, by tempting them to act as spies on one another. (5) Where the system has been introduced, it has failed lamentably in all save a few cases. It is almost invariably adopted with some such purpose as breaking up Trade Unions.

PSYCHICAL RESEARCH.

Pro: (1) There is a vast body of evidence in favour of occultism, dating from the earliest ages to the present day. (2) The number of so-called coincidences within everybody's experience is too great to be attributed to mere chance. (3) The scientific world as a whole uninquiringly dismisses these phenomena; yet instances of facts which once contravened the *consensus* of scientists, but subsequently gained it, abound (*e.g.* the revolution of the earth round the sun, mesmerism). The *general consensus* of mankind is rarely "based on educated common sense," or "ready to accept the *dicta* of experts": experts are unable by direct experimental treatment to prove their case, and decline to be present at the experiments of others, on the ground of their predetermined futility, and have ultimately no other defence of their position than the inherent incredibility of the opposing testimony, thus not only forming a handful of men who, in their own opinion, are sane whilst all the rest of the world is mad, but actually disappearing as a separate class. The common tendency to regard new "facts" as improbable or impossible on the ground of absence of evidence, and then, when evidence is offered, of refusing to examine it on the ground of this very improbability or impossibility, is an unscientific and unfair attitude, and effectually bars progress. The questions in point entirely transcend the region of scientific authority or experiment. The *rationale* of individuality, of matter and spirit, of life and death, are not laboratory questions. If men of science treat them as such, the result is bad philosophy, not science. (4) Negative inductions from experience are, by their very nature, not final: to try to make them final, is to close the door on the possibility of new conditions which may affect the result. (5) (Some) Observation of facts has often outrun the knowledge of their conditions, and opinion as to the facts has been in such cases widely led astray, either in the direction of credulity or of incredulity, according to the temper of the individual or of the age; and then, after a time, analogies have presented themselves, or the special conditions which made the facts possible have been more completely elucidated; then it has been found that there has been no breach of continuity and no contradiction—only a further extension and determination—of natural law. There is no ground for supposing that new or unusual facts will cease to appear and gradually make good their position in the natural scheme.

Con: (1) Most of the "facts" of occultism are traceable to two sources: (*a*) the tendency to attribute whatever is not immediately understood to occult agencies; (*b*) the myth-making tendency, which is implanted in almost every human being, and in yielding to which the average imagination finds its easiest and most congenial exercise. Other of the "occult" phenomena of the past and of the present are to be credited to the various forms of hysteria and other neuropathic conditions, which are as little occult as any other mental or moral phenomena. (2) It would be more than a coincidence if the number of coincidences were fewer than they are. The human mind takes no note of coincidences which, so to speak, do *not* happen, and correspondingly exaggerates the strangeness of those that do. (3) In abstruse questions lay evidence and lay opinion are almost worthless; they usually increase in confidence in proportion not so much to the possibilities of proof, as to the impossibilities of disproof; and highly-educated people are deceived by jugglers.* Long-continued experiment by trained specialists can alone lead to any trustworthy results. Evidence as to new "facts" must correspond in strength with the degree of their incompatibility with doctrines generally admitted as true; and, where statements obviously contravene all past experience and the general *consensus* of mankind, based on "educated common sense," any evidence is inadequate which is incomplete. (4) The hypothesis of new conditions demands most careful use. There are cases where the existence of the supposed condition is, in itself, quite as improbable as the occurrence of the alleged fact; and in such cases, the *à priori* improbability of the new fact is not at all diminished by the assumption of the new condition; the issue is merely thrust a step further back.

RAILWAY NATIONALIZATION.

Pro: (1) Railways are a natural monopoly, and while competition may seem to have advantages, experiences in England and America have shown that competition can only be worked at such a ruinous cost that in England at least the Companies have always come to terms. (2) The State in most

* See Hodgson and Davey's papers on "The Possibilities of Mal-Observation," in the *Proceedings of the Society for Psychical Research*, vol. iv.

European countries owns and works its lines most successfully. Among others the Belgian, Prussian, Bavarian, Austrian, and Hungarian Railways are owned and worked by the State, and for comfort, speed, and cheapness come in no way behind those of Private Companies. (3) Whilst a Private Company would only make a new Railway if it was likely to pay, or, in rare instances, in order to keep another Company out, the State would only consider the needs of a district. (4) The Railway vote in the House of Commons is disproportionately large, and presents a standing menace to the purity of our public life. (5) With State Railways would follow the substitution of one central authority for scattered bodies working independent of each other, thus avoiding the present great discomfort to the public, due to the refusal of the various companies to work into one another's hands. This method alone would make it possible to introduce into England the "Zone" system of travelling now obtaining on the Austrian and Hungarian State Railways, and which possess enormous advantages in cheapness and simplicity of working both for officials and the public. (6) A great economy would be effected by dispensing with directors—who are useless, because in the hands of the general manager—and by substituting a small number of responsible commissioners. The number of officials might also be reduced by the abolition of the competing systems, and of the number of competing trains. (7) Private companies spend so much money on a few racing expresses, and in competing with other companies, that the great majority of their trains fall far below the mark, and many districts get badly served. (8) In America the Railways have, by preferential rates, rebates, etc., favoured the growth of giant monopolies, such as the Standard Oil Trust, etc., and in England they have in like manner enabled the foreigner to undersell the home producer. (9) By carrying half-empty first and second-class carriages the Companies naturally increase the cost of travelling, since these classes, being carried either at a loss or at very small profit, have to be paid for out of the profits of the third-class passenger. (10) State Railways, by enabling workmen and third-class passengers generally to obtain season tickets, would enable them to live in the country, away from their work, and thus contribute enormously to the health of the community. (11) State Railways would aid commerce generally by simplifying the rates of carriage for goods, and by putting them on an intelligible system, so that a man might always know what he would have to pay on a particular class of goods. (12) The Italian experience really decides nothing on the main question of State ownership, since the conditions were so peculiar that the experience cannot be applied elsewhere. (13) The expense of State purchase has been greatly exaggerated, and could easily be met in the same way as in Prussia—at that time a very much poorer country than England is now; the transaction has paid, and the profits of the Railway are a great relief to taxation. (14) The introduction of State Railways would greatly reduce the hours worked by Railway servants.

Con: (1) The English Railways are in no sense monopolies, since Parliament is always ready to sanction the making of rival lines if it will serve a useful purpose. The countries where competition and private ownership of Railways are found are those where the greatest comfort and speed to the passenger is met with combined with cheapness. (2) Continental State Railways are proverbial for their inefficiency and expensive rates. (3) Private Companies frequently make lines which are never likely to pay, or not for many years, entirely at their own cost, whereas the English Post-office will not establish a new telegraph station without being guaranteed against loss. Where the State departs from commercial principles scandals arise, such as those connected with the so-called Strategic Railways in France. (4) It rests with the electors to choose their own members; if they choose Railway directors, that is their concern. It is also only natural that where the Railway Companies find themselves menaced by predatory legislation they should seek to protect themselves. The task of keeping State Railways free from party politics is almost impossible in a democratic country. (5) The advantages due to the cessation of competition would be as nothing compared with the inertia engendered by the absence of all stimulus to exertion and progress. (6) The economy due to the abolition of directors would be insignificant. The chief difficulty of State Railways is how to keep them clear of party politics, as it is obvious that such a complex business could not be managed, as the Post-office is, by a chief who would probably have to resign just as he had learnt his work. In Australia the system of non-political commissioners holding their posts on the same terms as Her Majesty's Judges has not been very successful, and in Victoria has been definitely abandoned. (7) The country districts are better served in England than in Germany. (8) Uniform rating has often been tried—notably on the Prussian State Railways—but given up in all cases as impracticable; and it is only right that when one man can, by taking a whole train or by filling a truck, save the Company certain expenses, he should be charged at a lower rate. (9) If the Companies choose to carry first and second-class passengers at a loss they must be allowed to do so at their own cost. (11) There must always be great difficulty in classifying different kinds of goods, and there is no reason to believe that the State Railways could do anything in this direction which the Private Companies cannot do. (12) Commissioners appointed by the Italian Government to inquire into the working of the Italian State Railways, and to examine the relative merits of the State and Private Railway Systems, reported in favour of the latter, on the ground that nothing which the former could do would not be better done by the latter; while the latter, besides giving their customers many facilities which the former did not give, were much better and more economically worked, and, above all, were free from all political influence. (13) The expenses of State purchase would be so heavy that the transaction could never pay. The profits made by the Prussian State Railways are quite illusory, since a more than equal sum is spent on them, and figures in the Budget. (14) State ownership would involve the State in all the dangers of strikes, etc., and leave Parliament open to undue influence from the votes of Railway men.

RATES: their division between owner and occupier.

Pro: (1) The occupier pays all the rates, whilst the owner (or the various owners, where there are several interests) gets a portion of the benefit. Each class should pay in proportion to the benefit received. (2) It would be quite feasible to divide the burden near enough for all practical purposes, and to ensure that it shall be fairer than the present haphazard system. (3) It would be much more simple, and avoid many difficulties (such as yearly assessment), were a fixed proportion of the whole rates, not merely one or two special rates, to be thrown on the property as a whole. It could be easily worked through the existing machinery, and could be calculated by the ratepayer, who would only have to deduct from his rent payments a certain fixed sum, just as he now does in the case of the Income Tax. (4) The principle, though in force in connection with the Income Tax (Scotland and Ireland), has not been found to raise rents. (5) It was recommended by committees in 1866 and 1870.

Con: (1) The present system has grown up gradually, and represents a very just division. No occupier takes a house in ignorance of the approximate amount of the rates. (2) That it is impossible to arrive at an absolutely fair division of the burden is a sufficient argument against disturbing existing arrangements, under which at least rough justice is done. (3) The present system is the most simple; the occupier is always to be found, whilst it is not always easy to trace the landlord. (4) The proposed system would undoubtedly raise rents in the end.

REFERENDUM, THE.

Pro: (1) The adoption of the compulsory Referendum, and possibly the Initiative, would be the greatest possible safeguard against sudden tampering with the constitution; as it would be applied only on important questions of constitutional change, it would not involve any serious change in the routine of government. (2) English statesmen who are wont to congratulate themselves on the democratic nature of our Constitution, and on their subservience to the will of the people, can hardly object to any measure the sole purport of which is to increase the efficiency of popular control. . (3) The checks to over-hasty legislation exercized by the House of Lords in this country, and the various Senates abroad, are inefficient, for they constitute in the eyes of the masses a defiance on the part of the aristocracy and plutocracy to the wishes of the people; whereby the issue becomes a different one, and measures which may have had their support before, do so no longer on account of their merits, but because they have been identified with the cause of popular rights. (4) General Elections are supposed to be an appeal to the country on particular measures; the issues are, however, so obscured by various side issues, that it is often impossible to attribute success to any specific cause. The Referendum would abolish this uncertainty, and render it impossible for a measure of which the people disapprove to become law. (5) It would force the electors to vote for measures, not for men; this they are perfectly competent to do; candidates are supported less because of their individual fitness than because they represent a party or are pledged to support a particular policy or statesman of whom the electors approve. (6) The Referendum would be most valuable as an educational factor, encouraging in the electors the habit of thinking for themselves on all questions of the day. (7) The adoption of the Referendum would not render Parliament unnecessary: it would make it more necessary, for it would be the duty of Members to decide how each measure should be drawn up, and to settle all questions of detail connected therewith, these being points on which the people would not be competent to act. (8) The Referendum has been at work for many years in Switzerland, and partially tried in several States of the American Union; in all cases it has been a great success. (9) There are many points connected with our legal and commercial systems on which the people would express a more unbiassed opinion than a House of Commons made up of lawyers, bankers, and Company promoters. (10) The adoption of the Referendum would weaken the detrimental influence exercized by the Party System over English politics: oratory and argument no longer weigh in a House of Commons made up of Members who vote in accordance with the orders of the Party Whip—it would be otherwise in view of an immediate appeal to the country. (11) (Some) A partial application of the Referendum might be made as an experiment. (12) The fact that the Referendum is not demanded by a large section of the people is no argument against its introduction. Its advantages are much more likely to be recognized after than before its adoption. (13) Between the General Elections, questions sometimes arise that were never discussed between a Member and his constituents; the former then acts without consulting the wishes of the latter, and occasionally in opposition to them. (14) The people have no temptation to compromise principles.

Con: (1) Sufficient checks to hasty legislation already exist in the Press and in public opinion; moreover, it would always be in the hands of the legislature or executive to decide what questions were or were not questions of constitutional change, and they would thus be able to defy the opinion of the House of Commons. (2) The English Constitution already errs on the side of democracy, and in a society where private property is recognized, and there are wide differences in the relative possessions and capacities of the citizens, it is unwise to leave the final decision on all vital matters in the hands of the populace. (3) The House of Lords, as representing the wealth, the intellect, and the culture of the country, is the most efficient check to ill-considered legislation. So far from weakening the House of Lords, the attacks on it have merely strengthened it. (4) In a General Election, statesmen are so identified with the measures they propose or oppose, and candidates elected so often on the ground of their support or opposition to a particular policy, that it is clear that the opinion of the majority on the main issue is the decisive factor in the situation. (5) The electors, while perfectly competent to decide between the capacities of two candidates, are not fit to decide on questions of general policy. (6) The efficiency of the Government is a much more important aim than the education of voters, who ought to obtain their education in a less expensive manner than by tampering with the Constitution. (7) The adoption of the Referendum would destroy the responsibility of the House of Commons, and deteriorate the tone of its Members. (8) Switzerland is too small, and its inhabitants too poor, to afford any precedent for the successful working of a similar system in a densely populated and wealthy country like England. The experiment in the United States has been so very partial that it is impossible to say how far it would be a success if tried all round. (10) Under the Referendum the Party System would be as rampant as ever, since the mass of voters, being ignorant on general questions, would follow one side or the other, and men keen to carry a reform would buy support for their particular hobby by promising support to other men's hobbies. Debates in the House of Commons would rapidly deteriorate under the Referendum, and would be left almost entirely in the hands of men anxious to distinguish themselves in the eyes of the people. (11) A partial application of the Referendum would prove nothing as to its applicability in its complete form, and would tend to produce an impression that the Constitution might be altered to suit a mere whim of the moment. (12) Until the Referendum is asked for, it would be absurd to introduce it. (13) (Some) The adoption of shorter Parliaments would supply the want of touch between a Member and his constituency better than any violent change in the constitution.

REGISTRATION OF TITLE TO LAND.

Pro: (1) Since the present Land Transfer is very cumbersome and expensive, it would be better to substitute for it one whereby a purchaser could, on payment of a small fee, obtain all necessary information respecting his intended purchase. Land Registry Offices should be established, and all owners be required to register their holdings and give evidence of their title within a specific time. (2) (Some) Registration of Title might be left to the discretion of the landowner; most would avail themselves of it. (3) It would facilitate the transfer of land, and would render the sale of portions of estates more easy. (4) It would facilitate the purchase of land by a tenant farmer or small holder, by diminishing the costs of transfer, which are now out of all proportion to the value of a small property. (5) The present system is responsible for delay and litigation. Under Registration, the titles would be fixed once for all, and there could be no dispute, whereas now transfers become more costly at each transaction. (6) The proposed system would make the process of raising money on mortgage much safer for the mortgagee, for the landlord would have to register all mortgages on his estate, hence there could be no doubt as to possible prior mortgages. This would not subject the landlord's affairs to inquisitive people any more than is the case with wills at Somerset House. (7) Registration would remove all danger of fraud by forged title deeds, etc., in the selling of land. (8) Registration in some shape prevails in Scotland, Ireland, and Australia, and has succeeded very well.

Con: (1) The proposed scheme would be impracticable, and would cause hardship to the landowner, inasmuch as he would be compelled to expose his titles to public view, whether he wanted to sell his land or not, with the danger that a flaw might be discovered in them. (2) If purely voluntary, any Act would be a dead letter. (3) It would destroy the old families, and concentrate the land in the hands of rich business men, who would regard it purely as a speculation. (4) It is impossible that a mere reduction in the cost of Land Transfer could enable a man to buy his farm if he were not otherwise able to do so; it does not do so in America or Australia; and even if it did the capital outlay involved would merely diminish the working funds at his disposal. (5) The proposed system would lead to much litigation concerning disputed titles, and would be a boon to none but needy lawyers. (6) It would be a great hardship to compel a landowner to make the transaction public every time he raised a mortgage, especially in the case of business men, who very often tide over difficulties by raising money on their residential estates—transactions which must be completed as secretly as possible, for the sake of maintaining credit intact. (7) Registration of Title would prevent fraud; but this solitary advantage offered by it would not outweigh the hardships it would inflict.

REVERSIONISTS, RATING OF.

Pro: (1) In order to repay the capital borrowed for the purposes of permanent improvements a separate rate should be imposed on owners, for under the present system the greater part of the benefit goes to them, whilst the occupier pays for them. (2) The tenant gets little advantage from a sinking fund, since few are likely to be in possession when the loan is finally repaid; thus the whole benefit is really reaped by the landlord. (3) Whilst the occupier would pay the interest on the loan raised to meet these improvements, the *onus* of repaying the capital would rest on the owner, as the permanent interest in the property is vested in him. (4) Such a measure would help towards a fair readjustment of the incidence of rating.

Con: (1) Permanent improvements benefit the occupier for the time being far more than the owner, and it is not fair to tax him on a prospective benefit, which may perhaps never accrue to him. (2) It is impossible to accurately apportion the benefits received in this or in any other similar case. (3) The actual sinking fund itself, or the part which goes to the extinction of debt, is infinitesimal in proportion; and, as this is the only sum that can rightly be called the landlord's, it is not worth while to alter the whole rating of a locality on its account. (4) No reform of local rating can be piecemeal; it must be comprehensive.

RIGHTS OF ANIMALS.

Pro: (1) In the sense that men have rights, animals also have rights, though in a lesser degree. These rights consist in what Herbert Spencer calls the "restricted freedom" to live a natural life in harmony with the permanent requirements of the community. (2) Though the public is only just beginning to recognize these rights, the subject is one which has attracted attention in the earliest times. One of the maxims of the Buddhist and Pythagorean canons was "not to kill or injure any innocent animal." Jeremy Bentham asserted the rights of animals. (3) Animals have already certain limited rights, which are recognized in private usage and by legal enactment. But legislation (in Great Britain, at least) allows men to torture or burn alive a hare or a rabbit, or any other animal which the law does not consider "domestic." (4) The most urgently needed now is some intelligible principle which shall consistently indicate the true lines of man's moral relation towards the lower animals. The rights of animals now are subordinate to almost anything that can be construed into a human "want," including flesh eating, fur and feather wearing, hunting, and scientific research. (5) As animals live (if left to their true selves) their own lives fitly, and indicate a marked sense of individuality, they show the highest moral purpose, and there can be no higher in man. (6) Animals are weak, and need man's protection ; and before pain or death is inflicted, we must be assured that it is necessary. (7) If rights to exist must be reciprocal, what claim can a lunatic or an infant have on our protection ?

Con : (1) It is purely arbitrary to say that animals have rights in the sense in which men have them, even if the rights claimed for animals are less comprehensive than those of men. We may be said to have duties of kindness towards animals, but it is incorrect to represent these as strictly duties towards the animals themselves. (2) A flesh diet being necessary for the inhabitants of colder regions, at any rate, it is not possible to put into practice the teaching of the Buddhists or Pythagoreans on this point. (3) Animals are protected because they are valuable, and not because they have "rights." In the case of wild animals they are destroyed and hunted, because either they may be dangerous, or the hunting may give pleasure. (Some) It is wrong in man to ill-treat animals unnecessarily, inasmuch as it is demoralizing to his own finer instincts. (4) It is impossible to draw any but a purely arbitrary line between animals which should be protected by law and those which should not. That such a line is necessary appears self-evident, however, when we reflect that, otherwise, on the evolution hypothesis, it would be impossible to stop anywhere short of protoplasm, unless, indeed, we are prepared to show exactly where intelligence begins. (5) It is absurd to say that animals have a moral purpose of their own. Even the dog seems to have no higher motive than to please his master. (6) Animals are not always the weaker, and in some cases man has to be protected from them. If in order to live man must kill, then he is justified ; the same argument would apply to scientific research to save him from disease, to hunting to give him pleasure, and to the wearing of animal products to give him warmth and comfort. (7) The infant and the lunatic have this claim on the protection of society : to preserve itself, if for no natural reason, society must protect the young, and all men feel that they themselves might become insane.

SCIENTIFIC RESEARCH, STATE ENDOWMENT OF.

Pro : (1) Beyond a few temporary endowments of small value, no direct pecuniary encouragement is at present given to the scientific worker. Only exceptionally constituted minds are fitted for the work of scientific discovery, and it is impossible to calculate what discoveries are lost to the world through the fact that these few exceptional minds have to spend most of their energy on bread-winning. (2) As the highest kind of scientific work research should be endowed with special prizes ; but, instead, every difficulty is put in its way, and every other kind of work is paid rather than this. (3) The gifts of the teacher and of the discoverer are totally distinct. The discoverer is rewarded by a professorial chair, because there is no other reward to give him, and the result often is that his pupils get the worst possible teaching. Thus the cause of education suffers indirectly, because research is not paid. (4) The principle of division of labour is in this case utterly ignored, though everyone must realize how much the world would have lost had Darwin or Newton had to spend his time in lecturing and examining.

Con : (1) The worker is the best judge of the value of his work, and, under the present system, he is left to the task of enforcing his merits on those around him as best he may. The Endowment of Research would necessitate the organization of a special Board, whose duty it would be to criticize the value of the research work done. Such a Board would inevitably tend to become conservative, and to refuse reward to discoverers whose investigations were novel. (2) Endowment of Research by the State would render the ratepayer the real adjudicator regarding the value of any given research; an arrangement which would tend to hinder the pursuit of truth, rather than to further it. (3) Teaching would degenerate if the men of insight were all told off to another duty. Teaching helps the scientist enormously, and forces him to be clear in his own mind. (4) Under this system, a tendency to theorise in Science would be fostered, as there would be a motive for seeking novelties, which would not be counterbalanced by the necessity for constantly going over the work of previous observers in the process of teaching. Darwin and Newton were not lost to the world: true genius always "will out."

SEA SERPENT, THE: ITS EXISTENCE.

Pro: (1) There is abundant evidence that huge Sea Serpents, or marine monsters more or less like serpents but at present unclassified, inhabit the sea. The evidence is continuous, and dates from Olaus Magnus (16th century) to Dr. Farquhar Matheson (Sept., 1893) and Capt. R. J. Cringle (Dec., 1893). Possibly the number of such monsters is small. (2) The evidence cannot be explained away by any theory of optical illusion. For example, in the most recent authenticated instance of its observation (1893), Dr. Matheson said, "What I saw precludes all possibility of such an explanation. In the case of optical illusion, what the eye sees becomes attenuated, and thus gradually disappears. But in the case of the creature I saw, it slowly descended into the water; it reappeared the same way, gradually ascending. I saw it move its head from side to side, and I noticed the glistening of the light on its smooth, wet skin." Capt. Cringle said, "I have been so ridiculed about the thing that I have many times wished that anybody else had seen that Sea Monster rather than me. I have been told that it was a string of porpoises, that it was an island of seaweed, and I do not know what besides. But if an island of seaweed can travel at the rate of fourteen knots an hour, or if a string of porpoises can stand fifteen feet out of the water, then I give in, and confess myself deceived. Such, however, could not be." (3) The evidence as to Sea Monsters is likely to be minimised because anyone reporting to have seen one gets so laughed at for his pains. Until comparatively recently tales of gigantic cuttle-fishes were regarded with incredulity; yet the existence of such creatures is now as much a recognized scientific fact as that of the whale.

Con: (1) Sea Serpents and Sea Monsters are in most cases merely creations of superstitious wonder-mongers or "enterprizing" editors. In England they occur only when the "silly season" arrives with its showers of frogs and monster pike; and in America in the columns of obscure local papers. (2) A long trail of seaweed rocking upon the sea surface, or a procession of porpoises, is enough to account for a report of a Sea Serpent. As a rule, the reporter is a superstitious sailor, often at a great distance from the object of his observation. Dr. Matheson's and Capt. Cringle's reports, though interesting, are wanting in sufficient scientific verification to be accepted as scientific evidence; and it is doubtful if the intrinsic unlikelihood of the existence of these monsters can be disproved until we have an actual specimen in our hands. (3) Though it is wise to keep an open mind in all matters of natural science, it is almost certain that examples of dead Sea Monsters would have turned up, if they had existed.

SECOND BALLOTS.

Pro: (1) The system of Second Ballots, by forcing the successful candidate to have a clear majority of the votes polled, would lead to a truer representation of the people. (2) Without a Second Ballot it is quite possible for a man to be elected who has gained little more than one-third, or even less, of the votes polled. (3) Second Ballots would destroy the force of the argument brought by the local caucus managers, etc., against Labour candidates and others, that they are going to split the party.

(4) The greater the number of the candidates, the greater the choice of the electorate.   (5) It is very difficult for the party officials to decide which of two or three candidates will be likely to secure most votes ; which difficulty would be abolished by a system of Second Ballots.   (6) Such a system would tend to counteract the tyranny exercised by party feelings, and to reduce the power of caucus managers and others.   (7) It would enable opinions to be heard that now have no chance of being discussed at all.   (8) It would reveal the strength of different sections of a party, and thus prevent small but noisy minorities from obtaining an undue amount of attention.   (9) As candidates would not be forced to compromise so much on various questions, they would be much more independent.   (10) Undue multiplication of candidates might be checked by demanding a deposit from each, to be forfeited in the event of his not obtaining more than a fixed proportion of the votes polled.   (11) The multiplication of Liberal candidates of various shades of opinion already threatens the Liberal party with disruption, and has lost them many seats. (12) The system is very common abroad, and works well there.

Con : (1) There is no necessity for change ; under the present system the people are adequately represented.   (2) To constitute an effective majority there must be a common body of opinion, strong enough to hold a party together ; and it may be presumed that where there is not enough in common between two parties to enable one to give way to the other on an important point, the binding force of those common opinions is not very great.   (3) Friction would have been engendered to such an extent within the party by the First Ballot, that the conflicting members of a party would not be so willing to co-operate at the Second. Besides which, the extra expense involved would make it much harder for the Labour candidate to stand. (4) The system would encourage the multiplication of parties, as in the French Chamber.   (5) It is no part of our electoral machinery to help the political parties to know their own minds, nor is there sufficient reason why the whole machinery of government should be thrown out of order for that purpose.   (6) The evils of the caucus are much exaggerated : party discipline is a very valuable factor in our political life.   (7) Such a system would multiply fads and faddists in the House of Commons. (9) Second Ballots would not abolish the necessity for compromise, at least during the second election, if not during the first. Would a Radical teetotaler vote for a Liberal brewer, even though he were the elected of the party ? would he not rather vote even for a Tory ?   (10) A deposit system would constitute a property qualification and introduce a speculative element, since no man can accurately forecast the number of votes he is likely to poll.

SEX IN FICTION.

Pro : (1) The sex problem, *i.e.* the relation of the sexes to one another, is the most important social problem, and forms the basis of most fiction. (2) If treated with restraint, it affords both instruction and amusement to the reader. All books cannot be written for the " young person."

Con : (1) The novel reader of to-day is sick of the so-called "sex-problem," which does not really exist for pure-minded people. Each new writer seems to go more and more fully into prurient details. This is specially noticeable in books written by women ; and society should make a stand against it, as it tends to lower the standard of purity.   (2) Girls secretly obtain possession of books of this kind, whether their parents like it or not. The result is that a girl to-day often knows a great deal more than is good for her. Knowledge leads to conversation on topics which used to be, and should still be, held sacred ; and conversation sometimes leads to actual misconduct. In any case the mind is degraded, and the instincts get warped.

SOCIALISM. (*See* COLLECTIVISM.)

SOCIALISM AND NATURAL SELECTION.

Pro : (1) Socialism, by securing to each member of the community adequate means of subsistence and by maintaining him in comfort, would be incompatible with the effective working of Natural Selection, since not only would the Socialist State support all its members alike, but would also encourage them to perpetuate their species. (2) Some such form of Artificial Selection as is proposed by Socialists to meet the case, would be repellent to and rejected by the members of any healthy-minded society, and would not be half so effectual as the more simple method of Natural Selection. (3) Statistics show that, whereas the average human life has increased during the last 30 years, the relative number of those living to old age has decreased, leading us to think that the vitality of the race is decreasing, though weakly people are, by improved methods, kept alive longer than formerly. If this be the case under our present system of society, it may confidently be predicted that the evils will be greatly enhanced in society under a Socialist State, in which so much care is to be bestowed on its weakly members.

Con : (1) The system of private property means that weakly, diseased people, who under a healthy system would die out, are pampered, kept in the height of luxury, and married by beautiful women, thus being encouraged to perpetuate their species; whilst men physically most fit and healthy are, owing to poverty, unable to marry till late in life. (2) As preventive medicine becomes daily more perfect, so the selective agencies, *i.e.* the various diseases which attack the weakly, lose their force; as it is impossible in the present state of public opinion to allow certain diseases to go unchecked, it becomes necessary that some artificial substitute should be found to perform their work, that at least certain members of the community be prevented from perpetuating their species. Competition does not lead to the preservation of the best, but the most cunning, members of society.

SPECIAL ASSESSMENT OF LAND AND BUILDING VALUES.

Pro : (1) In every house there are two values, which are radically distinct —(*a*) that of the building itself, (*b*) that of the land it occupies. They should naturally be separately assessed. (2) The value of the building is a temporary one, that of the land is permanent. Justice, therefore, demands that each person enjoying these values should pay his own assessments. (3) The tenant already pays the full amount that the property is worth; it would be unlikely that the landlord could obtain much more rent from him. (4) There would be no difficulty in separating values in this way; it is done by surveyors in assessing them under the present system.

Con : (1) Rating should be as condensed as possible, and the simpler the basis of its calculation the better. (2) Under Special Assessment it would be impossible to apportion the charges accurately, as the terms on which buildings and land are held by tenants and sub-tenants differ materially. (3) Separate Assessment would lead to the tenant paying the landlord's rates, in the shape of increased rent; and he would thus gain nothing. (4) It would be most difficult to make a distinction in such a manner as to avoid disputes. For a surveyor to do a thing for his own convenience is very different from his undertaking it as a public duty.

SPELLING REFORM, ENGLISH.

Pro : (1) The importance of good English elocution is beginning to be recognized. Even amongst the well-educated, a clear and beautiful pronunciation is exceedingly rare; and it is not common to meet with uniformly accurate spelling. Philologists agree that acquaintance with the written symbols of a language is not an adequate knowledge of the language itself, and they are almost unanimous in favour of some reform. (2) English spelling is a great hindrance to the intelligent study of phonology: the same sounds are always masquerading in a new dress. Spelling should be reformed on the basis of phonology. (3) Such a reform would save an immense amount of time now wasted by the young in attempts to master spelling. (4) It would preserve rather than destroy the continuity of the language. Our early writers spell in very different ways from that of the present day. It is not proposed to create a sudden break, but to introduce a new system gradually, and when once it is established, to maintain it for all time.

Con: (1) A change in our Spelling would cause an enormous and unnecessary amount of trouble. Adults would have to relearn their language, or be considered antiquated. No such reform is needed. The time a child is said to waste on learning to spell is not really wasted. Education is not only a means of storing accurate information, but consists in the culture of the mind, for which purpose language studies are specially suitable. (2) An artificial system would destroy the whole continuity and beauty of our language and our literature; our classics would become unreadable to most people of the next generation, and our libraries be rendered almost useless. Languages grow, and no artificial checks should, or probably could, be put in the way of their natural development.

SPORT.

Sport is here used in the sense of field sports—shooting, hunting, and fishing.

Pro: (1) Sport is one of the best elements in our national life, tending to keep the race hardy and manly, and to maintain the idea that physical strength is an object to be aimed at. It does for England what military exercises attempt to do for the great Continental nations. (2) In many ways Sport obviates the evil effects of city life by bringing man closer to nature and to an observation of her ways; this is so especially in shooting and fishing. (3) The keen sportsman does not mind undergoing a very large amount of discomfort in pursuit of it, and this calls out in him the power of sacrificing the present to the future, one of the signs of the superiority of man over the brutes. (4) Sport encourages the growth of the powers of observation, of quick calculation, and of rapid decision. (5) The chief objections to Sport are made on behalf of so-called humanitarianism, which claims that animals should be admitted to "rights," and be regarded as existing for their own end. Man can tolerate the existence of animals only in so far as they subserve his aims, and those which are either useless or harmful to men must disappear. We cannot tolerate poisonous animals on the ground of some kindness owed by us to them. Rights must be reciprocal, or they cannot exist. (*See* RIGHTS OF ANIMALS.) (6) Sport has been an element in the spread of civilization and in giving us a knowledge of unexplored parts of the world. It has given to the English that roving spirit which has placed them in the forefront of the nations of the world.

Con: (1) No question of "manliness" can justify men in *killing animals merely to gratify their pleasure.* Games like football, cricket, polo, etc., are more efficacious than Sport proper in promoting the manliness of the race. (2) The study of nature through the methods of science will give a much deeper and better knowledge of nature than the stray notes of the sporting man. (3) Whatever may have been the case in the past, Sport is now largely accompanied by luxury of all kinds. (5) The denial of rights to animals involves the denial of rights to men, since the evolution theory has shown the error of assuming that there is any difference of kind between the two. The fact of treating animals as a means to their own gratification is demoralizing to men. Animals must be seen to have ends of their own in nature before man can really advance in his knowledge of nature. As in astronomy the geocentric, so in biology the anthropocentric view must be abandoned. (6) While Sport in the past may have opened out many lands, and thus have promoted the spread of civilization, yet in the future it will probably be found that it will sink into the background, especially as the world advances in civilization.

STREET MUSIC, LEGISLATION AGAINST.

Pro: (1) Mental work is rendered more difficult by the noises which disturb the rest of dwellers in big towns. Bad enough when these noises are confined to the rumbling of vehicles, it is worse when to this are added the discordant notes of an instrument out of tune. Literary people as a class are not in a position to live where they like; and much good work is probably spoilt by the impossibility of obtaining the necessary quiet. (2) No one should be allowed to make himself a nuisance to his neighbours. As street music can be as great a nuisance as many other annoyances forbidden by the law, it should be made illegal, even though it may be a means to an honest, if not honourable, livelihood. (3) Street Music is a form of blackmail, for street musicians draw the chief part of their money from those who pay them to go away. The poor may like the music, but they are not willing to pay for it. (4) That street musicians are foreigners does not give them a right to torment us, and they would not be tolerated in any country but England.

Con: (1) Street Music is a source of pleasure to the children of the slums. People who require quiet must go into the country, and not seek protection against the harmless recreations of their neighbours. (2) The calling of a street musician is an honest one. (3) As long as householders are apathetic in the matter of Street Music no number of laws will check the nuisance. The police have power to remove the evil, and would do so did they think such action would be popular. Blackmail in this matter is inevitable just as long as there are those who will pay. (4) Most street musicians being foreigners, we should be careful lest we awake in the mind of foreign nations an idea that hostile action is prompted by race hatred.

SUGAR BOUNTIES: shall England protect her Colonies against the competition of foreign bounty-fed sugar?

Pro: (1) The refusal of England to enter into a Sugar Convention, and the determination to allow herself to be swamped by foreign bounty-fed sugar, has already reduced the sugar growers and refiners in the West Indies to the verge of bankruptcy. (2) Sugar-refining, which formerly was a trade carried on in England, has dwindled to infinitesimal proportions. (3) Even if some benefit can be shown to have accrued to certain trades in England, it must be remembered that such benefit is very uncertain, and depends on the caprice of others; and that, in the meantime, an industry is being destroyed, and a colony being driven to revolt by the apathy of the Home Government. (4) The sugar refiners of the West Indies have laid down the most expensive plant, and adopted the most approved and economical methods of production; it is untrue to say that they have been beaten through adhering to outworn, antiquated methods. It is unreasonable to expect them to compete successfully against such a highly artificial state of affairs as is created by the foreign Bounties. (5) Protection to the extent of the Bounty would not be protection in any known sense of the word—it would simply be a resolution on the part of England to accept no benefits which meant the ruin of a Colonial industry. (6) If England had joined the Sugar Convention of 1888, the other countries affected would have been bound to join too, before long, or would have found themselves shut out of the English market. (7) Foreign governments, far from abandoning Bounties, are increasing them, and there is no sign that such Bounties are unpopular as they are aimed at England.

Con: (1) England not unnaturally refused to ratify a one-sided convention, calculated to deprive her of the great advantages she derives from free sugar, in order to secure a doubtful benefit to her Colonies. (2) Sugar-refining has not declined in England, as, though the number of sugar-refining firms has decreased, the output remains the same. (3) Cheap sugar has been a boon to many English trades—such as jam-making and brewing. The Colonies can hardly expect us to throw men out of employment at home, or to give up the benefits we already derive from cheap sugar, to please them. (4) The sugar refiners in the West Indies adhere to obsolete methods, wasting about a third of the total product. As a matter of fact, were the Bounties removed to-morrow, there would be very little difference in the price of sugar, which is low, owing to improved methods, etc. (5) Protection to the extent of the Bounty would be protection pure and simple, and open to all the same objections. (6) Considering that the United States and France refused to join the Conference, and as these two are by far the greatest sugar-producing countries, the Convention was bound to fail; in any case the price of sugar would have risen enormously had England cut herself off from the supplies of these nations. (7) There are signs that foreign governments are getting tired of supplying England with cheap sugar, for which their own people have to pay three or four times the price, to the great encouragement of the English trades depending on cheap sugar. The rise in German and Austrian Bounties is insignificant, as things often get worse just before they improve—and public opinion in France seems to be going against Bounties.

SUICIDE: is it immoral?

Pro: (1) Suicide is wrong, because a man's life, being a gift from God, belongs to God, and God has reserved to Himself the right to say how long a man shall live, and when he shall die. (2) Suicide is at variance with the natural instincts of mankind, which prompt healthy-minded men to take a pleasure in life, with all its opportunities for happiness. (3) Suicide is a dereliction of duty on the part of any member of society. "We are all members one of another," and should make ourselves useful members of the community to which we all belong. (4) Incurable disease is not a sufficient excuse for suicide. The progress of medical science renders it impossible to say what diseases really are incurable. (5) Advance and progress are possible only through struggling with adverse circumstances, and such struggle alone moulds character; the man who, when things look their blackest, resolves to face out his difficulties has a finer character than he who deserts life. (6) The law is a great deterrent from Suicide, nor is a person who once has gone through the police court charged with the offence likely to repeat it. (7) Abolition of the law would open the door to grave dangers.

Con: (1) Many religions, including the Indian, have commended Suicide. Neither in the Old nor in the New Testament is suicide condemned, nor was it denounced by the Christian Church till the Council of Arles, A.D. 623. Suicide was common amongst the earlier Christians, and some who died thus have been canonised. (2) Natural instincts are no guide to conduct: the whole progress of medicine is a rebellion against nature. (3) So far from being a dereliction of duty, suicide may be a fulfilment of a duty; for instance, where a man is suffering from an incurable disease, and is likely to become a burden on others. (4) The progress of medicine is slow, and remedies for fatal diseases are rare. (5) Suicide involves a considerable amount of courage and will-power; where this is not so, and the perpetrator has committed suicide in order to evade the law, etc., society does not lose much; she is at least saved the maintenance of a criminal or weak person. (6) The law rarely acts as a deterrent; it often prevents a man from reconsidering his resolve, and eggs him on in order to escape the ignominy of being brought up before the magistrates. (7) The cases where one man could persuade another to take his own life would be very rare, and would probably be held murder under any law.

SUNDAY CLOSING OF PUBLIC HOUSES.

Pro: (1) Public Houses should be closed throughout Sunday. Wages being paid on Saturday, labourers naturally gravitate on Sunday to the only place of enjoyment open to them; hence Sunday drinking is probably heavier than that of any other day of the week. (2) It is wrong to tempt the working classes, who should be protected as far as possible. (3) Drinking is bad for a man's work; and consequently Monday has earned the name of "Blue Monday," as on it men recover from the effects of their Sunday's debauch. Even when they go to work, the work is of an inferior quality. (4) The liquor trade is the only important one which has the privilege of trading on Sundays. (5) Sunday opening is a hardship to the *employés* and *employées*, as well as to their principals, who are compelled by competition to do as others do. (6) The Clubs of the rich are different. Drinking is merely incidental to them, and Clubs are less frequented on Sunday than on any other day. (7) (Some) The question as to Sunday Closing ought to be left to the local authorities.

Con: (1) Sunday Closing would not prevent excessive drinking on Sundays. In Edinburgh, where the Closing obtains, Sunday drinking is often the heaviest of the week; drinkers lay in a store of liquor on Saturday night, and consume it at home. It also leads to secret drinking in the Public Houses, and the formation of bogus Clubs. (2) It is unwise to treat working men as though they were children. The greater the liberty given to grown-up men and women, the greater their education; where there is no temptation there is no virtue. (3) The absence of a workman from his work on "Blue Monday" causes him a loss of wages. If a workman chooses to sacrifice a day's wages to his own pleasures, and his employer does not object, it is not for the State to interfere. (4) Business is permitted in several other trades, *e.g.* eating-houses, tobacco shops. (5) Public House *employés* receive a holiday on some other day of the week as compensation for the partial loss of their Sunday. Publicans are their own masters, and if they do not take holidays it is because they prefer to earn money. (6) The rich have their Clubs; why should the poor not have their places of social intercourse and enjoyment? (7) Sunday Closing, wherever introduced, has been disastrous. (8) It would be very hard on *bond-fide* travellers.

SUNDAY OPENING OF MUSEUMS.

Pro: (1) Museums are maintained out of the national income, so should be accessible to all classes of the community. (2) Sunday is the only day on which the working classes can visit these institutions. (3) Sunday Opening of the Museums would constitute them a counter-attraction to the Public House. (4) Seeing works of art has a refining influence, and to some extent accounts for the superiority of the foreign over the British workman. (5) Everything that helps to make Sunday bright and pleasant should be encouraged. (6) Divine injunction applies to Saturday as the Sabbath, not Sunday; were this not so, the Sabbath was "made for man, not man for the Sabbath." (7) There is a vast difference between opening Museums and opening theatres on Sundays. (8) The evils of the Continental Sunday are much exaggerated; even were they not, Trade Unions would be able to protect their members from undue labour. (9) The number of Sunday workers involved would be small, and the work could be undertaken by volunteers. The labour of those employed to look after Museums is no greater than that of the vergers, etc., in churches. (10) The advancement of culture which would accompany Sunday Opening is out of all proportion greater than the trouble it would inflict, while the religious convictions of a small minority should not be allowed to weigh against the advantage of the many. (11) Sunday Opening has been tried in many places with great success. The assertion that Sunday Opening has been a failure is, in some cases, false. The particular cases quoted in Newcastle, Birmingham, Leicester, Manchester, and Liverpool, the Museums are still open, though the allegation as to their failure was made five years ago, in 1892. (12) No one supposed that when the first excitement of the opening was over, the crowds would not diminish; it has always been held that the real influence of Sunday Opening, in inducing working men to visit our great national collections, must be gradual. (13) Sabbatarianism was practically unknown till the time of the Puritans, and Luther's idea of Sunday was one that would meet with furious protests from our modern Puritans.

Con : (2) The working classes can, as a rule, go to Museums on Saturday afternoons, if they want to. (3) The people who would visit the Museums would not be those who would go to the Public House; on the contrary, people coming to Museums from a distance would be compelled to seek refreshments, and would often go to the Public Houses. (4) The mere fact of gazing at works of art is not itself of any great educational value: special instruction must accompany inspection. (5) Absolute rest one day in seven has benefited the nation in every way. (6) The divine injunction against working on the Sabbath applies with equal force to the Christian Sunday. (7) The Opening of Museums, etc., would in time lead to the opening of theatres and music halls, and the substitution of seven days for six. (8) The Continental Sunday would have a most disastrous effect on national life and character. (9) The number employed at the Museums would be very much greater than is usually supposed; the tendency at the present day is to decrease rather than to increase Sunday work. (10) It is wrong for the State to tamper with the religious convictions of a large number of its members. (11) Sunday Opening, where tried, has not always been a success, and in some cases has had to be withdrawn. (12) The change is not wanted by the working classes themselves, and it is in their interest that it is claimed.

TAXATION, INDIRECT: ABOLITION OF.

Pro : (1) Indirect Taxation violates the first principle of taxation, for it causes more to be taken from the taxpayer, ultimately the consumer, than it brings to the State. (2) It falls more heavily on the poor than on the rich. (3) It diminishes consumption, and so acts as an incubus on trade. (4) It is an uncertain means of increasing the revenue: the income derived from it fluctuates. (5) It takes from the taxpayer all incentive to check expenditure, as it deprives him of all knowledge of what he pays. (6) It necessitates an army of Inspectors, and is very liable to evasion.

Con : (1) Indirect Taxation affords a fruitful source of revenue, and could not be spared. (2) It forces the poor to contribute something towards the taxation of the country—an important point in a tax now when there is so strong a tendency to allow the poorer classes to dictate what the expenditure shall be. (3) It need be imposed only on trades or on articles such as alcohol, the consumption of which it is desirable to check. (4) Income Tax, and other forms of direct taxation, also fluctuates with the prosperity of the year. (5) It is quite easy for the taxpayer to find out the rate of taxation levied, if he wishes to do so. (6) It is not so open to evasion as Income Tax, or other direct forms of taxation.

TAXATION, VOLUNTARY.

Pro : (1) Taxation ought to be voluntary, since no man or body of men has a moral right to call himself or themselves the Sovereign, the Government, the Nation, etc., and to take a man's money against his will for purposes which he may not approve of. (2) The grant of Franchise might be made dependent on the payment of a voluntary Income Tax, as the only form of taxation. Such a system would probably not reduce the revenue ; even misers would be got at by exposure to public criticism.

Con : (1) Voluntary Taxation is a contradiction in terms. Inasmuch as men, being members of a civilized community, are indebted to the labours of that community, both past and present, for the benefits they enjoy, and to orderly government for their welfare and security for their possessions, it is clear that there is a moral obligation on the part of all to contribute towards the cost of the State, and that, otherwise, men would receive benefits gratuitously. "Freedom," in any case a relative term, scarcely comes into consideration here ; it is obvious that many things over which they can have no personal control must be demanded of members of a community as a *sine quâ non* of citizenship. (2) If "Taxation" were "Voluntary," there would be next to no State revenue. Social ostracism could not affect misers, or even others disinclined to pay.

THAMES STEAMBOAT SERVICE: MUNICIPALIZATION.

Pro : (1) The Municipality ought to undertake the control of the Thames Steamboat Service, because the present management is unable to supply the public with a regular and rapid service, cheap transit, and comfortable boats. (2) The present piers are too few and inconvenient, and their approaches often dangerous, and always dirty.

Con : (1) The Victoria Steamboat Association would be quite competent to manage the passenger traffic on the Thames, if it were not hampered by the Thames Conservancy. (2) Such exorbitant demands are made by the Thames Conservancy for the rent of piers, that it is impossible for the Company to spend more money on the steamers, piers, and approaches to piers ; if equitable terms could be obtained, there would be no need for change in the management.

THEISM.

Pro : (1) The wonderful order and regularity with which the Universe is governed, and the purposiveness which we see everywhere in the adaptation to an end of all the organisms, alike testify to the presence of a Designing Mind. Science has not destroyed the need for a Theistic explanation of the Universe ; by revealing the presence of a fixed order in Nature she has made some such explanation more necessary than ever ; and when we call an organ useless, we thereby mean to say that we do not know what its use is. (2) Man's existence as a self-conscious being, which raises him above the animals, and makes it all but impossible to suppose that he could have come from them, shows him to be a being *sui generis ;* for it is inconceivable that self-consciousness could have arisen from that which was not self-conscious ; nor is it possible to conceive that thought could have been evolved from that which was not thought. The attempt to trace a continuous evolution from the lowest beings, which are merely sensitive, to man, as a thinking being, and to show a clear line of connection between sensation and thought, is doomed to failure, for no amount of sensation can make knowledge in the absence of a mind which experiences those sensations ; sensations can be interpreted only by something that is essentially higher—they cannot interpret themselves. (3) Language as a medium of communication between men is of so complex a structure, and so well adapted to its end, that it is impossible to think that it could have arisen by accident; also, without speech, no thought is possible; a further proof that language was not invented by man.   (4) Theism accounts for the origin of the idea of duty and the moral ideas generally, and supplies an incentive to the ethical life, and a satisfaction of the higher aspirations in man's nature.   So far is the belief in God necessary to man's moral nature, that even those who professedly reject the belief have endeavoured to make up for the void by Comte's apotheosis of Humanity, Herbert Spencer's Unknowable, and such vagaries of Spiritualism as belief in mahatmas, etc.   (5) The universality of the belief among all nations which have reached a certain stage of culture, proves the presence in all men of certain aspirations after the eternal and unchangeable; though man's idea both of morality and of God continually progresses as his spiritual nature gets more enlightened—much as his knowledge of the external world improves with more exact habits of observation and knowledge of the laws which guide it.

Con : (1) The adaptability of the Universe to certain ends does not prove the existence of an Infinite Mind creating and controlling; it is impossible to jump from finite effects to an infinite cause; even then it does not prove the existence of a Creator, but only an Adapter.   Natural Selection, by the explanation it affords of many things otherwise obscure, leads us to dispense more and more with the Theistic explanation of the Universe; and the more science advances the more true this will be.   (2) The attempt to explain the existence of mind in man by showing that it could have arisen only from another mind, merely moves the difficulty a step further back, for we have still to explain how that other mind arose.   We can trace an almost continuous line of evolution from the simplest and least differentiated protozoon, which can only feel, up to man, with his marvellous powers of thought. (3) Language can be proved to have been a perfectly natural product, and to have arisen more or less spontaneously to meet the needs of man.   While thought (in the sense here intended) cannot exist without language, yet thought must have existed previously in a rudimentary state, as it is evident that animals have a certain power of thought without any means of expressing it in language.   (4) The value of Theism to meet man's requirements as a moral being must depend on its truth, not its truth on the fact of its necessity for man.   (5) The religious beliefs of nations vary as widely as those of individuals, so that it is not easy to discover any truly common grounds of faith.

THOROUGH (OR DEEP) CULTIVATION.

Pro : (1) A thorough aeration of the soil and subsoil is necessary in England at the smallest cost to obtain the maximum yield of crops, without impoverishing the soil.   If such aeration be adequately given, crops of all kinds may be increased from five to seven times the average usually obtained by the ordinary farmer—say from 100 to 240 bushels of wheat per acre ; 30 to 35 tons of potatoes ; 50 tons of cabbages ; 10 tons of hay, etc.   (2) Under Thorough cultivation the land retains and absorbs the moisture and dews from the atmosphere in the driest seasons, and during the heavy rains takes up the water, thus preventing floods and the swamping of lowlands. (3) This mitigation of the severity, and provision against the capriciousness, of the English climate, and consequent increase in the crops, would render unnecessary the importation of food from abroad, and England would no longer be dependent on foreign countries for a great part of her supplies. (4) Thorough Cultivation would prevent the land from going out of cultivation.   It would employ many more, and thus check the depopulation of the villages ; it would also attract city-dwellers back into the country, where profitable occupation under healthy conditions would soon re-establish our rural homesteads.   (5) The system is not new ; it has long been successfully practised in Oriental countries, and may now be seen in Japan, China, India, and elsewhere; here from 12 to 20 men are employed on every acre, tilling the soil, with good profit. Nor is the system new to England: it was carried on by Fitzgerald in the 16th century; Blith in the 17th; Tull in the 18th; the Marquis of Tweeddale, etc., in the 19th; it has been brought to perfection by General Sir Arthur Cotton, and is now adopted by many.

Con: (1) The opinion that by Thorough Cultivation it is possible to largely increase the produce of the soil, and at a lower cost, is opposed to the experience of many, *e.g.* Sir John Lawes maintains that the last bushel of increase per acre is relatively more expensive than the first. That such abnormally large yields as those stated have really resulted from actual experiments on any considerable scale is disputed; Sir John Lawes' challenge to produce evidence has not been accepted. (3) If the amount of corn grown in England were so increased as to render importation unnecessary, it is probable that the population would at once swell to such an extent as soon to bring us back again to our old state of dependence on foreign countries. (4) Thorough Cultivation, if a proved success, would be adopted wherever practicable, and with greater success in the great wheat-growing countries than in England, and the ratio between output and population would remain practically unaltered. Good farm drainage has doubled, perhaps even quadrupled, the yield of English land; but it has failed to protect us from the foreigner, nor has it rendered machinery less necessary. (5) Oriental farming and gardening operations are entirely unsuited to the circumstances existing in this country.

TIED HOUSES, ABOLITION OF.

Pro: (1) The Tied House system deprives the licence-holder of all responsibility for the good conduct of his house, and puts it under the control of a third party, in no way responsible to the magistrates. (2) Those who own Tied Houses impose onerous terms on their tenants; and by making their tenure terminable at very short notice, keep them completely under their own control. (3) The quality of the beer suffers by this, since the brewers are able to sell whatever beer they choose to their tenants, who are bound by agreement not to return any; and for the beer thus sold to them the tenants are bound to pay a higher price than the owners of free houses pay. (4) The tendency of the owners of Tied Houses is to extend the system to every article sold on the premises—spirits, wines, tobacco, etc. (5) The system has often ended in throwing the trade of a whole district into the hands of one brewery, or amalgamation of breweries, thus destroying all competition. (6) The uncertainty of tenure and the onerous terms oblige the tenants of Tied Houses to increase their sales to the utmost, so that they may make money whilst the business remains in their hands; thus the system is a direct incitement to drunkenness. (7) The system is illegal, since a licence, which is granted to one man, is granted to him alone, without power to assign it; any such transfer would be null and void; a brewery owning a Tied House in pursuance of such a transfer would be guilty of a breach of law if it sought to turn out the original licence-holder. (8) The evils of the system are felt by all connected with the trade, and the system is almost universally condemned. (9) Brewers, etc., very often fix the rent at a low figure in order to lower the assessment, and thus are able to evade their fair share of taxation. (10) The drink trade, being a licensed one, cannot be compared with any other, and the publican must be regarded rather in the light of a public servant than of a tradesman. (11) Brewers cannot complain if their "rights" are ignored, since knowing the law, they yet choose to risk their money on the chance of the law not being applied. The publican has never been recognized as having a "right" to demand a renewal of his licence.

Con: (1) It is to the brewer's interest that the tenant should conduct his house in a proper manner, so that the licence may not be endangered. Tenants of Tied Houses are often themselves largely interested in them. (2) No publican need take a Tied House, nor is it likely that he would, were the terms too onerous: that Tied Houses are the subjects of eager competition disproves all assertions as to the tyranny of the brewers. (3) No brewer is likely to sell bad beer consciously in a house under his own name. Most brewers allow their tenants to return beer if not good; and, if the tenant has to pay a higher price for his beer, he gets an excellent *quid pro quo* in the fact that he has to pay nothing for the goodwill of the business, and gets possession for a lower rent than would be possible on any other system. (4) The tenant is rarely tied for anything beyond beer; but, even where the tie extends to wine and spirits, these must be good or the public would not buy them. (6) The public buy the liquor which they want—no more; nor are they likely to increase the amount at the bidding of the publican. (7) If the Tied House system is illegal, why is it necessary to introduce an Act of Parliament to say so? (8) Magistrates have, as a rule, declined to interfere with the system. In cases where they have interfered it has been most unwise; for instance, where the Crewe magistrates objected to a provision in the agreement fining the publican £100 every time he endangered his licence by illegal conduct or mismanagement of his house —though this was a strong guarantee for the good management of the house —they insisted on its being exscinded. (9) It is a matter for the authorities to see that the assessment is put at a right figure; and it cannot be charged as a fault against the Tied House system if they fail in their work. (10) The Tied House system prevails in every country business where large firms have branches; and there is no reason why a distinction should be drawn between the drink trade and others. (11) An enormous amount of money has been spent by brewers in improving their properties; to hand this over to the publican without compensation to the brewer would be spoliation.

TRADES UNIONISM.

Pro: (1) From the point of view of labour, the organization of the workers in Trades Unions is a matter of imperative necessity, in face of the fearful evils of low wages, excessive overtime, and inhuman conditions of life. (2) Moreover, an immense growth of concentration or disciplined organization on the part of labour is needed to cope with the growing concentration and combinations which are so strongly marked on the side of capital. (3) Unrestricted competition of workers having dragged down the standard of life among large masses of our population to an unprecedented depth, this great weapon of Trades Unionism has to be used for the purpose of raising this standard before it is too late. (4) For the maintenance of a high level of industrial efficiency, specialized organizations of workers are required; and this idea—the portion of the old Trades Guilds which alone survives in modern Trades Unions—showed signs of a strong revival at the '95 Trades Union Congress at Cardiff, in the new Standing Order then adopted, by which all delegates to that Congress were required to be either present workers in, or permanent Union officials of, their particular trade. (5) The only available weapon for a worker against the horrors of the impersonal form which mastership has assumed in Joint Stock Companies, directorates, rings, trusts, and so on, is that of the strike of workers: this weapon can only be wielded by the workers when organized in Trades Unions. (6) As a method of provision against sickness or accident, the work of the Trades Union funds is for many reasons to be preferred to schemes of State insurance, or to provident or benefit funds worked in conjunction with the employers; the latter *may* serve as powerful weapons against the self-betterment of the men, in the hands of unscrupulous exploiters of labour. (7) Trades Unionism as a present-day factor provides an admirable training ground for working-class statesmen, such as the needs of the time require. (8) Trades Unions again form a powerful agency through their Congresses, Parliamentary Committees, the pressure they bring to bear upon Labour Members, and so on, for the furtherance in the political and Parliamentary field of the workers' interests, which they embody and seek to enforce. (9) Trades Unionism exists in all the civilized countries of the world, and affords an unrivalled rallying ground for the workers of all nations to carry forward their efforts in the direction of international solidarity of labour. The organizing of strikes forms only a small portion of the work done by the Unions, and is often necessary only when the Union is weak: where both employers and employed are strongly federated, the strike, though always a possibility, is seldom or never resorted to.

Con: (1) Trades Unionism is calculated to set the workers as a class against the employers as a class; it is a weapon primarily of class warfare, and leads from rather than towards the true social interests of the whole community. (2) It is not desirable in these days of minute subdivision of work to specialize the interests of the various workers by this form of organization, on the supposed analogy of the old Trades Guilds, which existed under such different conditions. (3) Although at the present industrial and social crisis the bitterness and standing dangers of labour disputes cannot be ignored, these should be met by the changes in the political and economic system which are slowly growing out of the deeper-lying moral revolution now proceeding, and which points to co-operation instead of to competition as the basis of organized social life: and even in fact the action of the Trades Unions complicates these disputes by embittering the situation. (4) The opportunities afforded by Trades Unions have often been utilized by clever and unscrupulous persons for the exploitation of the needs of their fellows in their own selfish interests. (5) While we look for a large improvement in political methods and the conditions of public life from the larger infusion into it of that working-class element which constitutes the real strength and backbone of the country, it is a mistake to turn aside working-class energies into the channels of trade conflicts and class warfare. (6) Trades Union action presses heavily upon the older workers in the industrial field, tending to deprive the community of the valuable use of much slowly and painfully-acquired skill. (7) As against the argument that Trades Unionism is necessary as a weapon of the class warfare, it may be urged that it cuts both ways: it forges a weapon for the hands of the masters, who, by setting free labourers or blacklegs against the organized or Trades Union workers, can sharply *divide*, and thus more easily *govern*, the working classes as a whole. (8) The object lesson of America and isolated occurrences in this country show clearly that Trades Unionism has a tendency to promote civil warfare, which cannot be held to be to the advantage of any classes, still less to the cause of progress in the race as a whole. (9) Further, the strike as a weapon of warfare is wholly insufficient to achieve in any permanent degree the very object with which it is wielded; (*a*) because far-reaching resources of capital make the fight an uneven one, and shift the ultimate decision from the strike itself to the moral sense of the community as a whole, and (*b*) because, organization apart, the repeating rifle and the Maxim gun remain available (as is shown by the Featherstone incident) for use against the workers, whether strikers or not, by magistrates and officials who are either employers themselves or leagued with employers.

TRAMWAYS (LONDON), MUNICIPALIZATION OF.

Pro: (1) No monopolies ought to remain in private hands; they should be devoted to the relief of taxation, or some other public interest. (2) The present Tramway Companies are, by their monopolies, able to levy a tax on the locomotion of Londoners.   (3) The hours worked by the Companies' employés for comparatively small pay are too long ; but it is obvious that no Trades Union or other voluntary action can help the men so long as the Tramways remain the property of private Companies.   (4) Though the London County Council has in some cases given the Tramways notice that it intends to resume possession of the lines, it has only done so to re-lease them to the Companies ; yet it is hard to see why it should not work them itself.

Con: (1) The great consideration in deciding on a question of private monopolies is expediency ; and it will be found in the end that a cheaper and more efficient service will be secured by leasing the lines to a Private Company, than by leaving it in the hands of a public body.   (2) The present Companies do not pay exorbitant dividends ; and the shareholders are entitled to a fair return on their capital. There is no surplus from which to increase wages or reduce hours of work.   (3) The work of Tramway men is light and unskilled ; therefore an Eight Hours' Day, such as is worked by the Huddersfield men, is ridiculously short ; high wages, if paid by the municipality, would be a bounty paid to a particular class of labour.   (4) By allowing the Tramway Companies to re-lease the lines, the County Council ensures to itself a certain profit, and can impose what conditions it thinks fit.

UNEMPLOYED, THE: STATE INTERVENTION FOR.

Pro: (1) Since the problem of the Unemployed is an acute and growing one, and since the welfare of its citizens is the purpose of a State, the burden of dealing with this problem must rest with the State.   (2) Repeated investigations have established the fact that the majority of the Unemployed are in that condition entirely from the force of economic circumstances over which they have no control.   (3) Since private enterprize has entirely failed to cope with the problem, as was inevitable, in view of the gigantic dimensions to which industry has grown, the State must deal with it if the Commonwealth is not to be ruined.   (4) It is the duty of Government to maintain a balance of power between the various kinds of workers within its jurisdiction ; but the existence of this shifting surplus of Unemployed labour puts the *labouring* class necessarily in a relatively powerless position, as compared with the *managing* class ; to adjust this balance, the State must devise some means for the absorption and utilization of this surplus labour. (5) As a result of the change which has come over public opinion in regard to the spirit of government, there has sprung up a demand that the State should register the demands of the public conscience ; among other things, by assuring the possibility of human conditions of life to every one of its citizens.   (6) An investigation of the origin of the Unemployed problem in the large and acute form in which it presents itself to-day, makes it clear that it is the result of the wrong use of State machinery, on the part of the stronger in the industrial partnership, viz., Capital, against, viz., Labour. (7) The contention that, because examination shows in almost every individual case that some moral defect is responsible for the man's position, therefore the problem is not economic, but purely moral, is false : granted that at a time when trade grows slack the men who lose their positions will be those who are, from one cause or other, the weaker workers, yet, if all workers were of equal strength, some would have to be turned away because of deficiency of work.

Con: (1) The proportion of the deserving Unemployed will be found to be small. The majority of those dismissed on account of bad trade, etc., consists of the less effective workers ; these it would not be wise to encourage : with the small number of really hard cases private charity is perfectly competent to deal. Partly from dangers inherent in itself, and partly from its effect upon the medium in which it works, State action is an evil (though necessarily within certain defined limits). All fresh departures in the way of extending it must be deprecated.   (2) It is a law of nature that some should fall out of the ranks in the struggle for existence. The State, therefore, should not attempt to deal with the problem, which lies in the nature of things, and which it can never solve.   (3) If the State were to deal with the Unemployed by undertaking large public works, it would be incurring too heavy a responsibility in the domain of finance, and aggravating the evils of officialism, jobbery, and corruption; neither would it be a help to the individual worker, who would not be able to work at his own trade, and would probably be inefficient at any other. The work would be costly, and would probably throw such a burden on the rates as to seriously affect other industries. The Government tried to pull down Millbank Prison by means of the Unemployed, but failed.   (4) If the State should intervene to supply work for the workless, until they could once more find a footing on the industrial ladder, it would tend to undermine those qualities of self-help upon which alone a healthy body politic can stand.   (5) All large schemes for the introduction of State insurance to protect the worker are open to the objection of creating fresh armies of small officials; and would probably break down owing to the unwillingness to keep up steady payments on the part of precisely that class of person to which the *chronic Unemployed* belong.   (6) Again, it is held that State intervention, in whatever form, would dislocate the complex machinery of the world's markets, interfering with the natural balance and interaction of supply and demand, and handicapping the great industrial capitalists, financiers, and brain-operators in the performance of their functions in the body politic. (7) The Unemployed will usually be found to be that part of the population which, being unfit morally, physically, or intellectually, has found its way to the bottom. The question occurs, then, how far the nation can afford to burden its capable members with the support of the incapable, and whether in so doing it will not be helping to deteriorate the race by maintaining members who would otherwise die out, and also in removing all stimulus from those just about to keep out of this class.

UNIVERSAL LANGUAGE.

Pro : (1) Language, of purely human origin, and devised as momentary needs suggested, has come down to us with all its imperfections. It should be replaced by a scientific language, the invention of which would be quite feasible.   (2) The diversity of the languages of the world impede the interchange of thought, and help to keep alive international jealousies and misunderstandings, thus postponing the attainment of the ideal of the universal brotherhood of mankind, which has so long been preached by the best and the wisest of the world's religious teachers.   (3) A Common Language has already been successfully adopted to some extent in the use of Latin within the Roman Church, in scientific and philosophical treatises, in the Hungarian Parliament; also in the use of Volapük, World English, and other artificial languages in commerce.   (4) The tendency of two or three languages to become universal (in spite of the recent attempts to revive local dialects), is an indication of the want of a Universal Language, and of the comparative ease with which it might be introduced. If it were made a school subject in England, France, and Germany, it would rapidly spread throughout the world.   (5) A Universal Language would not cut us off from the great thinkers of the past; the languages of Homer and Plato and even Chaucer are not the languages of to-day.

Con : (1) Language grows, and, though it may be modified, cannot be created by individual men or generations of men. It is in a state of constant change, to meet the needs of successive ages, and can no more be kept stable than can anything else which is subject to the laws of evolution.

(2) Languages are essentially natural, embodying the sentiments, traditions, history, and philosophy of the different races. The adoption of an artificial language would deprive a nation of its past. All beauty, all historical associations would disappear; even accurate thinking would be impossible. (3) If introduced, a Universal Language would, in a short time, become broken up into dialects. (4) If anything of the kind were attempted, it would be easier to adopt an existing language already spoken by many. (5) Language forms the link whereby we communicate with the great thinkers of the past; a communion necessarily more perfect in the case of those who have written in our own language. In the event of a Universal Language being adopted, all existing languages would, in a generation or two, become "dead languages."

UNIVERSITY, A NEW TEACHING, FOR LONDON.

Pro: (1) The present University of London is merely an Examining Board for the Empire, and has no special adaptation to the wants of London. (2) It does not require, except in the Faculty of Medicine, any regular and methodical course of study as a preliminary to admission to the examinations; thus, while a degree of the older Universities of Oxford and Cambridge is some evidence that the student has been educated, a London degree only means that he has answered so many questions. (3) Its examinations have no direct relation to the teaching in London institutions, and these have more and more withdrawn from any attempt to prepare students for the examinations in question. (4) As the centre of national life in its widest sense, and as the headquarters of all the learned societies, London ought to be the educational centre for England. (5) In Medicine the requirements for the M.D. degree are on the one hand so extensive, and on the other so ill-adapted to the wants of professional life, that many of the best men after a London education go to other Universities for a degree. (6) It is proposed to form a University which, while continuing to act as a degree-giving body for the Empire, shall be in touch with the London Colleges, and take from London the reproach of being the only capital in Europe without a teaching University. (7) Owing to the shifting and uncertain character of the majority in Convocation, and the small fraction of the body of graduates which attends the meetings, the new Constitution should not, in accordance with the Charter, be submitted to that body for approval; but a Statutory Commission should be constituted by Parliament for the purpose. (8) These proposals have the support of the Senate, of the authorities of the London Colleges, and of a majority of the graduates living in and near the Metropolis.

Con: (1) The present University has done and is doing good work, as evinced by the ever-increasing numbers of candidates for degrees; it would be calamitous to imperil this success for the sake of bolstering up decadent institutions. (2) In the Faculty of Medicine, attendance at a London school is compulsory; while in Arts the ill-success of such institutions as King's and University Colleges seems to show that London is not the best place for a University education in the ordinary sense. (3) The proposed University would be under the domination of the London teachers, and would run the risk of losing its high character for impartiality; while its examinations, specially adapted to the actual teaching in a few institutions, would press unfairly on those students, spread over the whole empire, who have hitherto enjoyed the privileges of the University without having gone through the curriculum in question, and thus these few institutions would gain an unfair advantage. (4) The wide area over which the London Colleges are spread, and the fact that the students would nearly all be non-resident, would render impossible all but the faintest shadow of that corporate life which gives such value to Oxford and Cambridge. (5) The M.D. Examination of the University of London has hitherto held an unrivalled position; and the tendency of the proposed change, judging from the language of its advocates, would be to lower the standard of this and of other degrees. **(6)** (Some) If the London teaching bodies are to be organized, it should be by means of a new "Gresham" or "Albert" University, leaving to the older body its present functions. **(7)** (Some) The new University would be accepted provided (*a*) that the privileges and veto of Convocation are retained; (*b*) that a larger representation on the Senate, than is at present proposed, be given to the graduates of the University; and (*c*) that the teachers of the London Colleges receive a consultative instead of a commanding voice in the management of the Examinations. **(8)** A majority of the whole body of graduates is opposed to the scheme in its present form.

UNIVERSITY EXTENSION MOVEMENT, THE.

Pro: **(1)** University Extension fulfils valuable purposes of culture amongst those who have intellectual cravings, yet have nothing wherewith to satisfy them. It stimulates interest and suggests study. **(2)** Like all other movements of its kind, it has had its ups and downs. The present is a period of depression. **(3)** State aid is indispensable. It would be a great error to disperse the existing machinery, which has gradually been accumulated after much effort and cost.

Con: **(1)** The scope and method of University Extension preclude it from being a real educational force, and it can be considered only as one among many methods of intellectual recreation. It lacks the elements of continuity and mental discipline, which are essential to true education. **(2)** It has been tried for more than twenty-one years, and has been found wanting. If there were a real demand to be satisfied, the Movement would now be self-supporting: there is, on the contrary, a rapid decrease in the numbers attending, the large majority of whom have been ladies desirous of obtaining a smattering of superficial knowledge on many subjects. **(3)** The grants made by the County Councils for technical education have had the effect of enervating and disabling it. No grants should be made in aid of the University Extension Movement until it has proved itself capable of supplying a real want.

VACANT LAND: ITS RATING.

Pro: **(1)** In rating Vacant Land its actual, not its present, value should be the basis. **(2)** Under the present system much valuable land is held vacant, or let at nominal rentals, in order to keep up the price of land generally. Under the proposed system, owners would be more readily induced to part with vacant land, and the price of land generally would be depreciated, and more be acquired for public purposes, such as parks, etc. **(3)** A distinction should be drawn between land which is suitable for public purposes, and that which is held back for speculative purposes. **(4)** Landowners reap enormous advantages out of the industry of their fellow-citizens, and should be made to share in their burdens.

Con: **(1)** The best test of the value of land is the present rate at which it lets, not what a surveyor may estimate it at. The proposed new rating would destroy many existing Open Spaces. **(2)** Holders of vacant land do not often fail to sell it when they can get a fair price. **(3)** It would be almost impossible to distinguish between land held back for building purposes and agricultural land near towns. **(4)** Landowners do not get much advantage from public expenditure, as a rule, in places where there is much vacant land. It would be the small rather than the large holders who would be affected by the proposed new rating, which would thus tend to concentrate land in a few hands. **(5)** The taxation of empty houses would be a discouragement to the building trade, and raise the price of existing houses.

VACCINATION.

Pro: (1) Vaccination, efficiently performed in infancy, and repeated at the age of puberty, has shown itself to be an almost absolute protection against smallpox, whilst in the few cases in which smallpox occurs after vaccination, the disease is always modified to such an extent as not to be recognizable in its early stage. Whereas, in pre-vaccination days, 80 per cent. of deaths from smallpox occurred in children attacked under five and 15 per cent. between five and ten, this ratio has been totally altered by Vaccination. (2) Statistics show an enormous difference between the relative numbers of cases of smallpox among the vaccinated and the unvaccinated, greatly in favour of the former, which also show far fewer fatal cases. The assertion that smallpox obliterates the vaccination marks is entirely without foundation, and entirely refuted by the experience of the most competent medical observers. (3) At Leicester, where Vaccination has been practically suspended, an attempt has been made to substitute for it a much harsher system of compulsory isolation and quarantine of from twelve to fourteen days: this has proved ineffectual, and the proportion of deaths among the unvaccinated is enormous compared with those among the vaccinated. (4) The Registrar-General's annual returns show beyond discussion that smallpox has decreased within the present century, and especially within the last fifty years. Improved sanitation and habits do not account for the change in the age-incidence of smallpox, since improved hygiene affects all ages. While the general death-rate of the country has decreased 9 per cent., the deaths from smallpox have decreased 72 per cent. Apart from Vaccination there is no reason why smallpox should be affected by sanitation to a greater degree than, say, measles or whooping-cough. (5) It has never been claimed for Vaccination that it is an antidote to smallpox. The protection it affords diminishes with time; hence, re-vaccination is essential. (6) Like any other trivial wound, Vaccination has occasionally caused inflammation, erysipelas, and possibly (though unproved) death. These diseases are invariably the result of improper treatment of the vesicles, and can be avoided by proper care and antiseptic precautions. The risk is practically infinitesimal; if Vaccination were really the cause of disease and death, a crusade against the practice would be unnecessary, for it would not be countenanced by the medical profession. (7) No diseases are conveyed by Vaccination, if proper precautions are taken; syphilis, for example, has been thus inoculated, but always as a result of gross carelessness. (8) If Vaccination were to any appreciable extent responsible for the inoculation of syphilis, it would be expected that a town like Leicester, where Vaccination has been in abeyance for some years, would show a marked decrease in the percentage of deaths from syphilis among infants; yet we find that, whereas in England and Wales the infantile deaths from such a cause have increased 25 per cent., in Leicester they have increased as much as 69 per cent. (10) The Gloucester epidemic has strikingly confirmed the efficacy of Vaccination. Here, in consequence of the neglect of Vaccination, the severest attack of smallpox recorded in modern times occurred. It is untrue to say that sanitary conditions caused the outbreak, for the disease was confined almost entirely to the better and more recently built parts of the town; and the houses, so far from being jerry-built, had all, together with their sanitary arrangements, been approved by the authorities. It is also curious that if the town suffered from bad drainage in any part, as was alleged by the anti-vaccinators, that the deaths from typhoid were so few. The conditions at the hospital were not good, but there is every evidence from the statistics to show that the want of isolation was aggravated by the neglect of Vaccination having left the disease such a mass of material to work upon. The sudden manner in which the disease declined when Vaccination was initiated proves its efficiency.

Con: (1) The only definition that can be found for "efficient" Vaccination is that which is not followed by smallpox, for smallpox of every degree of severity does follow Vaccination of every other sort. A large proportion of smallpox cases occur in children under ten, and it has been allowed by medical men before the Royal Commission that primary Vaccination is a very fleeting protection indeed; cases have occurred in which Vaccination had been performed a fortnight before the disease broke out. The claim that Vaccination mitigates the attack may be described as an unprovable assumption, involving a claim to know how badly each individual would have taken smallpox had he remained unvaccinated. (2) Statistics show that Vaccination not only confers no immunity from disease, but even increases the liability to it, as was shown by an outbreak in London in 1884, when the proportion of vaccinated persons to the whole number of cases inside the hospital, was shown to be slightly larger than the proportion of the vaccinated to the unvaccinated of the whole population of London. As regards the increased ratio of deaths among the so-called unvaccinated, the figures may be said to be impossible, for the real fact is, that severe cases of smallpox make the marks invisible, and thus the bad cases do not die because they are unvaccinated, but are returned unvaccinated because they die. It has further to be accounted for that, whereas in pre-vaccination days the fatality was a little over 18 per cent., it is now 35 per cent. among the unvaccinated. (3) At Leicester, in 1872, when Vaccination was universal, there was a larger number of deaths from smallpox than there was of cases in the recent outbreak, in spite of the absence of Vaccination and the increase that has since taken place in the population. Leicester, so far from adopting much harsher methods, has simply adopted the provisions of the Public Health Act, and in putting these in force no man's child has been removed from home against his will; on the other hand, poor parents have been, in other places, fined for the non-vaccination of a second child, where their first had died from the effects of disease induced by Vaccination. (4) It is not denied that smallpox has decreased, but not to such an extent as other diseases, such as typhus and typhoid. The first compulsory Vaccination Act was passed in 1853; since that date there have been three epidemics of smallpox, killing respectively, in round numbers, 14,000, 20,000, 44,800 of our population. It is since this last and greatest epidemic that the great decline in smallpox has set in, concurrently with a great increase in the default in Vaccination. The true cause is the sanitary awakening of the people, of which the Public Health Act of 1875 was both an integral part and a striking evidence. (5) It has been strenuously claimed for Vaccination that it is an antidote to smallpox—from the original claim of Jenner, that it would protect the patient "for ever after," down to the *Lancet* of 16th January, 1892, declaring that "no one need have the smallpox unless he likes; that is, he can be absolutely protected by Vaccination once repeated": in regard to which the return of the Metropolitan Asylums Board Hospital Ships for 1890 may be quoted—total cases of smallpox returned were twenty-six, of which nineteen vaccinated all recovered, five unvaccinated all recovered, two revaccinated both died. (6) Coroners' inquests have over and over again proved that Vaccination has been the cause of death. Mr. Jonathan Hutchinson in his *Archives of Surgery* records no less than 679 deaths from cowpox from 1881-93, or more than a child a week. If these are instances of medical carelessness, the doctors ought to be tried for manslaughter. (7) It has been testified by some of the greatest doctors that, in spite of precaution, syphilis has resulted from Vaccination. (8) Vaccination is one of the causes of infantile syphilis, though for many years the medical profession denied this. (9) Calf lymph is not safe except in respect of syphilis, since it conveys tuberculosis. As a matter of fact, the use of calf lymph has never been encouraged by the Local Government Board, on account of its inefficiency; the majority of Vaccination inquests are a result of the use of calf lymph. (10) There can be no doubt that the Gloucester outbreak was due to bad sanitary conditions, especially in that part of the town where the smallpox was worst, and also to the polluted water supply. The arrangements at the hospital—which stands so in the centre of the town as to render effective isolation impossible—were disgracefully bad, and broke down utterly, a fact admitted by the Medical Inspector sent down by the Vaccination Commission. How much Vaccination had to do with the decline of the epidemic may be seen from the fact that, while all authorities allow that Vaccination requires fourteen days, some a month, to become an effective check, the smallpox had begun to decline sixteen days before Vaccination was resorted to on a wholesale scale, and had almost died down before it could have had any effect.

VEGETARIANISM.

Pro: (1) The slaughter of animals is degrading, when animals are bred for the purpose; and hence man's view of his relations to the animals is distorted. (2) The slaughter of animals is accompanied by much cruelty, as when calves and lambs are separated from their mothers; animals also suffer much in transit; and while the cruelties at present associated with the slaughter-house might be abated, they never could be quite abolished by the erection of public slaughter-houses; all observers testify to the horror shown by animals on smelling blood, probably the cause of intense suffering to them. Humane methods must always be expensive, and hence not likely to be adopted by butchers. (3) The work is brutalizing, and therefore employment from which we should relieve fellow-citizens. (4) The formation of man's teeth and the general nature of his intestines proves him to be frugivorous by nature. The apes, which are nearest to man, are wholly Vegetarian in diet. (5) It is quite possible to get as much nourishment from a Vegetarian diet as from a meat diet; for, while the consumer of meat takes, in addition to meat, wholly proteid, a large amount of starchy food, the Vegetarian balances his by living on pulses and cereals, which contain a large proportion of proteids mixed with starch: this solution of the food problem has attracted much attention in various works on physiology. (6) The craving for stimulants in many cases is the result of the undue strain upon the digestive system, produced by excess of animal foods; and the craving for stimulants, etc., has been combated by a Vegetarian regimen, when carried out thoroughly. (7) Vegetarian diet is capable of as much variety as any meat diet can afford. Vegetarians have introduced to the masses new vegetables, such as haricot beans, tomatoes, lentils, etc. The general recognition among educated people of the Darwinian theories adds special force to the argument against domesticating cattle for the purposes of slaughter; for, in the case of these, "artificial selection" with a view to the table only, is substituted for the healthy operation of "natural selection," and the animal is thus deprived of its capacity to improve and rise in the scale of being.

Con: (1) Unless animals, such as cattle, sheep, pigs, etc., are to be used as food, they are not likely to survive, since land is far too valuable to be given up to the use of animals. Nor is it likely that a dairy farm would pay, unless some use were found for the non-milking cows, superfluous bulls, etc.; hence milk, cheese, butter, etc., would disappear from our list of foods. Pasture land would also disappear, and with it one of the chief beauties of the country. (2) Cruelty could easily be much mitigated by the substitution of public abattoirs for private slaughter-houses; a certain amount of pain is inevitable in nature, which, though we can alleviate, we cannot eliminate. (3) The fact of a trade being disgusting is no reason for its abolition; otherwise, we should abolish sewers, drains, etc. The necessities of the community often demand the execution of particular classes of work which may or may not be improving to the character of the individuals who perform them, but which, by their nature, demand special training and skill. (4) Man has so far risen above the apes, that it is as impossible to judge of his necessities by analogy from theirs, as it is to argue from savage to civilized races. (5) It is of advantage to the human organism to receive a larger proportion of proteid food than can be obtained from vegetables; and the adoption of an animal diet has therefore been an advantage to the race. (6) The various instances in which a Vegetarian diet has been found beneficial are not cases of a general law, but merely instances of disease requiring a special regimen. The arguments against animal foods from a hygienic point of view apply only to their excessive use. (7) While in theory Vegetarianism offers a new and large variety of foods, in practice the reverse is the case; the food habitually consumed by Vegetarians, and served in Vegetarian restaurants, is singularly deficient in variety, and cooked in unappetizing ways. (8) It is absolutely impossible for natural selection to have free play among the domesticated or semi-domesticated animals of to-day. It would be impossible to allow them to breed at pleasure and run wild.

VIVISECTION.

Pro: (1) The healing art is dependent for its advance upon all the Sciences, but especially upon a knowledge of biology. The laws of biology can be discovered only by observation and by experimentation on animals, just as the laws of every other Science have been discovered experimentally. Observation may suggest a law, but the proof depends on experiment; clinical observation is useful, but not a single biological law has been discovered through clinical observation alone. The assertion that these laws might have been elucidated without experiments on animals is beside the point; we are not concerned with what "might" have taken place, but with what has actually happened. (2) Medical men are making daily use of the teachings of Vivisection. Such a simple process as ascertaining the fulness of the pulse is dependent on the knowledge of the laws regulating blood-pressure—knowledge which we have gained through an English clergyman's experiments on horses. Again, clinical observers entertained mistaken ideas as to the functions of the arteries and nerves, until Vivisection showed that arteries contained blood, and that nerves were conductors of motion and sensation; anatomy, on both these points, had led capable observers into hopeless error. (3) The oft-quoted saying of Sir Charles Bell is more than qualified when we remember that he did not discover the functions of the anterior and posterior roots of the nerves. This discovery was made through vivisection by Magendie, whose experiments were repeated and confirmed by Shaw. That the discovery of the circulation of the blood was due to Vivisection is asserted by Harvey himself, although no doubt his anatomical studies guided him to some extent. The Vivisections of Marshall Hall led to the discovery of reflex action; this important function was entirely missed by clinical observers, for though clinical observation "might" have discovered it, the fact remains that it did not do so. (4) The surgeon who has done more than any man living for establishing the operation of ovariotomy—Sir Spencer Wells— admits his indebtedness to Vivisection. With regard to the localization of function of the brain, clinical observers had reached no safe conclusions, in spite of thousands of *post-mortem* examinations, until the experiments on monkeys of Ferrier and Yeo, Horsley and others, enabled them to map out the motor centres of the brain; for the monkey's brain reacts to *stimuli* just as a man's does. What was before guesswork was now founded on accurate laws. The fact that savages had performed both ovariotomy and trephining, and that such operations had fallen into neglect until the time of Spencer Wells and Horsley, simply proves how dangerous such operations were before the laws which regulate them had been ascertained by experimentation. (5) Vivisection has not only shown us the true causes of infectious diseases, but to some extent has enabled us to prevent and cure them. The Pasteur treatment has reduced the mortality among those bitten by animals *proved to be rabid* from 15 per cent. at least to 1 per cent. at most. Koch's tuberculin has given us a safe method of diagnosing consumption in animals when all other methods fail; whilst the antitoxin treatment of diphtheria has reduced the mortality by 50 per cent. (6) The action and effect of drugs are the same on all animals; when there is a difference in the action of a drug on two animals, it is a difference of *degree*, not of *kind*. Chloroform and ether, for instance, have essentially the same action on any kind of plant or animal; and morphia will act on rabbits and man in the same manner, though much larger doses are necessary in the rabbit. Although anæsthetics were not actually discovered by Vivisection, such experiments have thrown a great deal of light on their action. Simpson showed that in animals the process of parturition went on normally even when the parturient animal was placed under the influence of chloroform, or when the spinal marrow was destroyed; this discovery has been the means of saving exquisite and prolonged suffering to thousands of women. The combination of atropine and morphia with chloroform, now so constantly used by anæsthetists, we owe to the experiments of Bernard and Dastre. (7) Medical opinion is practically unanimous in favour of experimentation on animals; it would be difficult to find a hundred medical men opposed to it, and among these there is not one of the first rank.

Con: (1) Medicine and Surgery are arts and not sciences, and can never be advanced by methods which are indispensable to pure sciences. The animal economy is much more than a piece of machinery, and the human stomach is not the least like a chemist's test-tube. The healing art can only be learned at the bed-side; and experiments on living animals so far from having advanced it, have had a tendency to retard it. It is no reproach to medicine that it is but a wise empiricism. The element of life and the personal factor must for ever prevent it being an exact science. Every patient must be treated on his own merits; there is no other road to medical success than patient clinical observation. (2) Harvey's discovery of the circulation was not made in consequence of his Vivisections, but, as he tells us, by a study of the position of the valves of the veins in the dead subject. Sir Charles Bell emphatically protested against the assertion that his discovery of the functions of the nerves was in any way due to Vivisection. He declared that experiments had never been the means of discovery, but had always tended to perpetuate error. No experiments at all are needed for demonstrating the process of reflex action. "Living pathology" suffices for the purpose. (3) Ovariotomy has been successfully practised by savages from immemorial ages, and nothing can be further from the truth than to say that the operation owes anything whatever to the practice of Vivisection. Brain surgery was well understood by prehistoric man. As it is in the brain that man differs most from the lower animals, he could have learned little or nothing from Vivisection here; it was, in fact, by clinical observation and *post-mortem* examinations that our knowledge of brain surgery has been acquired. (4) Although Pasteurism has taught us much as to the causes of disease due to microbes, it has been exceedingly barren in practical results. The failure of the Pasteur treatment of hydrophobia, of Koch's "consumption cure," and the disappointing results of Antitoxin treatment prove this. (5) As very few, if any, actual medicines have the same effect on animals as on human beings, it cannot be said that we owe any exact knowledge of the action of drugs to experiments on animals. (6) Testing poisons on animals in criminal cases is, for the above reasons, an unscientific and dangerous proceeding. (7) Chloroform and ether as anæsthetics were not discovered by experiments on animals, but by experiments which Dr. Simpson performed upon himself (chloroform), and which Dr. Morton, the dentist, made upon his patients.

VOLUNTARY SCHOOLS AND RATE AID.
(See also EDUCATION: VOLUNTARY SCHOOLS.)

Pro : (1) In order to enable the Voluntary or Denominational Schools to hold their own against the Board Schools, it is necessary that they should be allowed funds from the same source from which the Board Schools draw theirs, viz., the rates. (2) The proposed Exchequer grant of 4s. or even 6s. would be totally inadequate to meet the demands of the case. (3) Any Exchequer grant would be at the mercy of the majority in the House of Commons, who might, at any moment, refuse to vote the money. (4) There could be no objection to ratepayers being represented, provided that it were strictly understood that the right of the ratepayers to interfere only extended to the point of seeing that the money was properly spent, and that they were not allowed to interfere with the religious character of the school or the selection of the teachers. (5) It is untrue to say that Parliament has been responsible for the greater part of the increased expenditure; this has really been caused by the extravagance of the School Boards. (6) As far as subscriptions are concerned, rate aid might be made conditional on the school securing a certain proportion of subscriptions. (Some) Subscriptions ought to be unnecessary in a national system of education. The members of the great religious corporations are required to pay both rates and taxes, and should not be called upon to pay in addition to have their children taught in their own religious principles. (7) (Some) The matter had better be compromised by allowing rate aid in those parishes only where there are Board Schools, and extending the Exchequer grant to all Elementary Schools. Thus the agricultural parishes would not be burdened with heavy rates, and the opposition of the Dissenters would be deprived of most of its force by the removal of a seeming injustice to the Board Schools.

Con : (1) It would be quite possible to give the Voluntary Schools such aid from the Exchequer as would enable them to hold their own against the Board Schools without jeopardizing their existence, as would be the case were rate aid adopted. (2) The Denominational Schools must make the best terms they can, and while 6s. may not meet all their requirements, it will enable them to continue to exist, and will not raise awkward questions, such as ratepayers' representation, etc. (3) Local rate aid would be at the mercy of the ratepayers in each particular district. Besides, the Exchequer grant could always be made permanent by means of a Bill, which would have to be repealed before the grant could be withdrawn. (4) It is hopeless to expect that ratepayers' aid, if ganted, could be given on any other terms than those of full control on the part of the ratepayers, and there being no way, short of destroying all local control, of forcing the ratepayers to give this aid, the ratepayers could make their own terms. (5) Parliament, or at least the Education Department, has undoubtedly been responsible for the greater part of the expenditure in connection with the schools. (6) Rate aid would dry up the subscriptions. It seems only just that in a society where no decided priority is given to any one religion, and where the number of sects is infinite, that individuals should be called upon to pay in part for the religious teaching of their children.

VOTERS, ILLITERATE: DISFRANCHISEMENT OF.

Pro : (1) Unless a man is able to read, he is not fit to vote, as he is unlikely to be endowed with enough intelligence to enable him to see through the interested promises of professional demagogues. (2) The fact that he is unable to record his vote without assistance lays the Illiterate Voter open to intimidation by interested persons who are able to find out which way he has voted. So far has this intimidation been practised in Ireland, where there is a large proportion of Illiterate Voters, that Literate Voters are induced to "vote illiterate," in order that the manner in which they have voted may be known to the presiding officer, who is not always above suspicion. **(3)** An Illiterate Voter would be disfranchized purely through his own act, as it is always open to a man to learn just enough to enable him to mark his paper correctly, and the presiding officer is allowed a wide margin on which to decide as to intentions. **(4)** The proposed measure would act as a spur to all classes of the community to learn to read.

Con: **(1)** The mere power to read would not increase a man's efficiency as a voter—often, indeed, the reverse—unless he knew what to read, and had the taste to read it; it can hardly be said that the mental *pabulum* devoured by the artizan population of towns, varying, as it mostly does, between murders, horse-racing reports, and accounts of football matches, is likely to increase their general stock of intelligence. **(2)** The presiding officer, and all associated with him, are liable to heavy penalties should they violate the secrecy of the ballot. **(3)** An Illiterate Voter has as much interest in the good government of the country as the most highly-cultured member of the community, and has therefore an equal right to vote. **(4)** If not allowed assistance in voting, the Illiterate Voter would still exercize his vote, though in a haphazard manner; hence the result would be that while the evils from intimidation might be avoided, the way in which an Illiterate had voted would be quite uncertain. **(5)** If the blind are allowed to vote with assistance, why should a man be prohibited merely on the ground of illiteracy?

VOTING, COMPULSORY.

Pro: **(1)** The Vote is a trust, not a privilege. In events of great national importance every citizen should be under an obligation to record his opinion. **(2)** Such compulsion would checkmate the wire-pullers, who calculate on the abstention of many who are disgusted with their party, and would facilitate the election of independent candidates. **(3)** Compulsory Voting could readily be effected, and easily worked. Each man is separately registered already; to see who had voted, and to prosecute such as had neglected to do so, would be quite simple.

Con: **(1)** A Vote given under compulsion is as likely as not to be worthless. The essence of Voting is that it should be voluntary. **(2)** It often happens that a man is not able to conscientiously vote for either one side or the other, in which case it is far better that he should refrain from Voting altogether. **(3)** Compulsory Voting would be very hard to enforce.

WATER SUPPLY (LONDON), MUNICIPALIZATION OF.

Pro: **(1)** Just as other towns manage their own Water Supply, so London should be enabled to own and control hers, thus securing a supply of good water to her citizens. **(2)** The profits, if any, from the Water Supply ou_ _ to go to the relief of rates, not to the aggrandizement of shareholders. **(3)** This scheme has received the approval of a Select Committee (1891), which was strongly in favour of the County Council becoming the Water Authority for London. **(4)** By means of the quinquennial valuations, the Companies find their incomes constantly increasing without any effort on their part, but simply on account of the growing wealth of the community. **(5)** The London Water Companies have never possessed any statutory monopoly; on the contrary, on several occasions two Companies have been allowed to serve the same area. **(6)** Municipalization of the Water Supply would not involve any hardship on the Companies, since they would receive compensation. **(7)** A new Supply of Water for London must be found—away from the present sources, which are becoming altogether inadequate for the needs of the growing population. So late as the summer of 1895 East London was left with a limited supply of water for several months, putting the whole metropolis in great danger of an outbreak of an epidemic. As sanitary requirements grow, more and more water will be required. **(8)** It is only a central authority which could undertake so enormous a scheme as that by which water could be brought to London from a distance (say, from Wales). **(9)** As the County Council would have the same power as the Water Company to break up the roadways, etc., no difficulties would arise on this score. **(10)** Amalgamated into the hands of one authority, the Water Supply would be more economically managed than at present, and many expenses would be saved which now fall on the Companies: thus a considerable sum would be available for the relief of the rates after all due compensation had been paid.

Con: **(1)** The present Supply of Water is very satisfactory, and the Companies do their work well. **(2-3)** If the Municipal Authorities were to manage the Water Supply, it is unlikely that there would be any profit to go to the relief of rates. The County Council already has more work on its hands than it can properly perform. **(4)** Everybody benefits by the increased wealth of the community, to which the Water Companies contribute largely. As they are not allowed to charge by the amount of water used, but only by the ratable value of the house, their income naturally increases each time the valuation rises. **(5)** The Water Companies have a legally sanctioned monopoly, and as such Parliament has fixed the price at which they may retail their commodity. **(6)** If Water Supply is to be municipalized, compensation ought to be paid on a liberal basis, since the Companies have borne the risk, whilst the County Council would reap the permanent benefit. **(7)** The present sources of supply are sufficient, and are likely to remain so for many years to come. The East London Water Company failed to give an adequate supply mainly owing to the opposition of the County Council to its application for increased powers to build new reservoirs, etc., whereby it would have been able to meet all the extra demands arising from the long drought. (Some) The present Supply of Water would be more than sufficient for many years to come were the Municipal Authorities forbidden to use it for watering the streets, flushing the sewers, etc., for which purposes water might easily be brought from the sea. **(8)** The cost of bringing an extra supply of water from (say) Wales would be a needless addition to the rates. **(9)** A transfer of the Water Supply to the County Council would create a conflict between that body and the Local Authorities, who have the management of the roadways. **(10)** It is not likely that the County Council would manage the Water Supply as economically or as conveniently to consumers as the Water Companies do.

WOMEN AND UNIVERSITY DEGREES.

Pro: **(1)** It is absurd and unjust to refuse to women who go through the University course the legitimate reward of their labours, in the shape of the degree; and this refusal puts women at a disadvantage with men, in that, while the latter can in after life show their degree as a hall-mark of their powers, women have nothing to show, and thus the stupidest and the cleverest women stand on the same footing. A specially-created degree would have little or no value in the eyes of the world. Women need not be made members of the University. The authorities could easily make this a condition of giving the degree. **(2)** The evils of mixed education are imaginary. Co-education stimulates a healthy rivalry between the sexes, and encourages each to do its best. In physiology, etc., women have long been admitted to the lectures with men, and the Professors in these subjects find no difficulty in lecturing to mixed audiences. These Professors are among those who favour the granting of the degree. Co-education accustoms each sex to the presence of the other with beneficial effects to both. A separate University for women would be open to all the evils inseparable from convents, etc. **(3)** Some of the most experienced educational men are in favour of the change. **(4)** The best medical opinions agree that study does not unfit women to become mothers, and that "children suffer from the sins and self-indulgence of their parents, not from their discipline, self-restraint, mental activity, and industry." Women's health may break down if they are worried with home duties during their University career, and cannot give undivided attention to their work. **(5)** There is no reason why granting the degree to women should stereotype the education of either men or women. Admitting women to the degree might be the means of reforms in the men's course. Far from making the degree easier, the present proposal makes it harder for women than for men to take a degree. **(6)** The women who do not wish to go through the whole University course would be as free as they now are; but there is no reason why their wishes should prevent other women from taking a degree.

Con : **(1)** Women do not, as a matter of fact, go through the same course as the men. To give women the degree would be to make them members of the University itself, for the University having gone so far could not stop here. A Special Degree for women would give them the hall-mark without making them members of the University. **(2)** Co-education has been found in America to be a failure. In England it only succeeds because so few women attend the University, but this is hardly likely to be the case long. There are many objections to teaching physiology, etc., to mixed audiences, and this course is open to grave scandal. A separate University for women would be preferable. Women could then be given an education that would fit them to be good women, not bad imitations of men. Competition between the sexes is not desirable. **(3)** Some of the most experienced friends of the women's movement at Oxford and Cambridge —including at least one head of a woman's college—are opposed to granting the degree to women. **(4)** Women, as the mothers of the race, ought to do nothing which will unfit them for their duties in this respect—overwork unquestionably lowers their vitality. **(5)** It would be a pity at so early a stage in the movement to stereotype women's education. This must be the effect of assimilating it to that of men. **(6)** Women have domestic calls on them at home—which press on them far more than on men—which prevent their spending the requisite time away from home. It would be a shame to penalize them in favour of their more fortunate sisters.

WOMEN, HIGHER EDUCATION OF.

Pro : **(1)** It is unjust for custom and prejudice to debar women from the intellectual pleasure and strength derived from the severer studies. **(2)** The number of women in the country is greater than that of men, so it follows that many women must remain single. The majority of these must support themselves; and to enable them to do so, every kind of education should be thrown open to them. **(3)** The laws of heredity apply to both parents: to neglect the education of the future mother is to lower the intellectual standard of the race. **(4)** The demand for Higher Education has been initiated and maintained by women themselves; to place any obstacle in the way is an unwarrantable interference with their liberty. **(5)** Although the present system of Higher Education as it exists for men is faulty, *i.e.* in the abuse of the examination system and in the neglect of physical culture, and is therefore unfit to be extended to the other sex, yet the extension of it to women will eventually be necessarily a direct cause of reform. Women are endowed by nature with those intellectual gifts which are specially needful for the training of children, and make far better teachers than men. They have also more power of sympathy, and pause to think what is really best for their pupils, not pressing them forward unwisely. If women acquire a voice in the organizing of education, and mothers obtain an education which gives them a right to have an opinion about the training of their sons, the evils of the present system of Higher Education will soon be remedied for both sexes.

Con: (1) The physical organization of women is unfit to bear the strain of the severer studies or the excitement of examination pressure. (2) Approximation of the education of both sexes to the same standard increases the danger of female competition in the professions, and the concomitant danger of lowered rate of pay. (3) The tendency of heredity is to repeat the intellectual qualities of the father and the physical qualities of the mother; so the physical rather than the intellectual culture of the mother is of importance. (4) As men are educated to be bread-winners, the cultivation of the arts is apt to be neglected in their education, and also the physical culture necessary for health. It is, therefore, an advantage that the future mothers of their children should err on the side of a too exclusive cultivation of the accomplishments and graces. (5) The existing system of Higher Education for men is so faulty as to be not worth having; and far from women having gained by the approximation of their studies to those of men, in adding classics and mathematics to their curriculum, the reverse is the case: the education of boys has gained by its approximation to that of girls, in a more general study of English subjects, modern languages, and the arts and accomplishments, and by the consequently less exclusive study of classics and mathematics.

WOMEN, MARRIED, AS WORKERS.

Pro: (1) Women, married or single, have, as human beings, a healthy instinct for work, yet differ as much as men in the nature of that activity: married women, therefore, as much as single women, and, in fact, as much as men, should be able freely to determine for themselves whether, and how far, they shall limit their activities to domestic duties. (2) It is eminently desirable that married women, any of whom may at any moment become widows, should, during their married life (as well as before it), keep up as far as possible their wage-earning efficiency. (3) Since the economic helplessness of women has produced glaring evils—on the one hand prostitution, and on the other mercenary marriages, with the attendant evils of divided homes and sensational divorces—freedom for married women to work at any occupations for which they can qualify is a first step towards ultimate removal of these disintegrating conditions. (4) The universal testimony of trained nurses throughout shows that child-bearing is attended with far less suffering where the working energies of the woman are maintained up to the last, and her personal attention thus diverted from the incidents of maternity, than where the woman is discouraged from exertion; and it may therefore be taken as demonstrated that merely physiological considerations by themselves would dictate the advisability of admitting married women freely to the active pursuits of life. (5) The refusal of liberty to a woman when married places a premium on the unmarried state for all women of character and independence, which is entirely opposed to a vigorous social life and the continuous production of desirable offspring. (6) Since in all departments of life woman's interests are affected, the responsible action of women in these departments is a necessity, and its limitation to single women means the loss to the community of the most fully developed women, as well as of the element of motherhood.

Con: (1) A woman, once married, should merge her own individuality in that of her husband, acting as a completement to him; hence she should work only for him in the home and as the mother of his children. (2) Decrease of wages always follows where the wife enters the labour market; in fact, the united earnings of husband and wife may even sink below those of the man alone. (3) Wherever and in so far as married women have refused to be limited in their sphere of action, the result has been a general neglect of wifely duties. (4) Since child-bearing and bringing-up of children are the most important functions of woman, her whole life, especially when married, should be regulated with a view to this function. (5) The alarming increase of infant mortality where married women work in factories calls for the prohibition of such work. (6) (Some) Women are naturally weaker than men in brain-power and general physical force; therefore, especially when subjected to the additional strain of maternity, they should be kept to quiet pursuits. (7) Woman's influence loses its peculiar potency and charm the moment it intrudes into the sphere of male activities.

WOMEN, MEDICAL EDUCATION FOR.

Pro: (1) Many women, yielding to a natural dislike to consult a male physician, endure complaints which might easily be remedied, and eventually suffer serious injury. (2) Midwifery was originally exercised by women, and it is difficult to defend the practice of it by men on any other ground than the absence of women equally qualified to undertake the task. (3) Men are always apt to become rough and ready when not restrained by the influence of the opposite sex as equals; and nurses and women patients in hospitals do not always receive the treatment which would be enforced if ladies had equal authority with the male physicians. (4) No one has ever denied that the duties of the nurse are such as a woman may fittingly perform. These duties require as much nerve as the practice of medicine, and the nurse has to attend upon male patients, while the woman physician attends only her own sex. (5) When women are seen to undertake the work of the physician, we shall better know how to value and to remunerate the work of the ladies, often equally well educated and intelligent, who now enter the profession of nursing, in the exercise of which they are always overworked, and usually underpaid. (6) The influence of women is almost universally exercized in favour of morality. It was long ago suggested by the prophetic framer of an Ideal State that a body of women physicians is necessary as a safeguard to public morals.

Con: (1) Women of small intelligence and education usually have a poor opinion of their own sex, and patients of this type would not yield to a lady doctor that implicit obedience which they yield to a man, and which is so important a condition of successful treatment. It is improbable that any woman has ever neglected medical advice simply because she could not consult a doctor of her own sex. (2) Women, as a rule, have less nerve than men; and no examination test would fully prove fitness to act in emergencies: a brilliant scholar might easily be deficient in this respect. The difficulties attending the training of women students are numerous. The co-education of the sexes presents special difficulties here. Yet in schools and hospitals for women only the field of teaching and of experience would be narrower. (4) Women, as a rule, hate responsibility, and even if fully qualified would probably tend to assume the position of nurse rather than doctor. (5) In the medical, as in other professions, the competition of women would seriously affect the chances of a livelihood for many men already in the field; especially as they would probably reduce the rate of pay by accepting a lower remuneration than that now paid to men. (6) Public morals as dictated by a body of women doctors would soon become an organized hypocrisy, since the over-regulation to which women incline would lead to a general evasion of the law.

WOMEN SUFFRAGE.

Pro: (1) Every human being, and therefore woman, is the subject of political rights. (2) The franchise is denied to minors and lunatics, because they have not attained adult age, and because they are mentally abnormal; women who are adult, and who are not mentally abnormal, cannot have their exclusion from the franchise justified by analogy with either of these classes. (3) Therefore, those who justify the exclusion of women from the franchise by the analogy of minors and lunatics are bound to show, *on other grounds*, that the former exclusion is as necessary for the good of the community as the latter. (4) The franchise is an essential element of good citizenship. To deny the franchise to women is to strike a serious blow at their good citizenship. (5) It is highly desirable that women who are wives and mothers and companions of those who already possess the franchise, and who have, as such, great influence, should have that influence steadied and rationalized by political responsibility, and by the important moral education which such responsibility carries with it. (6) Women are in so many respects differentiated from men, not only on account of the many differences of function which a complex civilization has developed in them, but most of all by the great differentiation of sex, that it is peculiarly desirable that the woman's point of view should be expressed, and the more especially feminine interests safeguarded by direct representation. (7) Representation by others, no matter how intelligent, sympathetic, and trustworthy they may be, can never be a substitute for the mental and moral development involved in the exercize of personal responsibility. (8) Such mental and moral development through the intelligent exercize of the franchise will enable women to exercize more intelligently and efficiently the various other functions which may be theirs. (9) Women who are indifferent to politics would be more likely to have their interest aroused if they had the franchise. (10) The possession of the franchise would make women a power which politicians could not afford to despise; therefore, the interests of women would assume an importance which never attaches to the interests of the unenfranchised. (11) It is to the interest of the whole community that women should have public spirit and the social point of view developed in them as much as possible. (12) Narrowness of view, and family or local colouring of judgment, are best cured, whether in men or women, by participation in a wider interest. (13) That women do not serve as soldiers in the modern state is due (as history proves), not to a physical weakness incidental to sex, but to the customs and functional differentiation of civilized society. An analogous differentiation exempts clergymen from service in the army, but does not deprive them of votes; a similar, or sometimes greater, physical weakness prevents, absolutely, old men and male invalids from military service, but is not made a ground for depriving either of the Parliamentary vote. Women suffer from war as much as men. War and peace are not decided by popular vote. (14) The exercize of the franchise by women will tend to raise political and social morality. (15) Women being—as at present developed—less speculative than men, their admission to the franchise might balance the natural instability of a democracy. (16) We cannot exclude women from the franchise on the score of mental incapacity, so long as we fail to require any intellectual qualification from the male voter. (17) Women have been admitted to the municipal franchise. They can vote at School Board elections, and for members of other local bodies. The results justify the extension to them of the Parliamentary franchise. (18) Legislation in England is being brought more and more face to face with social and economic questions, in which the judgment of women would be most valuable. This has been shown by their work on School Boards, Boards of Guardians, etc. (19) The recognized maxim that taxation and representation should go together is violated by the exclusion of women from the franchise. In the case of minors and lunatics, the property that is taxed is held in trust, so no analogy can be established with that.

Con : **(1)** A human being, as a member of a community, is a subject of rights ; but it is desirable that different rights should be recognized by different people, at different times, and as attaching to different sections of the community.   **(2)** The denial of the franchise to minors and lunatics proves that the good of the community is the ultimate consideration by which the bestowal or denial of the franchise must be determined. The good of the community demands that women shall keep free from politics. **(3)** Good citizenship is realized through many functions. Some of the most important of these are open to women.   **(4)** It is unnecessary to give women a Parliamentary vote, as they already possess an important influence on the votes of men.   **(5)** The interests of women are so intimately bound up with those of men, that in safeguarding their own interests, men necessarily, throughout a large area of human interest, safeguard the interests of women also.   **(6)** It is desirable that women should devote themselves to work other than political, for which their mental and moral development makes them better fitted.   **(7)** Women are already indirectly represented by men of intelligence and sympathy, who have the interests of women closely at heart.   **(8)** Women can agitate, can speak in public, and can write ; therefore, there is little chance that their point of view should remain unknown.   **(9)** The majority of women are quite indifferent to politics.   **(11)** Women are deficient in public spirit ; their judgment is more apt to be vitiated by narrow or personal considerations than is the judgment of men. Their sense of justice is limited.   **(13)** As women are unfitted for military service, it is unfair to give them the chance of deciding questions of peace or war.   **(14)** The opinions of women on questions of public morality are apt to be more faddy than robust.   **(15)** Women are much more superstitious than men ; therefore their admission to the franchise might have a most undesirable effect on the relation of the State to education and religion.   **(16)** Women are, generally, less mentally developed than men.   **(17)** The questions upon which the Parliament of the country has to decide are much wider and more important than the questions that come before local bodies ; the fitness of women, therefore, to elect members for the latter is no argument as to their fitness to elect members for the former.

WORKMEN'S ACCIDENT INSURANCE.

Pro : **(1)** Experience shows that Employers' Liability Acts are inadequate to secure compensation for workmen against accidents, as, in the first place, they are usually unable to pay the costs of a legal suit ; and, secondly, the law is so full of obscurities, that its results—however clear a man's case may be—are very uncertain.   **(2)** Since a large part of the accidents arise from no fault of either the employer or even of fellow-workmen, they obviously cannot be prevented by any penalty on the employer. A man would not, under this scheme, receive compensation where his own carelessness could be proved.   **(3)** Even where employers do not contract out they insure against accidents, and thus avoid litigation, etc.   **(4)** It is quite open for England to profit by the experience of Germany in this matter, avoiding those defects which mar the German scheme. So successful has insurance been in Germany, that other countries have already imitated her.   **(5)** Under Accident Insurance it is found in Germany that accidents decrease : as the Employers' Association, being responsible, are careful to see that all employers use the latest safeguards in their works, under penalty of raising their premium. These associations are continually considering new ways of avoiding accidents, which, as practical men, they are far more qualified to do, and far better able to insist on, than our Factory Inspectors.

Con: **(1)** The workmen desire as much to prevent carelessness on the part of an employer as to secure compensation for themselves when injured. Very often the threat of an action is a quite sufficient deterrent, even under the present law, and under a more stringent one this would be still more effective. **(2)** To insure workmen against the results of their own carelessness is to put a premium on carelessness. **(3)** Were contracting out prohibited, much would be done to make Employers' Liability more real. **(4)** The scheme is not popular among German working men. **(5)** Accidents have enormously increased in Germany under compulsory insurance.

CONTAGIOUS DISEASES ACT (INDIA).

Pro: (1) The alarming increase of venereal diseases in the Indian (British) Army since the repeal of the Acts imperatively demands that drastic measures should be taken, if the efficiency of the army is to be restored. In 1895 the number of cases had grown to the alarming number of 522 per thousand men, and in July, 1894, it was calculated that only 37 per cent. had escaped the evil effects, which are bad not only in the immediate results they produce on the man, laying him up for the time and so on, but in their permanently debilitating effects on the individual, and in any children he may have. It is absurd to condemn the Acts because they did not entirely stamp out the disease—as well advocate the abolition of police because some crime exists in spite of them. The fact remains that whenever in India the Acts have been modified or repealed, as in 1885 and again in 1888, the number of cases has enormously increased. The numbers decreased again in 1890 because precautions were again taken in certain places, but on these being declared illegal and stopped the numbers have since then enormously increased. (2) Every care has been taken to provide the soldiers with healthy amusement, and the beneficial effect of this is well shown in the comparative statistics of drunkenness and crime—both of which have greatly diminished. The general health of the troops has also, with the exception of this disease, much improved, but "The hard fact remains that among a body of men, mostly very young, and nearly all obliged by the condition of the service to remain unmarried, removed from home ties and restraints into a country where climate and environment conduce to sexual indulgence, comparatively few are able to control the strongest passion in human nature." [Report of a Departmental Committee on the Prevalence of Venereal Disease among the British Troops in India (C. 8379, 1897)]. Moreover, however much amusement be provided for the men, it has still to be proved that healthy men in good exercise are more continent than those less healthy. It has been estimated in India now that were troops required for any expedition over and above those in hospital, quite 33 per cent. would have to be rejected before starting, and experience in the Chitral campaign shows that large numbers would have to be sent back besides. (3) The State confers no more authority on its officials in relation to the regulation of these diseases than it does in relation to smallpox, scarlet fever, or any other contagious disease. (4) The principal medical evidence goes to prove that under the Cantonments Acts not only was the number of cases very much smaller but their virulence was much reduced, and since the abolition the virulence of the disease has grown to an alarming extent. (5) The fact that the State took precautions to guard against the spread of these diseases affords no more encouragement to vice than would be afforded by private charity in curing the woman by means of public hospitals. The women are open to moral and religious instruction, and are, if they wish it, brought into contact with influences which may be the means of inducing them to adopt a better mode of life. Men, in consorting with these women, are yielding to an influence which the mere fear of disease is unlikely to check. It is curious, moreover, that the people who argue that it is wrong to protect the soldier from the results of his vice argue with almost the same breath that the measures in question afford no protection. (6) While it may be hard in particular cases to ascertain the presence of the disease, this is very unusual, and an experienced surgeon will rarely fail to detect it. (7) The Cantonments Acts cleared the Cantonments and towns of a crowd of wretched women who were mere vehicles of disease. (8) It is absurd to say that compulsory registration and treatment of the prostitute is in any way repugnant to the feelings of a people with whom prostitutes are attached to each pagoda and who in many cases practically dedicate their children to a similar life at the temples, especially when such registration, etc., concerns only the lowest class of all, who alone consorts with the British soldier. (9) Such legislation is not directed against all women: only against particular women who get their living in a particular way, and are required to pursue it under conditions which are consistent with the public welfare. (10) Women as a rule do not go to the Voluntary Lock Hospital, and if they go, do not stay there.

Con: (1) The present condition of the British Army in India is to be deeply deplored, but there is every evidence to show that the Army Sanitary commissioners were right when they said that "the hopes of reducing venereal disease among the troops by means of lock hospitals which were formed by the Sanitary Department in India were not realised. Not only did these hospitals fail to effect a reduction in the ratio of venereal cases among European troops, but as it happens these diseases increased during the term of years in which they were in full operation." (2) In giving characters, the authorities should take into consideration whether a man has spent much of his time in hospital suffering from these diseases. At present a man may have spent a long time in hospital and yet, because in respect of sobriety and discipline his record is good, he receives on discharge as good a character as the man who adds to these latter qualities the fact that he has been able to practise self-control. This encourages the view that the authorities look on sexual purity as a minus quality, whereas self-control in all its forms is perhaps more required in a soldier's life than in any other. The evil effects of any system of regulation are best shown by its effects on the French Army in Madagascar after 100 years of enforced regulation. Almost the whole army were struck down, thus showing what a small amount of stamina was left in the force, which it must be remembered was a picked force. In fact, the opinion of Sir Andrew Clarke is justified that "a man is likely to be all the better for being chaste till he is 25 years of age." (3) There is no analogy between the precautions taken under the Vaccination Acts or Public Health Acts for scarlet fever, etc., and those under these Acts against venereal diseases. Because while it casts no special stigma on anyone to say that he is suffering from small-pox, scarlet fever, etc., the same cannot be said of venereal disease, and it is a cruel hardship especially for a woman to be unjustly accused; and compulsory examination is an indecent outrage. Moreover, it lays women at the mercy of common informers, who may either compel them virtually to submit to this degradation or be branded as diseased. The fact, however, remains that the State is not in this case taking precautions against a disease which may be inflicted on all, but only on those who by their own choice or lack of self-restraint bring it on themselves. (4) If the virulence of the disease has increased, it must have increased while the Acts were still in operation. (5) The State in this case does encourage vice by the fact that, however praiseworthy attempts may be made to reform the woman, the primary object of the Acts was not so much to cure the woman as to guard the efficiency of the army through as far as possible guaranteeing the soldiers against their vices. The opponents of the Acts do not allow that they did succeed in this—the experience of more than 20 years during which the Acts were in operation proves this—but they say that physically bad as the Acts were in leading men to rely on a non-existent security they were morally far worse in the degradation they imposed on women. (6) The Army Sanitary Commissioners say "there was ample experience to show that a woman's examination was no guarantee that she might not communicate disease." "The question must soon be asked whether they [*i.e.* the regulations] are not positively injurious by leading men to depend on a security which does not exist." [Army Sanitary Commission, 1874-75; quoted from Joseph Edmonson's Enquiry.] (7) It was a constant complaint of the officers—medical and otherwise—appointed to carry out the Acts that they could not get hold of the unregistered women who prowled about the cantonment after dusk, and were a fruitful source of disease. (8) It seems rather curious if the Acts were not repugnant to the feelings of the people that the military authorities should have been obliged to send round circulars to their subordinates pressing them to obtain young and good looking women for the soldiers and telling them to attract as many women as far as possible. (9) The inequity of these Acts lay in the fact that they were directed against the women. Moreover a perfectly innocent woman was liable on the instigation of a man, possibly one whose advances she had rejected, to be submitted to the most horrible indignities.

IMPERIALISM.

Pro: (1) The growth of population in a vigorous nation like England, makes it impossible that all native-born Englishmen should find a means of a livelihood at home; and the question arises whether it is better to contrive that surplus members of society should have an opportunity, whilst remaining Englishmen, of retaining their allegiance and receiving protection as such, to form communities which shall be a source of strength to the mother country, rather than that they should lose their identity in a foreign, and possibly hostile population, with the chance always of finding even that cut off from them by the legislation of that country. (2) There can be no question that the policy of expansion in the past has been the means of establishing thriving communities of Englishmen in various parts of the world, and of providing us with Coaling Stations for the use of our fleet; and the more completely such Coaling Stations are surrounded by a friendly population of our own countrymen, by whom they can be defended instead of drawing large bodies of troops from other places, the more serviceable they are. (3) England, so far from being ashamed of her aggressiveness, has every reason to be astounded at her own moderation in the past. Left absolute mistress of the seas, she could have annexed the whole of Africa and assumed a protectorate over China, such as is now being achieved by Russia. All her recent annexations have been undertaken either to secure existing colonies or to prevent her trade from being cut off by the closing of existing markets. There is no reason why, when Great Britain has got a clear title to any possession, she should allow herself to be frightened out of asserting the plain rights of her citizens, for fear of wounding the susceptibilities of say France or Germany. The so-called conciliatory foreign policy, which aims at securing peace by the making of concessions where we get no substantial *quid pro quo*, is bound to fail of its object, for, by exciting the cupidity of our neighbours, it encourages them to raise unfounded claims, which, being compromised, leave them the better off to the extent of that compromise: the whole of our Empire might thus be gradually given away, in exchange for nothing but the contempt of our neighbours. It involves no disparagement of other countries to say that they would probably take, in fact have taken, advantage of the weakness or complaisance of Great Britain. Driven, for various reasons, to establish colonies, they found Great Britain barred their way with already existing colonies or undefined spheres of influence, and it has in many cases only been by trenching on these that they have founded colonies at all. It must be remembered that while Great Britain enjoys no superior privileges in her colonial markets, the markets of colonial possessions of other powers are as far as possible closed to us. (4) Trade does not, of course, follow the flag in the sense that we do more trade with our own colonies than with foreign countries. But the question is, Do we do more trade with countries if we annex them, than we should if we allowed a foreign Government to come and impose duties against English goods? Statistics undoubtedly show that we do. Moreover, can we afford to neglect any opportunities of acquiring open markets in view of the fact that foreign markets are being more and more closed to us by hostile tariffs? (Some) It would be better for us to encourage our colonial trade by a system of slight preferential tariffs which, while not cutting us off from our foreign trade, would encourage the Colonial trade.

Con: (1) As the population statistics show the impossibility of a further attenuation of British governing power, so the emigration statistics show that three-quarters of the total number of British emigrants deliberately choose to go outside the Empire. Most of our emigrants go to America; nor is there the smallest possibility that the United States will close their doors against her best class of emigrants, considering that even yet her enormous population is out of all proportion small to the extent of the area of the country and the magnitude of her still undeveloped resources. Moreover England, in her existing Colonies (which by the way are just as free as the United States to refuse to receive her immigrants, and probably would do so, did not our emigrants represent the flower of our working classes) possesses an enormous field hardly yet opened out. When we consider the small relative proportion of the existing population of Australasia, Canada, and the South African Colonies, it will be at once evident that not only do we need no more colonies, but that by setting up claims which we can defend only at enormous cost, both in money and men, we are needlessly increasing our risks. As a matter of fact, the necessity for emigration, while our country districts in England are being depopulated, points to an unsatisfactory condition of affairs at home. It must also be remembered that the population of England has in the last few years shown signs of a diminishing rate of increase. It may well be questioned whether it is worth while to risk the whole Empire with its immense resources for countries in Africa and elsewhere, where a nominal sovereignty over large areas populated by natives is always causing us trouble, and whose value is only very small. (2) Sea supremacy with its concomitants (*e.g.* coaling stations) may be necessary for a Power which has large colonial dependencies possessing a scattered population open to attack and possible annexation, and which invites attack by carrying on aggressive warfare elsewhere, but it is obvious that the best defence of our various colonies against open aggression must lie in contented populations ready to defend their own shores. As to India, the real danger comes from within. As long as our rule is just and in the best sense economical, it is not the interest of any class in India, much less the educated class who flourish under it, to encourage the anarchy which they know full well would follow our withdrawal, or to exchange our rule for Russian, since both of these contingencies they are fully aware would render their position impossible, or at least most difficult. But were this not so, it has been almost universally held by writers like Sir John Seeley and others that we hold India only by the fact that we are practically recognised as the best rulers under the given circumstances, and should any large section of the people be against us we could not hold our own for a moment. Moreover, the prospect of annexing India would probably never concentrate more than one Power against us, and with a reasonable recognition of our own interests, which are not to come into unreasonable antagonism with other Powers, where, as has been shown, we are only foolishly wasting our resources, we ought to be able to avoid coming into collision with bigger coalitions. If we wish to maintain coaling stations, we must keep soldiers there to defend them, epecially in an unhealthy place like Sierra Leone, where white men cannot settle permanently. As regards Egypt, its value for defence purposes must be very small, if, as we are told by experts, the Suez Canal would be useless to us in time of war, especially when we stay there at the cost of our pledged word. (3) Nothing could have been more fatal to the Imperialist idea than the full realization—were that not wildly impossible—of its dreams. Had England annexed, as Imperialists sometimes wish she had, Africa, China, etc., apart from the question of the difficulty of finding a sufficient population to efficiently defend our possessions, deprived of all stimulus from the outside by foreign Powers annexing as (Germany and France have done) islands in the neighbourhood of Australia, our Australian colonies for example would have had no impulse to help us. The Imperialist sentiment in the Colonies, not too strong even now, must have died before the centrifugal tendencies of local antagonistic interests. Moreover, her interests would have been antagonistic to those of the whole world, and the strain of maintaining her armaments when those Powers began to find out their common interest must have been crushing. Also, in spite of being enclosed by French colonies, Sierra Leone—a notable instance—still does a trade which shows no diminution. The question is not so much whether we should insist on our rights, as what are our rights? Are we going to allow adventurers to drag us into war to defend their rights to treaties made under circumstances which we do not know and where we had no voice in the matter? The claim to hold as against other European nations all parts of the earth where our traders had ever been is baseless. The great consideration for England is whether she can really administer a larger territory than she has already got, and whether it is really worth while to risk the whole commerce and Empire to get more. (4) Foreign countries have always been, and show not the smallest sign of ceasing to be, by far our best customers. Hostile tariffs notwithstanding, we send two-thirds of our exports to foreign countries—the fact being that countries which send goods here must receive payment indirectly in English goods. Moreover, whatever trade we do by annexing new countries is met by the increased cost of such a policy. Our defence must rather lie in the skill of our workmen and the honesty of our traders, to surmount any obstacle that tariffs may place in our way. Further, it must always be remembered that our self-governing colonies for the most part have been as highly protected against us as any foreign country, and that one-third of our total colonial exports are to India, whose fiscal policy we ourselves control. Trade breaks through toll-bars and overflows the most ingeniously constructed national barriers; and it was for the good of humanity and especially of an industrial nation which has, as we have, three foreign customers to every Imperial one, that it should be so. In whatever country they live, men will buy what is cheapest and best and not simply what comes under a certain flag. Trade is international: the day when we seek to make trade and flag co-extensive will be the last day of British mercantile supremacy.

RITUALISM, SUPPRESSION OF.

Pro: (1) There are in the Church of England a large number of clergy who use their position to teach doctrines and practise ceremonies directly contrary to the principles of the Reformation, and expressly forbidden by her laws (*e.g.*, Communion is frequently celebrated without any communicant save the Priest). This law-breaking has in the past been aided by the Bishops, by the prohibition of all legal redress to aggrieved parishioners, and by the preferment of notorious law-breakers to the highest offices in the Church. (2) A National Church must be based on a national authority, and the only national authority recognized is that of Crown and Parliament. The ecclesiastical hierarchy is not a national authority, and not the smallest change can be made in the doctrines or ceremonies of the Church except by the authority of Parliament. The Clergy are bound by their canonical oath to obey the State. (3) The practice of Reservation is forbidden by the Rubrics and is absolutely alien to the spirit of the Prayer Book. (4) Confession, as allowed by the Church of England, is a very different thing from the auricular confession of the Roman Church. Not only is the former non-compulsory, but "the English Church gives the minister no power to demand that the penitent shall confess anything more than the matter which perplexes or troubles him" (Abp. of Canterbury's Address). It is absolutely impossible that the Confessor should find out concealed sins without instilling vice. "How can he see where in the heart of his penitent purity and impurity, knowledge and ignorance, meet, so as to be quite certain that his questions teach no new sin?" (Bp. Magee, Ch. Ass. Tract, L.—13).

Moreover, his questions to young children must be founded on his knowledge of the most abandoned of his parishioners, or more than that, he has to consult the volumes of the Roman Casuist, in which confessor after confessor has recorded his experience till they form a museum of vice.

Con: (1) So far from being law-breakers, the Catholic Party in the Church have been the first to insist on the strict observance of the laws of the Church, which had been notoriously and openly flouted by the Low Church Party, *e.g.*, in regard to the Daily Service, Fasting, etc. Moreover, the clergy are not forbidden to re-marry, in defiance of the law of the Church, persons who have been divorced, and Priests are allowed openly to deny the Incarnation, Resurrection, etc. (2) The right of Parliament or the Civil authority to interfere with, or dictate to, the Church in spiritual matters can never be admitted, and the blundering of the last few years shows how unfit the Civil Power is to deal with matters which lie outside its sphere. Neither the Court of Arches nor the Privy Council is in any sense a spiritual Court. The Archbishops sat in the Privy Council only as assessors, taking no real part in the proceedings, and the judgments of that body, at least in one instance, were confessed by a judge taking parting part in the proceeding to have been one of policy not of law. The oath of the clergy binds them to obey Church and State—not the State alone when it is acting in opposition to the laws of the Church. For instance should the State adopt Arianism it would be the duty of the clergy to resist. (3) The practice of Reservation for the sick is not forbidden by the laws of the English Church. (See Kempe, "Reservation of the Blessed Sacrament." (4) Confession is enjoined by the rubrics: and in order to avoid the evils of an unregulated Confessional the Society of the Holy Cross requested the Bishops to provide for the education, selection, and licensing of duly qualified Confessors. This was refused. The book, "The Priest in Absolution," was published by the Society in order to guide the clergy in dealing with moral disease and had necessarily to be outspoken and contain much, like a medical work, which could not be advantageously read by the general public, consequently the 2nd part was never published openly, and attempts were made to keep the whole book only for those who would use it and not abuse it—one fact which differentiates it from those works of Protestants which have been openly hawked about the streets in large numbers, though those who sold them must have known the purpose for which they were bought. (*Truth*, September, 1898.) Moreover, the following directions were laid down for the Priest. He was to ask no questions unless the Penitent needs help, from timidity, etc., or from being tempted to keep something back, and then only very tentatively so as neither to teach evil nor inspire a desire to know something not yet understood. (A. H. Mackonochie, letter quoted in *Church Times*, June 29, 1877.) The practice being, moreover, purely voluntary, is resorted to only by those who feel a special need for it, and to whom it will probably be most beneficial. It is most unjust to judge a system only by its abuses.

BIBLIOGRAPHY.

(FIRST APPENDED TO THE FOURTH EDITION.)

Absenteeism.
Palgrave (R. H. Inglis) Dict. Polit. Econ., vol. i, pp. 3-4 (Macmillan, 1892), art. "Absenteeism," by F. Y. Edgeworth [impartial; with good bibliography].
Pro: McCulloch (J R.) Treatises and Essays on Subjects connected with Polit. Econ. (Edin., 1853), pp. 223-49, Essay on "Absenteeism."
Smith (Adam) The Wealth of Nations.
Con: Cairnes (J. E.) Polit. Essays.
Edgworth (Maria) Castle Rackrent [a novel].
Mill (J. S.) Polit. Econ., bk. v, ch. 4, § 6.
Raumer (F. von) England in 1835, letter 62.
Young (Arthur) Tour in Ireland, 1780, vol. 2, pp. 594 sqq. (2 vols., Bell, '92; 7s.).

Abstinence, Total.
Bibliography:
Gustafson (A. and Z. B.) Foundation of Death, pp. 469-576 (Hodder, 5th ed., 1888; 5s.).
Macdonald (A.) Abnormal Man, pp. 300-36 (Bureau of Educ., Washington, U.S., 1893; gratis).
Buck (Dr. Albert; ed.) Handbook of Medical Sciences, vol. i, pp. 102-5; art. "Alcohol," by L. L. McArthur.
Mackenzie (F. A.) Sober by Act of Parliament (Social Science Series, Sonnenschein, 1896; 2s. 6d.).
Moffat (R. S.) The *Times* Drinking Bout (Liberty and Property Defence League; 6d.) [a Summary of Letters to the *Times* between 15th Sept. and 27th Oct., 1891, by Dr. M. Granville, Sir W. Lawson, and other eminent men].
Wilson (Dr. G. R.) Drunkenness (Social Science Series, Sonnenschein, 1893; 2s. 6d.).
Pro: Encyclopædia of Temperance and Prohibition (Funk and Wagnalls. N.Y., '91).
Gaule (Justus) Alcohol and Happiness—in *Popular Science Monthly*, vol. xlvi, pp. 28-33; Nov., 1894.
Gustafson (A. and Z. B.) *ut supra*.
Kingsbury (Dr. G. C.) Alcohol: its Use and Abuse—in *Humanitarian*, Jan., 1894.
Richardson (Sir B. W.) Alcohol (Macmillan, 1878; 1s.)
Con: Bramwell (Lord) Drink (Liberty and Prop. Def. League).
Brunton (Dr. T. L.) Action of Medicines, pp. 126-9, 194-199, 324-5, 328-331 (Macmillan, 1897; 10s. 6d. net).
Duckworth (Sir D) Alcohol: its Use and Abuse—in the *Humanitarian*, Dec., 1893.
Evans (E.) Are you a Teetotaler? (Country Brewers Association, 1892).
Farquharson (Dr. R.) The Case for Moderate Drinking (Blackwood, 1892) [16 pp.; reprinted from *Blackwood's Magazine*].
Jones (H.) Total Abstinence—in the *Nineteenth Century*, Dec., 1896, pp. 875-880.

ABSTINENCE, TOTAL (*cont.*)
Paget (Sir Jas., and others) The Alcohol Question (Strahan, 1879) [a series of essays by the then most prominent medical men in favour of moderate drinking; reprinted from *Contemporary Review*].
Ringer (Dr. Sydney) A Handboook of Therapeutics, pp. 353-364 (13th ed., H. K. Lewis, 1897) [judicial statement, giving results of most recent investigations].
Rowntree and Sherwell, Temperance Problem and Social Reform (Hodder and Stoughton, 1899) [excellent].
Wilks (Dr. S.) Effects of Alcohol—in *Brit. Med. Jour.*, Aug. 29, 1891, pp. 459-64 [a paper read before Brit. Med. Assoc.; very guarded].

Adulteration Acts.
Hansard Parliamentary Debates: Adulteration of Food and Drink Bill (1860). 3rd Ser., vols. 156-7.
Select Committee (House of Commons) on Adulteration of Food, 1856, No. 379.
Encyclo. Brit.: art. "Adulteration," vol. i.
Pro: Hassall (A. H.) Food and its Adulteration (Longman, 1855) [comprises the report of the *Lancet* Sanitary Commission, 1851-4, of which Dr. Hassall was chief analyst, and which practically secured the passing of the first Act].
Con: Donisthorpe (W.) Law in a Free State, pp. 132-58 (Macmillan, 1895; 5s. net) [Mr. D. prepared an Adulteration Bill introd. into the House of Lords by Lord Wemyss, 1887].

Advertizing, Public Control of.
Pro: Evans (Richardson) Advertising Disfigurement—in *Westminster Rev.*, March, 1899 [a good summary of what has been done by the Society for Checking the Abuses of Public Advertisements, of which Mr. Evans may be called the father; temperate and practical]; Age of Disfigurement (Remington, 1893).
New Review, Nov., 1893, vol. ix, pp. 467-81: articles by W. E. H. Lecky, Sir W. Besant, Lady Jeune, Sir W. B. Richmond, R.A., and Julian Sturgis.
The Beautiful World. The journal of the above Society.

Advowsons, Sale of.
Elliot (Hon. H.) Church and State, ch. ix (Macmillan; 2s. 6d.).
Pro: Patrons' Defence Assoc., Remarks on Bishop of Peterborough's Bill, 1876 [B. M., Press mk. 4109, h. 7 (10)].
Con: Gore (Canon C.; ed.) Essays in Church Reform, pp. 198-236; art. by C. V. Sturge (Murray, 1898).
Jessopp (Rev. A.) Church Defence or Church Reform—in *Nineteenth Cent.*, Jan., 1896; vol. 39, pp. 138-189.

Agnosticism.
Pro: Guyau, Non-Religion of the Future.
Huxley (T. H.) Collected Works, 9 vols., *passim* (Macmillan; each 5s.).
Stephen (Leslie) An Agnostic's Apology (Smith & Elder, 1893; 10s. 6d.).
Con: Bodington (A.) Religion, Reason, and Agnosticism—in *Westminster Rev.*, May, 1893; vol. 139, pp. 369-80.
James (W.) The Will to Believe (Longman, 1897).
Lilly (W. S.) The Great Enigma (Murray, 1892; 14s.).
Wace (Prof. H.) Christian Faith and Recent Agnostic Attacks (Blackwood).

Agricultural Banks.
Reports from Austrian Co-op. Loan Societies (Eyre and Spottiswoode, 1883; 1s. 6d.).
Reports on Schutz-Delitzsch System (Germany, 1884; 2s. 6d.).
Report on Peasant State Land Bank (Russia, 1885; 5d.).
Wolff (H. W.) Agricultural Banks (Agricultural Banks Association, Westminster, 1894; 8d.); People's Banks (P. S. King, 1899; 10s.).

Agricultural Depression.
Bear (W. E.) The Agricultural Problem—in *Econ. Jour.*, Sept. and Dec., 1893; vol. 3, pp. 391-407, 569-83.
Channing (F. A.) Agricultural Depression—see Royal Com. on Agric. Min. Report; The Commission on Agric.—in *Fort. Rev.*, vol. 62, pp. 459-63.
Heath (R.) Agricultural Depression in East Anglia—in *Contemp. Review*, Sept., 1893; vol. 64, pp. 443-460.
Moore (H. E.) Revival of Farming—in *Contemp. Rev.*, Jan., 1894; vol. 65, pp. 58-73.
National Agricultural Conference—in *Times*, Dec. 8 and 9, 1892.
"Nunquam" [R. Blatchford] Merrie England, 1894, ch. 4 (*Clarion* Office, Fleet St., E.C. [Socialist view]).
Quarterly Review, April, 1893; vol. 176, pp. 521-548.
Royal Commis. on Agricultural Depression: Report, 1897; 3s. 1d. [Blue-bk. C. 8540].

Agricultural Light Railways.
Ackworth (W. M.) Note on Light Railways—in *Econ. Journal*, March, 1895, vol. 5, pp. 86-9.
Parliamentary Debates: Light Railways Bill. 4th S., vols. 37-8, 41-4.
Thompson (C. L.) Catalogue of Books, etc., on Light Railways (P. S. King and Son, 1895; 2s. 6d.).
White (J. W.) Light Railways (Widnes, Lancs., 1895).

Agricultural Rates Act.
Parlia. Debates, 1896; 4th S., vols. 39-43.
Pro: Garnier (J.) Agric. Rates Act—in *Econ. Review*, 1895.
Royal Commission on Agriculture, 2nd Report, 1896: Majority Report, pp. 7-22 [C.7981]; 6d.
Con: Roy. Commiss. on Agric., 2nd Report: Minority Reports, pp. 22-56.
True Significance of the Agric. Rates Bill—in *Investors' Review*, June, 1896, vol. 38, pp. 330-4.

Allotments.
Neutral: Moore (H. E.) Back to the Land (Methuen, 1893; 2s. 6d.).
Pro: Bear (W. E.) A Study of Small Holdings (Cobden Club; Cassell, 1893).
Hobson (J. A.; ed.) Co-operative Labour upon the Land (Social Science Series, Sonnenschein, 1895; 2s. 6d.).
Impey (F.) Three Acres and a Cow (Sonnenschein; 6d.).
King (Bolton) Parish Councils and Allotments—in *New Review*, vol. ix (1893), pp. 544-53.
Lefevre (G. Shaw) Agrarian Tenures (Cassell, 1893; 10s. 6d.).
Stubbs (Dean C. W.) The Land and the Labourers (Social Science Series, Sonnenschein, 1891; 2s. 6d.).
Con: Kebbel (T. E.) The Agricultural Labourer (Social Science Series, Sonnenschein, 1893; 2s. 6d.).

Alsace-Lorraine.
Schulz (A.) Bibliographie de la Guerre Franco-Allemande (1870-1) et de la Commune de 1871 (Paris, 1886).
United Service Magazine, 1892, p. 264 [on condition of A.-L.].
Pro: International Working-Men's Assoc.: Manifestoes put forward during the war of 1870. See Bax (E. B.) Short Hist. of Paris Commune, pp. 88-98 (Twentieth Century Press, 1895; 6d.).
Con: Capper (S. J.), Alsace and Lorraine—in *Contemp. Review*, vol. 66, pp. 13-34.

America and England.
Besant (Sir W.) Future of the Anglo-Saxon Race—in *North Amer. Rev.*, Aug., 1896, vol. 143, pp. 124-43.
Dicey (Prof. A.) A Common Citizenship—in *Contemp. Review*, April, 1897, vol. 71, pp. 457-76.
Grey (Sir Geo.) The Federation of the English-speaking Race—in *Humanitarian*, Aug., 1894.
Smith (G.) Anglo-Saxon Union—in *North Amer. Rev.*, 1893, vol. 157, pp. 170-85.

Anarchism.
Nettlau (M.) Bibliographie de l'Anarchie (Brussels, 1897).
Pro: Bakunin (M.) God and the State (Tucker, Boston, U.S., 1883).
Donisthorpe (W.) Individualism (Macmillan, 1889; 14s.).
Kropotkin (Prince) Anarchist Communism (Reeves, 1891; 2d.).
Proudhon (P. J.) Property, transl. by B. R. Tucker (Tucker, Boston; $3.50); System of Economic Contradiction, transl. by B. R. Tucker (Tucker, Boston; $3.50).
Reclus (E.) Evolution and Revolution (Reeves, 1891; 1d.).
Con: Pleckanoff (G.) Anarchism and Socialism (Twentieth Century Press; 6d).
Salter (W. M.) Anarchy or Government? Shaw (G. B.) Impossibilities of Anarchism (Fabian Society; 2d.).

Anglican Church.
Anglican: Answer to the Archbishops of England to the Apostolic Letter of Pope Leo XIII (Longman, 1897; 1s.).
Denny (E.) Anglican Orders (S.P.C.K., 1893).

ANGLICAN CHURCH (cont.)
  Gore (C.) Roman Catholic Claims (Longman, 6th ed., 1897).
  Littledale (R. F.) Plain Reasons (S.P.C.K., 1890).
  Pusey (E. B.) Eirenicon, 3 pts. (Parker, Oxford, 1865-70; each 7s. 6d.).
  Roman Catholic: Hutton (A. W.) Anglican Ministry; introd. by Cardinal Newman (Kegan Paul, 1879).
  Newman (J. H.) Letter to Dr. Pusey (Longman, 1866; 3s. 6d.) [a reply to the Eirenicon].
  Papal Bull on the Anglican Church: trans. (Burns and Oates, 1897-8; 6d.).
  Richardson (F. A.) The Catholic Answer; intro. essay by Luke Rivington (Kegan Paul, 1889).
  Rivington (Luke) Authority, or Reason for Joining the Church of Rome (Kegan Paul, 7th ed., 1897); Dust (Paul, 1888) [a reply to Canon Gore]; The Primitive Church and the See of St. Peter (Longman, 1894).

Anti-Semitism.
Pro: Anglo-Russian. The Tzar and the Jews —in *Contemp. Review,* vol. 59, pp. 309-26.
Reich (Dr. E.) Jew-Baiting on the Continent—*Nineteenth Cent.,* vol. 40 (1896) Sept., pp. 422-38.
Smith (G.) Essays on Questions of the Day (Macmillan, 1894; 9s.).
Con: Blind (Karl) A Good Word for Jews —in *North Amer. Rev.,* vol. 149, pp. 672-81.
Evvera (L.) Russian Jews; introd. by T. Mommsen (Nutt, 1894; 3s. 6d.).
Lanin (E. B.) The Tzar Persecutor—in *Contemp Rev.,* vol. 61, pp. 1-25.
Frederic (H.) The New Exodus (Heinemann, 1892; 16s.).
Leroy-Beaulieu (A.) Israel among the Nations: transl. (Heinemann, 1895; 7s. 6d.): article in the *Liberty Review,* 15 May, 1897; Empire of Tsars, 3 vols. (Putnam, 25s.).
White (A.) Truth about the Russian Jew —in *Contemp. Rev.,* vol. 61, pp. 695-708.

Arbitration, Compulsory Industrial.
Labour Commission 1892-93. 5th Final Rep.; 2s. Minority Rt p. reprinted (Mancs.: Labour Press; 2d.).
Crompton (H.) Industrial Conciliation (P. S. King; 7s. 6d.; O.P.).
Fabian Society: State Arbitration and Living Wage; 1d.
Jeans (J. S.) Conciliation, etc., in Labour Disputes (Lockwood, 1894; 2s. 6d.).
Schulze-Gaevernitz (G. von) Social Peace (Social Science Ser., Sonnenschein, 1893; 3s. 6d.).
Times, Dec., 1898; Jan. 18, 1899, Correspondence by W. P. Reeves, Bishop of Hereford, Sir E. Fry, etc.
Webb (S. and B.) Arbitration—in *Nineteenth Cent.,* Nov., 1896; Industrial Democracy, 2 vols. (Longman, 1898; 25s. net).

Arbitration, International.
Pro: Arnoldson (K. P.) Pax Mundi (Sonnenschein, 1892; 2s. 6d.).
Darby (W. E.) Internat. Tribunals (Peace Society, 1897; 1s.).
Russell of Killowen (Lord) Internat. Law and Arbitration—in the *Forum,* Oct., 1896.

ARBITRATION, INTERNATIONAL (cont.)
  Sidgwick (Prof. H.) Practical Ethics (Sonnenschein, 1898; 4s. 6d.).
  West (L. H.) International Quarrels—in *Internat. Jour. of Ethics,* Oct., 1892, vol. iii, pp. 64-74.
  Westlake (J.) Intern. Arbitration—in *Internat. Jour. of Ethics,* Oct., 1896, vol. vii, pp. 1-19.
  Con: Blackwood's Magazine, Oct., 1896, vol. 160, pp. 572-584.
  Bradley (F. H.) Limits of National and Indiv. Self-Sacrifice—in *Internat. Jour. of Ethics,* vol. v, p 17.
  Greenwood (F.) The Safeguards of Peace—in *Cosmopolis,* May, 1896.
  The Utopian, July, 1884, vol. i, pp. 1-16.
  Wilson (H. W.) The Working of Arbitration—in *Fort. Rev.,* Dec., 1896, N.S. vol. 60, pp. 785-794.
  Wilkinson (H. Spenser) The Command of the Sea and British Policy—in *National Rev.,* vol. 26, pp. 758-769.
  Wilson (H. W.) Peace and War—in *United Service Mag.,* Sept., 1897.

Aristocratic v. Democratic Government.
Aristocratic: Lecky (W. E. H.) Democracy and Liberty. 2 vols. (Longman, 1896).
Maine (Sir H.) Popular Government (Murray, 1887; 12s.).
Mallock (W. H.) Aristocracy and Evolution.
  Social Equality (Bentley, 2nd ed., 1885; 6s.).
Democratic: Mill (J. S.) Representative Government (Longman, 1894; 2s.).
Rose (J. H.) Rise of Democracy (Victorian Era Series, Blackie, 1897).
Webb (S. and B.) Industrial Democracy (Longman, 1898; 25s. net).

Armenian Question, The.
Correspondence—Asiatic Province of Turkey, 1895. Turkey, No. I, parts I and II; 2s. and 3s. [gives the proceedings of the Commission of the Powers to enquire into the massacres].
Pro: Bryce (J.) Case for the Armenians (Anglo-Armenian Assoc., 1893); Trans-Caucasia (Macmillan, 1896; 7s. 6d.).
Green (F.) The Armenian Crisis (Hodder, 1895; 2s.).
Lepsius (J.) Armenia and Europe (Hodder, 1897; 5s.).
MacColl (M.) England's Responsibility (Longman, 1895; 2s. 6d.); Sultan and Powers (Longman, 1896; 10s. 6d.).
The Massacres in Turkey—in *Nineteenth Cent.,* vol. 40, pp. 654-680 [by various writers].
New Review, vol. 9, pp. 201-210, 456-65, 648-54 [controversy between F. S. Stevenson, G. B. M. Coos, and Sadik Effendi].
Rosebery (Lord) Speech.
Russell (G. W. E.) Armenia and the Forward Movement—in *Contemp. Rev.,* Jan., 1897.
Wilson (Sir R. K.) Shall we Invite Russia to Constantinople—in *Contemp. Review,* Feb., 1897.
Wiotle (W. J.) Armenia and its Sorrows (Melrose, 1896; 1s.).

Army, Short Service.
Pro: Adye (Sir John) In Defence of Short

BIBLIOGRAPHY.

Service—in *Nineteenth Cent.*, Sept., 1892, pp. 358-369.
Headquarter's Staff (A Member of the) The State of the Army—in *Contemp. Review*, Feb., 1898, vol. 73, pp. 275-81.
Haliburton (Lord) Army Organization (Stanford, 1898; 1s.).
Wolseley (Lord)—in *Nineteenth Cent.*, Mar., 1881, vol. 9, pp. 558-572.
Con: Farquharson (Col. J., C.B.) Army Organization (Stanford, 1898; 6d.).

Asylums, Private.
Lunacy Law Reform Assoc., London, 1874.
„ „ Com. Report 28 March, 1878.
Report of House of Commons Committee on Lunacy (Harrison and Sons, 1878).
Balfour (W. G.) Address—in *Brit. Med. Jour.*, Feb. 28, 1880, vol. 1, pp. 319-320.
Bucknill (Dr. J. C.) Address—in *Brit. Med. Jour.*, Feb. 7, 1880, vol. 1. pp. 198-200; discussion, pp. 220-2 and 342-44.
East (E.) Private Treatment of the Insane (Churchill, 1886).

Authority in Religious Belief.
Balfour (A. J.) Foundations of Belief (Longman,).
Stanton (V. H.) The Place of Authority (Longman, 1891; 6s.)
Con: Martineau (J.) The Seat of Authority in Religion (Longman, 1890; 14s.)

Bakehouses, Municipalization of.
L.C.C. Report, No. 163. Report by Medical Officer on Sanitary Com., 1894; 2d.
Con: Truth about the London Bakeries—in *New Review*, vol. 10, pp. 607-14.

Ballot, The.
Con: Mill (J. S.) Parliamentary Reform (Parker, 1859, O.P.).
Romilly (H.) Punishment of Death (Murray, 1886; 9s.).

Betterment.
Neutral: Special Report from Com. on Strand Improvement Bill, 1890; 2d.
Town Improvements Committee, '94; 2s. 9d.
L.C.C. Reports, No. 113. Precedents for Betterment (P. S. King & Co., 1s. 4d.); see also Precedents for Ground-Values.
Pro: Hobhouse (Lord) The House of Lords and Betterment—in *Contemp. Rev.*, vol. 65, March, 1894, pp. 438-452.
Con: Argyll (Duke of) The House of Lords and Betterment—in *Contemp. Rev.*, vol. 65, April, 1894, pp. 483-95.
Bauman (A. A.) Betterment (Arnold, 1893); Betterment, Worsement, etc. (Stanford, 1894).

Bimetallism.
Dana (Horton S.) Bibliography of Money, 1878.
Internat. Monetary Conf. of 1878.
Jevons (W. S.) Bibliogr. of Money (Macmillan, 1874) [Investigation in Currency, etc.].
Pro: Bimetallic League: Publications of.
Foxwell (H. S.)—in *National Rev.*, vol. 24, pp. 637-660.
Gibbs (H. H.) A Colloquy on Currency (Effingham Wilson, 1894).
Walker (F. A.) International Bimetallism (Macmillan, 1896).
Con: Gold Standard Defence Assoc.: Publications of.

Bimetallism (*cont.*)
Farrer (Lord)—in *National Rev.*, vol. 24, pp. 165-189; Studies in Currency (Macmillan, 1898).
Free Review, April and May, 1895, vol. iv, pp. 1-24. 169-87.
Lawson (W. R.) India on a Gold Basis—in *Contemp. Rev.*, vol. 73, April, 1898, pp. 491-99 [against re-opening of mints].
Macleod (H. D.) Bimetallism (Longman, 1894); Indian Currency (Longman, 1898).

Bishops: their Exclusion from House of of Lords.
Pro: Denison (Archd. G. A.) Why should the Bishops, etc.? (Parker, Oxford, 1877; 1s.).

Blasphemy Laws, Abolition of the.
Pro: Macdonell (John) Blasphemy and Common Law—in *Fort. Rev.*, N.S. vol. 33, pp. 776-89.
Stephen (Sir J. F.) Blasphemy and Sed. Libel—in *Fort. Rev.*, N.S. vol. 35, pp. 289-318.
Verinder (F.) The Blasphemy Laws—in *Free Review*, Feb., 1897, vol. vii, pp. 449-59, and March, pp. 578-90.
Con: Aspland (L. M.) Law of Blasphemy (Stevens and Haynes, 1884).
Spectator, The, April 10th, 1886.

Cabinet Government.
Pro: Helps (Sir A.) Thoughts on Government (Bell & Daldy, 1872; 9s. 6d., O.P.).
Sidgwick (H.) Elements of Politics; 2nd ed., chap. 21 (Macmillan, 1897).

Canada: Should she join the United States?
Pro: Smith (Goldwin) Canada and the Canadian Question (Macmillan; 8s. net).
Con: Parkin (G. R.) Imperial Federation (Macmillan, 1892; 4s. 6d.).

Canals, Nationalization of.
Canal Committee, 1883 (252), p. 413.
Pro: Edwards (C.) Railway Nationalization (Methuen, 1898; 2s. 6d.).
Jeans (J. S.) Waterways and Water Transport (Spon, 1890) [most complete].

Canvassing.
Con: *Westminster Review*, 1892, vol. 138, p. 43.

Capital Punishment, Abolition of.
Macdonald (A.) Abnormal Man, pp. 409 sqq. (Bureau of Education, Washington, U.S., 1893; gratis).
Pro: Neuman (B. P.) The Case against capital Punishment—in *Fort. Rev.*, N.S. vol. 46, pp. 322-33.
Romilly (H.) The Punishment of Death (Murray, 1886; 9s.).
Con: Law of Murder—in the *Humanitarian*, March, 1898.
Tallack (W.) Penological and Preventive Principles (Wertheimer, 1889; 8s.).

Cathedrals. Nationalization of.
Pro: Massingham (H. W.)—in *Contemp. Rev.*, September, 1891.
Con: *Speaker, The*, September 5, 1891.

Catholic University for Ireland.
Times, Jan. and Feb., 1899 [correspon.].
Pro: University Educ. in Ireland—in *Dublin Rev.*, Jan., '90, vol. 23, 3rd Ser., pp. 1-32.
The Irish University—in *Quarterly Rev.*, April, 1898, vol. 187, pp. 566-89.

Channel Tunnel, The
Correspondence and Papers, with maps, plans, and sections (1875; 5s.).
Report of Commissioners of Proposed Treaty between Eng. and France (1876; 3d.).
Corres. and Rept. of War Office (1882; 2s.).
Rept. of Joint Com. and Evid., etc.; and memo. of Sir W. D. Jervois (1883; 8s.).
Nineteenth Cent., 1882, articles by Col. Beaumont, Lord Dunsany, Goldwin Smith, Sir L. Simmons, Sir E. Hamley, etc. [on both sides].
Pro: Contemp. Rev., Feb., 1883, vol. 43, pp. 240-50; March, 1882, vol. 41, pp. 522-41.

Charity Organization Society.
Macdonald (A.) Abnormal Man, pp. 300-36 (Bureau of Education, Washington, U.S., 1893; gratis).
Barnett (S. A.) C. O. S. and Christianity—in *Econ. Rev.*, April, 1894, pp. 189 sqq.
Bosanquet (B.) Aspects of the Social Problem (Macmillan, 1896).
" (H. and B.) Charity Organization—in *Contemp. Rev.*, Jan., 1897.
Hobson (J. A.) Social Philosophy of C. O. S.—in *Contemp. Rev.*, Nov., 1896, vol. 70, pp. 710-27) [against the Society].
Loch (C. S.) Charity Organization (Social Science Ser., Sonnenschein, 1890; 2s. 6d.) [by the Sec. of the Society].
Lowell (J. S.) True aim of C. O. S.—in the *Forum*, 1896.
Toynbee (H. V.)—in *Longman's Mag.*, 1891, pp. 409 sqq.

Child Labour (Half-Timers).
Pro: Church Gazette, Jan. 11th, 1899.
Moulder (P. E.) Child Labour—in the *Humanitarian*, March, 1898.
Con: Children's Labour Question, The (*Daily News* Office, 1899; 6d.).
Dunkley (H.) Half-Timers—in *Contemp. Rev.*, vol. 59, pp. 798-802.
Hird (F.) The Cry of the Children; illus. by D. Macpherson (Bowden, 1898; 1s.).
Manning (Card.) The Minimum Age—in *Contemp. Rev.*, vol. 59, pp. 794-7).
Reid (A.) Free Trade in Children—in the *Humanitarian*, Sept. 1895.
Tuckwell (G. M.) The State and its Children, pp. 137-57 (Methuen, 1894; 2s. 6d.).
Sykes (T. P.) The Factory Half-Timer—in *Fort. Rev.*, vol. 56, pp. 823-31.

Chinese, Exclusion of.
Board of Trade Report on Alien Immigration (1893; 1s. 7d.) [by Messrs. Schloss and Burnett on the Amer. Laws; contains a bibliog.] Blue-book C. 7113.

Christendom, Reunion of.
De Soyres (J.) Christian Reunion, Hulsean Lects., 1886 (McMillan, St. John's, New Brunswick).
Döllinger (I. J. von) Reunion of the Churches; transl. (Rivington, Oxford, 1872).
Earle (W.) The Reunion of Christendom made Practicable (Simpkin, 1896; 2s. 6d.).
Halifax (Lord)—in *National Rev.* vol. 26, pp. 415-21: Reunion of Christendom—in *Nineteenth Cent.*, May, 1896.
Huntington (Dr. W. R.) The Peace of the Church (Nisbet; 6s.).
Pusey (E. B.) Eirenicon, 3 vols. (Parker, Oxford, 1865-70, O.P.).

CHRISTENDOM, REUNION OF (*cont.*)
Con: Manning (Card.) The Reunion of Christendom (Longman, 1886; 2s. 6d.).
Newman (Card.) Difficulties of Anglicans, 2 vols. (Longman; 7s.).
Vaughan (Card.) The Reunion of Christendom (Roxburghe Press, '96; 2s. 6d., O.P.).

Christianity, its Divine Origin.
Nichols (Rev. J. B.) and Dymond (C. W.) The Practical Value of Christianity (Watts & Co.) [2 Prize Essays, pro and con].
Pro: Bruce (Prof. A. B.)—in his Apologetics (Clarke, Edin., 1893; 10s. 6d.).
Gore (Canon C.)—in Lux Mundi (Murray, 1891; 6s.); in The Incarnation (Murray, 1891; 7s. 6d.).
Harrison (Rev. A. J.) Problems of Christianity, etc. (Longman, 1891; 7s. 6d.); The Ascent of Faith (Hodder, 1893; 6s.).
Hettinger (F. L.) Revealed Religion, trans. and ed. by H. S. Bowden (Burns and Oates, 1895) [Roman Catholic].
Row (Rev. C. A.) Christian Theism (Hodder, 1890; 5s.).
Con: Greg (W. R.) The Creed of Christendom (Kegan Paul).
Huxley (T. H.)—in his Collected Works, 9 vols. (Macmillan; each 5s.).
Renan (E.) Life of Jesus, transl. (Kegan Paul; 1s. 6d.).
Strauss (D. F.) in his Life of Jesus, transl. by "George Eliot," with introd. by Prof. Otto Pfleiderer (Sonnenschein, 1899; 15s.).
Supernatural Religion, 3 vols. (Longman, 1879; 36s.).

Christianity, Is Dogma necessary to?
Pro: See Christianity: its Divine Origin—*ut supra*.
Con: Bartram (R.) Religion and Life (by Brit. and For. Unitarian Assoc., 1891; 2s. 6d.).
Martineau (J.) Studies of Christianity (Longman, 1873; 7s. 6d.); Essays, Theological, etc., 2 vols. (Longman, 1871; 21s.).
Smith (Dr. Vance) The Bible and Popular Theology (Sonnenschein; 5s.).

Christian Socialism.
See Churches and Social Reform.

Church Attendance by Non-Believers.
Pro: Greg (L.) The Agnostic at Church—in *Nineteenth Cent.*, Jan., 1882, vol. 11, pp. 73-6.
Quarterly Rev., Jan., 1899, pp. 103-36.
Rashdall (H.) Ethics of Religious Conformity—in *Intern. Jour. of Ethics*, 1896.
Shorthouse (J. H.) The Agnostic at Church—in *Nineteenth Cent.*, April, 1882, vol. 11, pp. 650-2.
Con: Clapperton (Jane H.) The Agnostic at Church—in *Nineteenth Cent.*, April, 1882, vol. 11, pp. 652-6.
Sidgwick (H.) Practical Ethics, pp. 113-77 (Sonnenschein, 1898; 4s. 6d.).

Churches and Social Reform, The.
Pro: Barnett (Rev. S. A.) Practical Socialism (Longman, 1888; 2s. 6d.).
Barry (Dr. A.) Christianity and Socialism (Cassell, 1890; 3s. 6d.).
Clifford (J.) Socialism and Teaching of Christ (Fabian Society; 1d.).
Gore (Canon C.; ed.) Essays in Church Re-

form (Murray, 1898) art. by T. C. Fry, pp. 291-319.
Ely (R. T.) Social Aspects of Christianity (Bellamy Library, No. 18, Reeves).
Holland (Canon H. S.) The Church and Social Reform—in *Progressive Rev.*, Jan., 1897.
Headlam (Rev. S. D.) Christian Socialism (Fabian Society, 1892; 1d.).
Kingsley (Canon C.) Alton Locke [and other writings].
Reid (A.; ed.) Vox Clamantium, Essays by writers, preachers, and workers (Innes and Co., 1894).
Stubbs (Dean C. W.) Christ and City (Macmillan, 1890; 6s.); Christ and Democracy (Sonnenschein, 3s. 6d.); Christ and Economics (Isbister, 1893; 3s. 6d.); Church and Labour Problem—in the *Humanitarian*, July, 1894.
Con: Cunningham (Dr. W.) Path towards Knowledge (Cassell, 1890).
Free Review, Feb. 1894, vol. i, pp. 401-9.
Peterborough (Bishop of) The State and the Sermon on the Mount—in *Fort. Rev.*, n.s., vol. 48, pp. 33-46.
Quarterly Rev., July, 1894, vol. 179, pp. 1-26.

Civil Service (England).

Royal Commission [Ridley Com.] on Civil Establishments at Home and Abroad.
Pro: Sidgwick (H.) in his Elements of Politics (Macmillan, 1898; 14s. net).
Con: Hamilton (Sir R. G. C.) The Ruin of the Civil Service—in *Nineteenth Cent.*, Sept., 1890, vol. 28, pp. 460-70.
Helps (Sir A.) Thoughts on Government (Bell and Daldy, 1872; 9s. 6d., O.P.).
Quarterly Review, O t., 1872, pp. 241-76.
See also Examinations, Competitive.

Civil Service (India).

Official: Parliamentary Debates, 2nd June, 1893, 4th S., vol. 13, pp. 102-40.
Papers relating to Simultaneous Exams. (Eyre and Spottiswoode, 1894; 11d.) Blue-book C. 7378.
Despatch of Secretary of State and Minutes of Dissent by members of the Council of India (Eyre and Spottiswoode, 1893; 1¾d.) Blue-book C. 7075.
Pro: Indian National Congress, British Committee of: reports, 1885 and onwards (Palace Chambers, 9 Bridge Street, Westminster).
Con: Strachey (Sir Jno.) India (Kegan Paul, 1894).
Chesney (Sir Geo.) Indian Polity (Longman, 1894).

Civilization in Savage Lands.

Pro: Seeley (Sir Jno.) Expansion of England (Macmillan, 1884; 4s. 6d.).
Con: Petrie (W. F.) British Assoc. Trans., 1895, pp. 816-24.

Codification of the Law.

New Century Review, symposium: A Plea for the Codif. of Engl. Law, April, May, June, and July, 1897 [incl. art. by Sir C. Ilbert and Sir R. Wilson].
Pro: Stephen (Sir J. F.) Hist. of Criminal Law of Eng., 3 vols., vol. 3, ch. 34 (Macmillan, 1883).

Collectivism.

Pro: Bliss (W. O. P.) Handbook of Socialism (Social Science Series, Sonnenschein; 3s. 6d.).
Engels (F.) Socialism, Utopian and Scientific (Social Science Ser., Sonnenschein, 1892; 2s. 6d.).
Fabian Essays in Socialism (Fabian Soc., 1990 Scott: 1s., 2s., 6s.).
Hyndman (H. M.) Historical Basis of Socialism (Kegan Paul, 1883; O.P.); Economics of Socialism (3s.).
Manifesto of Eng. Socialists, pub. by Joint Com. of Eng. Socialists.
Morris (W.) and Bax (E. B.) Socialism, Its Growth and Outcome (Sonnenschein, 1893; 3s. 6d.).
"Nunquam," Merrie England (*Clarion* Office, 1894; 1d., 3d., 1s.).
Fabian Society: Publications.
Independent Labour Party: Publications (53 Fleet Street, E.C.).
Social Democratic Federation: Publications (3 Bolt Court, Fleet Street, E.C.).
Con: Bramwell (Lord) Economics v. Socialism (Lib. and Prop. Def. League, 1888; 1d.).
Donisthorpe (W.) Individualism (Macmillan, 1889; 14s.).
Kidd (Benj.) Social Evolution (Macmillan, 1894; 5s. net).
Levy (J. H.) Outcome of Individualism (P. S. King & Son, 1892; 6d.).
Mackay (T.; ed.) A Plea for Liberty (Murray, 1892).
Mallock (W. H.) Aristocracy and Evolution.
Spencer (Herbert) Man v. the State (Williams and Norgate; 1s.).
Naquet (A.) Collectivism (Social Science Series, Sonnenschein; 2s. 6d.).
Con: Schaeffle (A.) Quintessence of Socialism (Social Science Series, Sonnenschein; 2s. 6d.); Impossibility of Social Democracy (Social Science Ser., Sonnenschein; 3s. 6d.).
Ely (R. T.) Socialism (Sonnenschein; 6s.).
Liberty and Property Defence League: Publications (7 Victoria Street, S.W.).
Personal Rights Defence Assoc.: Publications (Victoria Street, S.W.).
Neutral: Bliss (W. D. P.; ed.) Encyclopædia of Social Reform (contains full information and arts. by men of all schools of thought on social questions).
Bibliography: What to Read (Fabian Society, Tract 29; 3d.).
Sonnenschein (W. Swan) Bibliography of Social Economics—extracted from the "Best Books" and "The Reader's Guide" (Sonnenschein; 6s. net).
Bliss (W. D. P.)—in his Handbook to Socialism, *ut supra*.
Stammhammer (J.) Bibliographie des Sociali-mus und Communismus (Jena, 1893; 10 mk.); Bibliographie der Social-Politik (Jena, 1897).

Common Lands, Enclosure of.

Debate in House of Lords, 27th July, 1893.
Law of Commons Amend. Act (Parl. Debates, 4S., vol. 13, pp. 602-11).
Con: Hunter (Sir Robt.) Footpaths, Commons, etc. (Cassell, 1895).
Lefevre (G. Shaw) English Commons (Cassell, 1894).

Compensation to Publicans.

Pro: Federated Brewers' Assoc.: Review on

some Points in Licensing Laws with Counsels' opinion as to transfer of Licence.
Mancestrian: The Drink Trade (Heywood, Manes., 1893; 1d.).
Russell (T. W.) Compensation or Confiscation—in *Nineteenth Cent.*, July, 1890, vol. 28, pp. 23-38.
Watson (P.) Equitable Compensation (C. E. T. S.).
Con: Cyclopædia of Temperance, etc., pp. 88-96 (Funk and Wagnalls, New York, 1891; $3·50) [gives the history of the question in America and England].
Pearson (E.) Parliamentary Precedents (Simpkin; 2d.).

Conscription.
Memo. of War Office, Dec., 1870, on "That form of Military Conscription known as the ballot for the Militia"; with Appendices (6d.).
Jour. of Royal United Service Institute, April, 1897, January, 1894 [controversy].
Pro: Dict. of Pol. Econ. (Macmillan) art. by Spenser Wilkinson on Defence, Cost of, in vol. I. 1894.
Goltz (von der) A Nation in Arms (Allen, 1887; 15s.).
Liberty Rev., April 15th 1897.
Con: Allan (Sir H. H.) A General Voluntary Training to Arms, etc.—in *Fort. Rev.*, vol. 61, Jan., 1897. pp. 85-97.
Liberty Rev., May 15th, 1897.
Maude (F. N.) Vol. v. Com. Service (Stanford, 1897).
Thompson (A. M.) Towards Conscription (*Clarion* Office; 1d.).

Constitution, A Written.
Borgeaud (C.) The Adoption of Courts of Constitution (Macmillan, 1895).

Contagious Diseases Acts.
Special Report on C. D. Acts, 1866, and Lord's Report and Evidence (1s. 9d.).
Report on the Pathology, etc. of C. D., 1868 (3s. 6d.).
Report of Committee on Working of C. D. Acts, 1869 (1s. 9d.).
Report of Commission on Administration of C. D. Acts. 1871 (21s.).
Memorials from Royal College of Physicians and Others, 1868-73 (9d.).
Report from Select Committee, and Evid. and App., 5 parts. 1879-82 (20s.).
Report of the Assistant Com. of Police on years 1875-8 (1s. 6d.); 1878-81 (1s. 8d.).
Mems. from Portsmouth, etc., also from Assoc. for Promoting C. D. Acts, 1879-83 (6d.).
Returns of Admissions to Hospitals, 1860-84, 4 parts, 1883-5 (1s.).
Report of Commissioner on Working of Act in Hong Kong, 2 part., 1880-81 (1s. 6d.).
Corres. with Govt. of India, 1883 (1s.).
Corres. with Govt. of India and Mem. by Quartermaster-General in India and Minutes of Dissent, 5 p'ts, 1888 (2s.).
Report of Committee on Rules, etc., of Indian Cantonments, 1893 (4s. 5d.).
East India Cantonment Acts Return, 1895 (11d.).
Rept. Dept. Comm. Ven. Dis (East Ind., Cont. Dis., No. 1, 1897; 6½d.).

Contagious Diseases Acts (*cont.*)
Memorandum by Army Sanitary Com. (East I. C. D., No. 2, 1897; 1d.) [comp. with East Ind. Cant. 1895].
Royal Colleges of Surgeons and Physicians (East I. C. D., No. 3, '97, 1d.).
Despatch to Govt. of India (East I. C. D., No. 4, '97, 1d.).
Memorials to Sec. of State (East I. C. D., No. 5, '97 1d.)
Further Correspondence (East I.C.D., No. 6, '97, 1½d.).
House of Lords. May 14 and 17, 1897. Parl. Deb., 4th S. 48, pp. 467-91, 49, 581-611.
United Service Mag., Jan.-Dec. 1897.
Pro: Dashwood (Maj r-Gen. R. L.) Health of Brit. Troops, 1897 (Killher & Co., 2d.).
Hunter (Surg.-Gen., Sir W.) Necessity for re-establishing the C. D. Acts—in the *Humanitarian*, Oct., 1894.
New Century Rev., Sept. and Dec., 1897.
Playfair (Sir L.) Speech in H. of C. (James Walton, 1870, O.P.).
Con: British Committee of the Fed. for the Abolition of the State Regulation of Vice (17 & 18 Tothill St., Westminster).
Ethelmer (E.) C. D. Acts in *Westminster Rev.*, May, 1897.
Mayne (Major C. B.) Past Legislation (H. Marshall, 1897, 6d.).
"Physician" Army Statistics re C. D. Acts (Nottingham).
Stuart (J.) A Reply to Sir W. Moore in the *Humanitarian*, Dec., 1894.
Nevins (Dr. J. B.) Réglimentation a Failure (British Com., 1897; 6d.).
Taylor (C. B.) Speech (Effingham Wilson, 1883).
Wilson (H.J.) History of a Sanitary Failure (Brit. Com., 1897; 1d.).
See also India Cantonment Acts.

Contracting Out.
Hansard Parlia. Debates, 1893-94, vols. 18-21, esp. vol. 19, pp. 750-804. 29, pp. 1-63.
Con: Nash (V.) Employers' Liability Bill—in *Fort. Rev.*, n.s. vol. 55, pp. 244-54.
Webb (S. and B.) Truth about Employers' Liability—in *Progressive Rev.*, Jan., 1897.

Co-operation v. Capitalism.
Pro: Holyoake (G. J.) The Co-operative Movement To-day (Methuen, '91; 2s.6d.).

Co-operation: Can it supersede Capitalism?
Pro: Vivian (H.) Producers' Co operation in England—in *Humanitarian*, May, 1893.
Con: Schloss (D. F.) Methods of Industrial Remuneration (Williams and Norgate, 1894; 3s. 6d.).

Co-operation v. State Socialism.
Pro: Holyoake (G. J.) Co-op. Movement—*ut supra.*
Con: Potter (B. = Mrs. S. Webb) The Co-operative Movement (Social Science Ser., Sonnenschein, 3rd ed., 1899; 2s. 6d.).

Corporal Punishment in Schools.
Pro: Byrne (J. R.)—in the *Humanitarian*, Aug., 1895—a letter.
Con: Olivier (S.) Mr. Squeers. M.P., in *Time*, 3rd Series Jan.-June, 1890 (vol. 1.) pp. 651-7.
Simpson (L.)—in the *Humanitarian*, July; 1895—a letter.

Cremation.
Pro: Thompson (Sir H.) Modern Cremation (Kegan Paul, 1891).
Wells (Sir Spencer) Cremation—in *Humanitarian*, Oct., 1893).
Con: Cremation and Christianity—in *Dublin Rev.*, April, 1890, vol. 23, 3rd Series, pp. 384-402.
Horden (F. S.) Cremation as an Incentive to Crime—in *Journal of Society of Arts*.
Roman Catholic decree on Cremation—in the *Month*, 1892, pp. 17, 499.

Criminal Appeal.
Howard Association, Publications of.
Tallack (W.) Penological Principles—*ut supra*, s. v. Capital Punishment.

Death Duties, Graduated.
Parlia. Debates, April, 1894 (4th S., vol. 23).
Pro: Bastable (C. F.) The New Budget—in *Econ. Jour.*, vol. 4, 1894, pp. 352-4.
Buxton (S.) and Barnes (G. S.) Handbook of Death Duties (Murray, 1890; 3s. 6d.).
Farrer (Lord) Sir W. Harcourt's Budget—in *Contemp. Rev.*, Aug., 1894, vol. 66, pp. 153-64.
Con: *Blackwood's Mag.*, 1894, art. Sham Soc. Budget.
Lubbock (Sir John)—in *New Rev.*, July, '94.

Deceased Wife's Sister.
Annual Debate in House of Lords.
Pro: Huth (A.)—in his Marriage of Near Kin (Longman, 1887; 21s.)
Lecky (W. E. H.) Democracy and Liberty (2 vols.) vol. 2, pp. 177-84 (Longman 1896).
Marriage Law Reform Assoc., Publications (2 Deans' Yard, Westminster).
Con: Luckock (H. M.) Hist. of Marriage (Longman).
Marriage Law Defence Union, Publications (1 King Street, Westminster).
Watkins (O. D.) Holy Matrimony, 1895.

Decimal System.
Pro: Arnold-Foster (H. O.) The Coming of the Kilogram (Cassell, 1898).
Coste (F. H. Perry) Advantages of Decimal Coinage—in *Westminster Rev.*, Jan., 1893, vol. 139, pp. 22-31.
Donisthorpe (W.) Measures (Spottiswoode, 1895).
Manning (J.) Future of the Metric and Imperial Systems of Weights, Measures, and Coinage (Sonnenschein, 1899; 6d.).
Palgrave (R. H. I.; ed.) Dict. of Pol. Econ., art. by F. Hendriks (Macmillan).
Con: Noel (E.) Science of Metrology (Stanford, 1890; 2s. 6d.).
Spencer (Herbert) Against the Metric System (Williams & Norgate, 1896).

Degeneration.
Pro: Adams (Brooks) The Law of Civilization and Decay (Sonnenschein; 7s. 6d.).
Nordau (Max) Degeneration, translation (Heinemann; 17s. net).
Con: Dunn (H. P.) Is our Race Degenerating?—*Nineteenth Cent.*, Aug., 1894.
Regeneration: a reply to Nordau (Constable; 17s. net).

Disarmament.
Pro: Czar of Russia, Eirenicon.
Simon (J.) Disarmament—in *Contemp. Rev.*, May, 1894, vol. 65, pp. 609-15.

DISARMAMENT (*cont.*)
International Peace and Arbitration Assoc., Publications (40-1 Outer Temple, E.C.).
Con: Wyatt (H. F.) War as the Supreme Test—in *Nineteenth Cent.*, Feb. 1899.
Howorth (Sir H. H.) Some Plain Words—in the same.
Navy League, Publications (13 Victoria St.).

Disestablishment (England).
Neutral: Elliot (Hon. A.) The State and the Church (Macmillan, 1882; 2s. 6d.).
Pro: Liberation Society, Publications of.
Miall (E.) Title Deeds (Longmans, 1885; 6s., O.P.).
Richard (H.) and Williams (J. C.) Disestab. (Sonnenschein, 1886; 1s.).
Reid (A.; ed.) Why I would Disestablish (Longman, 1886) [a series of papers by prominent men].
Russell (G. W. E.) Ritualism and Disestab. —in *Nineteenth Cent.*, Feb., 1899.
Con: Freeman (E. A.) Disestablishment (Macmillan, 1874; 2s. 6d.).
Fuller (Rev. M.) Our Title Deeds (Griffith, 1890; 7s. 6d.).
Garnier (T. P.) Title Deeds (S.P.C.K.; 3s. 6d.).
Gore (Canon C.; ed.) Essays in Church Reform (Murray, 1898).
Grey (Lord) and Fremantle (W. H.) Church Reform (Sonnenschein, 1853; 1s.).
Selborne (Lord) Defence of Church of England (Macmillan, 1888; 2s. 6d.).

Disestablishment (Scotland).
Neutral: Elliot (Hon. A.)—*ut supra*.
Pro: Reid (A.) Why I would Disestablish—*ut supra* (papers by Professors Calderwood, Taylor, and Mr. A. T. Innes, pp. 117-48).
Con: Gore (Canon C.; ed.) Essays in Church Reform, art. by Lord Balfour of Burleigh, pp. 79-100 (Murray, 1898).
Johnston (C. W.) Handbook (Hill, Edin., 1892).
McClymont (Rev. J. H.) Church of Scotland (Johnstone, Aberdeen, 1892; 1s.).
Macleod (D.) Scotland and Disestablishment—in *Contemp. Rev.*, Aug., 1893, vol. 64, pp. 259-72.

Disestablishment (Wales).
Welsh Rev., Jan. and April, 1892.
Review of the Churches, April and May, 1892.
National Review, Jan.—June 1893.
Pro: Darlington (T.) An Alien Church—in *Contemp. Rev.*, June 1893.
Reid (A.) Why I would Disestablish—*ut supra* [papers by prominent Welshmen, pp. 151-262].
Con: Bromley (Bp. A.) Tasmanian Precedent—in *Contemp. Rev.*, June, 1893.
Newbery House Mag., April and May, 1893.

Distress for Rent, Abolition of.
Pro: Richards (R. C.) The Landlords' Preferential Position—in *Fort. Rev.*, vol. 47, pp. 880-95.

Divorce.
Report of the Commissioners to enquire into the law of Divorce, 1853 (75 pp.).
Wright (C. D.) Marriage and Divorce, 1867-86 (W.S.A. Commissioner of Labour, Washington).
Parlia. Debates, 1857, vols. 145, 146, 147.

Divorce (cont.)
  Pro: Browne (M. E.) Marriage and Divorce
—in the *Humanitarian*, Jan., 1897.
  Dolph (J. N.) Is Divorce Wrong?—in *North Amer. Rev.*, vol. 149, pp. 646-52.
  Geogehan (H. C.) Divorce Extension justified (Robertson. Melbourne, 1888).
  Ingersoll (R. G.) Is Divorce Wrong?—in *North Amer. Rev.*, vol. 149, pp. 529-38.
  Lecky (W. E. H.) Democracy and Liberty, 2 vols., vol. ii, pp. 158-75 (Longman, '96).
  Potter (H.C.) Is Divorce Wrong?—in *North Amer. Rev.*, vol. 149. pp. 524-29 [gives the view of the Amer. Epi-c. Church].
  Stephen (A.) The Law of Divorce—in *Contemp. Rev.*, vol. 59, pp. 802-13.
  Winslow (Dr. F.) Insanity as a Plea for Divorce—in the *Humanitarian*, Jan., '98.
  Con: Chapman (E. R.) Marriage Questions in Modern Fiction, etc. (Lane, 1897) [includes, among others, the tract pub. by M. R. W.].
  Gibbons (Card.) Is Divorce Wrong?—in *North Am r. Rev.*, vol. 149, pp. 517-24.
  Gladstone (W. E.) Is Divorce Wrong?—in *North Amer. Rev.*, vol. 149, pp. 641-44.
  Harrison (Fred.) Marriage (Newton Hall, 1889) [Positivist view].
  National Divorce Reform League (U.S.A.), Publications of.

Divorce for Women.
  Parlia. Debates, 1857. vol. 145, 146, 147.
  Equal Morality of the Sexes—in the *Humanitarian*, Nov. and Dec., 1894 [a symposium by Lady Burton. Rev. H. R. Haweis, Mrs. J. Butler, Clement Scott, etc.].
  Lewis (G. H.) Marriage and Divorce—in *Fort. Rev.*, n.s. vol. 37, pp. 640-53.

Docks, Municipalization of.
  Neutral: Palgrave (R. H. I.; ed.) Dict. of Pol. Econ., art. by J. Mavoo vol. 1, pp. 611-21 (Macmillan, 1894) [gives a good bibliography].
  Labour Com. Index, vol. 4 (1894; 10½d.) [Blue-book. C. 7063, III].
  Pro: Webb (S.) The London Programme (Sonnenschein; 1s.).

Drama and Social Questions.
  The Problem Play: a Symposium—in the *Humanitarian*, May, '95 (by R. Buchanan, G. B. Shaw, S. Grundy, Dorothy Leighton, etc.).
  Pro: Archer (W.) The Free Stage and the New Drama—in *Fort. Rev.*, vol. 50, pp. 663-672.
  Con: Chapman (E. R.) Marriage questions in modern Fiction, etc. (Lane, 1897).
  Edward (H. S.) Social Science on the Stage—in *Fort. Rev.*, n.s. vol. 37, pp. 490-9.

Drink, Free Trade in.
  Hake (A. E.) and Wesslau (O. E.) The Coming Individualism, pp. 193-216 (Constable, 1895).

Education.
  Hall (G. S.) and Mansfield (J. M.) Bibliography of Education (Boston, 1893).
  Sonnenschein (W. Swan) Bibliography of Society, extracted from "The Best Books" and "Reader's Guide" (Sonnenschein; 6s. net).

Education. Mixed.
  Con: Hawtrey (M.) The Co-education of the Sexes (Kegan Paul, 1896).

Education, Moral.
  Pro: Adler (F.) The Problem of Unsectarian Moral Instruction—in *Intern. Jour. of Ethics*, Oct., 1891, vol. 2. pp. 11-20; Moral Instruction (Arnold, 1892; 6s.).
  Bryant (Dr. S.) Short Studies in Character (Sonnenschein, 1894; 4s. 6d.); The Teaching of Morality (Sonnenschein, 1897; 4s. 6d.); The Teaching of Christ on Life and Conduct (Sonnenschein, 1898; 2s. 6d.).
  Matthews (F. D.) Moral Education: a Dialogue (Sonnenschein, 1899; 3s. 6d.).
  Moral Instruction League, Publications (Surrey House, Thames Embankment, London).
  Con: Field (The Teaching of Holy Scripture, pp. 151-68 (Rivington 1891) [13 essays.]
  Gallway (Father) Practical Notes (Burns and Oates, 1857; 2s. 6d.).

Education, Religious: Dogmatic.
  Both Sides: *Journal of Education*, June-Dec., 1896 [a controversy].
  Pro: Diggle (J. R.) and Riley (A.) Re-opening the Religious Settlement—in *Nineteenth Cent.*, vol. 39. pp. 44-57.
  Con: Macnamara (T. J.) Religious Teaching in Board Schools—in *Contemp. Rev.*, Jan., 1896.
  Stanley (Hon. L.) A reply—in *Nineteenth Cent.*, vol. 39 pp. 328-31.
  Commission on Popular Education, 1861, 6 vols. (18s. 3d.); Working of Elemen. Ed. Acts, 1886, Report (5s. 6d.); Evid., etc., 10 vols. (48s. 1d.); Schools Enquiry Commission, 1868, 21 vols. (69s. 3d.).

Education, State: Compulsory.
  Arnold (M.) Elementary Schools (Macmillan, 1889; 7s. 6d.).
  Craik (H.) The State and Elementary Education (Macmillan; 2s. 6d.).
  Chadwick (E.) The Health of Nations, 2 vols. (Longman 1887).
  Manning (Card.) National Education (1889).

Education, Free.
  Pro: Radical Programme, The; with Preface by Joseph Chamberlain (Chapman, 1885).
  Con: Mackay (T.; ed.) Plea for Liberty, art. by Rev. B. H. Alford on Free Education, pp. 261-72 (Murray, 1891).

Education: Voluntary Schools.
  Parliamentary Debates, 1896, 4th S., vols. 40-41, 1897. Voluntary.
  Schools Bill, 4th S., vols. 46-7.
  Pro: *Church Quarterly Review*, April, 1897.
  Carpenter (W. B.) Efficiency of Vol. Schools —in *Fort. Rev.*, Jan., 1887.
  Gorst (Sir J.) Voluntary Schools—in *Nineteenth Century*, Nov., 1896.
  Gregory (Dean) Education—in the *Humanitarian*, Sept., 1893; Elementary Education (National Society, 1895; 3s. 6d.).
  Manning (Cardinal) National Education (Burns and Oates, 1889).
  Woodhouse (E. R.) The Claims of Voluntary Schools—in *National Rev.*, Jan., 1897.
  Con: Clifford (Dr. J.) Primary Education and the State—in *Contemp. Rev.*, March, '96.
  Fairbairn (Rev. A. M.) The Education Bill —in *Contemp. Rev.*, June, 1896.
  Fitch (J. G.) Flaws in the Education Bill —in *Nineteenth Cen.*, June, 1896.

EDUCATION: VOLUNTARY SCHOOLS (*cont.*)
    Horton (Dr. R. F.) The Doomed Board Schools—in *Fort. Rev.*, N.S., vol. 60, pp. 110-22.
    Macnamara (T. J.)—in *Nineteenth Cent.*, May, 1896.
    National Education Assoc., Publications of (Surrey House, Victoria Embankment).
    Rogers (Guiness)—in *Nineteenth Cent.*, May, 1896.
    Stanley (L.) Education Bill—in *Contemp. Rev.*, May, 1896; Position of Education Question—in *Contemp. Rev.*, Nov., 1897.
    White (J. D.) Our Educational Finance—in *Fort. Rev.*, N.S., vol. 59, pp. 84-93.

Egypt: Evacuation of.
  Pro: Blunt (W. S.) Lord Cromer and the Khedive—in *Nineteenth Cent.*, vol. 33, 1893, pp. 571-85.
    Keay (J. Seymour) Spoiling the Egyptians (Kegan Paul, 1882; 1s.).
    Reid (Sir W.) Our Promise—in *Nineteenth Cent.*, vol. 39, 557-66.
  Con: Dicey (E.) Egypt, 1881-97—in *Fort. Rev.*, May, 1898, vol. 63, pp. 681-99.
    Milner (Sir A.) England in Egypt (Arnold).
    Traill (H. D.) The Difficulties—in *Nineteenth Cent.*, vol. 39, pp. 544-56.

Eight Hours' Day.
  Bradlaugh (C.) and Hyndman (H. M.) The Eight Hours' Movement (Freethought Publis'ing Co., 1890; 6d.) [a debate].
  Pro: Hadfield (R. A.) and Gibbins (H. de B.) A Shorter Working Day (Methuen, 1892; 2s. 6d.).
    Mather (W.) Report on One Year's Work (Manchester; id.).
    Rae (J.) Eight Hour Day and Foreign Competition, Feb., 1894, vol. 65, pp. 189-206; Eight Hours for Work (Macmillan, 1894; 4s. 6d.).
    Webb (S.) and Cox (H.) Eight Hours' Day (Scott; 1s.).
  Con: Bradlaugh (C.) Labour and Law (Bonner, 1891; 5s.); The Eight Hours' Movement (Freethought Pub. Co., 1889; 2d.).
    Robertson (J. M.) The Eight Hours' Question (Social Science Series, Sonnenschein, 2nd ed., 1899; 2s. 6d.).

Elgin Marbles, The.
  Pro: Harrison (F.) Give Back the Elgin Marbles—in *Nineteenth Cent.*, Dec., 1890, vol. 28, pp. 980-7; Editorial Horseplay—in *Fort. Rev.*, April, 1891, vol. 49, pp. 642-55 [a reply to Knowles, *ut infra*].
    Curzon (G. N., Lord Curzon) A Suggestion—in *Fort. Rev.*, May, 1891, vol. 49, pp. 833-5.
  Con: Knowles (J.) The Joke about the Elgin Marbles—in *Nineteenth Cent.*, March, '91, vol. 29, pp. 495-506.

England: Why is She Unpopular?
  Darling (C.) The Isolation of England—in *National Rev.*, April, 1896.
  Dicey (E.) Why England is Unpopular—in *Cosmopolis*, Dec., 1896; The Isolation of England—in *Fort. Rev.*, vol. 59, 1896, pp. 330-40.
  Mahaffy (Prof.) Internat. Jealousy—in *Nineteenth Cent.*, April, 1896.

Entail, Abolition of the Law of.
  Palgrave (R. H. I.; ed.) Dict. of Pol. Econ.,

vol. 1 (Macmillan) art. by F. S. Montague [in favour; and a special art. on the Law in Scotland, by J. W. B. Innes].
  Pro: Arnold (Sir A.) Free Land, pp. 93-165 (Paul, 1880).
    Brodrick (G. C.) English Land and English Landlords (Cassell, 1881).
    Lefevre (G. Shaw) Agrarian Tenures (Cassell, 1893).
  Con: Cecil (E.) Primogeniture (Murray, '95).
    Garnier (R. M.) The English Landed Interest (2 vols.), vol. 2, pp. 390-8 (Sonnenschein, 1892-3; 21s.).

Equality, Religious.
  Pro: Radical Programme, The (Chapman, 1885).
  Con: Pollock (Sir F.) Religious Equality—see Oxford Lectures (Macmillan, '90; 9s.).

Equality, Social.
  Pro: Inequalities of Wealth—in the *Humanitarian*, Oct., 1892.
    Robertson (J. M.) Equality (South Place Religious Society Publications, No. 13).
    Webb (S.) Difficulties of Individualism (Fabian Society; 1d.).
  Con: Mallock, Social Equality (Bentley, 1885; 6s.).
    Stephen (Sir J. F.) Liberty, Equality, and Fraternity.
    Stephen (Leslie) Social Rights and Duties, 2 vols. (Sonnenschein, 1896; 9s.).
  See also Collectivism.

Ethical Movement, The.
  Pro: Adler (F.) Creed and Deed (Philad.; $1).
    Bosanquet (B.) The Civilisation of Christendom (Sonnenschein, 2nd ed., 1899; 4s. 6d.).
    Ethical World, The: weekly, 1d.
    Intern. Jour. of Ethical: quarterly; 2s. 6d. (Sonnenschein).
    Salter (W. M.) Ethical Religion (Roberts, Boston, U.S., 1893; $1.50).
    Sidgwick (H.) Practical Ethics (Sonnenschein, 1898; 4s. 6d.).
    Sullivan (W. R.) Morality as a Religion (Sonnenschein, 1898; 6s.).
  Con: Bartram (R.) Religion and Life (Brit. and Foreign Unit. Assoc., Essex Hall, W.C., 1891; 2s. 6d.).
    Carus (Paul) The Ethical Problem (Open Court Pub. Co., Chicago, 1890; 30c.).

Ethics as an Experimental Science.
  Con: Nobili-Vitelleschi, Inductive Morality—in *Nineteenth Century*, vol. 40 pp. 439-53.

Examinations, Competitive.
  Pro: Scoones (W. B.) Is Examination a Failure—in the *Nineteenth Cent.*, Feb., '89.
  Con: The Sacrifice of Education to Examination—in *Nineteenth Cent.*, Nov., 1888, and Feb., 1889.
    Helps (Sir A.) Thoughts on Government (Bell and Daldy, 1872; 9s. 6d. O.P.).
    Jevons (W. S.) Methods of Social Reform, Art. Cram. (Macmillan, 1883; 10s. 6d.).
    Pollock (Sir F.) Examinations and Education—see Oxford Lectures, etc. (Macmillan, 1890; 9s.).

Experiment in Politics, The.
  Pro: Jevons (W. S.)—in his Methods of Social Reform (Macmillan, '83; 10s. 6d.).
    Mackay (T.) Empiricism in Politics—in *National Rev.*, vol. 25, pp. 790-803.

Fair Trade v. Free Trade.

Protectionist: Carey, Harmony of Interests (Philad., 1883; $1.50).
Curtis, Protection and Prosperity (Low, 1896; 18s.).
List (F.) National Systems of Pol. Econ. (Longman, 1885; 5s.).
Patten (S. W.) Economic Basis of Protection (Lippincott, Philad., 1890; 5s.).
Sullivan (E.) Free-Trade Bubbles (Stanford, 1883; 1s.
Williams (E. E.) Made in Germany (Heinemann, 1896; 1s.); The Foreigner in the Farmyard, 1897; 2s. 6d.).
United Empire Trade League (St. Stephen's Chambers, Westminster).

Fair Trade: Bastable (C. F.) Commerce of Nations (Methuen; 2s. 6d.); Internat. Trade (Macmillan, 1897; 3s. 6d.) [the standard work].
Bastiat (F.) Popular Fallacies (Cassell, 1888; 6d.).
Farrer (Lord) Free Trade v. Fair Trade (Cassell, 1887; 5s.).
Fawcett (H.) Free Trade and Protection (Macmillan, 1885; 3s. 6d.).
Medley (G. W. E.) The German Bogey (Cassell, 1896; 6d.).
Cobden Club, Publications of (Cassell).

Fair Wages Clause.

Lords' Committee on Sweating, Final Report, 1890 (1s. 2¼d.), No. 63.
Select Com. Govt. Contracts (Fair Wages), 1896-7. Evid., 1896 (1s. 5d.), No. 277; Final Report (3d.), No. 334.
Labour Commission [esp. vols. C. 7063-1 (4s. 11d.), and C. 7063 III A. (3s. 1d.) 1894] [evidence of Webb (S.) and Farrer (Sir T. H.)].
Pro: Webb (S.) Economic Heresies (London Pub. Office).
Con: Farrer (Sir T. H.) The London County Council Wages Bill.

Farm Colonies.

Pro: Booth (C.) Life and Labour, vol. 1 (Macmillan; 7s. 6d. net).
Booth (Gen.) In Darkest England (Salvation Army Warehouse; 3s. 6d.).
Moore (H. E.) Back to the Land (Methuen, 1893; 2s. 6d.).
Con: Bosanquet (B.) In Darkest England (Sonnenschein; 1s.).
Dwyer (Canon P.) General Booth's Submerged Tenth (Sonnenschein; 1s.).
Loch (C. S.) Examination of General Booth's Scheme (Sonnenschein; 1s.).
See also Unemployed.

Federalism in Great Britain.

Pro: Spalding (T. A.) Federation and Empire (Henry, 1896; 10s. 6d.).
Con: Edinburgh Rev., Oct., 1892, vol. 176, pp. 506-20; Oct., 1896, vol. 184, pp. 341-67).

Free Libraries.

Pro: Crunden (F. M.) The Free Public Library (St. Louis Mo., U.S.A., 1893).
Greenwood (T.) Public Libraries (Cassell, 1894; 2s. 6d.).
Jevons (W. S.)—in his Methods of Social Reform (Macmillan. 1883; 10s. 6d.).
Ogle (J. J.) The Place of the Free Public Library (London, 1891).
Con: Mackay (T.; ed.) Plea for Liberty (Murray, 1894; 2s.): art. by M. D. O'Brien on Free Libraries.
Millar (F.) Thou Shalt not Steal (Stewart & Co., 1890).

Free Meals.

London School Board Rept. of Spec. Com. on Underfed Children, 1895 [contains a bibliog. Appendix].
Prize Essays on Feeding School Children, with Pref. by W. Bousefield (Causton & Sons, 1891; 1s.).
Pro: Kerr (Dr. J.) School Hygiene—in *J. R. Stat. Soc.*, vol. 60, 1897, pp. 662-4.
Morley (Rt. Hon. J.) Speech at Eighty Club Dinner, Nov. 19th, 1889 — reprinted in *Times*, Nov. 20th, 1889.
Pickard-Cambridge (F. O.) State Maintenance (Twentieth Cent. Press; 1d.).
Con: School Children in want of Food (Charity Organization Society, 1881; 6d.).

Free Shelters, Soup Kitchens, etc.

Con: Charity Organisation Society Reports, etc.

Gambling, Commercial.

Con: Bear (W. E.) Market Gambling—in *Contemp. Rev.*, June, 1894, vol. 65, pp. 781-94.
Smith (C.W.) Commercial Gambling (Low, 1893; 3s. 6d.).
See also Royal Commission on Agriculture.

Gambling, Morality of.

Barnett (A. T.) Why are Betting, etc., wrong? in *Econ. Rev.*, April, 1897.
Lambert (J. M.) Gambling: Is it Wrong? (Simpkin, 1890; 6d).
Pro: Marson (C. L.) Gambling—in *Progressive Rev.*, Jan., 1897.
Peterborough (Bishop of) Betting, Gambling, etc.—*Fort. Rev.*, n.s., vol. 46, pp. 754-63.
Con: Investors' Rev., June, 1897 [reply to Lyttelton, *infra*].
Lyttelton (E.) Betting and Gambling—in *Econ. Rev.*, Jan., 1897.
Mackenzie (W. D.) Ethics of Gambling (Sunday School Union, 1895; 1s.).
Parker (J.) Gambling (Bowden, 1897; 3d.).

Gambling, Suppression of.

Pro: Lecky (W. E. H.) Democracy and Liberty, 2 vols., vol. 2., pp. 107-11 (Longman, 1896).
Hawke (Jno.) Our Principles—in *New Rev.*, vol. 10, pp. 705-17.
Con: Mortimer (G.) The Betting Craze—in *Free Rev.*, vol. 2, pp. 308-14.

Game Laws, Abolition of.

Report of Select Committee on Game Laws, 1873.
Pro: Connell (J.) Game Laws (Humanitarian League; 1d.).
Palgrave (R. H. I.; ed.) Dict. of Pol. Econ.—art. by J. B. Kinnear (Macmillan).
Shaw-Lefevre (G.) Game Laws (Ridgway, 1874; 6d.).
Welford (R. G.) Influence of the Game Laws; with appendix by Jno. Bright (London, 1846; 3s. O.P.).
Con: Game, etc., in England—in *Quarterly Rev.*, vol. 161, pp. 218-45.

Gas, Municipalization of.

Amer. Economic Assoc. Pub., vol. 6, Nos. 4 and 5 Saratoga.

GAS, MUNICIPALIZATION OF (*cont.*)
    Bemis (E. W.) Municipal Ownership of Gas (Sonnenschein; 2s. 6d.).
    Dolman (F.) Municipalities at Work (Methuen ———; 2s. 6d.).
    Foote (A. R.) No Government should own, etc.—in *Municipal Affairs*, June, 1887.
    Grout (E. M.) New York should own gas supply—in *Municipal Affairs*, June, 1897.
    James (E. J.) Municipalities and gas supply, Economic Assoc., vol. 1, Nos. 2-3, Saratoga.
    Shaw (A.) Municipal Government in Great Britain ; Munic. Govt. in Europe.
    Webb (S.) The London Programme (Sonnenschein ; 1s.).
    Societies: London Municipal Society. London Reform Union.

Gothenburg System.
    Pro: Chamberlain (J.) Public-house Reform (Public-house Reform Assoc.) (Cassell, 1894, 1d.) [speech delivered at Grosvenor House, July, 1894].
    Chester (Bishop of) The Reform of the Public-house — in the *Humanitarian*, Nov. 1893.
    Goadly (E.) The Gothenburg System (Chapman & Hall ; 1s.).
    Gould (E. R. L.) Gothenburg System (U.S.A. Bureau of Labour, Washington, U.S., 1893) ; [bibliog. on pp. 243-4] Popular control of the Liquor Traffic (Public-house Ref. Assoc., Cassell, 1894) ; [with intro. by J. Chamberlain].
    McKenzie (F. A) Sober by Act of Parliament, pp. 122-32 (Social Science Series, Sonnenschein, 1894. 2s. 6d.)
    Municipalization of Drink Traffic (Fabian Society, 1898 ; 1d.)
    Pease (E. R.) Liquor Licensing (Fabian Society, 1898 ; 1d.).
    Shadwell (A.) A Model Public-house—in *National Rev.*, vol. 25, pp. 632-40.
    Wilson (T. M.) Gothenburg System—in *Contemp. Rev.*, June, 1894, vol. 65, pp. 836-46.
    See also English Consular Reports.
    Con: Cyclopædia of Temperance and Prohibition, art. Sweden (pp. 623-4) by C. A. Wenngren (Funk and Wagnalls, New York, 1891).
    Lewis (D.) Civil Government and the Drink Trade (Nat. Temper. League, 1894).
    Mortimer (R.) The Gothenburg Licensing System : a statement of facts (Country Brewers Soc., 1892) [personal investign.].

Greek, Compulsory.
    Pro: Bury (J. B.) Compulsory Greek—in *Fort. Rev.*, vol. 50, 1891, pp. 811-21.
    Field (T. W.) In behalf of Greek—in Thirteen Essays on Educ., pp. 239-53 (Rivington, 1891).
    Jebb (R. C.) In defence of Classical Study —in *New Rev.*, vol. 9, 1893, pp. 494-501.
    Con: Lyttelton (E.) Compulsory Greek, and Rendall (M. J.) The Teaching of Greek—in Thirteen Essays, *ut supra*, pp. 295-315.

Ground Values, Taxation of,
    Town Holdings Committee : Report on 2nd part of Enquiry (1892 ; 1s.).
    See also evidence of S. Webb and others on the same subject.
    London County Council Repts. (P. S. King and Son) No. 17, Rept. Local Govt. and Tax. Com. (9d.) ; No. 127, Rept. Local Govt. and Tax. Com., 1893 (1½d.) ; No. 131, Mem. by V. Chrm. of Council on Land Val. Bill, 1893 (2d.) ; No. 165, Conf. of Local Govt. and Tax Com. with Assess. Authorities, 1893-94 (5s.).
    Pro: Costelloe (B. F. C.) Incidence of Tax (Ward and Foxlow, 1893 ; 3d.).
    Moulton (J. F.) Taxation of Ground Values (Lond. Ref. Union).
    Ratepayer and Landowner (Land Law Ref. Assoc., 1898 ; 1d.).
    Con: Beken (G.) Taxation of Ground Rents (Lib. and Prop. Def. League, 1893 ; 1d.).
    Sargant (C. H.) Urban Rating (Longman, 1890 ; 6s.).
    See also Rates, Division of ; Vacant Land ; Betterment, etc.

Hospital Nationalization.
    Lords' Committee on Hospitals, 1888 (7s. 10d., Index, 1s. 4d.).
    Pro: Ellis (Havelock) Nationalization of Health (Unwin, 1892 ; 3s. 6d.).
    James (J. B.) State Organization of Hospital Management (J. Bale & Sons, 1888).
    Roberts (H.) Public Control of Hospitals (Humanitarian League, 1895 ; 1d.).
    Webb (S.) The London Programme (Sonnenschein, 1892 ; 1s.).
    Con: Hake (A. E.) Suffering London (London, 1892).

Immigration of Destitute Aliens.
    Stride (E. E.) Bibliography of works relating to Huguenot Refugees (King, Lymington, 1886).
    Rept. Select Com. and Evidence, 1888 ; 4s.
    Board of Trade Report [Blue-book C. 7113] (1893 ; 1s. 7d.) [by D. F. Schloss and Burnett, on America].
    Reports on Volume, etc., of Recent Immigration (Board of Trade, 1894 ; 1s.).
    Pro: Cunningham (W.) Alien Immigrants to England (Sonnenschein, 1897 ; 4s. 6d.).
    White (Arnold ; ed.) The Destitute Alien (Social Science Series, Sonnenschein ; 2s. 6d.).
    Wilkins (W. H.) The Alien Invasion (Methuen, 1892 ; 2s. 6d.).

Immorality and Public Life.
    Con: Brett (R. B.) The Nonconformist Conscience—in *Nineteenth Cent.*, Feb., 1891, vol. 29, pp. 202-13.
    Mallock (W. H.) Studies in Contemporary Superstition (Ward and Downey, 1895).

Immortality.
    Abbot (E.) The Literature of the Doctrine (Widdleton, New York. 1871).
    Alger (Rev. W.) Critical Hist. of Doctrine of Future Life (Philadelphia, 1885 ; $4.50).
    Pro: Immortality : a Clerical Symposium (Nisbet. 1885 ; 6s.).
    James (W.) The Will to Believe (Longman, 1897).
    Myers (F. W. H.) Science and a Future Life (Macmillan).
    Perowne (Dr. J. S.) Immortality (Bell, 1869 ; 7s. 6d.).
    Reynolds (Preb. J. W.) The Natural Hist. of Immortality (Longman, 1891 ; 7s. 6d.).
    Con: Bradley (F. H.)—in his Appearance and Reality (Sonnenschein ; 12s.).
    Hume (David) Immortality—in his Works, ed. by Green and Grose (4 vols.) vol. 4, pp. 399-406 (Longman, 1875).

Imperial Federation.

Pro: Dilke (Sir C. W.) The British Empire (Chatto and Windus, 1899; 3s. 6d.); Problems of Greater Britain (1890; 12s. 6d.);
Dilke (Sir C. W.) and Wilkinson (H. S.) Imperial Defence (Constable; 2s. 6d.).
Parkin (G. R.) Imperial Federation (Macmillan. 1892; 4s. 6d.).
Seeley (Sir John) Expansion of England (Macmillan. 1883; 4s. 6d.).
White (A. S.) Britannic Confederation (Philip. 1893; 1s.).
Con: Clarke (Wm.) Expansion of England [a review].
Freeman (E. A.) Greater Greece and Greater Britain (Macmillan, 1886).
Morley (J.) Critical Miscellanies, vol. 3.
Smith (G.) Essays on Questions of the Day (Macmillan, 1893).

Imperialism.

Giffen (Sir Rob.) Relative Growth of the Component Parts of the Empire (1899).
Pro: Greswell (W. P.) British Colonies, pp. 7-35 (Victorian Era Series, Blackie, 1898) [gives a history of the view of prominent men in the early Victorian Era on the Colonies].
Lord, Lost Possessions of England; Lost Empires of Modern Worlds.
Seeley (Sir John) Expansion of England— *ut supra*.
Stillman (W. J.) The Peace Crusade.
Watton (J. L.) Imperialism—in *Contemp. Rev.*, March, 1899.
Wyatt (H. J.) Ethics of Empire—in *Nineteenth Cent.*, April, 1897, vol. 41, pp. 516-30.
Con: Farrer (Lord) Does Trade follow the Flag?—in *Contemp. Rev.*, Dec., 1898, vol. 74, pp. 810-35.
Hobson (J. A.) Free Trade and Foreign Policy—in *Contemp. Rev.*, Aug., 1898, vol. 74, pp. 167-80.

Income Tax, Progressive.

Pro: Seligman (E. R. A.) Progressive Taxation (Amer. Econ. Assoc., vol. 9, Nos. 1 & 2 (Sonnenschein, 1894; 2s. 6d.).
Con: Bastable (C. F.) Public Finance, bk. iii, ch. 3 (Macmillan, 1895).

Increased Armaments, The Danger of.

Pro: Czar, The, of Russia, Eirenicon, 1898.
Empire, Trade, and Armament—, Increased Arm. Prot. Com., 40 & 41 Outer Temple, E.C. [and other pubs. by same Society].
See also England: Is further Expansion Necessary?
Con: Navy League, Publications of (13 Victoria Street, S.W.).
Wilson (H. W.) The World's Armaments—in *Nineteenth Cent.*, May, 1898; The Struggle before us—in *Fort. Rev.*, vol. 60, pp. 731-45.
See also Disarmament.

Independent Labour Party.

Pro: Reports of the Annual Conference of Independent Lab. Party (53 Fleet Street, E.C.; 2d. each).
Fabian Society, A Plan of Campaign for Labour (1894; 1d.).
Hardie (J. Keir) The Case for an I.L.P.—in *New Rev.*, vol. 10, pp. 718-25; in *Progressive Rev.*, Dec., 1896.
Hardie (J. Keir) and Macdonald (J. R.)

INDEPENDENT LABOUR PARTY (*cont.*)
Ind. Lab. Party Programme—in *Nineteenth Cent.*, Jan., 1899, vol. 45 pp. 20-38.
"Nunquam." Merrie England (*Clarion* Office, 1894; 6d.).
Con: Annand (J.) Forgotten Liberalism (54 Fleet Street, E.C.; 1s.).
Essays in Liberalism by six Oxford men.
Samuel (H.) The I.L.P.—in *Progressive Rev.*, Dec., 1896.

India, Prohib. of Child Marriages in.

Malabari (B. M.) Infant Marriage, etc. (Bombay, 1887; 3s. 6d.)
Risley (H. H.)—in *Asiatic Quarterly*, Oct., 1887, July, 1888 (Sonnenschein; 5s. each).
Pro: Petrosokino (J. T.) Enforced Widowhood (Unwin, 1892; 6d.).
Con: Raj Coomar Roy—in *N. Amer. Rev.*, 1888, vol. 147, pp. 415-23.

India: Home Rule.

Papers relating to Question of Simultaneous Examinations (Eyre and Spottiswoode, 1894; 11d.) [Blue-book C.7378].
Pro: Dilke (Sir C. W.) The British Empire (Chatto and Windus, 1899).
Dutt (R. C.) England and India (Chatto, 1897; 2s.).
Hyndman (H. M.) The Bankruptcy of India (Sonnenschein, O.P.).
Indian National Congress, Annual Reports (British Com. of I. N. C., 84 & 85 Palace Chambers, S.W.).
Con: Chesney (Sir G.) Indian Polity (Longman, 1894).
Duff (Sir M. E.) A Bird's Eye View of India—in *Nineteenth Cent.*, June, 1889.
Strachey (Sir J.) India (Kegan Paul, 1894).

Indian Defence: is Retrenchment possible?

Correspondence rel. to Chitral, 1895 (6½d.) [Blue-book C. 7864]; 1896 (3d.) [C. 8037].
Pro: Colvin (Sir A.) Perilous Growth—in *Nineteenth Cent.*, Oct., 1894.
Hanna (H. B.) Can Russia invade India? India's Scientific Frontier; Forwards or Backwards.
Con: Napier of Magdala (Lord) Brief Note—*Nineteenth Cent.*, March, 1898, vol. 44, pp. 370-5.
Rawlinson (Sir H.) England and Russia (Murray, 1875).
Wilkinson (H. Spenser) Chitral—in *National Rev.*, vol. 26, pp. 246-57.
Younghusband (G. J.) Permanent Pacification of Indian Frontier—in *Nineteenth Cent.*, Feb., 1898, vol. 43, pp. 250-55.

Individualism.

Pro: Donisthorpe (W.) Individualism (Macmillan. 1889; 14s.); Law in a Free State (Macmillan, 1895; 5s.).
Herbert (Auberon) Ethics of Dynamite—in *Contemp. Rev.*, May, 1894, vol. 65, pp. 667-87; A Voluntaryist Appeal—in the *Humanitarian*, May, 1898; Salvation by Force—in the *Humanitarian*, Oct., 1898.
Levy (J. H.) The Outcome of Individualism.
Mackay (T.; ed.) A Plea for Liberty (Murray, 1894; 2s.); Free Exchange (Murray, 1894).
Montague (F. C.) The Limits of Liberty (Rivington, 1884; 10s. 6d.).
O'Brien (M. D.) Natural Right to Freedom (Williams and Norgate, 1893; 3s. 6d.).

INDIVIDUALISM (cont.)
Spencer (Herbert) Man v. the State (Williams and Norgate, 1884; 1s.).
Con: Hobson (J. A.) A Rich Man's Anarchism—in the *Humanitarian*, June, 1898; Salvation by Force—in the *Humanitarian*, Oct., 1898.
Ritchie (D. G.) Darwinism and Politics (Social Science Series, Sonnenschein, 1891; 2s. 6d.); Principles of State Interference (Social Science Series, Sonnenschein, 1891; 2s. 6d.); Natural Rights (Sonnenschein, 1895; 10s. 6d.).
Salter (W. M.) Anarchy or Government.
Sidgwick (H.) Elements of Politics, vol. 1 (Macmillan, 1897; 14s.).
Webb (S.) Difficulties of Individualism (Fabian Society, 1d.); also repr. in his Problems of Modern Industry (Longmann, 1898).

Infallibility, Papal.
Pro: Addis and Arnold, Catholic Dictionary, art. Church of Christ, pp. 184-95; Honorius, pp. 449-53 and others (Kegan Paul, 1897; 21s.).
Rivington (Luke) The Primitive Church (Longman, 1894); Authority (Longman, 1897); Dust: a Reply to Gore (Longman, 1898).
Benham (W.) Dict. of Religion, pp. 549-51 (Cassell, 1887).
Döllinger (I. I. von) Declarations, etc. (Clarke, Edin., 1891; 3s. 6d.).
Gore (Canon C.) Roman Catholic Claims (1897).
Littledale (Dr. R. F.) Petrine Claims (S.P.C.K., 1889; 5s.).
Salmon (Prof. G.) Infallibility of the Church (Murray, 1890; 9s.)

Insurance of Children.
Report of Select Committee (House of Lords), 1890-91, 293 (4½d.); Evidence, 344.
Pro: Marshall (Capt. P.) Child-Life Insurance—in *Fort. Rev.*, 1890, vol. 48, pp. 830-43; also, 1891, vol. 49, pp. 939-46.
Con: Gardiner (F. G.) Child Insurance—in the *Humanitarian*, Jan., 1897.
Waugh (Rev. B.)—in *Contemp. Rev.*, July, 1890; Pamphlets.

Inter-Imperial Communication.
Pro: *Blackwood's Mag.*, Feb., 1897, vol. 161, pp. 269-79.
Hurd (P. A.) Our Telegraphic Isolation—in *Contemp. Rev.*, June, 1896, vol. 69, pp. 893-908.
A. S., An All-British Cable—in *Nineteenth Cent.*, Feb., 1899.
Parkin (G. R.) Imperial Federation—*ut supra, s.v.* Imperial Federation.
Con: "Imperial" Canadian Pacific Railway Imposture, The—in *Investor's Rev.*, Jan. 12th, 1896.
Smith (G.) Canada and the Canadian Question (Macmillan, 1891; 8s).

Internationalism.
Pro: Bluntschli (J. K.) The Theory of the State: transl.; pp. 24-35 (Oxford, 2nd ed., 1892).

International Money.
Report of Royal Com. Int. Coinage with Evidence and Appendix, 1868; 4s.
Palgrave (R. H. I.; ed.) Dict. Pol. Econ., art. by C. A. Harris.

INTERNATIONAL MONEY (cont.)
Pro: Jevons (W. S.) Money, ch. 14 (Kegan Paul, 1887; 5s.).
Shaw (W. A.) Internat. Money (Edin., '95).
Stone (C. W.) A Common Coinage—in *North Amer. Rev.*, July, 1896, vol. 143, pp. 47-55.
Con: Delmar (D.) Science of Money (E. Wilson).

Intestacy, Law of,
Report Com. on Law of Intestacy, etc., in S. Australia (1874; 1s. 10d.).

Ireland. Abolit. of the Lord Lieutenancy.
Pro: Jephson (H.) Irish Viceroyalty—in *Fort. Rev.*, N.S., vol. 37, pp. 500-11.
Strachey (St. Loe) Shall we Abolish the Lord Lieutenant?—in *National Rev.*, 1888, vol. 11, pp. 788-95.
Swift-Macneill (J. G.) The Irish L. L. and a Royal Residence—in *Fort. Rev.*, vol. 62, pp. 504-12.

Ireland, Home Rule for.
Pro: Parl. Debates, 1886, Govt. of Ireland Bill, 3rd S., vols. 304-6; Mr. Gladstone's Speech, pp. 1036-85, 1893; Govt. of Ireland Bill, 4th S., vols. 8-16 (H. of C.), 17 (H. of L.).
Bryce (J.) Handbook of Home Rule, with pref. by Earl Spencer (Kegan Paul, 2nd ed., 1887).
McCarthy (J. H.) The Case for Home Rule (Chatto, 1887; 5s.).
Gladstone (W. E.) Special Aspects of the Irish Question (Murray, 1892; 3s 6d).
Nineteenth Cent., Aug., 1892, vol. 32, pp. 177-93; a Symposium on, "Why I voted for Mr. Gladstone."
O'Brien (W.) Irish Ideas (Longman, 1893).
O'Connor (T. P.) Home Rule and the Irish Party—in *Contemp. Rev.*, Aug., 1896, vol. 70, pp. 179-90.
Robertson (J. M.) The Saxon and the Celt (Sonnenschein, 1897).
Con: Argyll (Duke of) Irish Nationalism (Murray, 1893; 3s. 6d.).
Case for the Union, The, 2 vols. (Cassell, each 6d.).
Chamberlain (J.) Speeches (Sonnenschein, 1891; 1s.); Unionist Policy (Sonnenschein, 1888; 1s.).
Dicey (A. V.) England's Case against Home Rule (Murray, 1887; 7s. 6d.); A Leap in Dark (Murray, 1893; 3s. 6d.).
Nineteenth Cent., July, 1892, vol. 32, pp. 151-76; a symposium on "Why I shall vote Unionist."

Ireland: is she Overtaxed?
Royal Commission on Financial Relations, Final Rep., 1896 (1s. 10d.) [Blue-book C.8262]: Parliamentary Debates, 1897, 4th S., vols. 47-8.
Pro: Lough (T.) England's Wealth, Ireland's Poverty (Unwin, 1896).
Con: Bastable (C. F.) Ireland's Place—in *Econ. Journal*, vol. 6, pp. 185-203.

Irish Land Acts.
Parl. Debates, 1896, Land Law (Ireland) Bill, 4th S., vols. 41-4, 1897; Motion in H. of Lords, 4th S., vols. 49-50.
Report of Com. of Enquiry (Lord Bessborough), 1881 (9d.); Evidence to same, Index and Appendices, 2 vols. (10s.);

IRISH LAND ACTS (cont.)
Select Com. House of Lords, 4 repts. and Evid. and App., 1882-83 (7s. 6d.); Observations of Irish Land Com. on last above, 1883 (3d.); Rept. of Ld. Cowper's Com., 2 pp., 1887 (4d.); Rept., Evid. and App. and Index 2 vols., 1887 (10s.); Annual Repts. of Irish Land Com., 1881-82, and on; Rept. on Evicted Tenants Com. (Matthew), 1893 (10d.); Rept., Evid., etc., 1893 (5s. 6d.); R pt. Com. Inquiry (Fry Com.).
Pro: Bear (W. E.) The Principle of Tenant Right—in *Contemp. Rev.*, April, 1882, vol. 41, pp. 645-55.
Lefevre (G. S.) Agrarian Tenures (Cassell, 1893; 10s. 6d.).
Mill (J. S.) Speeches on Irish Land Question (Longman, 1870; 2s. 6d.).
Wallace (Alfred Russel) Land Nationalization (Sonnenschein; 2s. 6d.).
Con: Argyll (Duke of) Essay on the Com. Principles, etc. (Cobden Club; Cassell, 1877).
Mahaffy (J. P.) The Irish Landlords—in *Contemp. Rev.*, Jan., 1882, vol. 41, pp. 160-76.
National Rev., May, 1897, arts. The Spoliation of the Irish Landlord.

Irish Members in Imperial Parliament.
See Parliamentary Debates, 1893; Govt. of Ireland Bill, 4th S., pp. 1111-9, 1159-1245.
See also, Ireland, Home Rule for.
Con: Dale (R. W.) The Exclusion of the Irish Members—in *Contemp. Rev.*, vol. 49, pp. 761-71.
Harrison (F.) Clause Nine—in *Contemp. Rev.*, Jan.-June, 1893, vol. 63, pp. 305-10.

Irish Ministry of Agriculture.
Recess Committee Report (Unwin, 1896; 1s.)

Journalism: are Signed Arts. Desirable?
Pro: Zola (M.) Address at Inst. of Journalists, Nov. 22rd. 1893.
Con: Macintyre (J.) Theophraste Renaudot —in *Nineteenth Cent.*, Oct., 1893.
Traill (H. D.) The Anonymous Critic—in *Nineteenth Cent.*, Dec., 1893.

Jury System.
Century Magazine, vol. 26, pp. 299, sqq.; Both sides of the Jury question: a symposium.
Lessner (M. A.) Historical Development of the Jury System (Rochester, N.Y., 1894).
Routledge (J) Chapters in the History of Popular Progress (Macmillan, 1876; 16s.).
Pro: Rollins (D.) The Englishman's Right (Boston; $1, 1883).
Upward (A.) Trial by Jury and the Labour Movement (Manchester, 1892).
Con: *Spectator, The*, art. The Decay of Trial by Jury, vol. 72, Jan., 1894, p. 8.

Kindergarten System.
Pro: Smith (W. A.) The Children of the Future (Gay and Bird. 1898).
Wiggin (K. D.) and Smith (M. A.) The Republic of Childhood 2 vols. (Gay and Bird, 1895-6; 20s.).

Land Nationalization.
Reports of the Royal Com. on Mining Royalties, etc.; 1st Rept. and Evid., etc., 1889 (3s.); 2nd Rept. and Evid., etc., and maps, 1891 (4s. 10d.); 3rd Rept. and Evid., etc., 1891 (2s.); 4th Rept. and Evid., etc., 1893 (2s. 9d.); Final Rept. and App., 1893 (1s. 9d.).
Levy (J. H.) Symposium on the Land Question (Unwin, 1894; 1s.) [Articles by Socialists, Individualists, Reformers, and Anti-Reformers of all schools].

Single Tax v. Social Democracy.
Debate between H. George and H. M. Hyndman, July 2, 1889.
Pro: Fluerscheim (M.) Rent, Interest, and Wages (Reeves, 1891; 4s. 6d.).
George (H.) Progress and Poverty (Kegan Paul; 1s.).
Wallace (Alfred Russel) Land Nationalization (Social Science Series, Sonnenschein; 2s. 6d.).
English, Land Restoration League, Publications of.
Land Nationalization Society, Publications of (47 Victoria Street, S.W.).
Con: Cox (Harold) Land Nationalization (Methuen, 1892; 2s. 6d.).
Garnier (R. M.) The English Landed Interest, 2 vols. (Sonnenschein, '92-3; 21s.).
Palgrave (R. H. I.; ed.) Dict. of Pol. Econ. art. by F. C. Montague [a polemic].
Property Protection Society; The Nationalization of Land, with special reference to N. Wales (Prop. Prot. Soc., 45 Parliament Street, S.W.).
Spence (J. C.) Property in Land (Liberty and Property Defence League, 1892).
Walker (F. A.) Land and its Rent (Boston, U.S., 1883.)

Leasehold Enfranchisement.
Leaseholds: Reports of H.M. Representatives on Tenure in Foreign Countries ('84; 6d.).
Town Holdings Committee, Report, 1st pt. of enquiry (1889; 1s. 8d.).
Pro: Broadhurst (H.) and Reid (R. T.) Leasehold Enfranchisement (Sonnenschein, 1885; 1s.).
Land Law Reform Assoc. [among whose publications are: Evans (H.) The Case against Leaseholds, 2 pts., 6d. each; Reports of the Debates on L. E. in 1889 and 1891; 6d. each] (17 Cockspar St., S.W.).
Con: Bramwell (Lord) Leasehold Enfranchisement (Lib. and Prop. Def. League, 1888; 1d.).
Fabian Society, Truth about Leasehold Enfr. (1d.).

Liberty of Speech, etc.
Pro: Mill (J. S.) Liberty (Longman, 1884; 1s. 4d.).
Paine (Thos.) The Rights of Man (1s.).
Con: Stephen (Sir J. F.) Liberty, Equality, and Fraternity (Smith & Elder; 14s.).
Lilly (W. S.) A Century of Revolution (Chapman, 1889; 12s.).

Life: Is it Worth Living?
Con: James (W.) The Will to Believe, pp. 32-62 (Longman, 1897).
Mallock (W. H.) Is Life worth Living? (Chatto).

Livery Companies, Reform of.
Royal Commission on London Livery Companies, 1884, Rept. and Evid. (3s. 10d.); Returns, etc. (17s. 8d.); Charity Com. Repts. (12s. 2d.).
Pro: Firth (J. F. B.) Reform of London Govt. and City Guilds (Sonnenschein, 1887; 1s.).

LIVERY COMPANIES, REFORM OF (cont.)
  Webb (S.)—in the London Programme (Sonnenschein, 1892; 1s.).
  Con: Hazlitt (W. C.)—in his Livery Companies, Intro. (Sonnenschein; 25s. net.).
  Vindication of the London Livery Companies (Gilbert and Rivington, 1885, O.P.)
  [Evidence before Royal Com.].

Local Option.
  Fanshawe (E. L.) Liquor Legislation in U. S. and Canada (Cassell, 1893).
  McKenzie (F. A.) Sober by Act of Parliament (Social Science Ser., Sonnenschein, 1894; 2s. 6d.).
  Wines (F. H.) and Koren (J.) The Liquor Problem. pp. 4-6, and 22-140 [on prohibition in Maine and Iowa] (Houghton, Mifflin and Co., Boston. U. S., 1897).
  Pro: Caine (W. S.) and Hoyle (W.) and Burns (D.) Local Option (Sonnenschein, 2nd ed.; 1s.).
  Con: Jevons (W. S.)—in his Methods of Social Reform (Macmillan, 1883).
  Harrop (H. B.) The Direct Veto, (Lib. and Prop. Def. League, 1893; 2d.).

London Self-Government.
  L.C.C. Rept. 52, Powers of the Council (6d.); 148, statement to Royal Com. (10d.).
  Municipal Year-book (annually).
  Pro: Firth (J. F. B.) Municipal London, (1876, 12s. 6d.).
  Webb (S.)—in the London Programme (Sonnenschein, 1892; 1s.).

London, Unification of.
  Papers put in by L.C.C. before the Royal Com., L.C.C. Repts., pp. 147-152 (6s. 9d.).
  Report of Royal Com. on Amalgamation.
  Pro: Harrison (F.) The Amalgamation of London.
  Gomme (G. L.) Future Govt. of London—in Contemp. Rev., Nov., '94, vol. 66, pp. 737-60.
  Con: Report of Special Com. of Corporation, Jan. 10th, 1895.

Lords, Abolition of House of.
  Pro: Bradlaugh (C.) How are we to Abolish the H. of L.? (Freethought Pub. Co.; 1d.).
  Free Review, Dec., 1894, vol. 3, pp. 193-209, art. The Second Chamber.
  Hobhouse (Lord) The Position of the H. of L.—in Contemp. Rev., Dec, 1894, vol. 66, pp. 774-94.
  Spalding (T. A.) The House of Lords (Unwin, 1893; 10s. 6d.).
  Con: Macpherson (W. C.) The Baronage and Senate (Murray, 1893; 16s.).
  Sidgwick (H.) Elements of Politics, ch. 23 Macmillan, 2nd ed., 1897; 14s.).

Markets, Municipalization of,
  L.C.C. Rept., No. 63, Rept. of Pub. Control Com. (P. S. King and Son; 2s. 6d.).
  Royal Commission on Markets, 1890-91; Final Rept. (3s. 10d.); Minutes, etc. (5s. 4d.); Numerous appendices, Complete set, 16 pts; 40s.
  Jones (H. A.) Middlemen and Parasites—in New Rev., June, 1893.
  Webb (S.)—in London Programme (Sonnenschein, 1892; 1s.).
  See also Gas Supply.

Military Council, A.
  Hartington Commission on Administration, Military and Naval, 1890, Report (1s. 3d.).

MILITARY COUNCIL, A (cont.)
  Pro: "Vetus"; Administration of War Office (Cassell, 1893; 1s.).
  Con: Wilkinson (H. Spenser) The Brain of an Army (Constable, 2nd ed., 1895).

Minorities, Rights of.
  Rept. Select Committee on School Board Elections and Evid. and App. (1885; 3s. 6d.).
  Pro: Commons (J. R.) Proportional Representation.
  Hare (T.) Proportional Representation; Coming Steps—in Fort. Rev., N.S., vol. 37, pp. 216-22.
  Lubbock (Sir J.) Representation (Sonnenschein; 1s.).
  Con: Ritchie (D. G.)—in Internat. Jour. of Ethics, Jan., 1891, vol. 1, pp. 129-42.
  Shaw-Lefevre (G.) The Crusade for Prop. Rep.—in Fort. Rev., N.S., vol. 87, pp. 202-15.

Monarchy.
  Pro: Lilly (W. S.) British Monarchy and Modern Democracy—in Nineteenth Cent., June, 1897. vol. 41, pp. 853-64.
  Con: Linton (W. J.) The English Republic (Social Sc. Ser. Sonnenschein; 2s. 6d.).
  Lynch (A.) A Possible Republic—in Free Rev., Oct. 1893-Mar. 1894, vol. 1, pp. 59-73.
  Robertson (J. M.) Arrest of Eng. Republic—in Progressive Rev., June, 1897.

Monogamy.
  Pro: Brinckman (A.) The Marriage Question (Innes; 1s.).
  Chapman (E. R.) The Marriage Question (Lane, 1897).
  Humphrey (W.) Christian Marriage (Kegan Paul, 1886; 1s.) [Roman Catholic view].
  Marriage—in the Humanitarian, Dec., 1892 and Jan. 1893.
  Con: Caird (Mona) The Morality of Marriage (Redway, 1897).
  Carpenter (Edw.) Love's Coming of Age (Sonnenschein; 3s. 6d).
  Ruedbusch (E.) The Old Ideal and the New (pub. by Author, Mayville, Wisconsin, U.S., 1896).

Municipal Dwellings.
  Report of Housing of Working Classes Com.—see Minutes of Council, 29 Nov., 1898; see Debates in L.C.C.
  Thompson (Ald.) Memo. Housing of Working Classes (P. S. King, 1899; 2s. 6d.).
  Royal Commission on Housing of the Working Classes, 1885. Rept. 8d., Evid. 7s. 8d.).
  Eighth Special Report of U.S.A. Commissioner of Labour: Housing of the Working Classes (Washington, 1895; gratis).
  Worthington (L.) Dwellings of the People (Social Science Series, Sonnenschein, 1894; 2s. 6d.).
  Bowmaker (E.) Housing of the Working Classes (Methuen, 1895; 2s. 6d.).
  Pro: Bowmaker (E.) Financial Aspect—in Progressive Rev., June, 1897.
  Fabian Society: Houses for the People (1897; 1d.).
  No Room to Live (1899; 1s.) [repr. of arts. in Daily News].
  Williams (R.) London Rookeries, etc. (Reeves, 1895; 1s.).
  Con: Mackay (T.; ed.) Plea for Liberty, art. by A. Raffalovich (Murray, 3rd ed., 1892; 2s.).

National Party in Politics.
Pro: Low (S.) A Plea for a Coalition—in *Nineteenth Cent.*, Jan., 1899, vol. 45, pp. 10-19.
Wilkinson (H. S.)—in The Great Alternative (Sonnenschein; 7s. 6d.).

Naval Adviser, A.
Briggs (Sir J. H.) Naval Administration, 1827-92 (Low, 1897).
Hamilton (Sir R. V.) Naval Admin. (Bell, '96).
Wilkinson (H. S.) The Brain of the Navy (Constable, 2nd ed., 1895).

Naval Reserve.
Nautical Magazine, 1897 [numerous articles].
Navy League, Publications of (13 Queen Victoria Street).

Old-Age Pensions.
Rept. Select Com. on National Prov. Insurance, 6 pts., 1885-87 (5s. 9d.).
Repts. from Abroad [numerous] (1d. to 6d.).
Rept. Royal Com. on Aged Poor.
Royal Com. on Old-Age Pensions (1898).
Central Poor-Law Conference, 1899 (P. S. King; 1s.).
Drage (G.) The Aged Poor (Black, 1895).
Pro: Booth (Chas.) Pauperism and the Endowment of Old Age (Macmillan, '92; 6d.).
Fabian Society, The Case for Old-Age Pensions (1d.).
Hobson (J. A.) Some Neglected Aspects of Old-Age Pensions—in *Ethical World*, Feb. 4th and 11th, 1899.
Holland (Hon. L.) Problem of Poverty in Old Age.
Robertson (J. M.) Fallacy of Saving (Social Science Ser.. Sonnenschein, 1892; 2s. 6d.). [on this point see also Hobson (J. A.) Evolution (Scott; 3s. 6d.); The Unemployed (Methuen; 2s. 6d.); also art. in *Contemp. Rev.*, Nov., 1896, on Charity Organisation].
Spender (J. A.) The State and Pensions in Old Age (Social Science Series, Sonnenschein 1892; 2s. 6d.).
Con: Charity Organisation Society, Insurance and Saving (Sonnenschein, 1892; 2s. 6d.).
Loch (C. S.) Old Age Pensions and Pauperism (Sonnenschein, 1892; 1s.).
Mackay (T.) Working-Class Insurance (Stanford, 1892; 1s.).
Wolff (H. W.) Old Age Pensions in Practice, June, 1894, vol. 65, pp. 887-902.

Opium.
Royal Commission on Opium, Final Report, 1895 (Eyre and Spottiswoode; 1s. 6d.).
[See also Minut.s of Evidence, pub. in 1894-1895].
Royal Commission, note by the Maharaja Bahadur of Durbhanga, 1895 (Eyre and Spottiswoode, 1895; 1d.) [Blue-book, C. 7751].
Anti-Abolition Pro: Foster (A.) Report of Royal Commission compared with evid. (P. S. King and Son, 6d.).
Rowntree (J) Opium Habit in the East (P. S. King, 1895).
Japp (A. H.) The Opium Question—in *Free Rev.*, vol. 1, pp. 410-30.

Outdoor Relief, Abolition of.
Poor Law Com., 1834 (repr., 1885; 2s. 9d.).
Poor Relief (Lord's Committee) 1888 (7s. 10d., index 1s. 4d.).

Outdoor Relief, Abolition of (*cont.*)
Pro: Chance (W.) Indoor *v*. Outdoor Relief—in *National Rev.*, vol. 25, pp. 667-89; Better Administration of the Poor Law (Sonnenschein; 6s.).
Con: Booth (C.) The Aged Poor (Macmillan, 1894; 8s. 6d.).
Hunter (W. A.) Outdoor Relief—in *Contemp. Rev.*, March, 1894, vol. 65, pp. 305-25.
Marshall (Prof. A.) Poor Law Reform—in *Econ. Journal*, June 1892.
Webb (S and B.) Problems of Modern Industry (Longman, 1898) Reform of the Poor Law (Fabian Soc.; 1d.).

Parliament, Delegates or Representatives.
Con: Sidgwick (H.) Elements of Politics, 2nd ed., ch. 27 (Macmillan. 1897).
Webb (S. and B.)—in Industrial Democracy, 2 vols. (Longman, 1898).

Parliament, Payment of Members.
Parl. Debates, April 5th, 1870, 3rd S., vol. 200, pp. 1334-68; July 6, 1888, 3rd S., vol. 328, pp. 631-79.
Buxton (S.)—in Political Questions of the Day (Murray, 1892; 10s. 6d.) [gives the Pros and Cons].
Pro: Duffy (Sir C. G.) An Australian Experiment—in *Contemp. Rev.*, April, 1893.
Mann (T.) Democ. of Parl.—in the same.
Elliston (W. R.) Is it a Constitutional Change?—in the same.
Radical Programme, the Pref. by Joseph Chamberlain (Chapman, 1885).
Taylor (P.) Payment of Members (Trübner, 1870, O.P.).
Con: Tulloch (Maj.-Gen.) An Object Lesson —in *Nineteenth Cent.*, July, 1895.

Parliaments, Shorter.
Buxton (S.)—in Political Questions of the Day (Murray, 1892; 10s. 6d.) [gives the Pros and Cons].
Pro: Fordham (G.) Annual Parliaments, 1817 (repub. by Unwin, 1891).
Snow (T. C.) The Shortening of Parliament—*Contemp. Rev.*. Jan., 1898, vol. 73, pp. 115-29 [favours annual Parlts.].

Parochial Boards.
Pro: Gore (Canon C.; ed.); Essays in Church Reform, art. by H. J. Torr, pp. 177-197 (Murray, 1898).
Grey (Lord) and Fremantle (W. H.) Church Reform (Sonnenschein, 1883; 1s.)

Party Government.
Neutral: Greenwood (F.) The Decay of Party Government—in *Contemp. Rev.*, Sept., 1896, vol. 70, pp. 352-364.
Pro: Kebbel (T. E.) Is the Party-System breaking up?—in *Nineteenth Cent.*, March, 1899.
Sidgwick (H.)—in Elements of Politics, 2nd. ed., ch. 29 (Macmillan, 1897).
Con: "A. B. C." The Nemesis of Party—in *Fort. Rev.*, Jan., 1898, vol. 63, pp. 1-11.
Froude (J. A.) Short Studies (4 vols.) vol. 3, pp. 429-76 (Longman; each 3s. 6d.).

Pauper Children, Boarding out of,
Departmental Committee on Metropolitan Poor Law Schools; Rept. on Boarding out in Scotland, 1893 (3d.); Rept. of Mr. G. J. Henley on Boarding out, 1870 (2s.)

PAUPER CHILDREN, BOARDING OUT OF (cont.)
　Rept. of Inspectors on Home, etc., Systems, 1878 (3s. 6d.).
　Pro: Aveling (H. F.) The Boarding Out System (Sonnenschein; 1s. 6d.).
　　Barnett (Mrs.)—in Contemp. Rev., Aug., 94, vol. 66, pp. 243-458.
　　Hill (Miss D. H.) Children of the State (Macmillan, 1889).
　　Tuckwell (Miss G. M.) The State and its Children (Methuen, 1894; 2s. 6d.).
　Con: Criticism of Rept. of Depart. Com. on Poor Law Schools, by Conf. of Met. Guardians (P. S. King, 1897; 6d.).
　　Chance (W.) Children under the Poor Law (Sonnenschein, 1897; 7s. 6d.).
　　Lidgett (E. S.) Poor Law Children—in Contemp. Rev., Feb., 1897.

Parochial Boards.
　Grew (Earl) and Fremantle (W. H.) Church Reform (Sonnenschein, 1883: 1s.).
　Gore (Canon C.) Essays in Church Reform (Murray, 1898).

Peasant Proprietorship.
　Pro: Arnold (Sir A.) Free Land, pp. 280-337 (Kegan Paul, 1880).
　　Cobden Club: Land Tenure in Various Countries (Cassell, 1881).
　Con: Kebbel (T. E.) The Agricultural Labourer (Social Science Series, Sonnenschein, 1893; 2s. 6d.).

Police, Metropolitan.
　Annual Repts. of Com. of Police (6d.).
　Report of Home Office on Admin., etc., 1886; (2d.).
　L.C.C. Rept. No. 176, Table Comp. Met. and City Police (P. S. King, 1894; 3d.).
　Pro: Webb (S.) London Programme (Sonnenschein, 1892; 1s).

Population.
　Pro: Besant (Mrs.) The Law of Population.
　　Bonar (Jas.) Malthus and Work (Macmillan, 1889).
　　Malthus, Essay on the Principle of Population (Ward and Lock; 5s.).
　　Malthusian League, Publications of,
　　Robertson (J. M.) Population (Forder, 1897; 1d.).
　Con: Cunningham (Dr. W.) Path towards Knowledge.
　　Medicus, Problems of Population—in the Humanitarian, April, 1898.
　　Nitti (J. B.) Population and the Social System, transl. (Social Science Series, Sonnenschein; 2s. 6d.).
　　Strahan (S. A. K.) The Depopulation of England—in the Humanitarian, Nov., '96.
　　Ussher, Neo-Malthusianism.

Post Office.
　Pro: Farrer (Lord) The State in relation to Trade, pp. 98-108 (Macmillan; 2s. 6d.).
　Con: Mackay (T.) A Plea for Liberty; Essay by F. Millar on Evils of State Trading, pp. 305-25 (Murray).

Prisons Reform.
　Report of the Departmental Committee, 1895 [Blue-book C.7702] (5½d.); Minutes of Evidence and Appendix and Index [C. 7702-1] (6 . 6d.).
　MacDonald (H.) Abnormal Man ut supra, s.v. Capital Punishment [contains a bibliog.].

PRISON REFORM (cont.)
　Pro: Ellis (Havelock) The Criminal (Scott; 3s. 6d.).
　　Morrison (W. D.) Crime and its Causes (Social Science Series, Sonnenschein, 1891; 2s. 6d.); Prisons and Prisoners—in Fort. Rev., vol 63, pp. 781-9.
　　Orme (Miss E.) Our Female Prisoners—in Fort. Rev., vol. 63, pp. 790-6.
　　Whiteway (A. R.) Prison Reform—in the Humanitarian, Aug., 1898.
　　Wines (F. H.) Punishment and Reformation (Sonnenschein, 1895; 6s.).
　Con: Du Cane (Sir E. F.) The Prison Com. Report—in Nineteenth Cen., Aug., 1895.
　　Horsley (Rev. J. W.) Prison and Prisoners (Pearson, 1899).
　　Tallack (W.) Penological Principles—ut supra, s.v. Capital Punishment.
　　Vicars (G. R.) Modern Penology, Feb., '98.

Profit-Sharing.
　Bliss (W. D. P.; ed.) Encyclopædia of Social Reform, art., pro, by N. P. Gilman, and a statement of objections by editor (Funk & Wagnalls, New York, 1897).
　Schloss (D. F.) Report on Profit Sharing (Board of Trade, 1894; 10d.); Methods of Industrial Remuneration (Williams and Norgate, 1894).
　Pro: Bushill (T. W.) Profit Sharing (Methuen, 1893; 2s. 6d.).
　　Jevons (W. S.) Methods of Social Reform, art., Industrial Partnerships (Macmillan, 1883).
　　Katscher (L.) Usefulness of Profit Sharing in Free Rev., vol 2, pp. 135-51.

Psychical Research.
　Pro: Gurney (E.) Phantasms of the Living (Kegan Paul, 1886).
　　James (W.) The Will to Believe, pp. 299-327 (Longman, 1897).
　　"M.A., Oxon.," Spirit Teachings.
　　Myers (F. W. H.) Science and a Future Life (Macmillan, 1893).
　　Podmore (Fk.) Apparitions and Thought Transference (Scott).
　　Society for Psychical Research, Proceedings.
　　Stead (W. T.) Letters from Julia (Richards, 1898); Real Short Stories (Richards, '97).
　Con: Bradley (F. H.) Evidences of Spiritualism—in Fort. Rev., 1886, N.S., vol. 38, pp. 811-99.
　　Ellis (R. P.) Case against Telepathy—in Ethical World.
　　Hart (E.) Hypnotism, Mesmerism, and the New Witchcraft (Smith & Elder, 1893, 4s. 6d.).
　　Robertson (J. M.) Logic of Ghosts—in Free Rev., Aug., 1895, vol. 4, pp. 397-418.
　　Weatherly (L. A.) The Supernatural.
　　White (E.) Modern Spiritualism (Stock, 1893; 1s.).

Railways, Nationalization of.
　Bibliography, etc., on Railways generally.
　Catalogue of Hopkins' Railway Library by F. J. Teggart (Leland Stanford Junior Univ., Palo Alto, (Lond., P. S. King).
　Report of Royal Com., 1867 (5s.) Minutes of Evid., 1865 and 1866 (9s. 4s.); Appendices, etc., 1867 (14s.).
　Report of Joint Com. on Amalgamation of Companies, 1872, and Evid., etc. (30s.).
　Report of Com. on Rates, 1881-82 (23s.); Rept. of Joint Com. on Do., 1891 (14s. 8d.).

RAILWAYS, NATIONALIZATION OF (cont.)
Rept. of the Railway Commissioners (annual).
Jeans (J. S.) Railway Problems (Longman, 1887; 12s. 6d.).
Pro: Dixon (F. H.) State Railroad.
Edwards (C.) Railway Nationalization (Methuen, 1897; 2s. 6d.)
Hole (J.) National Railways (Cassell, 1894; 2s. 6d.).
Perris (G. H.) Railways and the Nation (Rly. Nat. League, 1898; 3d.).
Railway Nat. League, Publications (40 Outer Temple, Strand, W.C.).
Con: Acworth (W. M.) The Railways and the Traders (Murray, 1891; 1s.).
Hadley (A. T.) Railroad Transportation (Putnam, 1886; $2.50).
Jevons (W. S.)—in his Methods of Social Reform (Macmillan, 1883; 10s. 6d.).
Mackay (T.; ed.) Free Exchange: essay by W. M. Ackworth (Murray, 1894; 2s.).

Rates, Division of between Occupier, etc.
Goschen (G. J.) Report on Local Taxation, 1870 (2s. 6d.).
Fowler (H. H.) Rept. on Local Taxation, 1893 (1s. 7d.).
See also Ground Rents, Betterment, Vacant Land.

Referendum.
Pro: "Dangle" (A. M. Thompson) Hail Referendum! (Clarion Office; 1d.).
Direct Legislation League, Newark, U.S.A., Publications of.
Dicey (A.)—in *National Rev.*, March, 1894.
Oberholzer (E. P.) Referendum in America, (P. S. King, 1893; 6s.).
Strachey (J. St. Loe) A Poll of People—in *Cosmopolis*, April, 1897.
Wuarin (Prof. L.) Genuine Democracy—in *Progressive Rev.*, July, 1897.
Con: Deploige (S.) The Referendum in Switzerland (Longman, 1898) [contains a bibliog.].
Droy (N.) The Referendum in Switzerland—in *Contemp. Rev.*, March, 1895.
Tonun (Miss L.) The Latest Phase—in *Progressive Rev.*, July, 1897; R. in Australia, etc.—in *Contemp. Rev.*, Aug., 1897.
Webb (B. & S.) Industrial Democracy, 2 vols. (Longman, 1898; 25s.).

Registration.
Four Reports of Com. on Real Property Law, 1829-33 (25s.).
Report of a Com. on a Special Register, etc., 1832 (4s.).
Reports of Commissioners on Registration, 1850 (8s.).
Reports of Commissioners, 1857 (5s.).
Report of Royal Com. on working of R. in Middlesex, 1870 (1s. 10d.).
Report of Select Committee on Simplifying Title (1878 & 79 (3s. 4d. and 2s. 10d.).
Royal Com. on R. in Ireland, 1st Rep., 1879 (2s. 4d.), 2nd Rep., 1887 (1s. 9d.).
Parliamentary Debates, 1874, vol. 220, pp. 1226-1264.
Bar Committee, Land Transfer, 1896 (1s.).
Arnold (Sir A.) Free Land (Kegan Paul, '80).
Brickdale (C. F.) Reg. of T. in Prussia (1888; 1s.).
Garnier (R. M.) English Landed Interest, 2 vols., vol. 2, pp. 95-109 (Sonnenschein, 1892-3; 21s.).

REGISTRATION (cont.)
Incorporated Law Society, Council of, Statement on Land Law (1884; 1s.).
Kay (J.) Free Trade in Land (1s.).
Land Transfer Bill, 1889: Member of Inc. Law Soc. (1888; 6d.).
Leech (H. B.) Registrn. of Title (Ridgway, '91).
Lefevre (G. Shaw) Agrarian Tenures (Cassell, 1893; 10s. 6d.); Freedom of Land (Cassell, 1880; 2s. 6d.).
Watson (J.) Tenancy and Ownership, Cobden Club Prize Essay (Cassell, 1891) [For Government Reports see P. S. King & Son's List of Parl. Papers, Land Ag., etc.; gratis].

Rights of Animals.
Pro: Salt (H. S.) Animals' Rights (Bell, '94) [with a bibliography]; The New Charter (Bell, 1896).
Con: Addis and Arnold, Catholic Dictionary, art. on Lower Animals (Kegan Paul) [Roman Catholic view].
Austin (P.) Our Duty tow. Animals (1885).

Ritualism, Suppression of,
Pro: Canterbury (Abp. of) Charges (Macmillan, 1898; 1s.).
Church Assoc., Publications of (Buckingham Street, Strand, W.C.).
Harcourt (W. Vernon) Lawlessness in the National Church (Macmillan, '99; 1s. net) [reprint of his letters to the *Times*].
Nye, Story of the Oxford Movement (Bemrose, 1899; 3s. 6d.).
Rogers (Guiness) The Nations and the Ritualists—in *Nineteenth Cent.*, Mar., '99.
Walsh (W.) The Secret History of the Oxford Movement; with a reply to Critics (Sonnenschein, 52nd thousand, 1899; 3s. 6d. net); Secret Societies in the Church of England—in *National Rev.*, Mar., '99.
Con: English Church Union, Publications of (Wellington St., Strand, W.C.).
Gore (Canon C.; ed.) Church Reform (Murray, 1890).
Halifax (Viscount) The Present Crisis in the Church—in *Nineteenth Cent.*, Jan., '99.
„ and Russell (G. W. E.) Addresses at Engl. Church Union Meeting, Dec., 1893 (E. C. U., 1898; 2d.).
Kempe (J. W.) Reservation of the Host in the Church of England.
Protestant Mare's Nest (Church Times Office; 4d.) [a review of Walsh, *ut supra*].
Roberts, History of the English Church Union (Church Printing Co.).
Russell (G. W. E.) Reservation in the Church of England.

Second Ballot.
Reports on Practice obtaining in certain Europ. Countries in contests for election, etc., Miscellaneous Repts, No. 7, 1881 (Harrison & Sons; 4d.) [Blue-bk C. 2987].
Report on the Operation of Second Ballot, etc., Germany, No. 1, 1893 (Eyre & Spottiswoode; 1d.) [Blue-bk C. 6953]
Buxton (S.)—in his Political Questions (Murray, 1892; 10s. 6d.).
Channing (F. A.) Speech on Second Ballot (National Press; 2d.).

Sex Questions in Fiction.
Pro: Shaw (G. B.) Quintessence of Ibsenism (Scott, 1891; 2s. 6d.).
Con: Chapman (Ella R.) Marriage in Fiction (Lane, 1897).

Socialism and Natural Selection.

Pro: Maine (Sir Hy.) Popular Government (Murray, 1887; 12s.).
Spencer (Herbert) The Man v. the State (Williams & Norgate, 1884; 1s.).
Stephen (Leslie) Ethics of Socialism—in *Contemp. Rev.*, Aug., 1893, vol. 64, pp. 157-70; in his Social Rights and Duties, 2 vols. (Sonnenschein, 1896; 9s.).
Con: Pearson (Karl) in The Chances of Death, etc.. 2 vols., vol. 1, pp. 103-39 (Arnold, 1897) [repr. fr. art. Socialism and Nat. Sel. in *Fort. Rev.*].
Ritchie (D. G.) Darwinism and Politics (Social Science Series, Sonnenschein; 2s. 6d.).

Special Assessment of Land.

Report of Town Holdings Committee, 2nd part issued 1892 on Local Taxation (1s.), whole set, 5 vols., with Evid. and App.; 25s.
L.C.C. Rept. on Sep. Val., Rept. No. 137, 1894 (1d.).

Spelling Reform, English,

Pro: Bell (A. M.) World English (Trübner).
Ellis (A. J.) Plea for Phonetic Spelling (Bath, 1896).
Gladstone (Dr. J. H.) Spelling Reform (Macmillan; 1s. 6d.).
Müller (F. M.) On Spelling—in *Fort. Rev.*, 1876, N.S., vol. 19, pp. 556-79.
Skeat (W. W.) Princ. of Eng. Etymology.

Sport.

Con: Salt (H. S.) Animals' Rights (Bell, 1894; 2s.) [contains a bibliography].
Humanitarian League, Publications of (Chancery Lane, W.C.).

Sugar Bounties.

Pro: Chisholm (H.) Choice for Sugar Consumer—in *Fort. Rev.*, Nov., 1897.
Powell (Sir G.) Doom of Cane-Sugar—in *Fort. Rev.*, Feb., 1897.
Williams (E. E.) The Case of Sugar Bounties—in *New Rev.*, Oct., 1896.
Con: Cox (H.) West India Sugar—in *Econ. Jour.*, Dec., 1897.
Farrer (T. H.) Sugar Convention (Cassell, 1889).
West India Sugar Com., art. in *Investor's Rev.*, Nov., 1897.

Suicide.

Bibliography: Macdonald (A.) Abnormal Man pp. 296-300 (Bureau of Educ., Washington, U. S., gratis, 1893).
Motta (E.) Bibliografia del Suicido (Bellinzona, 1890).
Statistical: Journal of Statis. Soc., June, 1874, vol. 37, pp. 187-92, art. by W. H. Millar; also March, 1886, vol. 49, art. by Dr. W. Ogle.
Encyclo. Britannica, vol. 22, pp. 629-31, art. by W. Hooper.
Morelli, Suicide, transl., 1881.
Neutral: Is Suicide under any Circumstances justifiable?—in the *Humanitarian*, July, 1896 [a symposium by Rev. S. D. Headlam, Paul Sudermann, Helen Mathers, and Dr. Forbes Winslow].
O'Dea (Dr. J.) Suicide (Putnam, 1882).
Pro: Archer (W.) Ethics of Suicide—in *Free Rev.*, Nov. 1893, vol. 1, pp. 113-29.

Suicide (*cont.*)
Hume (D.) Essay on Suicide—in Collected Works (4 vols.), vol. 4, pp. 406-14, (Longman, 1875; 56s.).
Schopenhauer (A.) On Suicide—in his Studies in Pessimism, pp. 40-50 (Sonnenschein, 1891; 2s. 6d.).
Strahan (S. A. K.) Suicide and Insanity (Soc. Science Ser., Sonnenschein, 1893; 2s. 6d.).
Westcott (Dr. W. W.) Suicide (H. K. Lewis, 1885).

Sunday Closing.

Rept. of Royal Com. on Sunday Closing (Wales), 1890 (4½d.) [Blue-book, C. 5994]; Evidence, 1890 (5s 6d.), [C. 5994-1].
Pro: Causer (J. W.) The Sunday Closing in Wales—in *Welsh Rev.*, June, 1892 (6d.) [now extinct; summarized in *Rev. of Reviews*, June, 1892, vol. 5. p. 591.]
Malins (J.) Sunday Closing, its progress and results (National Temperance Depot, 1889; 1d.).
Con: Stephen (H. L.) Sunday Closing in Operation—in *Contemp. Rev.*, vol. 60, pp. 285-90.

Sunday Opening.

Parl. Debates, 1896.
Lord's Committee on Lords Day Act, 1896, 2nd Report (6d.).
Westminster Rev., May-Oct., 1896, arts. by Rev. F. H. Peake, Mr. Judge, and others.
Pro: "Barrister, A"—in his Christianity and Commonsense, (Chapman and Hall, '83).
Lecky (W. E. H.) Liberty and Democracy (2 vols.), vol. 2, pp. 81-99 (Longman, '96).
Tree (H. B.) The Sunday Question—in the *Humanitarian*, Jan., 1895.

Taxation, Abolition of Indirect.

Pro: Financial Reform Assoc., Pubs. of,
Reid (A.) Bold Retrenchment.
Con: Bastable (C. F.) Public Finance, Bk. 3, ch. 4 (Macmillan, 1895).
Times, The, Feb. 13, 16. 21, 28, 1899; arts. Twenty Years' Finance.

Taxation, Voluntary.

Pro: Herbert (Hon. A.) A Voluntarist Appeal—in the *Humanitarian*, May, 1898.
Spence (J. C.) Freedom our Birthright (Lambert & Co., Newcastle-on-Tyne,'87).

Theism.

Pro: Flint (R.) Theism (Blackwood. 1886 7s. 6d.); Anti-Theistic Theories (Blackwood, 1880, 10s 6d.).
Hettinger (F. L.) Natural Religion, transl. with introd. by H. S. Bowden (Burns & Oates, 1891) [Roman Catholic position].
Knight (Prof. W.) Aspects of Theism (Macmillan, 1893; 8s. 6d.).
Momerie (A. W.) Personality (Blackwood, 1888; 3s.).
Tait (Rev. Jas.) Mind in Matter (Griffin, 2nd ed. 1892; 6s.).
Ward (W. G.) Essays on Philosophy of Theism (Kegan Paul, 1884; 21s,) [R. C.].
Con: "Physicus" [G. J Romanes] A Candid Examination of Theism (Kegan Paul, 1878; 7s. 6d.)
See also Agnosticism.

Trade Unionism.

Labour Commission, 67 pts. (£5 5s.); Final Report (2s.); Minority Report, (re-pub. by Manchester Labour Press; 2d.).
Trade Unions Com., 1838 (6s.); Com., '67-69 (20s.); Rept. on Sheffield Outrages, 1867 (5s.).

Strikes.

Mavor (Prof. Jas.) The Scotch Railway Strike (Edinb., 1891; 1s.).
Nash (V.) and Smith (H. L.) The Dockers' Strike, 1889 (Unwin, 1890; 1s.).
Board of Trade, Strikes and Lock-Outs (annually, Eyre and Spottiswoode).
Wright (Carrol D.) Rept. of Dept. of Labour Washington, U. S. (gratis).
Pro: Hobhouse (T. T.) The Labour Movement (Unwin, 1893; 3s. 6d.).
Howell (G.) Conflicts of Labour and Capital (Macmillan, 1890; 7s. 6d.); Trade Unionism, New and Old (Methuen, 1891; 2s. 6d.).
Webb (S. and B.) History of Trade Unions (Longman, 1894; 18s. net.); Industrial Democracy, 2 vols. (Longman, 1898; 25s. net.) [Both above works cont. excellent bibliographies].
Con: Birks (J.) Trade Unionism (Lib. and Prop. Def. League; 6d.).
Cree (T. S.) Trade Unions.
Taylor (B.) A Study in Trade Unionism—in *Nineteenth Cen*. April, 1898, vol. 43, pp. 677-92.

Tramways Municipalization.

L.C.C. Report No. 45, Hopkins (A. B.) Tramway Leg. (P. S. King and Son, 3s. 6d.).
Richmond Corporation, Rept. by Alderman Thompson, Memorandum on Municipal Tramways (Fabian Society; 6d.).
See also Gas, Municipalization of,

Unemployed, The.

Report by Mr. Llewellyn Smith on Methods, etc.; with map, 1893 (1s. 11d.).
Report of Com. on Com. Unemployment, 1896 (1s. 6d.).
Bousfield (W. R.) The Unemployed—in *Contemp. Rev.*, Dec., '96, vol. 70, pp. 835-52.
Drage (G.) The Unemployed (Macmillan, '94).
Hobson (J. A.) Problem of the Unemployed (Methuen, 1896; 2s. 6d.).
Macdonald (J. A. M.) The Problem of the Unemployed—in *New Rev.*, Dec., 1893, vol. 9, pp. 561-76.
Con: Bosanquet (B.) Aspects of the Social Problem (Macmillan).

Universal Language.

Academy, The, vol. 34, pp. 56 and 107.
Athenæum, The, 1888. p. 530.
Pro: Bell (A. M.) World English, pp. 24-7 (Trübner).
Haines (C. C.) Universal Language—in *Macmillons's Mag.*, March, 1892.
Mahaffy (J. P.) The Modern Babel—in *Nineteenth Cent.*, Nov., 1896.
Phillips (H.) An Attempt at an Internat. Language (Holt, New York, 1889).
Post (A. A.) Volapük—in the *Arena*, vol. 5, pp. 556-66.
Steiner (P.) Summary of the Universal Language Pasilingua (Trübner, 1889).
Con: Ellis (Havelock) Babel Reversed—in *Progressive Rev.*, April, 1897 [against a World-English].

University for London, A.

Papers on the Organization of a London University, 1852 (?d.).
Report Royal Commission, 1889 (2s. 6d.).
Draft Charter for Gresham Univ., 1892 (2d.).
Rept. of Com. on Draft Charter and Dissent, etc., 1894 (6d.); Evid., etc., 2 pts. (11s.).
Pro: Playfair (Lord) A Great University for London—in *Nineteenth Cent.*, Oct., 1895.
Con: Cattle (Dr. C. H.) Objections to proposed Reconstruction of the Univ. of London—in *Medical Mag.*, Feb., 1896.

University Extension.

Pro: Mackinder (H. J.) and Sadler (M. E.) Univ. Extension: has it a future? (Clarendon Press, 1891; 1s.).
Sadler (M. E.) and Stuart (J.) Facts about Univ. Extension—in *Nineteenth Cent.*,1894.
Con: Whibley (C.) The Farce about Univ. Extension—in *Nineteenth Cent.*, Aug. and Oct., 1894.

Vacant Land, Rating of.

Royal Commission on Housing of Working Classes, 1885 (25s.).
Town Holdings Committee: Rept., 2nd part, 1892 (1s.) [See also Ground Values].

Vaccination.

Catalogue of Anti-Vaccin. Lit. (Allen, '95; 2d.).
Royal Commission on Vaccination, Final Report, 1896 (1s. 10d.)
Numerous vols. of Evidence and Repts. of particular outbreaks [very valuable].
Bond (Francis) Story of the Gloucester Epidemic (Jenner Soc., 1896; 6d.).
Hart (E. A. P.) The Truth about Vaccination Smith Elder, 1895; 1s. 6d.).
Humphreys (N. A.) English Vaccination—in *Jour. of Stat. Society*, vol. 60, 1897, pp. 403-51 [includes a discussion].
Jenner Society, Pubs., of (Dr. Bond, Hon. Sec., Gloucester).
McVail (J.) Vaccination Vindicated (Cassell, 1887; 5s.).
„ Rept. of Roy. Com.: Review of Dissentients' Statements (P. S. King, '98; 2s.).
Morris (M.) The Superfluous Vac. Com.—in *Nineteenth Cent*. Dec., 1896.
Con: Creighton (C.) Jenner and Vaccination (Sonnenschein, 1889 (4s. 6d.).
Crookshank (Prof. E. M.) Hist. and Pathol. of Vac., 2 vols. (H. K. Lewis, 1890; 20s.).
Hutton (A. W.) The Vaccination Question 1895 (2s. 6d.).
Milnes (A.) What about Vaccination, 1895 (6d.); Small Pox and Vaccination—in *Jour. of Stat. Soc.*, vol. 60, 1897, pp. 552-62.
National Anti-Vaccination League, Pubs. of (50 Parliament Street, S.W.).
Picton (J. A.) The Vaccination Commission —in *Cont. Rev.* Oct., 1896, pp. 484-503.
Tebb (Dr. Scott) A Century of Vaccination (Sonnenschein, 2nd. ed., 1899; 5s.).
Wallace (Alfred Russel) Vaccination a Delusion (Sonnenschein, 1898; 1s.).

Vegetarianism.

Springer (R.) Wegweiser in der vegetarianishen Literatur (Nordhausen, 1880).
Pro: Salt (H. S.) A Plea for Vegetarianism (Veget. Soc., Mancs., 1886); Humanities of Diet (Humanitarian League, 53 Chancery Lane, W.C.).
Smith (J.) Fruits, etc., the proper Food of Man (Ideal Pub. Union, 1897).

Printed in the United States
117004LV00010B/40/A